MILLER'S

100 YEARS OF THE
DECORATIVE ARTS

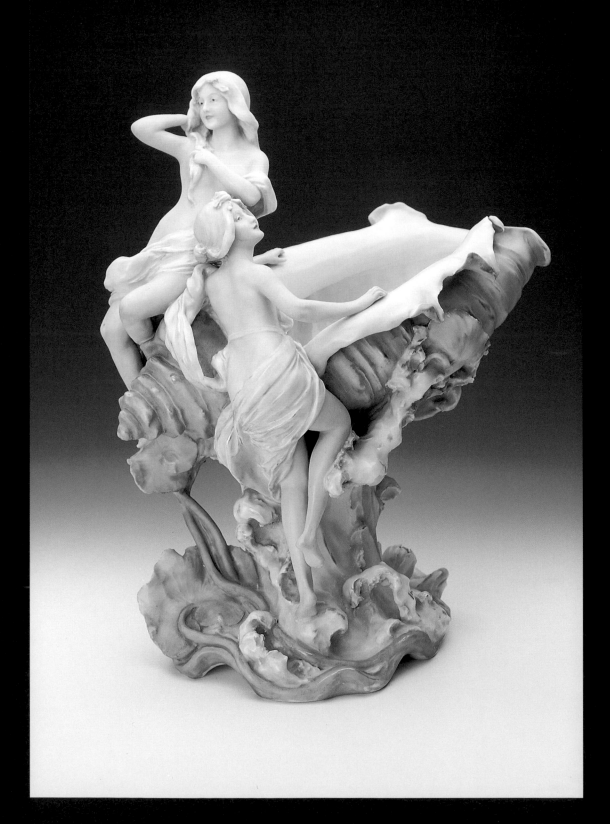

MILLER'S

100 YEARS OF THE
DECORATIVE ARTS
Victoriana, Arts & Crafts, Art Nouveau & Art Deco

ERIC KNOWLES

An Amphora Turn-Teplitz Bowl,
designed by Riessner, Stellmacher & Kessel, c.1900

First published in Great Britain by Miller's, a division of Mitchell Beazley,
imprints of Octopus Publishing Group Ltd,
2–4 Heron Quays, Docklands, London E14 4JP

Miller's is a registered trademark of Octopus Publishing Group Ltd

Executive Editor Frances Gertler
Editor Alison Macfarlane
Art Director Tim Foster
Art Editor Sarah Pollock
Index Hilary Bird
Production Ann Childers

First published in 1993 as *Miller's Victoriana to Art Deco*
Copyright © Octopus Publishing Group 1993
Reprinted 1994, 1998 (twice), 2000

The Publishers will be grateful for any information which will assist them in keeping future
editions up to date. Although all reasonable care has been taken in the preparation of this
book, neither the Publishers nor the compilers can accept any liability for any consequences
arising from the use of, or the information contained herein.

Some of the material in this book originally appeared in Miller's Antiques Checklists:
Victoriana, *Art Nouveau* and *Art Deco*, © Octopus Publishing Group Ltd 1991, 1992

A CIP catalogue record for this book is available from the British Library
ISBN 1 84000 052 X

Produced by Toppan Printing Co., (HK) Ltd.
Printed and bound in China
Typeset in Gill and Garamond SX Composing Ltd

Jacket pictures

Front: left, Sotheby's Picture Library; top, Octopus Publishing Group Ltd;
centre, Phillips, London; right, Bonham's, London
Back: top left, by kind permission of BBC *Homes and Antiques* magazine;
top right and bottom left, Sotheby's Picture Library;
bottom right, Christie's, New York

CONTENTS

FURNITURE

GLASS

CERAMICS

SCULPTURE

SILVER AND METALWORK

JEWELRY AND PRECIOUS OBJECTS

PRINTS AND POSTERS

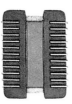

RUGS AND TEXTILES

INTRODUCTION

100 Years of the Decorative Arts covers one of the richest periods in history. Great advances were made in science, technology, the arts and travel, which were to have an effect on every aspect of the applied and decorative arts. Two World Wars were fought. It was the age of the Industrial Revolution, which had begun in Britain in the mid-18th century, and by the 19th century had led to the emergence of an industrial nation whose influence was to spread throughout the world. A vast range of new products entered the market, many of them for the first time, and many of which took advantage of the new mass-production techniques.

Because of the fast pace of technology and the numerous historical and cultural changes that occurred, the Victorian age was a time of continuous transformation in the applied and decorative arts. Initially, Victorian designers and craftsmen, keen to avoid the Neo-classical constraints favoured by their forebears, drifted towards a revival of Elizabethan and earlier medieval styles which was to manifest itself in the Gothic style championed by Augustus Welby Pugin and William Burges. Gradually, the Gothic gave way to the opulent excesses of French Baroque, favoured by many designers as the ultimate expression of wealth and importance, but often resulting in a vulgarized form where embellishment overpowered the form. Styles and period elements often became confused, resulting in elaborate and not always successful hybrids.

Industrial advances led to a new wealth and a new class of society. The arts had previously been strictly the domain of the rich aristocracy, but now art products were being bought by the rising new middle classes. The vogue for 18th-century French furniture produced by the top *ébénistes* and for Sèvres soft paste porcelain was often beyond the means of even the upper middle classes and for the most part remained the exclusive domain of such ultra wealthy bankers as the Rothschilds, Vanderbilts and Rockefellers. For the majority of Victorian households the prime concern was still with paying the rent and feeding the family, with any money left over going towards the purchase of elementary furnishings rather than new designs.

The breaking down of trade barriers and the introduction of "Free Trade" in Europe in the 1850s brought an even greater range of products to a greater number of countries. The cultural and artistic influences of Britain and Europe on the New World and colonial outposts are clear, but these countries in turn exerted their own influences on the arts. For example, Kashmiri shawls produced in India led to the mass-production of the Paisley shawl in Scotland. The influences of China and Japan became increasingly significant when world trade with Japan resumed after almost 200 years of self-isolation in the 1870s. The Japanese observation of nature and their subtle application and integration of decoration and form caught the imagination of mid-Victorian artists and the public. The arrival in Britain and Continental Europe of Japanese woodblock prints by such masters as Hokusai and Hiroshige was greeted with much acclaim by such influential western artists as James Whistler, Dante Gabrielle Rossetti and William Morris who emulated the bold use of colour and perspective in their work, while the importation of Japanese art and artefacts to Britain, Europe and the United States prompted a craze for the *japonais* style, which was later to manifest itself in the Aesthetic movement. Championed by Oscar Wilde and other literary figures the movement sought to improve the standard of design in everyday furnishings and utilitarian objects by avoiding the often vulgar and over-embellished in preference for the ebonized and simplified furniture designs of E. W. Godwin and the metalwork and ceramic designs of Christopher Dresser.

Later in the century this quest for honest design continued with the formation of arts and crafts guilds whose aims followed the medieval principals of producing hand-crafted objects of high quality at an affordable price. Unfortunately, these guilds failed as they could not compete with the low-priced mass-produced items of, for example, the furnisher and interior decorator Arthur Lasenby Liberty, who successfully retailed machine-made metalwork, jewelry and textiles that had the texture and outward appearance of being hand-crafted.

Although the Art Nouveau style was popularized throughout Europe and the United States, its origins can be traced to Britain. It was a style that incorporated naturalistic and organic forms, often with an element of fantasy. The female figure was a dominant motif, given erotic or ethereal qualities, and often held as an object of worship.

The horror and devastation of the 1914-18 war was to change the whole structure of society. Fortunes were gained and lost during these years, and a new class of *nouveau riche* emerged. The role of women changed significantly. The support they provided during the war by working in munition factories or by carrying out work usually done by men led the way to their emancipation and the right to vote. Women were no longer the subservient creatures of the 1840s or the ethereal women of the Art Nouveau period, but individuals in their own right. Women came into their own as sculptural subjects – often depicted in fashionable clothing and modern situations, such as smoking or playing sport, both inconceivable only a few years earlier. Their heroes were often the stars of the silver screen – Rudolph Valentino of the 1920s, Clarke Gable of the 1930s; and many heroines became role models – for example, Greta Garbo, Marlene Dietrich and Jean Harlow.

Attitudes to life changed, as those who survived the war, simply glad to be alive, wanted nothing more than to party and have fun. It was the age of jazz, cocktails and crazy American dances such as the Charleston and the Black Bottom. It was the "Roaring Twenties" and the emphasis was on speed, with new land, sea and air records continually being set and broken.

In these years the Art Deco style emerged, which derived its name from the 1925 Paris *Exposition Internationale des Arts Décoratifs et Industriels Modernes*. The term encompasses two very different schools of design – Traditional and Modern. The former was led by the French designers Jacques-Émile Ruhlmann and Jean Dunand; the latter by Ludwig Mies van der Rohe, Marcel Breuer and the German Bauhaus school of design.

COLLECTING

The period from 1837 to 1940 was one of great change, and is unparalleled for the variety of styles and objects it produced. It is a very fertile area for all collectors of antiques, whether a beginner or professional, and no matter what their taste or pocket. Hopefully, the information in *100 Years of the Decorative Arts* will provide the ideas and inspiration to go on searching for exciting new purchases.

Having been lampooned by antiques collectors and dealers alike in the 1950s and '60s as being vulgar or at best incongruous, "Victoriana" has gained a new respectability today, with many people recognising the virtues of the style. Prices have risen, sometimes dramatically, and the work of designers such as William Burges, Edward W. Godwin and Christopher Dresser has fetched astonishing prices at auction during the past decade. However, there are still bargains to be found, making it possible to put together an interesting collection relatively inexpensively. It is usually cheaper to buy good solid Victorian craftsmanship than its often shoddy mass-produced modern-day equivalent. Victorian glassware, especially Stourbridge art glass or the moulded wares of Sowerby and Greener and Davidson from the North East of England are still relatively inexpensive – as is much Georgian glass; and prints and etchings can be bought at very low prices, especially when compared to those asked for the photographic reproductions sold by today's chain stores, which have little or no resale value.

Any criticism levelled at Victoriana during the 1960s was minimal when compared to the critics' reactions to the Art Nouveau style that emerged in around 1900. However the past twenty years have witnessed a renewed interest and today the style has an unprecedented following and is one of the most popular collecting areas, combining at its best quality, originality and affordability.

Once again prices paid for the more important pieces by top Art Nouveau designers such as Alphonse Mucha, Emile Gallé, Josef Hoffmann and Charles Rennie Mackintosh are prohibitively expensive for the potential collector. However, a whole plethora of comparatively inexpensive industrially-produced objects were also made at the time which are gaining increasing popularity among collectors today. Mass-produced Art Nouveau jewelry, enamelled or mounted with semi-precious stones, is still plentiful but beware clever reproductions. Pieces retailed by Liberty & Co., Charles Horner and Murrle Bennet are still found at reasonable prices, especially when compared to modern day equivalents. It is important to establish the provenance of pieces when collecting Art Nouveau as there has been a wide range of honest reproductions and outright fakes which can mislead even the most experienced collector.

Antiques from the Art Deco period are sought after not only for their high quality of craftsmanship and inventive forms, but also because they invoke nostalgia, as many products conjure up the giddy age of the 1920s and '30s. Collectors of Art Deco should look for objects which not only display quality workmanship and inventive forms, but which also capture the mood of the period. Cocktail cabinets with mirrored and illuminated interiors regularly appear at auction at reasonable prices. Commercial perfume bottles from France and Czechoslovakia are becoming increasingly popular to collectors today, following the success of those designed by René Lalique and Baccarat. Look for perfect pieces, especially with original contents and container. Car mascots provide another new collecting area. Craftsman-made pieces, such as the glasswares of Maurice Marinot and the jewelry of Jean Fouquet, are hard to come by and can be prohibitively expensive. However the mass-produced hand-finished wares are more readily available and affordable.

ERIC KNOWLES

CHART OF THE MAJOR HISTORICAL, POLITICAL AND CULTURAL EVENTS

1837 Queen Victoria ascends the throne in Britain.

Isambard Kingdom Brunel completes the Great Western, the first transatlantic steamship.

The electrical telegraph is patented in Britain by Charles Wheatstone and the English electrical engineer William Fothergill Cooke.

1838 The first regular steamship communication is established between England and the United States.

1839 The Opium wars between England and China begin.

Photography is invented by Louis Daguerre in France and by William Fox Talbot in Britain.

1841 Augustus Pugin publishes a revised edition of *Contrasts*, an essay linking society and architecture.

The ballet, *Giselle* is first performed, choreographed by Jules Perrot and Jean Coralli.

1842 The Treaty of Nanking ends the Opium Wars, opening Chinese ports to Brititsh trade.

1843 John Ruskin begins *Modern Painters* which was to have an enormous influence on Victorian taste.

1844 Samuel Morse sends his first telegraph message between Baltimore and Washington.

1845 Robert Peel's "Free Trade" budget repeals all export duties and many import duties in Britain, facilitating trade with Europe and the United States.

1846 Eugène-Emmanuel Viollet-le-Duc, French Gothic Revival architect and medievalist, begins his first restoration project, the Abbey of Saint-Denis.

A potato famine in Ireland results in mass emigration to the United States.

1848 The Pre-Raphelite Brotherhood of painters was formed.

1849 John Ruskin publishes *The Seven Lamps of Architecture* which upholds the Gothic style for its truth to nature and moral worth.

1851 The first world fair, the Great Exhibition is held, and the Crystal Palace is built for it.

1851 The American inventor, Isaac Singer, invents the sewing machine.

1852 The French engineer Henri Giffard makes the first airship flight.

1854 The outbreak of the Crimean war.

1855 The Paris World Exhibition opens.

1856 End of the Crimean war.

1857 The first Atlantic cable is completed.

1858 Queen Victoria is made sovereign of India.

1860 The Anglo-Chinese war ends.

The internal combustion engine is invented by French engineer Etienne Lenoir.

1861 William Morris establishes his association of fine art workmen, Morris, Marshall, Falukner & Co., to reform the applied arts, particularly the Gothic revival.

1862 The French actress, Sarah Bernhardt, makes her debut at the Comédie-Française in Racine's *Iphigénie et Aulide*.

1863 The first underground railway is opened in London.

Viollet-le-Duc's writings on Gothic architecture, *Entretiens sur l'Architecture*, first appear (translated into English 1877-1881).

1876 Scottish-born Alexander Graham Bell invents the telephone in America.

The American, Thomas Edison, invents the phonograph.

Karl Benz builds a motorized tricycle with a maximum speed of 7mph.

The Philadelphia Centennial Exhibiton is held in the United States, showing a Renaissance revivial.

1880 The Arts and Crafts movement begins in Europe (ends 1900).

1883 Jazz and blues becomes popular through the songs of poor blacks at work and in church.

1885 The German engineer Karl Benz invents the motor car and Gottlieb Daimler patents a petrol engine to power a motorcycle.

1887 The *Théâtre Libre* is founded in Paris.

The German physicist Henrich Hertz transmits the first radio waves.

1888 The Kodak camera is developed, leading to a popular interest in photography.

1889 The Paris Universal Exhibition is staged, at which the potential of electricity is first demonstrated.

1890s The Aesthetic movement, headed by Oscar Wilde, begins.

1890 The Arts and Crafts movement is adopted in the United States.

1893 Alfred Gilbert's sculpture of *Eros* is erected in Piccadilly Circus, London.

1890s Art Nouveau develops (ends c.1920).

The dancer Loïe Fuller makes her first appearance in Europe with the *Folies Bergères* in Paris.

The Chicago World Fair is staged, showing many American designs.

1895 The first film, *Lunch Break at the Lumière*, was made by the Lumière brothers, Auguste and Louis.

1895 Italian physicist Guglielmo Marconi invents the wireless.

Samuel Bing opens his shop, *La Maison de l'Art Nouveau*, which became a gallery for French and international Art Nouveau designs.

Victor Horta created the *Maison du Peuple* in Belgium, which displayed his furniture and interior design.

1896 The Glasgow School of Arts is founded in Britain by Charles Rennie Mackintosh.

1898 Ragtime music is popularized in the United States by the black singer Scott Joplin.

Zepplin invents his airship.

1899 Start of the Boer War.

Joseph Maria Olbrich completes the Secession Art Gallery in Vienna,

Austria, the headquarters of the Austrian Art Nouveau movment.

1900 Antoni Gaudì completes the *Palacio Güell* in Barcelona, which epitomizes the curvilinear style of Art Nouveau in architecture.

The Universal Exhibition is held in Paris.

1901 Frank Lloyd Wright publishes his lecture, *The Art and Craft of the Machine*.

Queen Victoria dies. Edward VII, her eldest son, is made King.

Marconi sends the first transatlantic radio signal.

1902 The Exhibition of Decorative Arts is held in Turin, where the revolutionary designs of Carlo Bugatti are exhibited.

1903 The *Salon d'Autuomne* is built in France for annual exhibitions.

1903 The Wright brothers make the first powered flight at Kitty Hawk, North Carolina.

Mrs Emily Pankhurst starts the Woman's Social and Political Union.

The Wiener Werkstätte is founded by Josef Hoffmann and Koloman Moser in Austria.

1904 Theodore Roosevelt is re-elected as President of the United Sates.

1904 Charles Rennie Mackintosh designs the Willow Tea Rooms in Glasgow.

1907 The *Deutscher Werkbund* is founded in Germany, promoting standards for industrial design.

1908 The *Ballet Russe* is founded Sergei Diaghilev.

Paul Poiret revives fashion illustration with his *Les Robes de Paul Poiret*, illustrated by Paul Iribe, showing Oriental-inspired costumes.

1909 Cubism is introduced.

The *Ziegfeld Follies* first appear in New York.

1909 Louis Bleriot becomes the first person to cross the English Channel by plane.

Henry Ford introduces the assembly line for the production of his cars.

The *Ballet Russe* perform their first ballet in Paris, *Le Pavillon d'Armide*, with Louis-Quatorze décor and cos-

tumes by Alexandre Benois.

1910 Roger Fry, English critic and designer, coins the phrase "Post-Impression".

1910 *Schéhérazade*, with costumes by Léon Bakst, is first staged in Paris.

1910 The Argentine tango becomes popular in Europe and America.

1911 Paul Poiret's second book of fashion illustrations, *Les Choses de Paul Poiret vues par Georges Lepape*, is published.

1912 Nijinsky choreographs and performs the ballet, *L'Après-midi d'un faune*.

1913 The first great Expressionist ballet, Nijinsky's *Rite of Spring*, is produced.

1914 The Panama Canal opens to shipping, saving vessels the 6,000 mile trip around South America.

The outbreak of the First World War.

1917 The original Dixieland Jazz Band make the first-ever jazz recording.

1918 Peace is declared in the First World War.

The De Stijl group of architects and designers set out their manifesto, outlining their belief that art, architecture and design should have universal rather than individual appeal. Their magazine is edited by Theo van Doesburg until his death in 1931.

Gerrit Rietveld, influenced by de Stijl, designs his red and blue chair, one of the most famous "icons" of the Modern Movement.

British women over 30 are given the vote.

The German Bauhaus is founded by Walter Gropius (ended in 1933), whose members attempted to unite form and function in their designs.

1922 King Tutanhkamun's tomb is opened by Howard Carter, inspiring a host of Egyptianesque designs.

1923 Le Corbusier's *Towards a New Architecture* states that "A house is a machine for living".

The classical jazz song *Rhapsody in Blue* is written by Gershwin.

1924 An 18th century ban on female actors was lifted in China.

1925 The *Exposition des Arts Decoratifs et Industriels Modernes* is held in Paris, which was a showcase for Art Deco.

The Bauhaus headquarters are designed by Walter Gropius.

Josephine Baker appears with *La Revue Nègre* at the *Théâtre des Champs-Elysées*.

1926 Fritz Lang's film, *Metropolis* opens, which depicts an Expressionist vision of the future.

1926 Rudolph Valentino dies, causing mass hysteria at his funeral.

1927 Charles Lindbergh crosses the Atlantic in his monoplane.

Al Jolson speaks the first lines in a film when he appears in *The Jazz Singer*.

1928 Pierre Chareau's Modernist house of glass is completed in Paris, combining steel and glass.

Walt Disney's creates his famous character, Mickey Mouse.

Showboat, the classic American musical, is first performed.

Alexander Fleming discovers penicillin.

The age of voting for women in Britain is reduced to 21.

1929 "Black Thursday" launches a worldwide depression.

Broadway Melody, the first film musical, is launched.

1930 Jean Harlow stars in *Hell's Angels*, beginning an American craze for platinum-blonde hair.

1932 Franklin D. Roosevelt is elected president of the United States.

Norman Bel Geddes's *Horizons* is published, outlining his streamlined approach to design.

1935 Gershwin's *Porgy and Bess* is staged.

The *S.S Normandie* liner is launched, its interior the epitome of Art Deco.

1936 Edward VIII succeeds King George in Britain.

BBC broadcasts begin in London.

1939 The outbreak of the Second World War.

KEY EXHIBITIONS

Exhibitions of applied and decorative arts were primarily showcases, displaying the latest scientific and technological advances. They were greatly competitive; the host country in particular strove to outshine fellow exhibitors. A huge number of visitors attended, including designers who hoped to gain new ideas.

THE GREAT EXHIBITION 1851

This opened in Hyde Park, London to boost international trade. The largest international exhibition that had ever been held, it was housed in the Crystal Palace built specially for the occasion. Thirteen thousand exhibitors took part, of whom half were British. Other countries were given space according to their size. The applied arts were well-represented. The British mastery of ceramics was evident in the wares of Worcester and the Staffordshire potters. Majolica by Leon Arnoux for Minton was much admired. Glasswares, particularly cut glass, were exhibited, amongst others, by Webb & Sons. Furniture included the *papier-mâché* work of Jennens & Bettridge. Many pieces depicted the Crystal Palace. American exhibits included *The Greek Slave*, a hugely influential sculpture by Hiram Powers.

PHILADELPHIA CENTENNIAL EXHIBITION 1876

This represented the Renaissance revival; everything was on a huge scale, reflecting the modern mechanical influence. Neo-classical themes were combined with modern American motifs to create a peculiarly American style – porcelain and glassware in classical shapes were decorated with historical scenes, patriotic eagles and profiles of George Washington, as well as North American animals. Tiffany silverware attracted enormous attention. Some furniture followed English styles of firms such as Gillow and Cooper and Holt; a piece exhibited by T.E. Collcutt for Collinson and Lock helped set the style for the entire show, a style typified by straight lines, elaborate turning and inlaid marquetry panels in various woods, brass, and with surface carving.

COLUMBIAN EXHIBITION (EXPOSITION) 1893

Held in Jackson Park, Chicago, this attracted numerous British and European exhibitors, and was staged to show the United States' growing industrial, agricultural and artistic achievements; and the country's opulence. Several fine American Arts and Crafts pieces were on show; and Tiffany & Co. had their own pavilion, displaying silver and plate with Oriental motifs. Major British contributions included Webb's cameo ware and stoneware by Doultons. Other contributors were Wahliss (Austria), Royal Copenhagen (Denmark) and Muller (France).

PARIS EXHIBITION (EXPOSITION) 1900

This was primarily a display of French inspiration, although more than 40 countries participated. Spreading across a large area of central Paris and bisected by the River Seine, the exhibition consisted of numerous buildings, most of which contained few elements of Art Nouveau design whatsoever, and were instead often based on historicism. The most enduring pieces for the exhibition are Hector Guimard's Métro entrances. The two predominantly Art Nouveau pavilions were the *Pavillon Art Nouveau Bing* and the *Palais des Arts Decoratifs*. The former housed designs from the Paris School; and the latter works from the Nancy School. Other contributors included René Lalique, Henri Vever, Loetz, Christofle and Eugène Grasset. Dancing displays were given by the French actress Loïe Fuller, who inspired many sculptors.

TURIN EXHIBITION 1902

This was dominated by artists from Italy, Germany the Low Countries and Britain. Many English Arts and Crafts designers exhibited there, and Charles Rennie Mackintosh's British Pavilion achieved international recognition for the members of the Glasgow School. Of the Italian exhibits, the Moorish-inspired, exuberant designs of Carlo Bugatti showed remarkable talent. Carlo Zen also provided some interesting and relatively simple furniture profusely decorated in "spaghetti" style curvilinear inlay. Germany had a large section, but France sent relatively few exhibitors, with Lalique and the Nancy School designers being the major names.

PARIS EXHIBITION (EXPOSITION) 1925

Although international, this exhibition was dominated by the leading French craftsmen of the day. For the event René Lalique designed a 50-foot internally-lit glass fountain waterfall, and his light fittings were to be found throughout. Jacques-Émile Ruhlmann designed the central *Pavillon d'un Collectionneur*, featuring his furniture and the ironwork of Edgar Brandt, the glasswork of Lalique and a massive mural by Jean Dupas. Other pavilions included *L'Ambassade Française*, decorated by Groult, Dunand and Follot. In stark contrast was the *Pavillon de L'Ésprit* Nouveau, designed by Le Corbusier, and featuring Cubist designs and furniture by Thonet.

ARTS MOVEMENTS

From the reign of Queen Victoria through to the 1920s and '30s there were a number of movements which were to prove very influential in creating distinctive styles in the applied and decorative arts in Britain, Continental Europe and the United States.

THE GOTHIC REVIVAL

Beginning as early as the 1840s, this was the first of several new art movements to spring up in reaction to the excesses of the High Victorian style. Evident in the work of designers such as Bruce Talbert and William Burges who produced relatively simple, neo-Gothic furniture, the Gothic Revival was to have a profound effect on all areas of design throughout the rest of Victoria's reign.

THE AESTHETIC MOVEMENT

Confined to the decorative arts in the United States and Britain, this movement encompassed a group of people, including the poet Oscar Wilde, who believed in art as beauty. To its followers, who were almost obsessed with symbolism, it became a way of life. The Japanese influence was strong, and furniture was largely simple and often ebonized, with little unnecessary ornament. A chief exponent was William Morris, considered a leading arbiter of taste, whose company was the most important retailer of furnishing in the Aesthetic style.

THE ARTS AND CRAFTS MOVEMENT

The Aesthetic Movement gave way to the Arts and Crafts Movement. Its exponents strove to incorporate the ideals of the hand craftsmanship of the medieval age into the 19th century world of the machine. Guilds, such as Charles Robert Ashbee's Guild of Handicraft, were founded to practice traditional handicrafts and construction methods. Many were not successful, as their ideals proved incompatible with harsh economic realities, and in the early 20th century Liberty's affordable, mass-produced silverware with a hand-finished effect finally ended the Guild of Handicraft, who were unable to compete. The Arts and Crafts style continued into the Edwardian years, practised at such establishments as the Cotswold School, founded in 1894 by Ernest Gimson and Sydney Barnsley.

THE ART NOUVEAU MOVEMENT

The seeds of Art Nouveau were sown in in the early 1870s with the Aesthetic Movement. The name is said to have derived from Samuel Bing's gallery, *Maison de l'Art Nouveau*, which attracted the works of both French and international exponents of the new art including

Louis Tiffany, Max Läuger, Henri van de Velde, Eugène Gaillard and Edward Colonna. Its origins can be found in Britain; and the French regularly refer to it as *le style Anglais*, and to the Italians it is *lo stile Liberty*. Designs are characterized by sinuous lines and the use of naturalistic elements, often fantastical, especially in female forms, which usually have erotic or ethereal undertones.

THE TRADITIONALIST MOVEMENT

In the Art Deco period of the 1920s and '30s Traditionalist designers, led by Jacques-Émile Rhulmann and Jean Dunand, adapted and embellished 18th-century designs, using exotic woods and materials, and concentrating on comfort.

A fine Art Nouveau carved mahogany breakfront by V. Epeaux, exhibited at the Paris Exhibition of 1900

THE MODERNIST MOVEMENT

This was led by such designers as Ludwig Mies van der Rohe and the British firm of Isokon who advocated clean profiles, machine-made materials and mass production. Modernist pieces predominate in the 1930s, whereas the Traditionalist pieces are more prevalent in the 1920s, although both were produced throughout the Art Deco period.

MAP OF MAJOR CRAFTSMEN & FACTORIES

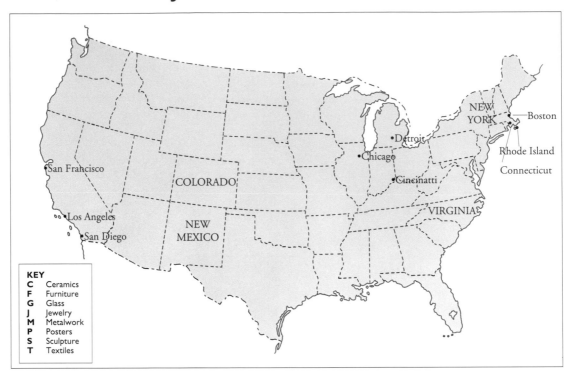

KEY
C Ceramics
F Furniture
G Glass
J Jewelry
M Metalwork
P Posters
S Sculpture
T Textiles

ENGLAND
Elton C
Michael Cardew P
Gordon Russell Heals F
Jennens and Bettridge F

LONDON
Century Guild
 A. H. Mackmurdo F
 Charles F.A. Voysey
Guild of Handicraft
 C.R. Ashbee
Archibald Knox S M
Liberty & Co F T S
William Morris & Co. F T
Rex Silver S
Bruce Talbert F T
E.W Godwin F T
Collinson & Lock F
James Powell G
Minton (Kensington) C
William de Morgan C
Sir Alfred Lord Leighton S
William A. S. Benson G M
Elkington S
Collie Foundry S
Doulton C
 Margaret E Thompson
 M V. Marshall
 Frank E. Butler
Betty Joel F T
Gilbert Bayes S
P.E.L F
Isokon F
E. McKnight-Kauffer P T
Marion Dorn T
Charles Vyse C
William Staite-Murray C

BRISTOL
Nailsea G

COTSWOLDS
Ernest Gimson F
Sidney Barnsley F

GATESHEAD
Sowerby G

George Davidson G

LEEDS
Burmantofts C

MIDDLESBOROUGH
Linthorpe Pottery C
Bretby Art Pottery C

MANCHESTER
Jackson & Graham F
Perry & Son F M

POOLE
Carter, Stabler & Adams C

STAFFORDSHIRE
James Macintyre C
Masons
Minton & Co. C
Doulton & Co., Burslem C
Trent Pottery (G. Jones) C
William Moorcroft C
Susie Cooper C
Carlton C
Shelley C
Wedgwwod C
Keith Murray C S G
Wilkinson & Co. C
Clarice Cliff C

STOURBRIDGE
Webb & Sons G
Richardsons G
Stevens & Williams G

ST IVES
Bernard Leach C
Shoji Hamada C

SUNDERLAND
Henry Greener
Jobling G

TORQUAY, Devon
Torquay Terracotta Co. C
Aller Vale Potteries C

WORCESTER
Worcester Royal Porcelain
Co. C

SCOTLAND
C. Dresser C G M T
Wemyss (Fife Pottery) C
Charles R. Mackintosh F
Herbert MacNair F
Frances and Margaret
Macdonald T
E.A. Taylor F
Jessie M. King J
James Couper & Sons G
George Walton F

IRELAND
Belleek (C)

AUSTRIA
VIENNA
Wiener Werkstätte
 Koloman Moser F M C J
 J. Hoffmann F C G M J
 Dagobert Peche M
 J.M. Olbrich F M J
 Michael Powolny G
Marcel Goldscheider C
Wahliss C
Ludwig Lobmeyr G
Loetz G
Josef Lorenzl S C
Hagenauer S
Ernst Dryden P

BELGIUM
Henri van de Velde F J C
Boch Frères C

DENMARK
Georg Jensen M S
Royal Copenhagen C

FRANCE
Pierre Jule Mêne S
R.. and I. Bonheur S
Christophe Fratin S

NANCY
Daum Frères G
Baccarat G
Louis Majorelle F
Eugène Vallin F
Émile Gallé F G
LIMOGES
Marcel Goupy G
Jean Luce C

GERMANY

BAVARIA
Rosenthal C

BERLIN
Ferdinand Preiss S
Bruno Zach S
Otto Poertzel S
Meissen C
KREFELD
Kayser Sohne M
STUTTGART
W.M.F. M

MUNICH
Richard Riemerschmid F C
Peter Behrens F J C

WEIMER
Bauhaus F (moved to
 Dessau 1925, Berlin
 1930)
 Walter Gropius F (moved
 to England 1934)
 L. Mies van der Rohe F

HOLLAND
Rozenburg C

HUNGARY
Zsolnay P

ITALY
Carlo Bugatti F C
Cantagalli C
Ginori C
Carlo Zen F

SPAIN
Antoni y Cornet Gaudi F

USA
Pairpoint M S

BOSTON
Mt. Washington Glass Co.
 G
Boston & Sandwich Glass
 Co G

CHICAGO
Frank Lloyd Wright F M

CINCINATTI
Rookwood Pottery C

COLORADO
Artus Van Briggle C

CONNECTICUT
Handel G M

NEW YORK
Roycrofters M
Gustav Stickley F
Quezal G
Tiffany & Co. G J
John Henry Belter F
Meeks & Son F
Herter Brothers F
Donald Deskey F
W. Dorwin Teague GM
Sidney Waugh G

RHODE ISLAND
Gorham S M
Tiffany S

VIRGINIA
Hobbs, Brokunier G

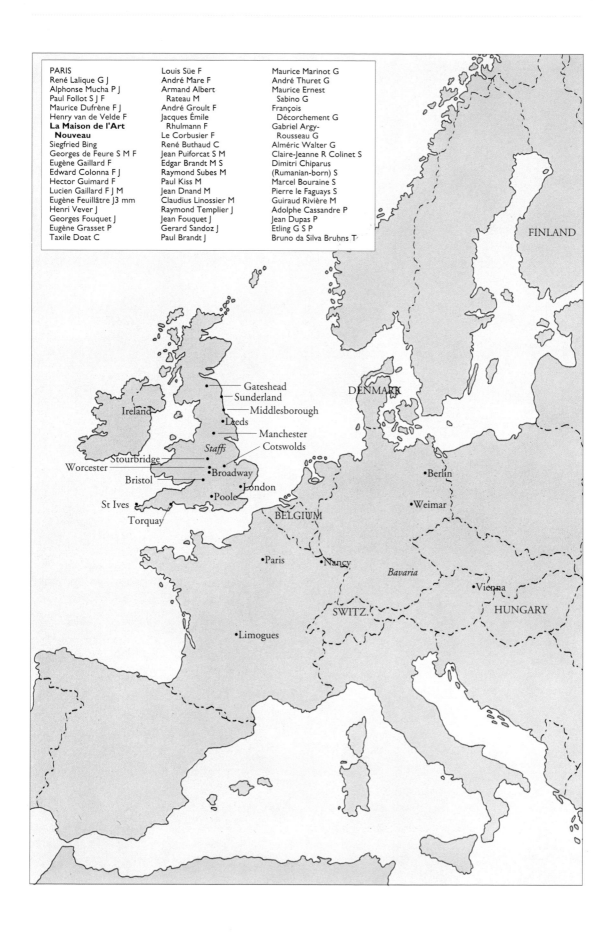

PARIS
René Lalique G J
Alphonse Mucha P J
Paul Follot S J F
Maurice Dufrène F J
Henry van de Velde F
**La Maison de l'Art
  Nouveau**
Siegfried Bing
Georges de Feure S M F
Eugène Gaillard F
Edward Colonna F J
Hector Guimard F
Lucien Gaillard F J M
Eugène Feuillâtre J3 mm
Henri Vever J
Georges Fouquet J
Eugène Grasset P
Taxile Doat C

Louis Süe F
André Mare F
Armand Albert
  Rateau M
André Groult F
Jacques Émile
  Rhulmann F
Le Corbusier F
René Buthaud C
Jean Puiforcat S M
Edgar Brandt M S
Raymond Subes M
Paul Kiss M
Jean Dnand M
Claudius Linossier M
Raymond Templier J
Jean Fouquet J
Gerard Sandoz J
Paul Brandt J

Maurice Marinot G
André Thuret G
Maurice Ernest
  Sabino G
François
  Décorchement G
Gabriel Argy-
  Rousseau G
Alméric Walter G
Claire-Jeanne R Colinet S
Dimitri Chiparus
(Rumanian-born) S
Marcel Bouraine S
Pierre le Faguays S
Guiraud Rivière M
Adolphe Cassandre P
Jean Dupas P
Etling G S P
Bruno da Silva Bruhns T

FINLAND

Gateshead
Sunderland
Middlesborough
Leeds
Manchester
Cotswolds
Staffs
Stourbridge
Worcester
Bristol
Broadway
St Ives
Torquay
Poole
London

DENMARK

Berlin

Weimar

BELGIUM

Ireland

Paris
Nancy
Bavaria
Vienna

SWITZ.
HUNGARY

Limogues

FASHION AND LIFESTYLE

An understanding of the fashions and lifestyles of the period covered within these pages can greatly enrich the collector's experience of antiques, as well as providing a useful dating aid. Changes in lifestyle directly affect fashion, and both have had a significant impact on the applied and decorative arts of the period.

Probably the greatest influence was the changing role of women in society. Women in the Victorian age had few rights and little autonomy. Artists, too, were restrained by Victorian prudery. For their female sculptures and ceramic figures they borrowed mainly from Classical themes, with, for example, Hiram Powers and John Gibson taking the figure of Diana as their subject. New methods of mass production led to the output of ceramic figures on a hitherto unprecedented scale. As well as celebrities and royals, the majority of these figures were everyday people in contemporary dress, which today are an accurate record of the fashions of the time.

Victorian fashions reflected the strict prudery of the age. Women wore long crinoline skirts and men wore trousers. Colours tended to be subdued and many garments featured medieval motifs. The introduction of the bustle made skirts flow out behind. Hair was long and ringleted, often worn *en chignon*. Men's clothes became less formal, with tweeds, caps and capes. After the death of Prince Albert Queen Victoria went into a period of mourning which was to pervade throughout the whole of Britain. Black was the predominant colour, and a new fashion for mourning jewelry emerged which featured black precious or semi-precious stones such as jet, or dark enamels. Pendants and pendant earrings, suggestive of tears, were popular and necklaces were long to complement low necklines.

An illustration from a 1920s edition of La Vie Parisienne *advertising contemporary fashion*

A costume design by Erté from c.1930

At the 1900 Paris Universal Exhibition the *Palais de la Femme* was dedicated wholly to women, heralding the rising importance of women in society. The new freedom of the age was reflected in the sculptural and ceramic figures from the Art Nouveau period in which women are frequently portrayed with long, flowing hair and dressed in diaphanous gowns. They are often draped round mirror frames, or in the extreme case of Carabin, they evolve out of chair backs. However, their role was still primarily a subservient one, and women were still portrayed as being decorative rather than useful.

The turn of the century signalled the Belle Époque and in France in particular a number of couturiers started to change the face of fashion. Paul Poiret, inspired by Diaghilev's *Ballet Russe*, was particularly influential in liberating women's clothes, designing among other garments, harem pants and skirts. After the First World War, as women became more emancipated and went out to work and had their own money, fashion was an increasingly important area of their lives. Skirts became shorter and necklines changed. Accessories were designed to complement the new fashions. Earrings became longer as the short bobbed hairstyle became the vogue. Brooches gained popularity and were worn in ways not seen before – for example, on coat collars. Wristwatches – such as those designed by Cartier – were also popular.

Several artists turned to fashion design, and the development of pochoir prints led to the emergence of the advertising fashion posters of George Barbier, Georges Lepape – and Erté, who worked in the studios of the French couturier Paul Poiret before the First World War and was then hired by *Harper's* magazine to design its covers from 1915-1936. These poster and magazine designs were recognized as art in their own right and are highly collectable today. Georges Lepape, George Barbier and Erté all worked on the important fashion periodical *La Gazette du Bon Ton*, published in France between 1912 and 1925.

In the 1920s and '30s figures in contemporary dress were treated as subjects in their own right, rather than as incidental features. Women were portrayed in their newly independent and confident guises. Bruno Zach's women often stand with legs astride, sporting a haughty expression – and attired in risqué clothes. (These can often help to date his work: pyjama suits and camisoles, worn by many of his women, were not introduced until the 1920s.) The Italian Lenci workshops' porcelain and earthenware figures portray women dressed in knee-length dresses, with short blond bobbed hairstyles, sometimes wearing berets; and in Britain Doulton produced porcelain figurines clothed in the costumes of the

Two stylized Hagenauer brass figures of a man and woman golf player, c.1920

1920s and '30s, such as elegant evening gowns, and many of which had a distinctly English look.

The world of sport and leisure was gradually opening up to women. They played golf, hockey, tennis, drove fast cars, smoked and danced. Posters by Alphonse Mucha use women to advertise *Job* cigarettes. The

An Austrian silver and enamel novelty cigarette case, c.1920 decorated with a Bugatti-type racing car and signed by the artist, F. Zwichl

sculptures of Hagenauer in Austrian, and Ferdinand Preiss and Otto Poertzel in Germany show women engaged in various sporting activities. The Rumanian sculptor, Demetre Chiparus depicts women dancing, and many other sculptors show women accompanied by the new symbol of elegance and speed, the borzois dog. Men, also, were frequently depicted wearing accurate clothing and indulging in contemporary pursuits.

Changing lifestyles led to a demand for new prod-ucts. The frivolous age of jazz popularized smoking which spawned a whole new area of collectables in the form of the highly enamelled and decorated cigar and cigarette cases of Gerard Sandoz, Jean Goulden and Cartier, all in France. Cigarette holders were also popular and table lighters became a feature of most homes in the 1930s, especially in the United States. Ashtrays were made in metal, and in glass – for example by Alméric Walter, who produced a series in *pâte-de-verre*.

The Art Deco period was essentially the age of fun and parties. Drinking alcohol, and cocktails in particular, became fashionable, and to meet the new demands cocktail glasses and metal "sky-scraper" cocktail shakers and trays were designed – for example, by Norman Bel Geddes in the United States – many of them in streamlined forms which reflected the new skyline. New pieces of furniture emerged – in France the modernist designer Jacques-Émile Ruhlmann created an innovative cocktail cabinet which he mounted on skis. Dressing tables, designed by Raymond Subes among others, became an increasingly important decorative feature of the bedrooms of the recently self-aware women. Dressing table accessories had already become popular during the Art Nouveau years, designed by William Hutton and Sons and Liberty in Britain, and they continued to be in vogue in the Art Deco years. As women began to use more perfume, glass perfume bottles became fashionable, and many fine examples were produced by the Czech firm of Baccarat and the French glass designer René Lalique. Lalique also produced a highly collectable series of car mascots which are a quintessential product of the modern age.

THE PERFORMING ARTS

One of the greatest influences on all aspects of the applied and decorative arts between the age of Victoria and the 1930s was the presentation of new cultures, fashions and lifestyles on the stages of the major cities, and in the films shown in cinemas. Actors and actresses became embodiments of their age and were taken as central decorative motifs by a number of important designers.

THE STAGE

The American actress and dancer Loïe Fuller was one of the earliest stars to exert an influence on the arts, when she made her first appearance in Europe with the *Folies Bergères* in Paris in 1893. The French artists and posterists Paul Colin and Jules Chéret produced advertising posters for her performances, and the French sculptor Raoul-François Larche's fig-

A poster advertising the appearance of La Revue Nègre *at the Théâtre de L'Étoile in Paris*

ural lamps modelled on the actress are among some of the finest bronzes ever made. Art Nouveau designers found inspiration in other dancers, too. The French sculptor Louis Chalon took the dancer Cleo de Merode as his subject. Henri de Toulouse-Lautrec depicted Parisian nightlife and *Le Moulin Rouge* in his famous and widely reproduced posters, which illustrate the central role women were taking on stage. Alphonse Mucha created many stage designs, and was specially commissioned by the actress Sarah Bernhardt to design posters for her appearances in productions as well as jewelry and costumes – one of his most famous pieces is an innovative snake bracelet in gold, enamel and diamonds in the form of a bangle joined

An incised and enamelled vase by René Buthaud c.1931

to a ring by a fine chain, which was executed by Georges Fouquet in 1899. The French sculptor Théodore Rivière also based his subjects on leading ladies – including Sarah Bernhardt who appears in his bronze group, *Carthage* (1901), which depicts a scene from the play *Salammbo* in which she starred.

When *La Revue Nègre* appeared with Josephine Baker at the Théâtre des Champs-Elysées in Paris in 1925 it was to have a profound influence on all areas of the applied and decorative arts. This was the first time that Negro art and culture had been given such a wide audience. Jazz dancing became synonymous with the frivolous 1920s. Negroes featured as prominent motifs on the products of a number of designers. The French ceramist René Buthaud incorporated them into his vases; the Austrian firm of Goldscheider produced Negro wall masks; and sculptors at the Hagenauer Werkstätte in Austria made numerous Negro figurines. The Frenchman Marcel Goupy decorated his glasswares with brightly coloured jazz dancers, and in Britain Clarice Cliff produced a series of dancing figures entitled *The Age of Jazz*. In the United States Cowan Pottery's brightly-coloured jazz bowls took the jazz image to its height, incorporating motifs of musical notes and instruments and other images symbolic of the jazz age in New York.

Josephine Baker herself also featured in the work of many designers. In 1925 Paul Colin, who designed posters for a number of other jazz musicians performing in France at the time, produced a series of posters advertising her appearances in *La Revue Nègre*.

The staging of Diaghilev's brightly-coloured *Ballet Russe* in Paris in around 1910 made one of the greatest contributions to the emergent Art Deco style. The new use of bright colours in unusual combinations not only provided the inspiration for Cubism, but also influenced interior design – for example, in the brightly-painted furniture of the American designer, Paul Frankl, and in the rugs of Bruno da Silva Bruhns in France. The exotic costumes designed by Léon Bakst and the sumptuous stage settings for the performance of *Schérézade* had an effect on every branch of the decorative arts, which began to display a new Oriental exoticism and exuberance. The French fashion designers and posterists, Paul Iribe, George Lepape and Georges Barbier, all became involved in designing costumes and stages for the theatre, and they all made the natural progression to Hollywood in the Art Deco years to work on film design. Designs for stage costume and jewelry – for example, those by Erté – are also collectable in their own right.

HOLLYWOOD

Although the stage established the importance of the Belle Époque and the new age, with its presentation of emancipated woman, jazz dancing, exotic settings and exciting lifestyles, it was really Hollywood

A costume design by Léon Bakst for Schérézade, *performed by the Ballet Russe*

and the introduction of the movies which had the most widespread influence on the public, largely because it attracted a much wider audience to its screens.

The cinema buildings themselves were the embodiment of the Art Deco style and design. Avant-garde exteriors revealed a world of make believe – of chromed and black-painted metal, luxurious fittings and cleverly-illuminated interiors – which was far-removed from the reality of the homes of the majority of movie-goers. Cinema furnishings reflected the Modernist streamlined creations of designers such as Jacques-Émile Ruhlmann and Paul Frankl; and although their furniture was very expensive and inaccessible to the majority of people it was successfully emulated by lesser-known designers at much lower prices which could be afforded by many households. Light fittings in cinemas were often futuristic, and their designs were repeated in the work of the French metalworkers, Raymond Subes

A Jean Dupas poster depicting a modern woman looking at a Hollywood film reel

and Edgar Brandt. The emphasis on luxury extended throughout the arts with designers such as Paul Iribe using sharkskin in his expensive furniture and Eileen

Gray, inspired by tribal art, incorporating animal skins in her interiors to set the modern against the savage.

The cinema became a showcase for the Art Deco style, portraying an exciting life of high fashion and new places and showing people dancing, drinking and driving fast cars. For many people Hollywood was the embodiment of success and its influence filtered into every aspect of life in the 1920s. Posters and magazines were designed to promote current films, and these are highly collectable. Although produced on a large scale at the time, they are rare today. Actors and actresses wearing stylish clothes were featured in the inexpensive figurines produced by the Staffordshire potteries in England, Goldscheider in Austria and a number of Czech potteries; and the firm of Rosenthal in Bavaria depicted ceramic groups of stylized dancers in colouful, exotic or futuristic costumes, clearly taken from Hollywood films.

The fashions of the stars themselves set a precedent for contemporary dress. The posterists Erté and Ernst Dryden designed film costumes which influenced their designs for everyday clothing; and when the couturier Coco Chanel visited Hollywood with her latest collection, she provided inspiration for the clothes of many of its stars. Accessories were important. Jewelry became increasingly modernistic in style and was highly exotic and often ostentatious, emulating the jewelry worn by the leading ladies of the day. Precious and semi-precious stones were replaced by brightly-coloured glass and enamels. Products from the cinema also created a new collecting area, as numerous souvenirs were produced, such as ashtrays and cigarette cards, and these, together with other film memorabilia, are highly collectable today, as is everything evocative of the giddy '20s and heady '30s.

TECHNOLOGICAL ADVANCES

By 1890 the steam age was drawing to a close and the late 19th century saw the beginnings of a great age of technology, with the development of many new machines and inventions which were to dramatically change the face of society, affecting not only industry, but also acting as a facilitator and inspiration to the applied and decorative arts. After the Industrial Revolution, which started in Britain in the 18th century, countries in Europe began to recognize the need to apply new industrial advances and technology to design, and organisations were set up to promote this new alliance, such as the Werkbünds in both Austria (1910) and Switzerland (1913) and the British Design Industries Association (1915).

Important domestic labour-saving machines were developed. The sewing machine, patented in 1830, was widely used after Isaac Singer developed the foot treadle in 1851. Many products could now be mass-produced and brought to the consumer at considerably lower prices. Textiles and rugs were no longer all hand-woven, but were produced on machines. Machines and tools were invented which could aid the hand-making process and this led to more affordable hand-crafted pieces, such as the jewelry and metalwork produced by Murrle Bennet and Liberty and Co. in Britain. Cheverton introduced the reduction machine in the 1850s and this led to the production of small-scale sculptures based on life-size originals. The machine age was at its height in the 1920 and '30s. The German Bauhaus (1919-1933) – made up of architects and designers – aimed to fuse art and industry, producing functional items with modern forms, using new materials. Ludwig Mies van der Rohe, one of the Bauhaus's chief exponents, applied the organization's machine-age philosophy to his use of chromed tubular steel, glass and leather for his primarily functional furniture designs. Betty Joel incorporated plate glass into her table tops, and Marcel Breuer, inspired by the construction of his bicycle, and recognizing the potential of tubular steel as a furniture material, developed his famous aluminium *chaise longue*. Increasingly, industrial design and the decorative arts became inextricably linked. In the United States in the 1930s Norman Bel Geddes and Walter Dorwin Teague, two of the most

A jug commemorating the laying of the first transatlantic cable

A Jean Desprès gold, silver, and ivory brooch c.1930

influential industrial designers, designed modern consumer goods. They not only applied their industrial skills to traditional items such as glass and ceramics, but created new products such as cars, telephones and toasters. Teague designed cameras for Kodak, and Bel Geddes created a streamlined range of metalwares, which included cocktail services, as well as designing commemorative medallions – one, for example, for the 25th anniversary of General Motors in 1933. Many people in the 1920s found it difficult to accommodate the new functionlist furniture in their homes, but they were far more receptive when the same principles were applied to personal decoration. The jewelry of the French designers Raymond Templier and Jean Desprès – which closely resembled the machine components themselves – proved very popular. Other pieces of jewelry incorporated Cubist designs or modern bright stones and glass in unusual forms.

The invention of the carbon filament lamp by Edison in 1879, and the development of electricity, created a new area within the decorative arts, as lamps and light fittings became an increasingly important decorative feature in every home. The favrile glass lamps produced by the Tiffany studios in the United States are particularly collectable today, as are the Modernist bronze and glass serpent lamps of the French designer Edgar Brandt. Writing desks and dressing tables were designed with light fittings incorporated into them, furniture desgners and glassmakers working together. Artificial light accentuated the properties of precious stones, and diamonds, particularly attractive in bright lights, were used more frequently.

This was also the great age of travel, and designers and artists turned their energies towards transport design, becoming actively involved in design technology – Norman Bel Geddes designed cars, trains and airliners. The development of the railways heralded the end of the stage coach and horse drawn carriage. 1879 saw the first electric train, and in 1920 the first diesel. Designers were also commissioned to furnish and decorate their interiors – the railway carriages built for the French *Compagnie des Lits* incorporated Lalique glass into their compartment panels, as well as featuring a number of his glass mascots. Sea travel was vastly improved when Isambard Kingdom Brunel developed the steamship, and his *Great Western* (1837), *Great Britain* (1843) and *Great Eastern* (1858) liners, and by the end of the century sea transport had become a far easier and safer mode of transport than it had been in the early 19th century. After the First World War ocean liners were built on a scale and with a standard of luxury never seen before. Early vessels included the ill-fated *Titanic* (1912). The French *S.S. Normandie* liner was launched in 1935 as a showcase for Art Deco. Top craftsmen were commissioned to furnish it. Lighting fixtures were designed by Marius-Ernest Sabino and René Lalique, who was also responsible for the wall panels and glass tablewares; murals were designed by Jean Dunand, Jean Dupas and Paul Jouve; furniture was provided by Jules Leleu and Jacques-Émile Ruhlmann. Raymond Subes created wrought-iron work, and Georg Jensen provided silver tableware. All these items are highly collectable today, as are the furnishings from a number of other liners, and souvenirs, artefacts and medallions produced to commemorate the liners; and indeed this collecting area has grown to such an extent that a new term, *linerania*, has emerged to embrace it.

A bronze medal commemorating the S.S. Normandie liner of 1933

The invention of the bicycle improved personal mobility and features in many posters. The *Penny Farthing* was patented by James Stanley in 1871, and John Dunlop developed the air-filled tyre in 1888, leading to the bicycle design of today. 1885 saw the invention of the car by Karl Benz and Gottlieb Daimler, and when Henry Ford introduced the assembly line to produce his model at low costs (1913) the car became accessible to far greater numbers. The two American brothers, Wilbur Wright (1871-1940) and Orville Wright (1867-1912), pioneered powered flight and soon air travel became widespread, initially on the battlefields in Flanders during the 1914-18 war, and later for passenger travel. When Charles Lindberg crossed the Atlantic in *The Spirit of St Louis* he opened up even more possibilities for travel.

A poster by Adolphe Cassandre advertising the Étoile du Nord railway service (1927)

The train, ship, bicycle, car and plane all became dominant motifs in the decorative arts in this age of travel and speed. The French artist Adolphe Cassandre produced a series of striking posters advertising French rail travel. Frank Pick, who ran the London Underground during the 1920s and '30s, commissioned posters from several well-known artists including Jean Dupas and Edward McKnight-Kauffer. Many were designed primarily as inducements to leisure travel and rarely show the method of transport, concentrating instead on the destination. Cars, trains, boats and planes were also frequently featured in the enamel work applied to jewelry, cigarette cases and lighters. The preoccupation with travel, and hence also with speed, had an influence on the sculpture of the period – the bronzes of Hagenauer in Vienna and Chiparus in Paris featured sleek women accompanied by borzois dogs, which were particularly symbolic of speed.

In 1837 Sir William Cooke and Sir Charles Wheatstone patented the first transatlantic cable, and soon the continents of the world were linked by transoceanic cables, and the main political and commercial centres were brought into instantaneous communication. The Scotsman Alexander Graham Bell developed the telephone in 1876 and telephones became a decorative item in their own right, designed in a variety of forms and made from a number of new materials, including plastic and bakelite. At the end of the century Guglielmo Marconi (1847-1937) popularized the wireless, and these, too, are collectable today.

It was not only the technological discoveries themselves that were important, but the way in which they offered up a whole new area of design. There was no area of the applied and decorative arts which did not benefit from the new technology of the age, whether it was from the improved methods of construction achieved with the development of new machinery, the new raw materials available, or the growing influence of technology as an inspiration for innovative motifs and forms.

FURNITURE

In Britain, Victorian furniture adopted the heavy forms of William IV's reign and earlier periods and added carving or inlay for decoration. A rise in demand for furniture necessitated mass-production techniques and the Victorians soon took advantage of advanced technology whereby hand methods could be transferred to machine. Nostalgia and a love of decoration led to over-embellishment and a variety of misinterpreted and confused historical styles, evident in the incongruous combinations seen at the 1851 Great Exhibition. This trend was checked by a group of architect designers, including Bruce Talbert, William Burges and Augustus Pugin, who borrowed from the old Gothic principles of simplicity to create pleasing and inventive pieces, initially for churches, but soon for the general public. New materials were used, such as metal for beds, and *papier-mâché*, and new forms were created – the grand piano became the smaller, elaborately decorated baby grand, and a new compact writing table, the Davenport, was popular.

The Aesthetic furniture of the 1870s and '80s was mainly ebonized, in simple forms and with decoration restricted to confined areas, and was produced with great success by the Herter Brothers in America. In the 1890s the furniture of the Arts and Crafts Movement harked back to medieval England. William Morris and Liberty & Co. produced affordable mass-produced furniture in heavy oak, which, hand-finished and of high quality, was aimed at the more *avant-garde* British buyer. Decoration was often limited to embossed brass or copper strapwork.

British Art Nouveau furniture was less innovative than elsewhere. The furniture of Charles Voysey, Ernest Gimson and the Cotswold School was strongly symmetrical; other pieces reflected the clean, often severe lines of the Glasgow style, which influenced the Vienna Seccessionists. Two important schools in France adapted Arts and Crafts organic elements and took them to the forefront of Art Nouveau design: Nancy used marquetry panels, local woods and local flora and fauna motifs; and Paris, inspired by Georges de Feure and Hector Guimard, adopted fluid forms and asymmetrical decoration using the wood veneer. In Italy, Carlo Bugatti's highly original style had a distinctive North African flavour, while designs in the United States were simple and undecorated, epitomized by the solid oak pieces of Frank Lloyd Wright's "Prairie" range.

After the First World War new luxury furniture emerged, such as elaborate dressing tables and cocktail cabinets, which were both decorative and functional. New materials were used alongside traditional forms – in France, plate glass was promoted by René Lalique and wrought iron by Edgar Brandt. French furniture from the 1920s typifies the more opulent style of Art Deco; J. E. Ruhlmann designed expensive well-sprung and luxuriously upholstered pieces for the *nouveau riche* élite. Polished and figured marble and rich woods, such as amboyna and macassar ebony started to replace wood veneer. Jules Leleu's and Jean Dunand's late traditionalist work made extensive use of lacquered surfaces, and Süe et Mare turned utilitarian furniture into objects of art. Extravagance reached its peak in 1925 when traditional forms were replaced by the Modernist creations of Le Corbusier and the German Bauhaus. The Bauhaus architects and designers experimented with new materials and applied functionalism and minimalism to everything from buildings to cutlery. Disbanded by the Nazis for being subversive, many members, including Walter Gropius and Ludwig Mies van der Rohe, moved to the United States, where they were widely accepted. American designers preferred painted furniture, lacquered in bold colours, often edged with a primary colour or with silvered or gilt decorative elements. Where featured, the wood grain is often contrasted with chrome. Pieces were mainly large, with a "skyscraper" range for smaller urban homes. Formalized flowers were replaced by Cubist decoration and motifs from Egyptian and African art. British furniture in the 1920s and 1930s was restrained, with the exception of the cantilevered and streamlined forms of Isokon and Betty Joel, in mainly pale woods and making a decorative feature of the wood grain. Some designers, such as Robert Thompson, still worked in oak and used traditional methods of construction.

Pieces by Liberty are highly desirable, as are those by any named designer. In France, a lot of work was unsigned, but pieces by Majorelle and Gallé are well documented. Large, commissioned furniture is rare, as are expensive and smaller functional pieces, but chairs are numerous; even those in need of reupholstery are desirable. Of Deco furniture, the finest is found in France, but pieces do appear in England and the United States. Contemporary journals and periodicals offer the most useful illustrations.

Above A vitrine made by the Bath Cabinet Makers Co. Ltd., c.1900
Right A fruitwood dresser by Gustave Serrurier-Bovy, c.1900

PAPIER-MÂCHÉ

Papier-mâché furniture became popular towards the latter part of the 19th century. The decoration is nearly always japanned (varnished) onto a black background, although there are some examples that use deep burgundy or dark green. Decoration tends to be hand-painted and elaborate, showing flowers, birds and sometimes even complete landscapes. Giltwork is often incorporated into the decoration and used in borders and rims of furniture, and in the ornate outlines found on papier-mâché trays. The mother of pearl inlay on the chairs in the main picture is a typical feature. Papier-mâché furniture was made by a variety of makers, but they are mainly anonymous.

Japanned papier-mâché chairs, inlaid with mother of pearl, made by Jennens and Bettridge c.1860; ht approx. 32in/81cm

Marks Pieces by Jennens and Bettridge tend to be impressed on the reverse beneath a crown. Copies are easily distinguished by the inferior quality of their decoration. No other papier-mâché companies are known to have signed their wares.

Although both useful and decorative, some trays, like this example with its sumptuous landscape, are so elaborate as to seem not intended for use. Like most paintings on papier-mâché furniture, they are not signed. Trays tend to have an ornate outline, accentuated with gilded edging. The Rococo scrollwork on this example is fairly common. The value of these trays is usually dictated by the quality of the painting and the condition in which they have survived. Copies of subjects by Sir Edwin Landseer were popular.

JENNENS AND BETTRIDGE (ENGLISH, active 1816-64)

In 1816, Aaron Jennens and T. H. Bettridge took over the successful firm of Clays of Birmingham, specialists in papier-mâché, to begin the great age of japanned papier-mâché with which their name is now synonymous. Their earlier pieces tend to be small, useful wares, such as bottle coasters (very popular at the time), writing slopes, trays, jewelry, glove boxes, fans and frames for miniature paintings and wax miniatures behind glazed windows. Later they produced some larger pieces, such as cabinets and dressing tables.

Japanning Oriental lacquered furniture first became popular in Britain during the 17th century. Japanning was the English attempt at the Oriental technique, with heavy varnishing used to imitate lacquer. The method had grown steadily in popularity since the Regency period. It was particularly successful in the decoration of papier-mâché objects and thus the two were frequently used together. The Victorians applied the traditional methods of furniture construction and japanning to contemporary styles – the balloon backed chairs are typical. Probably the most popular japanned wares were the large and often graduated sets of serving trays.
•The technique of japanning papier-mâché is different to that used to japan sheet metal (usually referred to as tole ware) and the two should not be confused.

Condition The condition of japanned papier-mâché furniture is a crucial factor in valuation. Papier-mâché needs to breathe and is liable to crack and warp if not given sympathetic conditions; the effects of modern central heating can be devastating. Restoration is difficult and generally unsuccessful.

The use of mother-of-pearl inlay in japanned furniture was introduced by George Souter at Jennens and Bettridge in 1825 and became extremely popular. This dressing table is a typical example. It also shows the elaborate gilded scrollwork characteristic of Victorian japanning.
•Other papier-mâché pieces, such as writing slopes, may feature inlaid shellwork.
•Large papier-mâché furniture is rare. Bedsteads, in particular, are hard to find, as are whole suites of furniture; if in good condition these are very valuable.
•Despite popular belief, the prevalence of black in furniture owes nothing to the death of Prince Albert; it was quite usual before the phase of national mourning that followed his death.

THE HIGH VICTORIAN STYLE

Queen Victoria's reign saw a natural progression, already begun in the Regency period, towards excessive embellishment, borrowing from many styles, such as Baroque and Jacobean. The craftsmanship was often fine, but there was sometimes an unfortunate mismatch of design techniques which reached a peak in the furniture for the 1851 Great Exhibition. Designers such as John Ruskin and William Morris endeavoured to move away from these hybrids, but change was slow. Some High Victorians did manage to produce fine-quality work, including the very collectable John Henry Belter, who combined deep upholstery with elaborately ornate carving. Many others, especially in England, worked anonymously (and a lot of High Victorian furniture is consequently unattributed).

A Jackson & Graham sideboard, exhibited in 1851

JOHN HENRY BELTER (THE UNITED STATES, 1804-63)

This chair illustrates Belter's predilection for "Rococo" patterns of realistic flowers and fruit. Typically, it is extensively carved and pierced, with well executed and extravagant designs, depicting flora, fauna, foliate and Baroque scrollwork. The cornocupia was a popular motif. Occasionally, Belter gilded the carving.

German-born John Henry Belter was one of the most collectable cabinet makers of the Victorian era. He emigrated to the United States in 1833 and developed a range of sumptuously carved and heavily proportioned pieces for the urban and suburban houses of the country's *nouveau riche* which included many parlour suites. By the 1840s he had assumed the title of "America's most fashionable cabinet-maker" and when he died, the term "Belter style" was applied to any large-scale, elaborate Rococo furniture, whether or not it was made by his firm. His company was taken over by his brother-in-law in 1863 and ceased trading in 1867.

Techniques The chair is made of laminated rosewood. The lamination technique, patented by Belter, involved gluing together long strips of veneer (usually rosewood) which were then steamed, compressed and moulded into forms that were especially suitable for the high backs of seat furniture. In later work Belter often used black walnut; other examples were ebonized. On drawer fronts and other flat surfaces, Belter frequently employed a four-layer laminate in place of a single sheet of veneer. This was both flexible and tough, and was epecially suitable for carving.

Collecting Belter furniture is hardly ever found outside the United States, where it was particularly fashionable in the wealthy French-speaking communities. Most collectable are the elaborate pieces, especially rare forms such as tables or those with figural motifs including portraits of famous historical personalities.

Marks Belter furniture is seldom marked, but some examples are inscribed "J.H. Belter & Co" in black ink on the frame. Printed labels are also occasionally attached.

This rare walnut and painted upright glass piano was made by the firm of Dimoline of Bristol for the Great Exhibition of 1851. Like many exhibition pieces, it is particularly striking in appearance and set a precedent for similar designs, some of which were less extravagant. The carving and decoration – featuring shamrocks, thistles and an Italianate scene – are typically excessive.
•A smaller version of this piano in a papier-mâché case was produced and exhibited by Jennens and Bettridge.

BRITISH MAKERS

Jackson and Graham (established in 1840) produced ornate and lavishly-decorated furniture which won them many awards, including the gold medal at the Paris Exhibition of 1855. The firm's designers included Owen Jones. In 1885 they were taken over by the firm of Collinson and Lock. The sideboard at the top of the page was exhibited at the Great Exhibition in 1851 and is a fine example of the kind of ornamental furniture produced in the Victorian period with its combination of Neo-Renaissance, Neo-Baroque and Jacobean styles.

THE GOTHIC STYLE

Victorian England saw a revival in Gothic furniture as early as the 1840s, as designers reacted to the excesses of the High Victorian Style (see p.25). Simple designs followed medieval forms and construction and solid materials of oak or ebony were used to produce predominantly large and perpendicular furniture. Decoration also showed a medieval influence and featured formal carved motifs or crenellations. Amongst the Gothic style's pioneers were Augustus Welby Pugin, William Burges and Bruce Talbert – all primarily manufacturers making for the wealthy. When Pugin decorated the interior of the Houses of Parliament in London he started a trend that led to the Gothic being adopted as the national style.

A painted bookcase made to a design by William Burges
c.1860; ht 72in/183cm

AUGUSTUS WELBY NORTHMORE PUGIN (ENGLISH, 1812-52)

Pugin epitomizes the Gothic revival in Britain with his style that combined heavy Gothic decoration and practical Victorian forms. He produced mainly solid, robust and utilitarian furniture, which was highly ornamented, and was usually made of oak. His stringent insistence on following medieval styles and methods – all minor details and joints were handmade – was in keeping with the return to the forms and methods of construction advocated by many 19th century cabinet-makers.

Commissions Pugin received most of his commissions from the wealthy, often for one-off commemorative pieces. These are much sought-after today, particularly if supported by documented evidence of the commission. His conversion to Roman Catholicism in 1835 led to ecclesiastical commissions – his altars and other furnishings can still be seen in several Catholic churches in Britain.

Chair legs are usually short. However, this chair was designed by Pugin's son, Edward, who was strongly influenced by his father, and the legs are longer than those of the elder Pugin's work. Typically, the chair appears to have been constructed entirely from wood, using pegs and wedges in an almost medieval style of craftsmanship. This example is also plainer than Augustus's designs, with decoration restricted to the form itself and the pierced supports and central seat rail.

Pugin's furniture designs for private houses favoured inlay rather than pierced work or elaborate carving, with fruitwoods used for decorative contrast – as in this burrwood sideboard from around 1850. In any applied decoration, brass, leather, steel or porcelain predominate.

The simple, solid lines of this desk typify Pugin's sympathy with Gothic ideals of design. It displays the linenfold panelling, chamfered and carved uprights and foliate motifs characteristic of his work. Other versions include a desk for the Prime Minister at the Palace of Westminster in 1849.

Recognition points Typical decorative features of Pugin's work include:

- rosettes, particularly on the side supports of chairs and tables
- flower heads on serpentine stems
- steel pendant loop handles
- blind tracery and crenellated decoration
- linenfold panelling
- pierced galleried top rail
- ornamented chamfered pillars
- inlay; some pieces incorporate initials or, in commemorative pieces, coats of arms, dates and so on.
- H-stretchers and column supports with multiple knops on tables.

WILLIAM BURGES (ENGLISH, 1827-81)

Primarily an architect, Burges was a designer in the early Gothic style. He designed an enormous array of items as well as a number of buildings, which included cathedrals and castles. Most of his furniture was of pure Gothic form, colourfully painted and gilded with medieval characters and motifs. He also designed pieces in the Moorish and Persian styles. He applied medieval decorative elements to everyday Victorian furniture – the painted bookcase, from around 1860, in the main picture is very much a 19th-century type of object executed in a medieval manner. Burges's medieval furniture tends to be solid, and very simple in construction. He favoured ebony or ebonized wood, as a basic material, although examples of his work exist in other woods.

Decoration Decoration – painted, carved, or inlaid – is generally ornate and colourful. Inlay is most common, in materials such as ivory, mother-of-pearl, cedar and boxwood. Ivory banding is also typical. Carved decoration, usually flamboyant, includes crenellations, crockets and other medieval motifs. The bookcase in the main picture is unusual in its lack of carving, but the painting – in this case of classical and medieval figures – is typical. Several artists assisted in the decoration of Burges's designs, including E. J. Poynter, Sir Edward Burne-Jones, Simeon Solomon, Thomas Morten, N. H. Westlake, W. F. Yeames, Henry Holliday, J. A. Fitzgerald and H. Stacy Marks. Often several collaborated on one piece – a bookcase exists with paintwork by all the above.

This ebonized table was designed by Burges for the Summer Smoking Room at Cardiff Castle.
•Burges's pieces are unsigned and can generally be attributed only by accompanying documentation. If this is unavailable, collectors should familiarize themselves with typical features of his style, such as the black and white chequered effect on the arched end supports of this table and on the legs, created from ivory-inlaid ebony.

GAULBERT SAUNDERS (ENGLISH, active mid-19th century)

Gaulbert Saunders' work is again strongly influenced by the Gothic. He sometimes worked together with Burges and similarities are evident between the hand-made cabinet, right, designed by Saunders, and Burges's bookcase in the main picture.

Saunders' pieces often feature panels with floral decoration, but these seem to be more inspired by the symmetry in Iznik tile paintings than the Gothic.

Availability Burges's and Saunders' work tended to be commissioned from wealthy clients and therefore rarely comes up at auction, and is generally expensive.

Saunders' cabinet makes use of Neo-gothic forms with highly decorative inset panels depicting medieval figures and stylized floral decorations that bear a striking resemblance to those of Burges's piece. The linenfold panels are a common Gothicizing device (first appearing in the 14th century).
•Unlike Burges, Saunders tended to sign his pieces, often flamboyantly. This cabinet has "Gaulbert" and "Saunders" carved in Gothic script just above the linenfold panels.

BRUCE TALBERT (SCOTTISH, 1838-81)

Born in Dundee, Talbert trained as an architect, moving to London in 1865 to design furniture for Holland & Sons. His furniture is of very high quality with strongly architectural forms and is usually of mahogany, oak or ebony. Designs tend to be massive and often, especially if ebonized, profusely inlaid, with ivory, marble and mother-of-pearl, and to display elements of both the Neo-gothic and the Aesthetic styles.

Makers The Juno sideboard was made by Jackson and Graham of Manchester, but Talbert also designed for Collinson & Lock, and Gillows & Co.

Marks Talbert's pieces are not marked and are not well-documented. Some are recorded by the maker – inlaid in the lid of this piano is the legend "Case by Gillow & Co Works by Erard". Some auction catalogues attribute pieces to Talbert without definite proof.

This "Juno" sideboard takes its title from the portrait of Juno inlaid into one of the five panels in the superstructure, and represents an Aesthetic extreme, with its use of ebony, coupled with ivory and its inlaid marquetry panels; the Gothic element is represented by the arches and the Renaissance-style panels. This piece was designed for exhibition, which may partly explain the elaborate decoration, but it is by no means exceptional in Talbert's oeuvre.

The Jacobean influence is clearly evident in this piano. The base is solid and simple, and the low stretchers are characteristic of many of Talbert's designs. The sunflower motif carved in the panels and on the legs was used originally in the 17th century. It was revived by the Aesthetic designers and often appears on Talbert's work, as does the cabling between the carved panels.

CHARLES LOCKE EASTLAKE (ENGLISH, 1836-1906)

Like Talbert, Eastlake trained originally as an architect, although he never practised. His theories of design, outlined in his book *Hints on Household Taste* (published in England in 1868), found an immediate following in Britain and subsequently in the United States, where his influence on furniture design was profound and where his name is still synonymous with the Gothic revival. His designs are similar to those of Talbert, but tend to be more rustic. His second book, *A History of the Gothic Revival in England*, appeared in 1872, and it is mainly on the strength of these two volumes that his reputation rests. He deplored the shoddiness of mass-produced furniture, and favoured hardy and solid designs.

Marks Eastlake's designs are not marked, and many pieces of furniture are attributed to him, some of them erroneously. Some documented proof can be gleaned from the records of contemporary cabinet makers, but as his pieces are not stamped, even by makers, this could be laborious.

Eastlake was another advocate of the Early English style. As with the designs of Edward Godwin, decoration on Eastlake's furniture is generally restricted to simple turning, as featured on this oak day bed. This piece is designed primarily for comfort and function and its simplicity would have been unusual for the time.

Comparison of this piece with the extravagance of Talbert's "Juno" sideboard above gives an idea of the extreme range of styles of furniture produced during the period.
•As well as the furniture for which he is most famous, Eastlake also designed wallpapers, textiles, metalwork, interior fittings and jewelry.

THE AESTHETIC AND ARTS & CRAFTS STYLES

An ebonized side cabinet after a design by E. W. Godwin c.1870; ht 78in/97cm, wdth 50in/29cm

The 1870s and '80s saw a growth in the Aesthetic movement with designers producing ebonized furniture in simple forms, and decoration restricted to confined areas rather than applied all over. Unnecessary ornament was rejected as vulgar. William Morris and his company were the most important retail outlet for Aesthetic-style furniture, while the Japanese influence was particularly evident in the work of Edward Godwin. The Aesthetic style was especially popular in the United States, where it was adopted with great success by the Herter brothers.

In the 1890s the Aesthetic Movement gave way to the Arts and Crafts movement, whose exponents strove to incorporate the ideals of the hand craftsmanship of the medieval age into the 19th century world of the machine. Furniture became heavier, with oak the preferred wood and styles that looked back nostalgically to medieval England. The influence of the Arts and Crafts Movement continued into the Edwardian years and was practised by such establishments as the Cotswold school (see pp.48-9).

EDWARD WILLIAM GODWIN (ENGLISH, 1833-86)

Makers and marks
Godwin's furniture designs were executed by several cabinet makers. His longest association was with William Watt, responsible for the side cabinet in the main picture. Other makers were Collinson and Lock, who produced the octagonal rosewood table, and J. G. Grace. The table bears the mark "Collinson and Lock London 5770", and a design number. Where pieces are attributed, it is to the maker; none bear Godwin's name. Attribution is based on stylistic similarities to his few known pieces or to his surviving sketches.

Initially an architect, Godwin's move to London at the age of 32 coincided with his diversification into interior design – as well as theatre sets and costumes, he designed textiles, wallpaper and furniture, including tables, chairs, cabinets, easels, shelves and bookcases.

Although Godwin's pieces were hand-made, they were produced in quantity, but never mass-produced. His cabinets are fairly rare and tend to feature door panels with quartered fronts and broad strapwork hinges. Any fittings tend to be made into a decorative feature, with gilding, to give a strong contrast to the body of the piece, which can be seen in the cabinet at the top of the page. The top gallery of this piece, with the supports standing proud of the rails, are also typical features.

Strongly influenced by the Orient, Godwin pioneered the "Japanesque" in Britain. His interest in novel construction techniques is shown in this table's finely-turned stretchers which radiate from a central cruciform block. This piece is made from rosewood; other pieces favoured ebony.

Above What painted or stencilled decoration exists in Godwin's work tends to be limited to symmetrical and stylized flower heads and geometric designs. These can be seen clearly on the hinged frame of this ebonized wood easel.
•Other decorative motifs include a Greek key-type motif.
•Ebonized furniture cannot easily be restored, so the value of any piece will be dictated by the amount of original finish it has retained.

Many of the firm's commissions came from wealthy American families for which the brothers provided high quality furniture, as well as exotic furnishings which they imported from France and the Near and Far East. In 1882 Christian completed an ambitious interior for the Vanderbilt mansion in New York. This marble and cherry-wood dressing table was made for this scheme. He died a year later and, although the company continued in production until 1905, little furniture of interest seems to have been made after his death.
•Throughout the 1880s the firm also produced revivals of Gothic, Renaissance and Egyptian styles, as well as some re-creations of late 18th-century English pieces.

THE HERTER BROTHERS (AMERICAN, 1865-1905)

At the same time as Godwin was working in England, the New York company of Herter was founded by the half-brothers Gustave and Christian, who like J. H. Belter (see p.25), emigrated to the United States from Stuttgart in the mid-19th century. Gustave concentrated on conventional and revivalist designs, but Christian produced more adventurous pieces inspired by the English Aesthetic movement and influenced by the contemporary fashion for Japonisme. It is the designs by Christian which are most collectable today while those of his brother hold little collectable interest. Gustave returned to Germany in the 1870s, but under Christian's directorship Herter became the most progressive furniture design company in the United States.

Aesthetic furniture Herter's Aesthetic furniture is relatively simple in outline, following the principles of design set out in Charles Locke Eastlake's *Hints on Household Taste* (see p.28). Most pieces are ebonized, or stained and polished. Gilding is common, and most examples are extensively inlaid with satinwood, mother-of-pearl, brass, ebony and ivory.
Anglo-Japanese furniture From 1876 Herter produced Anglo-Japanese furniture in simple forms and generally made of ebonized wood with Oriental marquetry designs picked out in lighter tones.

Typical of Herter's Japanese pieces are these ebonized chairs. The toprails are inlaid with flowers and bamboo sprigs over a lattice splat. Anglo-Japanese pieces tend to be on a small scale and to be made in cherry, rosewood or dark-grained hardwoods.

Marks Herter's furniture is rarely signed but most pieces can be easily identified by their characteristic style as well as well as by their high design and manufacturing standards.

MORRIS & CO. (ENGLISH, 1861-1940)

Established originally as Morris, Marshall, Faulkner and Co., this association of like-minded craftsmen advocated simplicity and good quality hand crafting in furniture construction. The main designer since its foundation, William Morris took sole control in 1875, and the company adopted the name by which it is still known today. Like Herter's, a lot of Morris's furniture had an Oriental influence.

Above Later pieces, like this breakfront dresser, tended to reflect styles popular during the 17th and 18th centuries, and were generally more elaborate in design and decoration. They often reflect an Italian influence. Mahogany was still used, with satinwood inlay, but designs tended to be more architectural. Doors are glazed, and pierced carving is evident, particularly on raised pediments, but the effect is modest compared to the excessive ornament of other contemporary designs.

Right Two distinct and different styles can be seen in Morris & Co. furniture. Earlier designs, like this fine buffet from around 1899, were Aesthetic in style. Such pieces are more traditional, heavy and solid, and were made principally from mahogany, and inlaid, possibly with satinwood, as here.

Marks Pieces are almost without exception marked, generally with the "Morris and Co." stamp. Some also carry a registration mark. Makers are not credited. Many designs were widely copied but the Morris stamp is not known to have been faked and is therefore confirmation of originality. Collectors should beware of labels attached to some heavy oak furniture of Arts and Crafts inspiration which may say "in the style of M and Co.", as such items are only copies.

Designers Although William Morris was the main designer for the company in the early years, he later diversified into textiles (see p.235), leaving the firm's furniture design to a number of others, including Philip Webb, Ford Madox Brown, George Jack (chief designer from 1890) and W. A. S. Benson (see p.80), who specialized in metalwork design and was responsible for the metal mounts on many pieces, for example, the buffet on the previous page.

The Sussex Chair The simplicity of traditional pieces, such as the rustic Sussex chair, had a wide popular appeal in the late 19th century. In the 1880s Morris & Co. produced many pieces in this style and the chair continues to be their most famous design.

• The Sussex chair was still being manufactured in the early years of this century, despite the fact that by the 1890s the new furniture designs produced by Morris & Co. tended to be far more sophisticated.

The Sussex Chair shown here harks back to the rustic style popular earlier in the 19th century, with its spindle back form and traditional woven rush seats. Typically, decoration is minimal, restricted to simple turned wood spindles. Multiple stretchers have been added for strength. The chair was mass-produced, although hand-made for the most part, in line with the ethos of the Arts and Crafts movement.

ARTHUR HEYGATE MACKMURDO (ENGLISH, 1851-1942)

Mackmurdo, primarily an architect, believed responsibility for the decorative crafts should be restored to the artist from the tradesman, and to this end, in 1882, he founded the Century Guild, the first of the English Arts and Crafts societies of designers, artists, architects and metalworkers.

Above Mackmurdo's forms usually have original elements, despite their basic adherence to tradition. This tall mahogany cabinet pre-empts the work of Charles Voysey with its vertical emphasis and long, slender, tapering legs. The painted panels, featuring typically late 19th-century organic motifs of leaves and flowers, are probably by Selwyn Image, a co-founder of the Century Guild.

Mackmurdo's furniture was created in the workshop using a combination of the talents of different craftsmen: this mahogany cabinet was designed by Mackmurdo but the features on the doors and drawers of cast bronze figurative finger plates, although small and unobtrusive in the manner of Mackmurdo's fixtures and fittings, were probably by Benjamin Creswick, a fellow member of the Century Guild. Mackmurdo's cabinet-making was always of a very high standard. His work shows a distinct transition from the earlier, High Victorian mode to a simpler, more traditional style based on solid craftsmanship and with a strong architectural feel. The mahogany cabinet is characteristic of his later work in its lack of elaborate decoration and its reliance on the colour and graining of the wood for much of its effect.

Under the direction of Wyburd decoration became slightly more elaborate, with beaten copper plaques, leaded glass panelling and ornate copper for fixtures such as hinges and handles; sometimes mottos were included. Furniture was designed in "ranges" – this wardrobe was part of Liberty's "Athelstan" range. Its pierced heart-shaped motifs are a typical Arts and Crafts application, while the very basic handles are reminiscent of rural traditional furniture. All Liberty designs had a typically British symmetrical emphasis.
•Later Liberty furniture, from c.1900, is less original and was mainly reproductions.

The Greene brothers worked mainly in Honduras mahogany. Joints are complex and visible, involving square pegs of a darker wood than that of the main body; the ebony and mahogany of this chair was the most common combination. Other pieces had inlay of metal or coloured wood.

LIBERTY AND CO. (ENGLISH, 1875-Present)

Liberty & Co. was set up in 1985, primarily as a retail outlet, by Arthur Lasenby Liberty to produce a vast and varied output of textiles, wallpapers, carpets, ceramics, silver and metalwork and furniture. Early furniture, from around 1880, was Anglo-Oriental, based on designs from China and North Africa, mainly in bamboo and designed by Monsieur Ursin Forter who worked for Liberty for many years. In 1883 Leonard F. Wyburd, a painter and architect, set up a Furnishing and Decoration department. Under his directorship Liberty produced furniture, largely in the Arts and Crafts style, using heavy oak in well-constructed solid forms based on rural designs. Mass-produced, but hand-finished and of a high quality, it is still available in fairly limited quantities, and is very collectable today.

Makers Liberty employed many important designers. These included Charles Voysey (p.46), George Walton (p.45), Ernest Gimson (p.48) and the Barnsley brothers (p.48). Most Liberty furniture is stamped or labelled "LIBERTY & CO.".

In the early years Wyburd specialized in Moorish furniture, based on original Egyptian designs. This four-legged mahogany Thebes stool, dated 1884, is one of several variations on a theme. Others were three-legged, with a seat made from a solid piece of wood; some were stained or lacquered in red. The solid, simple shape and minimal exterior decoration are typical.

CHARLES (1868-1957) & HENRY (1870-1954) GREENE (AMERICAN)

Charles and Henry Greene were both architects. They opened a studio in Pasadena, California, in 1893 to design buildings, furniture and furnishings. Their style shows the influence of Arts and Crafts, of Japanese and Chinese construction standards, and of the aesthetic theories of Frank Lloyd Wright (p.46), whom they both greatly admired. They worked exclusively to commission: the armchair on the left was designed for the Robert Blacker house in Pasadena. The Gamble House, also in Pasadena, completed by them in around 1909, is now a museum. The partnership was dissolved in 1916.

CHARLES ROHLFS (AMERICAN, 1853-1936)

As evident in this drop-front desk, Rohlfs worked almost exclusively in dark oak, which was sometimes stained black. He made a feature of hand-wrought iron or copper hardware. As well as desks, he produced storage chests, library furniture and sideboards.
•Most of Rohlfs' pieces bear an incised monogram, "CR". Some are also dated, and these tend to be preferred by collectors.

Charles Rohlfs opened his furniture practice in Buffalo, New York in around 1890. His style is unmistakably Arts and Crafts-influenced, and in particular he made extensive use of exposed joinery.

Value Because Rohlfs' furniture was exclusive, it is rare and collectable today. Pieces are not signed, but they are usually well-documented. Some designs have recently been commercially reproduced but these can be easily identified by their newness and inferior craftsmanship.

GUSTAV STICKLEY (AMERICAN, 1898-Present)

This table is typically simple and solid, its rectilinear construction designed to prevent warping or shrinkage. The firm used mainly American white oak, stained rich or light brown, or grey, in a fuming process developed at the factory. Wood was often riven and joined with mortice and tenon and any hardware was either handmade or had a hand-hammered surface. The leathered top of the table is held with brass tacks made in a 17th-century manner.
•Any upholstery used by the Stickley brothers is mainly leather, typically brown, red or green.

The Stickley name is associated with plain furniture in solid oak, often described as "Mission style", because of its similarity to pieces found in 19th-century American mission churches. Furniture bearing the Stickley name can be attributed to one of three factories, the best known and most collectable of which is the firm of Gustav Stickley. Gustav Stickley (1847-1942), opened his factory in New York State, to make original furniture with an Arts and Crafts feel, using traditional construction methods and hand-made hardware.

Marks and reproductions Most of Gustav's work is stamped in red with a joiner's compass device enclosing the Dutch motto "Als ik kan". The company still makes quality oak and cherry furniture in the Colonial style which presently is of no collectable value. They have recently reproduced a few of Gustav's early designs, but these are obviously modern.

"Craftsman" furniture From around 1900 Gustav made a range of "Craftsman" furniture which included textiles, metalwork and some woven furniture in willow and oak. The most collectable, progressive designs echo the work of Hoffmann (p.40) or Mackintosh (p.44).

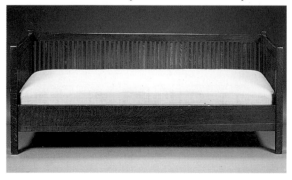

Above This music cabinet is one of the rare designs by English-born architect and furniture designer, Harvey Ellis (1852-1904), who worked with Stickley from 1902. The inlaid panel is typical of Ellis's work; he often used Jugendstil-style motifs (see pp.38-9) inlaid in contrasting materials, such as ivory or darker woods, as well as pewter and copper. Other motifs commonly include stylized flowers and Viking ships. Most inlaid Stickley pieces were designed by Ellis.
•Ellis's designs are so popular that some Stickley pieces have been fitted with modern inlay intended to deceive; poor quality of work usually identifies these.

Left This "Spindle" settle, designed by Gustav Stickley in around 1908, bears obvious design similarities to furniture designed by Hoffmann, and is consequently highly collectable. Other "Craftsman" versions of chairs and settees had high backs.

THE STICKLEY BROTHERS

George and Albert Stickley, two of Gustav's younger brothers, had a workshop in Michigan (1891-1910), making oak furniture, similar in style to the "Craftsman" line, and to conventional rustic "Quaint furniture". However, neither type equalled Gustav's furniture in quality, nor are they of value today. Of more interest is the work of two other brothers, Leopold and J. George Stickley (c.1900-present), who based their designs on later "Craftsman" models. They made simple, solid home and office furniture, which included bookcases and tables. Their more progressive pieces are the most popular today. Many pieces bear a branded signature or brass plate.

THE NANCY SCHOOL

From the latter part of the 19th century the Art Nouveau style dominated the French decorative arts. Two important schools working in this style were set up in Paris and Nancy. The Nancy School, made up of craftsmen and artists working in or around the Nancy area (Alsace), and epitomized by the work of Emile Gallé and Louis Majorelle, was more prolific and consequently the more readily synonymous with Art Nouveau design today. It was formed by Gallé in around 1890 to promote naturalism in design. Other significant members were the Daum brothers and Eugène Vallin. They were the first designers to use marquetry panels, which were often created from local woods, and depicted local flora and fauna.

A fruitwood and marquetry two-tier table by Emile Gallé 1895; ht 30in/76cm

EMILE GALLÉ (FRENCH, 1846-1904)

Known equally for his exquisite glassware (see pp.72-8), Emile Gallé designed furniture which is considered to be pure Art Nouveau. His inventive designs which drew inspiration from nature, particularly the flora and fauna of his native Lorraine, heralded the rise of more floral decorative forms. His use of marquetry led to its revival.

Gallé's designs Gallé's furniture shapes were symmetrical and highly inventive. He used mainly exotic or fruit woods, and treated the wood as a plastic medium, rather than following the grain. The structural elements, such as the supports, tend to be organic, zoomorphic or naturalistic. Rims or top rails often feature open-work relief carving. All his pieces were hand made. The sculptural quality of his designs can be seen in the legs of the table at the top of the page, which combine plant and animal forms and show one of Gallé's favourite motifs, the dragonfly. The inlay is of a typically very high quality. Designs include occasional furniture and dining and bedroom suites. Some pieces are inlaid with verses.

•Gallé signed his work, usually in a corner, and often in elaborate inlay. After his death, the firm produced more traditional pieces, often with less inventive inlay which are also signed "Gallé" (see p.53). Fakes are not known to have existed.

The form of this mahogany vitrine is simple, with emphasis on the inlaid and carved decoration, which itself is restrained. The shelves are undecorated. Larger pieces such as this (62in/159cm in height) generally command higher prices.
•Most of Gallé's furniture has survived in excellent condition as many pieces were commissioned, and owners have tended to covet each one. Even marquetry was laid so precisely as to have usually survived intact.

Gallé produced some novelty forms, such as this music stand, which adapted elements from other designs. This piece, from around 1900, is reminiscent of a Regency chiffonier, although it contains innovative variations that give it a strikingly original appearance. Characteristically, decoration appears on the sides and back as well as on the front. The quality of the fruitwood marquetry rivals that of the 18th century ébénistes. The motifs, of flowers and butterflies, are typical.

LOUIS MAJORELLE (FRENCH, 1859-1926)

Louis Majorelle, another important member of the Nancy School, took over his father's cabinet-making business in 1879. His early work was in a Rococo style but as a member of the Nancy School and influenced by Gallé, he produced hand-made furniture, adopting Art Nouveau forms to create an individual, elegant style. His furniture tends to fall into two types – either architectural, which featured mainly inlaid decoration, or sculptural, with mainly carved decoration. Both types used naturalistic motifs and sinuous forms. He favoured exotic and strongly grained woods, such as mahogany, and used the grain to complement the design and to provide decoration. He often used gilt bronze mounts (ormolu), especially on the feet or supports.

Right This carved mahogany side table is a typical example of Majorelle's sculptural designs, where decoration is confined chiefly to the supports. The legs, although reeded here, can equally often be fluted, and usually terminate in slightly outswept feet.
•Mounts on sculptural pieces are often integral to the design.
•On chairs with arms the leg often becomes part of the armrest.

Collecting Majorelle worked partly to commission, but also produced designs to be sold through a catalogue. Even so his work is rare. Chairs with original fabric command a premium. As well as pieces in Majorelle's style, some unmarked items exist that may well have been designed by him. His work is well-documented and if in doubt collectors should refer to a documented example. His style was often imitated, which can be confusing to collectors, but fakes are so far unknown.

Marks Most of Majorelle's work is marked, often on the doors, and may be branded, stamped, carved, or, as in the example right, inlaid in marquetry.

This credenza from around 1900 has the symmetrical form and inlaid decoration common to Majorelle's architectural pieces. Also typical in such pieces are the short, solid feet and supports (both embellished with metal mounts), the back panel, which is fitted with pleated silk, and the chicory leaf motif. Typically, the marquetry is of very high quality.

EUGÈNE VALLIN (FRENCH, 1856-1922)

Like Louis Majorelle, Eugène Vallin was a cabinet-maker turned furniture designer and also a member of the Nancy School. He later went on to design complete interiors for buildings, including the ceilings, panelling and furniture. Vallin's work tends to be sculptural and it is more sombre and imposing than that of Majorelle and Gallé. Vallin's work is rarer than Gallé's or Majorelle's but it commands similar prices today.

This mahogany bureau and chair demonstrate Vallin's preference for curvilinear forms. Here, the writing area is the only level surface. Decoration is supplied by the natural wood grain, and stalk elements – which often appear in supports, as they do here – are also included in the back plate. Here the supports are tapered and have outswept feet. Typically, mounts and handles are unobtrusive.

THE PARIS SCHOOL

Together with Nancy, Paris was a major centre of French Art Nouveau design. The designers of the Paris School were associated with the Parisian publisher and dealer, Samuel Bing (1838-1905), who sponsored several of them, including Georges de Feure, Eugène Gaillard, Edward Colonna and Hector Guimard, who all contributed furnishings to his *Pavillon de l'Art Nouveau* at the 1900 Paris Exhibition. Parisian styles were more sculptural than those from Nancy, and relatively restrained. Furniture, mainly in fruit woods, tended to be symmetrical, and often had a curved element. The designers managed to achieve a balance between elegant forms and strong organic elements, applying slender, sinuous stems or whiplash-type carving, which may appear in low relief. On chairs, upholstery tends to be sympathetic to the form, as the designers often designed the fabric themselves.

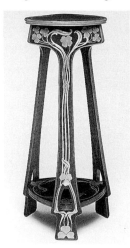

Right A fruitwood salon cabinet by Eugène Gaillard c.1901-02; ht 72in/184cm

EUGÈNE GAILLARD (FRENCH, 1867-1942)

This stand, designed c.1900, is typical of Gaillard, with its symmetrical shape and graceful design. Inlay, often featured in Gaillard's work, is here in copper and brass, and incorporates stylized floral motifs of stems and clover. Light and dark woods are contrasted as an additional decorative feature.

Eugène Gaillard was a French furniture designer, active from 1895-1911. For Bing's Pavilion he produced bedroom and dining suites. His work was typical of the Paris style, with bold, plain outlines and balanced proportions. The large fruitwood salon cabinet in the main picture incorporates strongly curved, plant-like elements. Typically, the flowing lines give an impression of lightness in spite of the considerable size of the piece.

HECTOR GUIMARD (FRENCH, 1867-1942)

Another member of the Paris School, Hector Guimard was an architect and artist craftsman, famous for his organic designs in iron for the entrances of the Paris Métro stations. His was often a distinctive interpretation of the Art Nouveau style, and his furniture tended to be more sculptural than that of the other Paris designers. He designed the interiors to some of his buildings.

This pearwood chair from around 1900 is characteristically light and elegant. The open-work backrest, carved with sinuous whiplash motifs, and the leather upholstery embossed with floral motifs, are redolent of his Paris Métro designs.

Guimard's early work (1886 - 99) concentrated on dark hardwoods in fluid forms with asymmetrical motifs for decoration. His later designs (1900-10) were more gently curved and more sparsely decorated and tended to use softwoods, such as the pearwood here.

GEORGES DE FEURE (FRENCH 1868-1928)

De Feure was a painter and graphic artist who designed stained glass as well as furniture. He moved from Holland to Paris in 1890 and studied as a pupil of Jules Cheret (see p.214) before joining the Paris School. He too worked with Samuel Bing at the 1900 Paris exhibition, where he achieved great success. His pieces were often light and fragile. Designs tended to be extreme and were either very ornate or remarkably restrained, like the cherrywood chair below.

Left The stylized floral and organic carved motifs, and the simple white cotton upholstery are typical of de Feure, but at other times he used embroidered silk or damask, which he often designed himself. On other pieces pale woods, such as birch or sycamore, appear in decorative combination with veneered figured panels.

Above This walnut wardrobe, designed by de Feure for Bing's Pavilion in Paris, is characteristically restrained in form. With its stylized floral motifs, the decoration is typical of the Paris School designers. It is only applied to the legs and corners, and to the bronze locks and handles, which are characteristic of de Feure, who often made decorative use of fittings by applying giltwork.

EDWARD COLONNA (GERMAN, born 1862)

This German designer emigrated to the United States in 1882, but moved to Paris in the 1890s, where he worked in the Art Nouveau style of the Paris School. His work with Samuel Bing included creating a drawing room for his Pavilion at the Paris Exhibition, but he also designed jewelry for Bing and for Tiffany's, for whom he also designed ceramic tablewares.

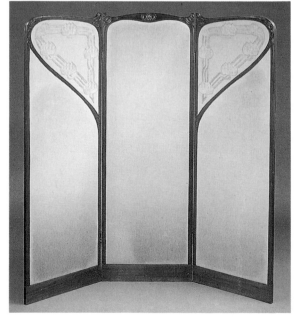

Above This chair, with its elongated back, incorporates both traditional and innovative elements in its design. Paris School chairs rarely include stretchers, but slender cabriole-type feet are common. Here, carved decoration is confined to the edges, with a whiplash motif at the top of the seat rail.

This screen is characteristic of designs from the Paris School, with its typically curvilinear frame made in walnut wood and its carvings of intertwining whiplash motifs. The upholstery is embroidered in golden threads with formalized water lilies and tendrils. Carving on Colonna's pieces is generally light and often incorporates scrolls.
•Colonna was also responsible for railroad car interiors in the United States and for furniture for the Canadian Pacific Railway in Montreal.

THE BELGIAN APPROACH

Three designers stand out as particularly strong exponents of Art Nouveau in Belgium – Henri Clemens van de Velde, Gustave Serrurier-Bovy, and Victor Horta. Working in a predominantly architectural style with the emphasis on function, they produced mainly furniture, but also ceramics, jewelry and metalwork.

Right A mahogany bronze-mounted coiffeuse by Serrurier-Bovy c.1899; ht 74in/188cm

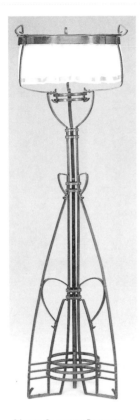

Above Serrurier-Bovy produced many lamps, hat and umbrella stands and ceiling lights in this style. The use of horizontal bands – in this case, three towards the base and two below the shade – is typical. There is no surface decoration, but the minimalist design incorporates some florid features, such as the curving vertical side-pieces and the D-shaped spurs on the top rim of the shade. The screw heads on the lower horizontals are left exposed.
•The firm also produced metalwork vases, usually combined with glass.

GUSTAVE SERRURIER-BOVY (BELGIAN, 1858-1910)

Born in Liège, Serrurier-Bovy became one of Belgium's leading Art Nouveau designers. His early work owes much to French and English design, particularly to that of William Morris and the Arts and Crafts Movement. His furniture tends to be symmetrical, with restrained curves. The mahogany coiffeuse above is architectural in form and although solid, it is enlivened by the use of brass fittings. Serrurier-Bovy's later work owes more to German or Viennese design.

"Silex" furniture From 1902 Serrurier-Bovy produced his inexpensive "Silex" range of ready-to-assemble furniture in kit form which he designed in response to his belief that everyone should have access to beautiful furniture. Pieces, which included tables, chairs and bedroom furniture, were usually produced out of light woods, such as pitch pine. They are relatively simple in form and employ circles and squares in any decoration, which are usually laid out in a symmetrical arrangement.
•As when first made, Silex furniture is less expensive today than other Serrurier-Bovy pieces.
Marks and value Serrurier-Bovy's work is usually signed, often with a branded signature. Silex furniture is stamped "SILEX".

This night table is typical of Serrurier Bovy's "Silex" furniture designs in its use of simple geometric forms, pale wood, painted sheet metal, stencilled motifs and decorative raised metal studs incorporated into the joints.

HENRI CLEMENS VAN DE VELDE (BELGIAN, 1863-1957)

Henri Clemens van de Velde trained as a painter, architect and graphic designer in Antwerp and Paris, and was instrumental in the evolution of the Belgian Art Nouveau style. He designed all manner of items, including whole interiors, but was particularly influential in furniture, ceramics, jewelry and metalwork. His work was produced mainly to commission.

Availability and marks Van de Velde's furniture is fairly rare and, as his importance as a designer is now fully acknowledged, is keenly sought after. It is rarely marked but contemporary photographs exist, which help in the search for the provenance of some pieces.

Above Van de Velde's furniture often combines innovative elements with tradition. It tends to be substantial, concentrating on restrained, sculptural well-balanced forms for interest, rather than applied decoration and inlay. The strongly traditional form of this screen incorporates an Art Nouveau whiplash motif on the tops and bottoms of the panels which is also used for the railing on the desk (**right**). An innovative feature is found in the glass panels.

Above This chair has a traditional feel despite the innovative interplay of uprights and horizontals. The way the arm rests overlap the upright back rails is typical of van de Velde's work.

Left Practicality is never sacrificed to design – the drawers of this desk (c.1898) are all in easy reach. Instead, design works with function – the light fitting is incorporated into the desk and the wire is trained through the metal gallery rail at the back. The leather upholstery is characteristically decorated with beaded studwork. These feet are simple, but others are chamfered.

VICTOR HORTA (BELGIAN, 1861-1947)

Horta was an architect and designer, who trained in Paris before studying under the Belgian royal architect Alphonse Balat. He found inspiration for his work in nature, Gothic designs and 15th-century Flemish paintings, as well as in the work of the French architect, Viollet-le-Duc, who introduced him to ironwork. Horta designed both buildings and their interiors to create a harmony of textures and colours. As a result, some of his pieces may appear incongruous if placed outside of their original context. His furniture is characterized by sinuous lines, with curves often forming the shape of the stems of flowers. Decoration often includes wrought iron and curved metalwork or inlaid woods.

Horta believed in hand-crafting his furniture and refused to accept modern machine methods. This, together with his insistence on using only first class materials (such as American stained glass and exotic woods from Africa), made his work very expensive.

Availability Horta's work is difficult to find and is very desirable for collectors today. Unfortunately, shortly before his death Horta destroyed a lot of important documentation relating to his furniture.

These chairs display Horta's preference for novel forms – for example, supporting pillars bisect the stretchers. Although solid, the pierced backs give the pieces a lightweight feel, an effect which is further enhanced by the central splat which creeps down into the well, and the strongly curved lines. Horta manages to combine an interesting form with comfort, making a decorative feature of the padded backrests and seats. The backs and the terminals of the front legs have a characteristic sculptural quality. Horta is likely to have designed the fabric on the chairs himself to complement the interior they were to appear in.
•Horta's furniture bears similarities to the work of van de Velde but it tends to be more decorative.

THE WIENER WERKSTÄTTE

Inspired by his association with the Vienna Secessionists and their attempts to bring more abstract and purer forms to design, Josef Hoffmann founded the Wiener Werkstätte in 1903, and together with Koloman Moser (who resigned in 1906) worked as its artistic director. Initially these two designed all the Werkstätte's work themselves, but by 1910 they received contributions from, among others, Josef Olbrich, Gustav Klimt and Dagobert Pêche. At one time the Workshop employed 100 workers, including nearly 40 "masters" who signed their work. As well as buildings and furniture, the group designed silver, glass (see p.82), ceramics and metalwork (see p.189).

A beechwood chair designed by Josef Hoffmann for the Wiener Werkstätte c.1905; ht 42in/106.5cm

JOSEF HOFFMANN (AUSTRIAN, 1870-1956)

These two chairs were designed by Hoffmann and made by Kohn in around 1900-1905. Workshop-made rather than mass-produced, these pieces represent a departure from Hoffmann's modern steam-moulded techniques towards more traditional methods of construction. Decoration is in the form of inlay applied to the back panel and studs fitted into the upholstery – a feature which was used throughout this period. The gilt sabots on the front legs of the chairs are both decorative and practical.

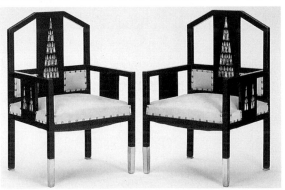

Hoffmann originally trained as an architect and was influenced by Mackintosh (see p.44) and the Glasgow School. His notable commissions include the interior of the Fledermaus Café in Vienna. In 1897 he founded the Vienna Secession, an association of artists and architects disillusioned with the work of the Viennese Society of Visual Artists. Unlike many Wiener Werkstätte designers, Hoffmann often used mass production techniques.

Hoffmann's designs Hoffmann designed all kinds of furniture, including tables, chairs and light fittings. His work uses severe, geometric or linear forms, rather than the sinuous forms of other Art Nouveau designers. The *Sitzmachine* (sitting machine) in the main picture typically combines simple oval and rectilinear forms. This example is adjustable – the knobs determine the

Some of Hoffmann's furniture is made from bentwood – laminated or solid wood steamed and bent into the required curvilinear shape. These pieces, exemplified by this simple bentwood table, typically have smooth or gently rounded corners. It was made to Hoffmann's design by Jacob and Josef Kohn, one of the largest Viennese furniture manufacturers who, together with the Viennese firm, Thonet Brothers, executed the majority of Hoffmann's designs.

angle of incline. Hoffmann often placed ball-shaped knobs at intersections. This chair also makes typical use of piercing in the squares in the back and the slender rectangular grilles in the sides. Other chairs had upholstered backs. Hoffman used little surface decoration.
• Although this piece is made from beechwood, Hoffmann often used more costly limed oak, mahogany and ebonized wood. The bases of some of his pieces are covered in beaten brass.

The Wiener Werkstätte produced several mantel clocks. This strongly geometric example, designed by Josef Urban, is made of such diverse materials as walnut, silver plate, ivorene, enamel and agate.

JOSEF OLBRICH (AUSTRIAN, 1867-1908)

Olbrich was an architect, artist and designer who made a valuable contribution to the output of the Wiener Werkstätte, and who, like Hoffmann and Moser, had been a member of the Vienna Secession. In 1879 he had worked at the Darmstadt Artists' Colony, where he designed the Darmstadt Room for the 1900 Paris Exhibition for which he won a gold medal. Previously, he had worked for the Matildenhöhe, which placed art and beauty at its forefront, and for which he designed both the buildings and the interiors. He produced items in metalwork, as well as designing furniture.

Olbrich's designs are not as severely geometric as those of Hoffmann and Moser, but are lighter and feature formalized decorative motifs, often borrowing from those of the Jugendstil (see pp.38-9). This walnut cabinet, entitled *Herbst* (Autumn) is made up of strong symmetrical elements. Decoration is restricted to panels inlaid with fruitwood and mother of pearl, and the carved lines along the sides.

KOLOMAN MOSER (AUSTRIAN, 1868-1918)

Left This rare cabinet was designed by Moser c.1900. The interior opens to reveal three maidens in marquetry among bubbles of silvered metal. The figural decoration used by Moser is similar to that of the Glasgow Four; however, Moser's maidens have faces.

Right The firm of Kohn made this mahogany and beechwood desk designed by Moser c.1902. Steam-moulded and laminated, it makes extensive use of new and modern technology. The design is avant-garde and very different from what was being produced elsewhere on the Continent.

Koloman Moser was a painter, graphic artist and designer. Along with Hoffmann, he was a member of the Secessionists, and a founder member of the Wiener Werkstätte. His work had a very strong influence on Austrian designs and is sometimes so close to Hoffmann's that it is very difficult to distinguish between the two.

Marks Wiener Werkstätte furniture is seldom signed. Attribution is usually made using contemporary photographic or original design material.

THE EXOTIC

A spectacular vitrine by Carlo Bugatti c.1900

Interpretations of the Art Nouveau style varied considerably. One very original approach was that of the Italian, Carlo Bugatti, whose designs looked back to 13th and 14th century Moorish Spain and North Africa. His interiors resemble theatrical settings for *The Arabian Nights*, with tribal and Middle Eastern fabrics embellished with cushions and tassels, and a sense of novelty that contrasts sharply with the work of the schools in Paris, Nancy, Vienna and Glasgow. Carlo Zen, working in Italy at the same time as Bugatti, produced furniture slightly more akin to popular Continental Art Nouveau designs, with symmetrical forms and floral inlay and an avoidance of metal *appliqués*, painted panels and exotic tassels. In Spain, Antoni Gaudí produced organic furniture with few straight lines or inlay, making full use of the wood grain. In France, Carabin took these sculptural elements to their height, constructing furniture in female forms. All these designers' pieces exhibit unusual and often extraordinary elements of design which separate them from mainstream Art Nouveau.

CARLO BUGATTI (ITALIAN, 1855-1940)

Cabinets, such as this ebonzied and rosewood writing desk, are architectural in form and make strong use of pillars and spindles. Some pieces combine function and form and tables may incorporate cabinets or seats may be designed with integral lamps.
•Colours tend to be subdued; brown and black dominate.

Bugatti produced a wide range of furniture, often for specially commissioned interiors. Interest in his work grew with increased European colonial expansion into North Africa and the resultant exposure to the Arab culture. Many of his interiors have a decadent, harem-like appearance, reinforced by the addition of exotic Middle Eastern carpets.

Decoration Although influenced by North African style, Bugatti's decorative approach was highly original – the vitrine in the main picture shows his preference for circular motifs. A large variety of materials feature in the decoration – he was particularly fond of brass, pewter or ivory inlay which is invariably of a high standard and often more inventive and of higher quality than the North African models that inspired him. He often used contrasting woods. He also applied strips of beaten or pierced metal, or embossed metal *appliqués* and tassels to his furniture. His characteristic use of vellum (fine calf or lambskin parchment) was particularly unusual; the vitrine in the main picture is covered in vellum and decorated with Japanese motifs of stylized insects and branches. Similar decoration is applied to his chairs and benches.

Marks A number of Bugatti's pieces have a painted signature incorporated within the vellum panels. His furniture is not known to have been faked.

Forms Many of Bugatti's pieces combine strong circular and rectilinear elements. The verticals in the writing desk, **left**, contrast strongly with the circular decoration. In his chairs, comfort was never a primarly concern.
•The elements of large sectional furniture were often produced as separate pieces.
•Turned legs often have blocks at terminals or junctions.

CARLO ZEN (ITALIAN, 1851-1918)

Zen's furniture appeared at all the major international exhibitions, starting with Turin in 1898. He often applied inlaid flowers with slender, sinuous stems which have recently been referred to as the "spaghetti style".

Left This mahogany cabinet, designed by Carlo Zen for the Turin Exhibition of 1902, shows his preference for using the wood grain as a canvas for exotic floral inlay of mother of pearl, silver and brass. The form, relatively restrained and with a definite perpendicular emphasis, anticipates the Art Deco furniture of Jacques Ruhlmann (see p. 54). The feet on this cabinet are typically short and solid.

Right This large mirror from around 1905 exhibits a similar use of "spaghetti style" inlaid decoration to that on the cabinet. His furniture is generally symmetrical in shape and always elegant – the only irregularity in this piece is the addition of a small compartment at the top of the mirror.
• Although Zen's design skills have been criticised, at its best his furniture is well constructed and innovatively designed.

RUPERT CARABIN (FRENCH, 1862-1932)

From 1878 Carabin worked as a wood carver with a cabinet maker in Paris and by the end of the 19th century he had become one of the city's most individualistic artists. He combined sculptures of women with furniture design, often carving a woman from a piece of wood which he would then attach to the furniture. His treatment of women differed from the sensuous treatment of other Art Nouveau designers in that they were portrayed in a subservient or enslaved position, often bound to the furniture, and always naked.

Marks Carabin's work is not usually signed, but it is possible to identify his distinctive style by looking in contemporary catalogues.

This pearwood book case from 1905 is more restrained than much of Carabin's work, as the women, depicting an allegorical scene, are carved in low relief. High relief decoration is confined to carved oak leaves trailing beneath the pediment. The women have ample proportions and hair *en chignon*. In contrast to the exotic decoration, the form is relatively simple. A rich patina is achieved by soaking the wood in linseed oil and then fine polishing. Other pieces include entire fireplaces in a female form.

ANTONI Y CORNET GAUDÍ (SPANISH, 1859-1926)

Gaudí was particularly famous for his architectural designs in Barcelona, Spain, which include work for the Güell Palace (1884-90) and the Vicens House (1883-5) both of which exhibit his highly personal Moorish style. However, as part of the Catalan movement, "El Modernisme", he also created a range of idiosyncratic furniture in a highly exotic, organic Art Nouveau style, with undulating curves and floral motifs. His earlier designs had more in common with Spanish historical elements than his later more sculptural work. Gaudí's furniture often displays an asymmetrical or amorphous element, which can also be found in his buildings.

Marks Little, if any, of Gaudí's work is marked and it is not known to have been faked.

This carved wood *étagère*, designed c.1900, shows how Gaudí's personal interpretation of the Art Nouveau had progressed from his earlier designs, which had more in common with Spanish historical themes. His sculptural style is evident in the novel apron, carved in low relief and shaped to simulate hanging foliage, and the inward-scrolling feet at the end of stylized legs. Further irregularity is added by the pierced centre through which the three stretchers pass. Gaudi treats his materials with plasticity, lending the piece an organic appearance.

ARCHITECTURAL ART NOUVEAU

An oak cabinet designed by Charles Rennie Mackintosh in 1898; ht 63in/159cm

Many Art Nouveau architects became involved in interior design, creating everything from the building itself through to fireplaces, furniture and even keyholes. Their furniture was hand-crafted rather than mass-produced, mainly in oak, with simple forms and perpendicular shapes. In Britain, Hugh Mackay Baillie-Scott tended to use inlaid decoration, whereas Charles Rennie Mackintosh, Ernest Taylor and George Walton made more use of leaded glass panels. Other designers applied architectural Art Nouveau motifs to more mundane objects; George Logan applied the Glasgow Rose to dinner services, and Wedgwood and Co. applied it to chamber pots, with little sympathy between form and decoration.

The Glasgow artists, who included Charles Rennie Mackintosh, Ernest Taylor and George Walton, became known as the Glasgow School.

CHARLES RENNIE MACKINTOSH (SCOTTISH, 1868-1928)

Architect-designer Charles Rennie Mackintosh was one of the most influential figures in the development of Art Nouveau and the Modern Movement and is still internationally admired. Like his Scottish forbear, Robert Adam who worked on Kedleston Hall, his commissions involved him in furnishing specific rooms in houses he had already designed. Mackintosh worked closely with the architect Herbert MacNair and the Macdonald sisters – Frances, who later married MacNair, and his own future wife, Margaret, who designed metalwork and embroidery. Together they were known as the Glasgow Four and were highly influential members of the Glasgow School.

This high-backed oak dining chair has a perpendicular emphasis and a sculptural quality common to Mackintosh's furniture. He was particularly fond of the tall, ladder-back form for chairs, with the ladder extending beyond the seat; the double spindle stretchers are typical. He often applied decorative motifs to the back; this oval back rail is pierced with the motif of a formalized bird in flight. Comfort was not a prime consideration; upholstery tends to be very simple – this chair has a rush seat.

Attribution
Mackintosh did not sign his work, although most of his furniture designs are well-documented. The cabinet at the top of the page has a brass panel which is signed "Margaret Macdonald". Many pieces are optimistically described by dealers and auctioneers as being "in the Mackintosh style", and

his name is often used as an umbrella term for a variety of general Arts and Crafts furniture.
Style Mackintosh's furniture has clean lines and minimal decoration. He often worked with dark stained oak, as in the large cabinet above, but he also produced a number of designs in white painted wood.

In contrast to the high-backed chair on the left is this contoured one, which is another typical Mackintosh design.
•Both these chairs were designed for Miss Cranston's Tea Rooms in Glasgow, the tall one for the dining room and the short one for the billiard and smoking room.
•Mackintosh also designed light fittings, pianos, cutlery (flatware) and wrought-iron work.

Decoration

Decoration may include painted or beaten brass panels and leaded and glazed windows. The oak cabinet pictured on the left has a combination of these. The brass panels bear enigmatic female figures, a motif which, because of its frequent use by the Glasgow Four, earned them the nickname of the "Spook School". The leaded glass panel is also typically decorated with the stylized Glasgow Rose. Piercing is usually of a chequered design and any brass fittings on Mackintosh's furniture, such as handles or escutcheons, are subtle.

•Mackintosh's later commissions, from around 1912, tend to be less exciting and less collectable than his earlier work. In 1920, he moved to France to pursue an interest in painting.

ERNEST ARCHIBALD TAYLOR (SCOTTISH, 1874-1951)

Above Taylor designed several screens in wood panelling, rather than the fabric or stamped leather more commonly used at that time. He makes use of the traditional rose motif.

Right The overhanging pediment on this writing cabinet from c.1903 is typical of Taylor. The leaded glass panels set into the upper cabinet are characteristic, as is the use of stained glass. The panels would have been designed by Taylor himself. The tiny, pierced, formalized flowerheads on the apron of this writing cabinet indicate Taylor's work, but are not exclusive to him. The handles, in ring form, provide an important decorative element and are also typical.

Little is known of Taylor. However, as a painter and furniture designer he was influential in bringing the designs of the Glasgow School to a wider public. Few pieces were directly commissioned; instead, Taylor's furniture was made commercially, mostly by the firm of Wylie and Lockhead. In 1908, Taylor moved to Manchester to work for George Wragge Ltd.

Design and style

Taylor's designs are often confused with those of Mackintosh, but his work is more similar to that of the British Arts and Crafts designers. Architectural in form, his pieces are always substantial, with strong vertical elements and spare but distinctive decoration. They are usually made of stained, ebonized or white-painted oak. Like Mackintosh, Taylor makes frequent use of the popular stylized rose.

Attribution Taylor's furniture is rarely found at auction today. His pieces are not marked, so the collector must try to establish the provenance. Useful contemporary documentation includes the London-based design publication, *The Studio*.

GEORGE WALTON (SCOTTISH, 1867-1933)

Walton studied architecture and design at evening classes at the Glasgow School of Art. He started his own interior design firm, George Walton & Co., Ecclesiastical & House Decorators, in 1888. Among his commissions were chairs in ebonized wood for the photographic firm, Kodak, and he began to work for Liberty (see p. 30) in 1897.

This mahogany desk, designed by Walton in around 1900, is typical of his designs – strongly linear, with a vertical emphasis created by the tapering legs.
•Walton also produced a large amount of metalwork and a range of Clutha glassware for James Couper (se p.68).

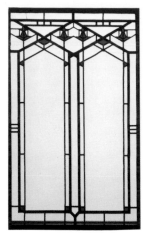

Above Stained-glass panels tend to be small-scale and designed with rectilinear panels of vertical emphasis. These sometimes include diagonals, as in the top section of this window, an arrangement inspired by the art of the American Indians. The use of colour tends to be minimal, and ornament abstract.

Most of Wright's work which is available today was designed for commercial interiors, such as offices and schools. This side chair was made for the Hillside Home School at Spring Green, Wisconsin. The simple structure and leather seat are typical of Wright's designs.

FRANK LLOYD WRIGHT (AMERICAN, 1867-1959)

Wright was a prolific architect who, until 1914, worked mainly in the "Prairie" style – a mid-Western interpretation of the Arts and Crafts movement of which he became a major exponent. He believed in thematic consistency in interior design and created the furniture for most of his architectural projects himself. He later worked with more modernist materials (see p.61).

Above Working in stained, fumed oak with a dark, reddish or brown patina, Wright created forms of revolutionary simplicity, based on architectural, rectilinear lines and intersecting planes, which relied on their imaginative construction for decorative effect. The undecorated spindles and slab crest rail of this chair are typical. Wright's domestic designs tend to be preferred to his commercial work – these pieces are rarer and more complex in design, and usually better made. The progressive pieces are most popular, particularly spindle- and high-back seat furniture.

Metal and glasswork
From around 1905 Wright produced some painted sheet metal furniture, as well as metal vases and lighting fixtures in bronze and stained or leaded glass, and stained-glass windows

Fakes and reproductions None of Wright's work is signed, but provenance is usually available. While no deliberate fakes exist, a lot of contemporary American furniture is misrepresented as Wright's work, particularly stained glass and furnishings in the Prairie style, but these are identifiable by their inferior design. Recently some of Wright's early designs have been reproduced; these can be distinguished by their obvious newness.
• Wright's later work, from the early 20th century, is inexpensive compared to his early pieces, but is bound to increase in value as the limited supply of his early work becomes exhausted.
• Early work was handmade, but later pieces were made commercially with metal screws and machined joints.

CHARLES ANNESLEY VOYSEY (ENGLISH, 1847-1941)

Charles Voysey was another architect who applied his design expertise to furniture as well as buildings, working in a style strongly influenced by the English Arts and Crafts movement. Towards the end of the century he began to design household items, such as cutlery, tea wares, and clocks. He worked mainly to commission.

Identification Voysey never signed his work, but many designs are registered at London's Patent Office. His unique style is unmistakable.

Decoration Voysey's designs are well-balanced and solid-looking. Decoration is usually sympathetic to the form and tends to make a feature of the wood grain. Any additional decoration is usually pierced or inlaid, but may be painted or in the form of metal *appliqués*. Motifs are generally entwined in a flowing organic style with obvious roots in Continental Art Nouveau. The central metal hinge of the writing desk on the right is pierced with the figures of two birds and a snake in a typical Art Nouveau style. The heart, a common Arts and Crafts motif, was frequently used by Voysey.

Voysey's style was strongly influenced by the English Arts and Crafts movement, with furniture hand-made in native woods such as oak and beech, and sometimes stained as in this writing desk. His distinctive designs tend to have a strong vertical emphasis, usu-

ally created by the use of long, tapering, upright elements, such as the octagonal columns supporting the desk. These sometimes terminate in rectangular finials.
• The overhanging top of the writing desk is characteristic of Voysey.

Chair backs, often innovative, tend to incorporate tapering uprights, perhaps at right angles to the arm rests. This oak chair's strong vertical element is characteristic of Voysey's style. Modified versions with shorter backs were produced for Liberty's (see p.30). Chairs have either four stretchers, as here, or none at all. Rush seating is a common alternative to a fitted cushion.

Baillie-Scott frequently used metal inlay; pewter roundels, similar to the design illustrated above, were typical.

MACKAY HUGH BAILLIE-SCOTT (ENGLISH, 1865-1945)

The architect, Mackay Hugh Baillie-Scott also produced furniture in a strongly architectural style, designing robust, utilitarian pieces, hand-made in mahogany and oak, with the natural grain of wood used to decorative effect. Baillie-Scott made much of his work to commission, including some interesting designs for keyboard instruments.

Above This mahogany wardrobe, made by cabinet-makers, Wylie and Lockhead, has chequered inlay in ebony and blond woods. Typically, the apron is curved and the cornice overhanging. Also characteristic are the panels outlined with ornate stringing.

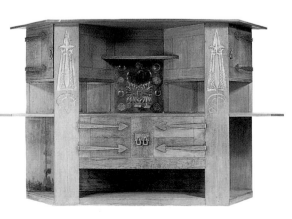

This large oak buffet makes typical use of bold, innovative inlay and incorporates a beaten *repoussé* panel. Baillie-Scott's original, even revolutionary, forms often turned a functional item into an art object. Decorative use has been made of the large gilt wrought-iron hinge and lock plates.
•Baillie-Scott's wide range of furniture is all unsigned, and much is erroneously attributed to him. Contemporary photographs or magazine articles may help establish provenance.

THE COTSWOLD SCHOOL

This loose association of English furniture makers, located first at Pinbury and then at Sapperton in the Cotswolds, Gloucestershire, was led by the architect and designer, Ernest Gimson and the brothers, Sydney and Ernest Barnsley. The School attempted to unite traditional rural craftsmanship with the hand-crafting principles advocated by the Arts and Crafts Movement. Designs were relatively sombre, with decoration sometimes restricted simply to chequered stringing. Their furniture was machine-made, but they spurned the use of screws in favour of the more traditional dovetail joints. Each member of the group has his own distinctive style. Other craftsmen associated with the Cotswold School include Peter Waals, the Dutch cabinet maker, who came to England to become foreman in 1901, and Gordon Russell.

Right A walnut and ebony cabinet by Ernest Gimson 1908; ht approx. 4ft/1.23m

Gimson's pieces always feature subtle inlaid decoration. In addition to contrasting woods, or inlays of holly, ebony and cherrywood, some more expensive pieces also include ivory, bone or mother-of-pearl. The latter appears on this cabinet in inset panels and a central escutcheon.

ERNEST GIMSON (ENGLISH, 1864-1919)

An architect and designer, Gimson's furniture, always hand-made, features simple geometric forms and decoration, and has a strongly symmetrical emphasis. He followed the principles of medieval craftsmanship. His work is typified by the use of figured and often contrasting woods or veneers. On many pieces he achieved the decorative effect purely through geometric arrangement of the grain on areas of veneer. He used both local and exotic woods, and had a particular fondness for ebony, which is featured in the large cabinet in the main picture. Such heavy cabinets tend to be supported on equally heavy, short feet. Although cabinets predominate, Gimson also made a small amount of dining room furniture, usually of relatively simple form.

This detail of the cabinet in the main picture shows the Cotswold craftsmen's preference for traditional dovetail joints rather than screws.
•Gimson produced a number of designs for execution in wrought iron and plaster.
•Most of his work was designed to exclusive commission.

SYDNEY (1865-1926) & ERNEST (1836-1926) BARNSLEY

Like Gimson, the Barnsley brothers used the colour and the grain of the wood for decorative effect. However, this mahogany sideboard designed by Sydney Barnsley makes use of painted decoration by the ceramic decorators Alfred and Louise Powell.

These brothers produced simple, well-proportioned, functional furniture, including dining and bedroom furniture and a range of occasional pieces, in mahogany and local woods, especially walnut and oak. Using traditional methods, they avoided the use of screws, and preferred chamfered legs to sharp edges. Their works closed down in around 1918.
• Pieces are not signed and the brothers' work is hard to tell apart.

PETER WAALS (DUTCH, 1870-1937)

Another member of the Cotswold School, Waals, although Dutch, designed furniture that was quintessentially British. His work is seated in the tradition of the Arts and Crafts and Art Nouveau movements rather than in the more modern style of Art Deco, although its functional appearance gives it something in common with the Modernist furniture produced elsewhere in Europe. He preferred country woods, especially walnut, cedar, oak and limed oak. Pieces are rarely signed, but many are commissioned and so have an available history.

Some Arts and Crafts features are evident in this Waals walnut and cedar wardrobe from 1928 – for example, the use of the wood grain as a decorative element, and the stout, masculine, heavy form, which borders on the utilitarian. Typically, ornament is absent.

GORDON RUSSELL (ENGLISH, 1892-1980)

The double hayrake stretchers on this table are an innovative element in an otherwise conventional form, but they also make an important structural contribution as they provide added strength to the piece. The peg construction is clearly visible in this table. Even those concessions to ornament, such as the ear pieces (the shaped sections between the legs and the frieze) and the spandrels in the corners of the table are primarily functional and only incidentally decorative.

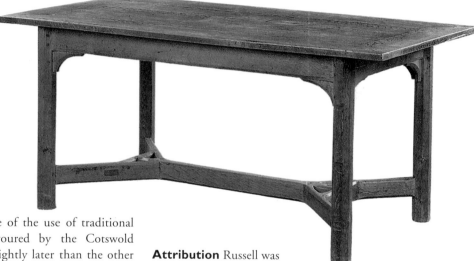

Russell was another advocate of the use of traditional construction techniques favoured by the Cotswold School. Although working slightly later than the other makers mentioned in this section, he never really made the transition to the use of Modernist materials and styles adopted in Continental Europe during the 1920s and '30s. He made a wide range of items, including dining room, bedroom and office furniture.

Forms and decoration Pieces are all hand-made with a hand-finished surface. They are often in oak, and are solid, with emphasis on the quality of construction. No use is made of carving or other decoration, as the form was considered sufficient in itself.

This fine sideboard makes only a few concessions to ornament, with carved laburnum handles, a moulded frieze and a waved apron. It has a solid, conservative appearance.

Attribution Russell was primarily a designer and it is unlikely that he made any of his pieces himself. Some furniture comes with a paper label; that of the oak dining table, above, is particularly detailed and reads: "This piece a dining table in English quartered oak was designed by Gordon Russell and constructed by hand by G. Cooke in the workshop of Gordon Russell and Sons Broadway Worcestershire England in May 1923". This workshop, established by Russell, is still in operation today.

Condition Ear pieces are vulnerable to knocks and damage. Make sure they are original by checking the wood corresponds in colour to the main piece. Collectors should expect to find some wear – for example, scratches or knocks on the feet and lower legs: this is not detrimental to value unless severe. Chairs are sometimes reupholstered – check modern springing or modern-looking hide covers for signs of age, as the piece may be recent.

THE TRANSITION TO ART DECO

An Omega Workshops dressing table mirror, decorated by Vanessa Bell in 1914; ht 26¼in/67cm

Before the end of the first decade of the 20th century Art Nouveau furniture had begun to lose favour, with designers and the public alike craving a new approach which borrowed nothing from that style's curvilinear excesses. Several French designers looked back to the late 18th and early 19th century to produce pieces inspired by Louis XIV and the French Empire. At the same time as Hoffmann in Austria created his Seccessionist furniture (see p.40), in Britain a group of artisans endeavoured to break away from the mainstream furniture productions of the 1900s of largely Georgian revivals or the Arts and Crafts furniture of Voysey and the Cotswold School. The Omega workshops produced relatively simple hand-made furniture, often with brightly-coloured decoration. In Holland, the Dutch designer, Gerrit Rietveldt designed the red and blue chair and with his early Art Deco forms created a landmark in furniture design.

THE OMEGA WORKSHOPS (ENGLISH, 1913-19)

Marks Furniture from the Omega Workshops usually bears the Greek omega symbol, painted on the underside. Few pieces survive today.

The Omega Workshops were established in 1913 by painter, art critic and potter, Roger Fry, to produce and sell applied art, which combined the Arts and Crafts ethic with Post-Impressionist art. He employed a number of artists, including Duncan Grant, Vanessa Bell, Wyndham Lewis, Frederick Etchells, Cuthbert Hamilton and Edward Wadsworth, who between them created whole interiors. They produced domestic furnishings which placed hand-painted decoration before form, and which, although a departure from the mainstream, were not avant-garde. Noticeable in most of Omega's work is an elegance of design.

These two chairs were designed by Roger Fry in around 1913. They are relatively subdued, with restrained hand-painting in a pattern of white on grey. They were retailed as "Queen Anne" chairs but bear no resemblance to chairs of that time and probably have been given the name because they were designed at the time of a Queen Anne revival in architecture. The simple linear shape and sparse decoration are close to the later designs in the Art Deco period.

Above Similarly quirky to the name given to the chairs on the left is the name of this "Egyptian" dining chair (also designed by Fry in around 1913) which bears no resemblance to anything in Ancient Egyptian furniture. Typically, emphasis is placed on applied decoration rather than form. The chair has a repeating painted geometric design on a yellow ground; the form is relatively simple.

Decorative techniques Abstract designs were inspired by Wyndham Lewis, and an Italian influence, which can be found in all aspects of the workshops' work, came from several visits Duncan Grant made to Italy. Although the workshop has been accused of poor workmanship, the decoration is usually of a high standard. Fry often applied his decoration to second hand Gothic or Medieval furniture, or the classical work of the Adam brothers.

The dressing table mirror in the main picture was decorated by Vanessa Bell in 1914 and is typical of the Workshop's designs, with its "modern" omega shape and the abstract frieze surround, painted in green and mustard on a black background.

GERRIT THOMAS RIETVELD (DUTCH, 1888-1964)

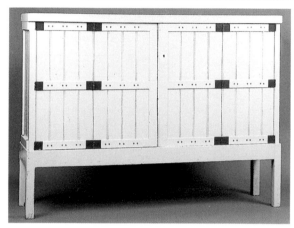

Gerrit Rietveld initially trained as a carpenter before becoming an architect and furniture designer, setting up a workshop in 1911. In 1918 he joined the de Stijl group, whose members believed furniture should have a universal, rather than an individual appeal. The majority of his work was experimental, but some designs were manufactured by the Dutch retail company, Metz, who promoted the work of modern designers.

Left Rietveld's early work was in the simple style of Dutch Arts and Crafts. This white-painted wooden linen cupboard from around 1911 is typical of designs from this period and shows a resemblance to the furniture of the Cotswold school, with its simple hand-made form. The only concession to the later "Modern" design is the red and white hand-painting.

Right Rietveld's name has become synonymous with his Red and Blue Chair, which he designed in 1919, and which pre-empted the Modernist designs of the Bauhaus and Scandinavian designers such as Alvar Aalto (see p. 63). The chair represents a departure from Rietveld's earlier, simpler designs, as, influenced by the de Stijl group which he joined in 1919, and by the works of such designers as Frank Lloyd Wright in America, his designs became more avant-garde and Cubist in form.
•Other "landmark" designs by Rietveld include his Zig-Zag chair and the "Crate" chair.

Later designs moved towards the Modernist styles of Art Deco. This chair, produced in around 1927, is made in bent laminated wood and steel and has an affinity with the chairs of Marcel Breuer and Isokon. It is purely utilitarian and functional, with the only decoration a contrast in painted wood.

PAUL FOLLOT (FRENCH, 1877-1941)

Paul Follot was one of a few Art Nouveau designers who made the transition to Art Deco. He was a French interior decorator, and as well as furniture, designed textiles, wallpaper, ceramics and silverware. His designs covered the entire style spectrum, and ranged from distinctly traditional to high Art Deco, and they always exhibit a high level of craftsmanship in both construction and decoration.

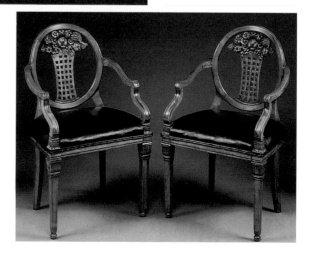

Early work Follot's early work, produced before the mid-20s, was based on late 18th-century forms, with an emphasis on comfort.

These sycamore chairs from around 1912 are a clear departure from Art Nouveau styles and take inspiration from the 18th century. The back splats are similar to those on Josef Hoffmann's chairs (see p. 40).

This chair and sofa were designed by Follot in around 1915-20. Giltwood frames with bright upholstery were a common feature of his furniture in this period. He preferred to design complete interiors or sets of furniture, and this sofa and chair are part of a set that includes a chaise-longue, three armless chairs and a small table. Designs tend to be restrained with controlled embellishment and an emphasis on simple forms. Typically, the upholstery provides the main decoration on these pieces. Additional decoration is in the form of carved flowers; these became gradually more stylized as Follot's career progressed, and were later dispensed with in favour of inlaid decoration. Although relatively heavy, Follot's furniture always manages to look lightweight and elegant.
• A carved budding rose, known today as the "Follot rose", is often found on Follot's work, especially on back rails and chair splats.
• The slightly less avant-garde designs are the most readily available. Pieces are seldom signed.

Materials Follot eschewed modern materials, and developed instead a growing interest in the possibilities of wood, particularly pale woods. He began by experimenting with inlays, gilding, veneers and lacquer, and then became increasingly preoccupied with bringing out the contrast between different woods. In his unupholstered pieces, the emphasis is on form as much as decoration.

Left This dressing table from around 1925 represents Follot's more Modernist designs. Even so, it is made from lacquered wood, rather than one of the "new" materials such as amboyna or macassar ebony. Not all his Modernist work dates from this later period and some pieces from the pre-war era seem to anticipate the move toward more streamlined, innovative forms that occurred in the early 1930s. Follot always concentrated on comfort and style even when creating modern pieces.

PAUL IRIBE (FRENCH, 1883-1935)

This chair from around 1913 is obviously inspired by the First Empire type of furnishings of the early 19th century, which in turn were influenced by Ancient Egyptian and Roman styles. Most notable is the return to comfort – the chair has heavy cushions and a heavily-padded seat back. The wood is elaborately carved with pendant berries, blossoms and leaves.

Paul Iribe was an illustrator famous for his cartoons in a range of Parisian journals. In the early 1900s he developed skills as an interior designer whilst working for Paul Poiret, and gained recognition when he was commissioned by the couturier Jacques Doucet to furnish his new apartment. His creativity was outstanding but short-lived, spanning only four years from 1910 to 1914, when he moved to America to design stage sets. Like Follot, his Art Nouveau designs made the transition to Art Deco.

Furniture designs Iribe's furniture is characterized by sinuous legs and the use of rich materials, such as velvet for upholstery, macassar ebony, zebrawood, mahogany and silver. His furniture looks towards the late 18th and early 19th centuries for inspiration, and designs display an elegant fluidity and a Louis IV flamboyance.

Left Sharing the First Empire influence evident in the chair on the opposite page, is this chest of drawers, dated 1914. The swag decoration and inlaid festoons were a popular late 18th century feature. Iribe's treatment of the feet – tapering with reeded and berried terminals – is distinctly modern. Each drawer pull has a carved flowerhead set against an inlaid leaf ground. The sharkskin cabinet may also originally have had a black slate or marble top.

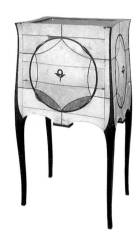

Left Iribe revived the use of sharkskin in furniture design; it had first enjoyed popularity in the late 18th century when introduced by M. Galuchat, who lent his name to the material in France. It was used throughout the Art Deco period, by designers such as Eileen Gray (see p.60). This cabinet, in sharkskin and ebony, was designed in around 1913-14, and is identical in form and material to furniture designed for Doucet's apartment. Surviving examples are very rare and display a fine balance between the curvilinear forms of Art Nouveau and the trend towards more rectilinear forms in the twenties. The fine tapering legs and elegance of design are characteristic of Iribe, as is the stylized rose motif in the centre of each panel (often referred to as the "Iribe rose"). Further decoration is in the form of inlaid ebony.

LES ATELIERS MAJORELLE (FRENCH, 1918-c.1939)

The 1909 Exposition Internationale de L'Est de la France, staged in Nancy, marked the end of the Art Nouveau style in France, as designers sought a new more conservative decorative style. Further changes were brought about by the First World War. Majorelle's workshops on the rue du Veiel-Aître were destroyed by fire in 1917 and when he had them rebuilt, he appointed his long-standing design assistant, Alfred Levy, as Deputy Director, and began to adapt to contemporary tastes. Majorelle attempted to move away from his earlier Art Nouveau furniture designs (see p.35), and by 1910 he had developed a more sober style, which he was to continue to adopt until his death in 1926. The flowing lines of his earlier pieces gave way to simpler, perpendicular shapes; and more stylized flowers and small abstract medallions replaced the extravagant motifs of the Art Nouveau style.

In later Majorelle pieces, such as this desk and chair, there is no evidence of the earlier inlaid floral and landscape designs. Instead, large unadorned surfaces feature, with the wood grain and small natural motifs in high relief used for decoration. This piece is closer to French historicism with a reliance on a traditional form. The simple lines of the armchair are closer to the Art Deco style than to Art Nouveau.

GALLÉ STUDIOS (c.1900-1933)

Although Emile Gallé died in 1904, Victor Prouvé, his friend and associate, became artistic director of the company to carry on the Gallé name, until the firm's closure in 1933. Like its contemporaries, the Gallé studios began the transition to Art Deco, rejecting Gallé's curvilinear and sculptural forms of Art Nouveau (see p.35) for simpler designs and more stylized decoration.

The construction of this table shows a complete departure from Gallé's Art Nouveau designs, and is strongly geometric, with no fluid forms or curvaceous lines. The table top provides a canvas for the inlaid design of two polar bears, standing on an island, against a background of icebergs.

TRADITIONAL ART DECO

A Süe et Mare macassar ebony marquetry giltwood and marble commode c.1925; 33 × 68in/84.5 × 173cm

Exponents of traditional Art Deco employed fine craftmanship and high quality materials to create forms which echoed the designs of the French Empire and Directoire periods. Designers concentrated on comfortable upholstery, designing luxurious and colourful materials specifically for individual pieces of furniture. Wood veneers gave way to polished and figured marble and luxury woods, such as amboyna and macassar ebony. The late traditionalists, including Jules Leleu and Jean Dunand, made extensive use of lacquered surfaces. Furniture of this period was very expensive, and was made for the *nouveau riche* élite.

The British designers of this period, such as Betty Joel and Heal & Son, interpreted the traditional Art Deco style in a very different way to the French designers, André Groult and Jules Leleu. They had to provide pieces that were acceptable to the British public, whose tastes were more reserved and retrospective.

SÜE ET MARE (FRENCH, 1919-28)

Later work In 1928 the designer Jacques Adnet took over the direction of the company, but Süe continued his activities there as artist and designer. Under Adnet the firm turned away from its sumptuous styles towards Modernism and an increased use of metal.

Marks Furniture is unmarked: the style itself was considered a sufficient trademark.

Copies A few lesser French companies copied the work of Süe et Mare. However, despite a superficial similarity, there is little likelihood of mistaking the copy for the original, which is always of the highest quality – for example, copies of Süe et Mare's lacquered furniture are painted rather than ebonized or inlaid.

Established French designers, Louis Süe and André Mare, set up their "Compagnie des Arts Français" in 1919, which soon became known by their surnames. Its work epitomizes the opulence of French high Art Deco style. Using a large team of designers such as Maurice Marinot, Pierre Poisson and André Vera, the company produced a range of furniture and coordinated interiors as well as pieces in wrought iron, and a number of decorative objects, including mirror frames and table lamps, all using stylized natural forms.

Many Süe et Mare pieces were commissioned rather than made for mass production and as such exhibit very high standards of workmanship.

Forms and styles The company aimed to produce a purely French style, with comfortable and luxurious furniture that looked back to the era of Louis-Philippe, and was often almost Baroque in its extravagance. Many pieces are massive, their traditional forms relieved by intricate decoration, such as inlays, often in pale woods, depicting large floral bouquets or flower vase motifs, and sometimes incorporating mother of pearl, and occasionally lacquer. Follot-style roses sometimes appear (see p.51). Even the most traditional forms are given unusual touches – the commode at the top of the page is essentially traditional in form, but has extraordinary, highly original stylized melon-like feet. On other furniture the feet often appear to be fixed to the outside of the body.

Although this fall-front bureau from around 1923 is less decorative than many of Süe et Mare's pieces, it has several recognizable features, including a marble slab top, scrolled feet, ormolu fittings, curved elements in the construction and the use of veneers to relieve a heavy form, with contrasting pale and dark woods and a delicate scalloped frieze around the top.
•Süe et Mare's furniture often incorporated bronze and metal embellishments by Maurice-Guiraud-Rivière and other leading metalworkers.

ANDRÉ GROULT (FRENCH, 1884-1967)

Also working in a traditional Art Deco style was the French interior decorator and furniture designer André Groult, whose designs were mainly executed by craftsmen working in his atelier in Paris. Furniture was luxuriously embellished with ropes and tassels, and upholstered in velvet, ivory and sharkskin. Groult used exotic veneers and the colour and grain of different woods to achieve harmonious effects.

The *galuchat* (sharkskin) veneer of this chair is typical of Groult's design, as is the U-shaped form of the back and seat, which shows his preference for curves.

JEAN MICHEL FRANK (FRENCH, 1895-1941)

This sharksin cabinet, designed by Frank in 1932, demonstrates his architectural and minimalist style. The piece is finely applied with *galuchat* in repeated rectangular sections. The interior is fitted with sycamore shelves and two small drawers. There is no other surface decoration. Although designed by Frank, the piece was executed by Adolph Chanaux's firm – Chaneaux and Co.

Frank was another French Art Deco interior decorator who also designed furniture. From 1927 he worked closely with fellow designer and craftsman, Adolphe Chanaux. Primarily concerned with form, his design and execution show a strong respect for French traditionalism. He preferred exotic wood grains to relief ornamentation, using sumptuous veneers such as straw parquetry, vellum parchment, snakeskin, sharkskin and suede to produce what has become known as the "Frank line". He concentrated on earth tones, working in ebony and sycamore and using ivory whenever possible. Frank often applied the veneers to whole rooms, decorating walls and doors as well as furniture.

JULES LELEU (FRENCH, 1883-1961)

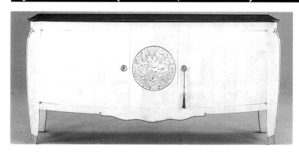

This sharkskin, mahogany and bronze commode from c.1930-5, is typical of Leleu's furniture with its exotic materials and rich ivory colour. The simple decoration relies on the wood grain. The central gilded motif incorporates Leleu's signature, exotic plants and a nude woman. The only other decoration is the red tassel hanging from the key.

Leleu, a French cabinet maker and decorator, expanded his father's painting firm with his brother, Marcel, to produce furniture and, later, lamps, carpets and fabrics, influenced by Jacques-Emile Ruhlmann. Leleu made extensive use of the lacquered surface, taking inspiration from the Japanese in his rectangular segments, but also adopted sharkskin, ebony, amboyna and mahogany, with ivory, *galuchat* or horn for marquetry. Forms were often heavy and enlarged but touches of luxury gave relief to his simple style.

Leleu worked mainly on commission, furnishing liners, and many buildings, including the 1936 *Grand Salon des Ambassadeurs* (known as the "*Salon Leleu*") at *La Société des Nations* in Geneva.

JEAN DUNAND (SWISS, 1877-1942)

Dunand, in Paris from 1896, was a prolific metalworker, lacquerist and furniture designer. He produced expensive high-quality hand-made pieces for the most exclusive end of the market, mainly to special commission. In 1912 he learned the technique of lacquer work for which he became best known. His early work featured naturalistic designs, but his style became progressively more geometric.

This two-tier table from 1925 is typical of Dunand's later furniture, with its simple form, geometric designs and highly polished surface. Eggshell – which appears on the top of this table – was often applied to both inner and outer surfaces to provide a textured effect.

Note Dunand's naturalistic work is very different from his highly stylized geometric designs and collectors should familiarize themselves with the full range of his work.
Marks Not all Dunand's work is signed. Some pieces have an incised signature, sometimes with a serial number. Others have the words "JEAN DUNAND 72 RUE HALLE PARIS MADE IN FRANCE".

Dunand applied lacquer work to his screens and panels, which often have a Japanese or African influence. The dentated lower edges here are a common decorative feature.
Dunand also worked in metal, particularly dinanderie (see p.193). At other times he uses silver inlay. These techniques were applied to his furniture, screens and vases.

JACQUES-EMILE RUHLMANN (FRENCH, 1879-1933)

Initially a painter, Ruhlmann became the best-known French cabinet-maker of his day, following the tradition of the *ébénistes*. He designed for a rich and exclusive clientele, using exotic wood and other expensive materials. After the First World War he took over his father's successful building firm, Ruhlmann et Laurent, and added workshops devoted to furniture and other aspects of interior design, including textiles, light fixtures and even wastepaper baskets. His furniture designs were mostly executed by craftsmen rather than by himself.

Earlier pieces, up until the mid 1920s, tend to be handmade in a traditionalist Art Deco style, based on simplified French Neo-Classical designs and are balanced in form, with subtle decoration and discreet ivory embellishments, such as stringing, chequering or corner trims. Pieces from around 1925 were more cubist and less symmetrical although always with a traditional concern for elegance and quality. Ruhlmann then began to incorporate functional metal components into his work, and during the 1930s he made more widespread use of metal, tubular steel and plastic, without moving towards the functionalism of the Modernists.

Small pieces, such as this lady's writing desk in macassar ebony and ivory from around 1927, have tapering, slender legs, often with ivory feet only at the front, as here.

Characteristically, the legs appear to emanate from outside the structure rather than supporting it from underneath. Drawers are always smooth-running and fit snugly.

Marks All Ruhlmann's work has a branded signature, followed by A, B or C, indicating the atelier from which the piece emanated. A is most desirable. After his death, his nephew, Alfred Porteneuve, took over and repeated some of his designs.

Many Ruhlmann pieces, like this unusual drinks cabinet on skis from around 1930, were made to individual commission. Its characteristically heavy form is relieved by the use of wood grain for decorative effect. Ruhlmann favoured exotic veneers of macassar ebony, amboyna and shagreen, often combining them with ivory escutcheons and handles or with decoration in mother-of-pearl or tortoiseshell.

BETTY JOEL (CHINESE, 1896-1984)

Betty Joel moved to England, adapting the traditional Art Deco style to suit more conservative English tastes. In 1921 she established a furniture workshop in Hayling Island, factories in Portsmouth and Kingston, and a shop in London. Much of her work was commissioned. Many pieces are built-in. Joel's furniture is large, intended for the spacious rooms of London mansion homes, and is usually highly practical and versatile. Joel also designed rugs and textiles. Pieces are hand finished, although some machinery was used in the construction.

Marks Furniture bears a glazed paper label affixed to the reverse of the piece, giving the date and signature of the designer and craftsman, and usually also, "Made at the Token Works, Kingston" (derived from a combination of the words teak and oak).

Materials Joel avoided the luxury woods popular at the time, preferring conservatively grained woods, which she arranged to achieve an almost monochromatic effect. In the 1930s she employed plywood laminates and other man-made materials. Chrome was sometimes used for plinths.

Decoration Designs from the early 1920s are often heavily upholstered and paired with signed rugs (see p.238). By the end of the 1920s Joel had developed a more distinctive style, with simpler and more geometric forms. Pieces are usually devoid of carved decoration and painted finishes, but some are lacquered.

Form is given priority over decoration, and furniture tends to be strong and solid-looking. Joel favoured ellipses and curved contours – such as the rotundas in the twin-pedestal desk. Dressing tables often incorporated large circular mirrors. The handles, with their scalloped design, are typically simple and of a grip rather than a hanging type. Drawer edges may be cross-banded, as here.

HEAL & SON (ENGLISH, 1810-Present)

Decoration on Heals furniture is very simple, as in the rectangular grill back and rush seat of this chair.

Ambrose Heal (1872-1959) designed all the furniture for the family firm from 1896 until the 1950s. Like the work of Betty Joel, his early pieces have a strong affinity with the English Arts and Crafts Movement and have an architectural look with the wood grain as the chief decorative element. Heal preferred light-coloured woods, especially limed oak. After the First World War the firm began to use weathered oak instead of unpolished wood. Work of the 1930s is more avant garde, but not to the same degree as French furniture, and tends to combine contemporary features with more traditional elements. All pieces are hand-finished, but made with modern techniques. Most are stamped or labelled.

Heals made a number of multiple utility items. This example is typical, combining a chair with a side table and bookcase. Examples with original fabric can still be found today.

NEW MATERIALS AND THE MACHINE AGE

New machine techniques led to a revolutionary use of new materials in furniture manufacture. The French cabinet maker, Jacques Adnet, took over Süe et Mare (see p.54) in 1928, rejected their traditionalism and moved their designs into the 20th century, providing furniture to fit the new concrete-built spacious homes lit by electricity. Tubular steel was adopted by Frank Lloyd Wright, Ludwig Mies van der Rohe and Eugene Schoen. Painted lacquer became popular, with Frank Deskey contrasting primary colours for effect. Paul Frankl's perpendicular furniture reflected the Manhattan skyline. In Britain, Isokon and Finmar used laminated plywood. Plate glass, perfected by René Lalique (see pp.90-1), was incorporated into table tops and other pieces and appeared in private homes, department stores, liners and churches. Working with similar innovative use of new materials was Eileen Gray, but she rejected the mass-produced man-made techniques of her contemporaries to create individual designs for the wealthy.

The Barcelona chair, designed by Mies van der Rohe, in steel and leather c.1931; ht 30in/75.5cm

The Barcelona chair

The Barcelona chair, right, first exhibited in 1929, is one of the most popular of all 20th century chair designs. Mass-produced after the Second World War, it has been in continuous production ever since.

The chairs are not stamped but one way to distinguish between early examples and later mass-produced models is in the construction: the top rail of this original version is in bent chromed flat steel, with separate sections joined by lap joints and screwed with chrome-headed bolts. In later versions the top rail is in cut and welded stainless steel. Leather straps, used for additional support, also made the chair more comfortable. Most of the chairs retain their original upholstery.

LUDWIG MIES VAN DER ROHE (GERMAN, 1886-1969)

In both his glass skyscraper architecture and his furniture design, Mies van der Rohe is the doyen of the Modernist approach. He was one of the chief promoters of the Bauhaus machine-age philosophy.

From 1927 to 1931 his furniture was produced by the small firm of Berliner Metallgewerbe Joseph Müller. Thereafter it was made by Bamberger Metalwerkstätten, and marketing was handled by Thonet-Mundus.

In his furniture designs Mies van der Rohe combines classical forms with Modernism, achieving a machine-made look, but with careful hand-finishing and close attention to detail. Form follows function and the furniture has clarity and elegance of line. Pieces are often in chromed tubular steel, combined with leather, raffia or glass, with upholstery contributing visually to the structure, as well as providing a degree of comfort. In 1927 he started to produce his famous cantilevered tubular range of armchairs, coffee tables and stools.

Collecting Original furniture dating back to Mies van der Rohe's time at the Bauhaus, and before mass-production began, fetches very high prices, particularly in the case of classics such as the Barcelona chair.

Identification
All Mies van der Rohe's furniture was made by machine and pieces are not stamped. Many are still in production, but with minor changes to the basic designs.

This armchair from 1927 is one of van der Rohe's cantilevered tubular designs, and is made in chrome-plated steel tubes. Often such chairs would be on X-stretchers with no feet. The leather seat is laced on the underside and the back is held in place with a metal strip and screws. Similar versions exist without arms.

MARCEL LAJOS BREUER (HUNGARIAN, 1902-81)

Breuer moved from Hungary to the Bauhaus in Weimar in 1920. Some of his designs were manufactured by P.E.L. in England, and by Thonet in Austria and he worked briefly for Isokon in England in 1936. In 1937 he joined his ex-colleague, Walter Gropius, in America. His laminated furniture shares design affinities with that of the Finnish Designer, Alvar Aalto.

Materials and styles
Breuer revolutionized utility furniture, promoting the use of tubular steel, laminated wood and aluminium with minimal decoration. In the 1920s he experimented with plywood. He made desks, cabinets, tables, folding or stacking pieces and designed furniture for specific interiors.

Attribution Breuer's work is not signed or stamped, but pieces for Thonet have a maker's label. Attribution can be ascertained by consulting contemporary catalogues. There are also catalogues for P.E.L. and Standard-Mobel, who produced a number of his tubular steel chairs.

Recognition point
Runners, instead of feet, were used increasingly after 1925, and add to the impression that Breuer's tubular steel furniture was made in one piece.

Reproductions
Modern reproductions exist, but these lack the characteristic signs of wear of the original pieces.

Left With its cantilevered construction and simple vertical and horizontal planes, this oak chair from 1922, made in several versions, is typical of Breuer's furniture of the period and may have been inspired by Rietveld's famous 1919 chair. The floating impression of the seat, suspended between the structural elements, and the apparently unsupported arms are typical, as is the compromise between comfort and function, in combining a hard frame with a soft seat. Later he used hide for upholstery rather than canvas.
•By c.1925, inspired by his new bicycle, Breuer began to use tubular steel in furniture.

Above In 1936 Breuer adapted some of his earlier designs to plywood – for example, this *chaise longue*, which became the Isokon "short chair" (see p.63).

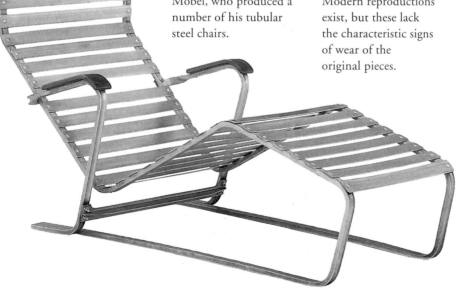

Left In 1932 Breuer produced his first furniture in aluminium, with a silvery finish which could be left dull or shiny. Designs tended to have more curves than those in tubular steel because aluminium was lighter and required more support.

EILEEN GRAY (IRISH, 1879-1976)

Above This pine and chromed metal table from c.1935 is typical of Gray's work, embracing Modernist ideals to create what became the basis of the Bauhaus style. Gray's work was mainly for commission and thus expensive. She designed for wealthy Parisians, creating whole interiors – in 1919 she was commissioned to decorate the apartment of famous fashion designer, Suzanne Talbot.

Eileen Gray, born in Ireland in 1879, moved to London to study art at the Slade School in 1898 where she took an apprenticeship in Oriental lacquer work. She moved to Paris in 1907 and opened the "Gallerie Jean Désert" in 1922 to exhibit her work. She was a complete decorator and interior designer and designed two houses, the first in 1927 in Roquebrune with the help of architect Jean Badovici, and the second in Castellar in 1933.

Design and materials Gray began by working in lacquer with the Japanese artisan Sugawara, with whom she perfected her technique, and later enlisted the help of Inagaki, a specialist in ivory carving and lacquer application. She often borrowed from tribal art and juxtaposed animal skins such as zebra with modernist materials in order to highlight each element.

This black lacquered wood screen, made c.1923, strongly two-dimensional and made up of perpendicular blocks, is typical of screens produced by Gray in the 1920s.

PRACTICAL EQUIPMENT LTD (ENGLISH, 1920's to present)

P.E.L. experimented with steel, adding a pitch filling to prevent it flattening, making it stronger and more suitable for furniture designs such as this Modernist desk, designed by Wells Coates for P.E.L. in 1933.
•Initially producing for the domestic market, P.E.L. now concentrates on large furnishing contracts, producing functional items, including a wide range of products for schools and colleges.

This leading British manufacturer of chromium-plated tubular steel furniture created designs which followed the principles of the Bauhaus, integrating form and function. Factory techniques and the removal of craftsmen turned the designer primarily into an engineer, leading to mass-produced furniture which was easily affordable. One of P.E.L.'s major innovations was the stacking chair, still popular today.

FRANK LLOYD WRIGHT (AMERICAN, 1867-1959)

Having been the foremost exponent of the Prairie School, an American interpretation of the Arts and Crafts style (see p.46), Frank Lloyd Wright's designs from around 1914, while still showing an unmistakably architectural influence, were more Modernist and adopted the new materials of the age. He also worked in other media, for example, designing ceramics for the Japanese/American firm Noritake (see p.145).

This enamelled steel, walnut and brass-plated desk and chair made in around 1937 for the S.C. Johnson Administration building in Wisconsin typically for Wright reflects both the interior and exterior architecture of the building. Also typical is the form, based on bold, geometric shapes and parallel lines and curves, and with no fussy detail or decoration.

Collecting As Frank Lloyd Wright is one of the most famous architect/designers of this century his work commands high prices, especially as many pieces were made to private commission. Unique designs and limited editions command a premium. Furniture is unsigned, but provenance of pieces is usually well documented. His architectural plates and drawings are also highly collectable.

Fakes Wright's furniture is not known to have been faked, although there are some honest reproductions, which, unlike the originals, do not have signs of wear and tear.

This oak chair (1916-22) is innovative in form. Shapes and motifs, often cubist, may reflect a Japanese, Mayan or Aztec influence, as in the zigzags. Colour is applied in simple solid blocks and upholstery is used to soften a hard form.

DONALD DESKEY (AMERICAN, 1894-1989)

By the late 1920s Deskey, who began his career in an advertising agency, had achieved recognition as a furniture and product designer. He combined a taste for functionalism with a specifically American flair and mastery of the "streamlined" style. His work for private commissions was of unique design and rarely appears on the market today.

These formica and aluminium side tables were designed by Deskey for Radio City Music Hall in New City in around 1932 and are typical of his furniture with their simple forms

based on rectilinear lines and geometry and complete absence of ornament. Metal or metallic surfaces were often contrasted with a bold primary colour.

Deskey-Vollmer Most Deskey pieces found today were produced between 1927 and 1931 with Deskey's business partner Phillip Vollmer. Designed to be economically manufactured on an industrial scale, many were ultimately produced in small quantities. Tables, seating, small desks, chests and a range of innovative lighting devices were made in brushed or chromium-plated steel in bent form, tubular steel and plate glass, and were often coloured to give them a "Bauhaus" look. Aluminium, bakelite and cork were also used.

Commissions In the late 1920s Deskey worked in collaboration with Frankl (below), and on commission for several New York manufacturers, including Eskey and Amodec, producing more conventional wood-veneered furniture which tends to be less collectable today. Finishes include macassar ebony, sometimes with brass, a variety of blond wood, and some painted surfaces. Commissions included designs for whole interiors.

Marks Much Deskey furniture is unsigned, although most designs are recorded in modern publications.

PAUL FRANKL (AUSTRIAN, 1886-1958)

Frankl emigrated to the United States during the First World War. He was one of America's pioneer Modernists and the first furniture designer to echo contemporary architecture in his work, a result of his early training in architecture and engineering. In the late 1920s he wrote five books and a number of influential articles on form and design. Work before 1920 is relatively undistinguished and European in style to satisfy his fashionable American clientele. Later work, from 1925, is more individual and thus more collectable.

Skyscraper furniture Frankl is perhaps best known for the range of Skyscraper furniture he pioneered in 1925 and continued working on until 1930. With its perpendicular lines, it evokes New York's remarkable Art Deco architecture and its awareness of the needs of smaller, urban spaces.

Identification Other American designers adopted the Skyscraper form and adapted it to other areas of the decorative arts in addition to furniture. However, their work is less collectable, so check that pieces bear the Frankl mark – a metal tag, stamped "Skyscraper Furniture, Frankl Galleries, 4 East 48th Street, New York".

There is an element of novelty about all Frankl pieces, seen in this "puzzle desk", from 1927, with its concealed seat and the asymmetrical placement of its drawers. Frankl's designs are geometric and their sometimes severe outlines are almost Neo-Biedermeier in style.
• Frankl furniture from the early 1920s favours oak and metal, often with ebonized frames. Later he used pale-coloured American woods, such as birch or maple.

Right Many of Frankl's pieces are multi-functional and combine cupboards, display units and bookcases, as here. They are often made of California redwood, usually with a red, silver or black lacquered trim and turquoise, blue or green interiors; some have plastic or metallic finishes. The standard of cabinetry on Skyscraper pieces is usually poor. They have not been commercially reproduced, but modern copies do exist.

Below This "Chinese" chair from around 1930, with its contrasted red and black lacquering and gold detailing, reflects Frankl's interest in Oriental styles and complements the highly popular Chinese style of 1930s interior design. Sets are rare.

Later work After 1930 Frankl abandoned the Skyscraper concept to concentrate on metal furnishings, producing tubular chromed chairs and consoles and Formica-topped metal tables which met with the strict standards of functionalism of the period, and can be compared with the work of Donald Deskey (see previous page).

•In the 1930s Frankl also produced an innovative range of sun parlour and patio seat furniture in wicker and other cane fibres, reviving a popular Victorian style, but adding angular corners and armrests in keeping with the spirit of Modernism.

Above This Skyscraper lacquered dressing table and stool are typical of Frankl's furniture designs. Lines are simple and uncluttered, with rectangular tops to the table and stool and triangular legs. The zebra-cloth upholstery demonstrates Frankl's use of unusual materials.
•Check the condition of lacquering and metallic paint, which are easily marked or scratched. A small degree of wear is acceptable provided decoration has not disappeared.
•Frankl's other furniture from the late 1920s is also in wood with brightly coloured lacquered and painted surfaces. He often used mirrored glass for tops of pieces, together with bakelite and metal fittings, to give an almost theatrical effect. Pieces from this period are usually innovative – for example, he designed bookshelves made up of many units which form a pyramid shape. These are highly collectable.

EUGENE SCHOEN (AMERICAN, 1880-1957)

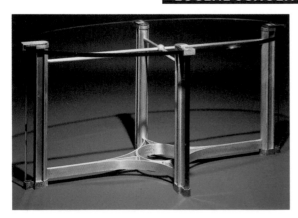

Initially an architect, Eugene Schoen began designing furniture, fabrics and rugs in 1920. Particularly influenced by the Wiener Werkstätte (see pp.42-3), he nevertheless used luxurious materials including exotic woods, often edged in silver leaf, with silk or calf skin upholstery. Products were small-scale and extremely elegant, showing traces of Neo-classical or Biedermeier influence and many are unique.

By the late 1920s/early 1930s Schoen was working in the more familiar materials and forms of modern American taste, exemplified by this glass and nickel table with its simple lines and scant decoration.
•Furniture may bear the name of the maker, Schmeig, Hungate and Kotzian.

FINMAR LTD (BRITISH, 1934/5-39)

Finmar Ltd was established as the British importers and distributors of furniture designed and produced by Alvar Aalto, a Finnish architect and designer (1898-1976). The first stacking furniture, made in 1927, included chairs and side tables. From 1929 Aalto began to use plywood, especially for chairs and tea trolleys. The stacking stools designed by Aalto and produced by Korhonen in Turko between 1930 and 1933 were very popular, because they were eminently versatile and practical. In 1935 he established his firm Artek to produce his furniture designs, door furniture and lighting.

Most Finmar furniture has a multiple construction element. A striking impact is achieved through use of bold blocks of strong strident colours, rather than through surface decoration, which is usually absent.

Marks Some of the furniture made by Aalto in Finland is marked "Aalto Mobler, Svensk Kvalitet Sprodurt". Finmar pieces are not signed. *The Decorative Arts Journal* shows the full range of their wares. Most items carry an applied metal label bearing the model number.

Above Most pieces, especially those required to bend, were made from plywood (although table tops are of solid wood), and are Modernist in every sense, with clean contours and no concessions to decoration. This birch and laminated wood tea trolley, typical of Finmar's pieces, was designed by.Alvar Aalto in 1935-6.

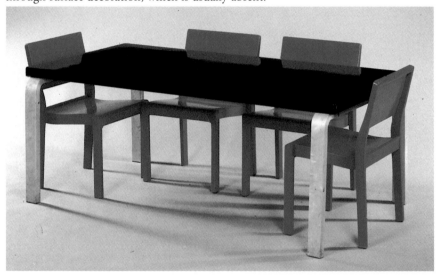

Left Pieces were designed to complement and harmonize with one another both stylistically and practically so that sets could be made using many different combinations of chairs, tables and so on. Some sets may have been made at different dates: the chairs of this dining room set were designed around 1929, and the table between 1933 and 1935.
•Laminated plywood tends to chip and flake, and furniture in this medium has not survived in quantity.
•Chairs and *chaises longues* were designed to accept loose-fitting padded cushions. Pieces that retain their original cushions command a premium.

ISOKON (BRITISH, 1932-39)

Plywood furniture was also made by Isokon. Jack Pritchard, who founded the firm, had been designing furniture since the end of the 1920s, but Isokon (from "Isometric Unit Construction") was not set up to produce the designs in quantity until 1932. In 1936 the firm was renamed Isokon Furniture Company and Walter Gropius, the creator of Bauhaus, became the Controller of Design, but he emigrated to America the following year. The firm closed down at the outbreak of the second world war but it was reopened by Pritchard in 1962.

The furniture designs of Isokon tended to be more adventurous than those of Finmar. Marcel Breuer (see p.59) was the leading designer. Most pieces were produced in plywood and some were built-in.

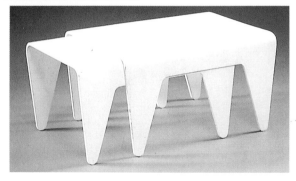

Isokon is mostly remembered for its "cut-out" furniture, especially side chairs and tables such as these white-painted plywood nesting tables

designed by Breuer in 1936, cut and moulded from a single sheet of plywood, lightweight and easily assembled. They exist in many versions.

GLASS

Queen Victoria's reign saw a revival in a flagging glass industry. New mass-production techniques, such as moulding, were developed, which led to glass replacing pewter in taverns. Early glass was in the safe clear shapes of the Georgian period, but the repeal of the glass act in 1845 saw a fall in production costs and a consequent rise in engraved glass, inspired by the French glass houses of Baccarat and Saint Denis. Imported Bohemian coloured glass stimulated demand in Britain, hitherto satisfied only by Bristol's cobalt blue and green glass tablewares. Thomas Webb's superb cameo wares exhibited an exemplary standard of craftsmanship, often with several people carving one piece. In contrast, the north-east England glassworks made small, inexpensive, often decorative moulded glass objects, in colours of vaseline and sapphire blue. Beaded glassware was popular for commemorative wares, which sometimes incorporated verses or mottos. The United States boasted manufacturers such as Steuben and the Boston & Sandwich Glassworks, which preferred moulded forms and pressed glass to hand-blown wares. Arts and Crafts Guild workers, whose principal makers and designers included Sir Edward Burne-Jones and William Morris in Britain, developed an interest in the stained glass of churches following the Victorian revival in church building. Unfortunately, little stained glass has survived today, as much of it was discarded in the 1950s and '60s when religious subjects were not popular with collectors.

In the Art Nouveau period glassmakers abandoned earlier elaborate cutting techniques to concentrate on sculptural and surface possibilities, often combining the skills of chemist and glassblower. In France, Nancy was established as the cradle of French art glass production by Emile Gallé and the Daum Frères, who developed industrial mass-production techniques to make cameo glass more readily available to the masses, as well as producing highly-collectable studio glass. Gallé also perfected the technique of *marquetrie de verre* and experimented with new possibilities for glass surfaces, such as iridescence. Forms tended to be impressionistic, and decoration relied on local flora and fauna. Controlled iridescence emulating lustrous peacock plumage was used in America by Victor Durand and the firms of Quezal and Steuben, and was exploited by America's highly collectable glass artist, Louis Comfort Tiffany. Loetz, in Austria, produced similar wares. Little Art Nouveau glass was produced in Britain, with the exception of Stevens & Williams in Stourbridge and Thomas Webb & Sons. Elsewhere, Meyr's Neffe, the Bohemian glassworks, produced wares inspired by the Austrian Otto Prutscher's geometric designs; Graal glass was made in Sweden by Orrefors; and in Russia, cameo glass was produced by the Imperial Glass Factory in St Petersburg.

Innovative glasswares, halted by the death of Gallé in 1904, enjoyed a revival in the 1920s and '30s, when architects and designers worked imaginatively with plate and mirror glass, adapting old techniques to new styles. René Lalique perfected moulded opalescent glass and his techniques were widely emulated. Enamelled glass was also popular, and as it was not as common as moulded glass, it commands high prices today. Engraved glass was made at Orrefors in Sweden and at the American Steuben Glass Works, as well as by several glassmakers in France, including Daum and Maurice Marinot, and by Thomas Webb in England. Also in France, Gabriel Argy-Rousseau and Alméric Walter made luxury items in *pâte-de-verre* and *pâte-de-cristal*. Changing lifestyles in the Art Deco years led to new forms. Perfume bottles and car mascots were popular. Lalique dominated this market, and also provided glass for light fixtures and architectural settings. Some low-budget domestic wares were produced, called "Depression glass", which, simple in form and in murky colours, is of little value today. More popular is the cloud glass by Davidson's of Gateshead in Britain, which is often dark brown with a random swirling effect.

Victorian glass is highly collectable – its value has increased by 500 per cent over the last 15 years. Cameo glass is expensive; the cameo glass plaques of George Woodall of Webb are particularly desirable. Art Nouveau fakes abound, especially of Tiffany and Gallé, but these lack the vitality of the originals. Loetz glass has also been faked. Art Deco wares can still be found at reasonable prices, but few glasses have survived, and apart from those by Lalique, the market for perfume bottles is still in its infancy. Elsewhere, there is some good Czech glass available, especially figural types and pieces with hand-engraving or geometric enamelling.

Above A Lalique "Pâquerettes" perfume bottle, c.1920
Right A Thomas Webb & Sons Queen's Burmese ware vase, c.1895

NOVELTY GLASS

A vase made in Stourbridge by Stevens & Williams c.1890; ht 8¾in/22.5cm

From the mid-19th century Bohemia-inspired coloured glass in novelty forms came into its own. A departure from earlier English coloured glass, pieces were now purely decorative, consisting mainly of vases and épergnes, but also pipes. Some show an Italian influence – the form of the vase in the main picture was probably inspired by the Murano-base firm, Salviati. Although Stourbridge was the main centre of production in England, fancy glass was also made in Gateshead, and in London, by James Powell (see p.70). The same techniques and styles were used by them all, so it is difficult to differentiate between the different centres. Glasswares were carried through the streets in processions by the members of various glass societies which were formed during the period.

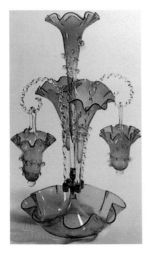

The firm of George Ernest Fox, near Stourbridge, made many épergnes in the late 1890s, including this cranberry example, with its characteristically irregular colours. No two are identical, and many show evidence of hand manufacture. The barley twist bracket supporting the baskets is typical, as is the trailing decoration. Some examples have as many as five or six vases radiating from a central trumpet.
•Cranberry-coloured épergnes are more popular than those in other colours.

STOURBRIDGE

The group of factories in Stourbridge is mainly remembered for the cameo glass made by Thomas Webb & Sons (see p.68) and Richardsons, and for the novelty glass produced by several factories, the principal one being Stevens & Williams, later Brierly Royal Crystal (see p.68). Not all glass makers signed their work and attribution often has to be made on the strength of subtle differences – for example, in the decoration.
•The wavy edge of the vase in the main picture was so popular in the 1870s that many Stourbridge firms patented their crimping method.

NAILSEA (ENGLISH, 1788-1873)

The Nailsea glassworks, based near Bristol, England, produced domestic wares in dark brown or green glass. To make their wares more attractive, they perfected a method of fusing or splashing on pieces of coloured or white enamel. The process was widely copied.

Spun-glass ornaments Fancy spun-glass ornaments housed under glass domes, many of them made in the Stourbridge area, are very collectable today. Exotic glass birds were popular but the most sought-after are those depicting stuffed birds within an ornamental glass cage. Ship subjects are also popular and are valued according to their size and the number of "extras". These ornaments are never marked.
Épergnes Coloured glass épergnes, or flower stands, were popular during the 1860s. They are invariably ornamental rather than functional.

The multicoloured feathering of this pipe has always been associated with the Nailsea glassworks, but it is becoming more apparent that the majority of feathered pieces are probably the work of either the Stourbridge factories or of those glass makers working in the Northeast of England.

Amongst the many types of novelty glass produced in Nailsea were lozenge-shaped flasks in a variety of colours and sometimes incorporating two necks, as here.

CONTINENTAL GLASS

During Queen Victoria's reign Continental glassmakers experimented with many techniques and styles. In the 19th century Bohemia produced a vast output of coloured glass, borrowing from the Ancient Egyptians who imitated precious stones in their glass to create ruby, agate and amber. Overlaid glass, cased glass and polished opaque glass were also popular, but perhaps most collectable is the engraved glass depicting woodland scenes, stags and huntsmen, soon copied in Britain, France and America. In France, the most notable development was the creation of a translucent milky-white glass called opaline in around 1810. Initially plain, it soon adopted contemporary decoration and shapes. Antonio Salviati headed a resurgence of glassmaking in Venice and a subsequent Venetian interest throughout Europe and America, with his revival of the early styles of the 16th and 17th century, which although interesting historically, were not very original.

An Italian coloured glass chandelier, Murano, c.1900; 3ft 9in/120cm high

Left This vase, engraved with a picture of Crystal Palace in London, commemorates the Great Exhibition there in 1851. Pieces were colour-flashed in ruby or amber; purple and amethyst were also used. Ruby is most sought-after. Later, cheaper examples were made of thinner glass.

BOHEMIAN ENGRAVED GLASS

Bohemian wares consisted of vases, liqueur sets, goblets, chandeliers and candelabra, often with heavy forms. Some are overlaid, with decorative overlay cutting or with engraved panels, hand-enamelled portrait medallions, or gilding. Pieces were often panel-cut, and if only decorated on one side, the reverse would have a prism panel. Signed examples are rare and expensive.

FRENCH OPALINE GLASS

French opaline glass was often used by decorators almost as an alternative medium to porcelain, which it resembles. This type of glass is usually heavier then its other Continental counterparts, and often exhibits polished and ground pontil marks.

Left Decoration on opaline wares tended towards asymmetrical sprays of flora trailing over highly formalized bands of gilt flower and leaf decoration, as in this example. Bases and footrims are often embellished with gilt bands of arabesques.
•Some opaline glass by Bohemian and lesser French makers is to be avoided. These pieces are light in weight, and often have a moulded base, which may exhibit a pontil mark.

MARY GREGORY GLASS

Named after a decorator at the Sandwich Glassworks in America who painted figures of small children on white enamel vases, dressing table sets and so on, Mary Gregory glass was mass-produced both in Europe and in the United States.

Bohemian examples, such as that shown here, usually depict older children, often with coloured facial detail. American versions tend to show infants, and to use only white enamel.

VENETIAN GLASS

The use of strong, often contrasting colours, typifies the glasswares made in Venice in the 19th century, especially on the island of Murano. Many 19th-century wares echoed earlier forms such as *latticinio* and *millefiori*. Murano wares are distinguished by their use of a range of differing techniques. The exuberant chandelier at the top of the page combines enamel, engraving, casing, air-twist and relief-moulded S-brackets. It also shows the typical, popular pleated and crimped rims.

VICTORIAN ART GLASS

Art glass became popular towards the last quarter of the 19th century, largely as a result of the development of new techniques, such as ribbing and beading, and a revival of cameo techniques, and the Venetian style, first popular during the late 16th and 17th centuries. Mass production techniques in moulding made glass available on a scale not seen before. Relatively inexpensive and hygienic, it was particularly appealing to the Victorians, and superseded pewter as tavern ware. English glassmaking was taken to its zenith by the glassworks of Thomas Webb, whose superb cameo wares illustrate an exemplary standard of craftsmanship.

The Dancers, a Webb cameo plaque ascribed to G. Woodall c.1880, dia. 12½in/32cm

The other prominent designer at James Couper & Sons was George Walton (1867-1933), who concentrated on using aventurine – green-tinted glass, sometimes randomly speckled with small particles of gold, copper or some other metal. This bowl is typical of his wares, which are invariably unsigned. It is difficult to distinguish between the styles of Dresser and Walton, although the latter's forms were generally the more restrained.
•Pink threading and silver foil inclusions and combed, white striations are especially desirable features of Clutha glass.
* It has long been accepted that "clutha" meant "cloudy" in Old Scottish, but it is also said to be the Gaelic name for the River Clyde.

Some decorators at Webb's introduced layers of pale pink and yellow as well as white into their cameo reliefs, as in this four-colour ovoid vase, a fine and rare piece made by Webb's in around 1880.

JAMES COUPER & SONS (SCOTTISH, c.1885-95)

James Couper & Sons is best known for its Clutha glass, developed around 1885 and remaining in production until around 1905. Clutha glass tends to be a cloudy yellow, green, amber or pink with variegated bubbles and streaks. Pink is the most collectable. The range included decorative wares, vases, bottles and tablewares. Shapes were often irregular, based on antique Roman and Islamic models.

Early Clutha designs were by Christopher Dresser. Many of these were sold by Liberty's, where Dresser's usual mark was placed in a circle surrounding Liberty's "lotus" trademark.

Christopher Dresser (Scottish, 1834-1904)

Initially Dresser trained as a botanist and his expert knowledge of plant forms can be seen in his designs, not only in his glassware but in the other media in which he worked.

Dresser designed this marbled, solifleur vase in the mid-1890s for James Couper's Clutha range. His pieces are often signed, but should show the maker's seal as fakes abound.

THOMAS WEBB & SONS (ENGLISH, 1856-present)

Thomas Webb's glassworks at Stourbridge began producing finest quality wares in 1856. Its main output was cameo glass, Burmese ware and rock crystal.

Value depends on the overall quality of design, size (larger pieces command higher prices), and in the case of cameo ware, how many layers of cameo the piece has: multiple layers are the most desirable.

Most of the cameo wares produced by Webb's were purely decorative, with the exception of scent bottles and flasks.

Burmese ware
Burmese glassware, in merging tones of pink to pale yellow, was developed by the Mount Washington Glass Company in the United States (see p.78). The combining of gold and uranium oxides had the unusual side effect of making pieces radioactive.

The most sought-after Burmese ware is enamelled, often with a floral motif. Gilt enamelling is the most desirable. Fakes and copies abound. Genuine wares should bear a ground circular stencil mark on the base. The surface should be semi-matt – granular surfaces indicate fakes.

Rock Crystal "Rock crystal" refers to engraved lead glass cut to simulate the natural facets of real rock crystal and polished to achieve the desired effect. Artificial leaves and berries were sometimes added as a surface feature, and later pieces show an Art Nouveau type of floral design. Typical wares included wine glasses and vases. At the time rock crystal was the main source of Webb's income, but today it is the least popular of their wares.

Overlay (Cased) glass Webb's overlay glass, mainly confined to vases, made an important contribution to Art Nouveau design but it never achieved the popularity of the cameo glass. Although similar to cameo, the design was on the outer layer upon an underlying clear glass form. The overlay process was more industrial than the intricate carving of the cameo process, and therefore simpler.

Marks All Webb cameo glass was etched on the base: "THOMAS WEBB & SONS". Rock crystal wares are stencilled with either "Webb" or, on later pieces, "Webb, England". They usually bear one of the marks on p.247. George Woodall signed most of his pieces "GEO. WOODALL".

Cameo glass Cameo glass, first developed by the Romans, was revived in England in the mid-19th century. Two or more layers of glass, often of varying colours, were laminated together, then carved on a wheel or etched to make a design in high relief. Webb's very high quality cameo glass was hand-made under the direction of the firm's main designer, George Woodall (1850-1925), and his brother, Thomas (1849-1926). Woodall's decorative themes tend to be based on Neo-classical subjects, but he avoids their usual stiltedness with his lively and subtle treatment. His almost three-dimensional figures are often partially visible through diaphanous drapes, as in the plaque in the main picture. Typically, relief decoration is highlighted in white. The underlying, translucent glass was often brown, as here, or yellow, plum or blue.
•Webb's cameo wares have a silky surface.

Webb's overlay wares are not as sophisticated as their cameo glass. The prismatic effect is achieved by broad martelé cutting, a distinctive feature of Webb's overlay glass. Overlay can also be green, and is always of a single colour. Others, instead of the prism-cut surface shown here, have a semi-frosted craquelure effect achieved by acid-cutting.

STEVENS & WILLIAMS (ENGLISH, c.1830-present)

This Stourbridge firm is most noted for the cameo wares of Joshua Hodgetts (1858-1933) and John Northwood (1837-1902), and the engraved rock crystal wares of Joseph Keller. Today, the firm operates under the name Brierley Royal Crystal.

Flashed glasswares Applying the surface of glass with a thin glass plating, usually in a stronger colour, was an inexpensive way to produce parti-coloured glassware. Stevens & Williams's flashed wares tend to be more inventive than their overlay counterparts.

This red and yellow vase was marketed as "alexandrite", after the greenish-brown gemstone that seems to change to red or reddish-brown in certain light. However, despite its name, the vase shown here does not have this quality.
Marks Some Stevens & Williams wares bear the firm's name or initials etched or impressed. Individual designers did not sign their wares.

This vase has several features typical of Powell's vases and drinking glasses of around 1885-90, including a fairly unconventional form, a slender stem, a wide, flat foot, fluted rim and undulating body. Powell's glass is usually thinly-walled. Ribbing was also common.

Above Vaseline glass, also known as yellow opaline, incorporates a type of pale yellow-green, opalescent colouring that thickens and changes colour at the rim. In Powell's glass, the vaseline often thickened to blue.

This centrepiece is typical of Powell's Art Nouveau pieces, with its furnace-wrought decoration and trailed emerald green feathering. Other examples used gold aventurine in knopped stems. The use of enamel work makes this a particularly valuable piece.

JAMES POWELL & SONS (ENGLISH, 1835-1980)

James Powell & Sons was one of the foremost makers of studio glass in the Victorian period. James Powell bought the London company, Whitefriars Glass Works, in 1834 to produce Arts and Crafts style goblets and wine glasses, carafes, decanters, table centrepieces, vases, candelabra and paperweights. From 1880 to 1914 Harry Powell controlled the firm.

James Powell also made vaseline glass for light fittings designed by A.S. Benson and green glass mounts used in Tudric pewter, Cymric silver and the silver-mounted wares of Ashbee's Guild of Handicraft.

Other types of Powell glass

- Early 1850s, "silvered" glass, with metal injected between two separate layers of glass via the pontil.
- Lead glass reproductions of ancient Roman designs.
- Table glass designed by Philip Webb in 1859, mainly in green, which exemplified Arts and Crafts utilitarianism and inspired many glassmakers.
- From around 1889, soda lime glass that exemplified the firm's practical and aesthetic ideals: although light in hand, it is far tougher than it looks. This lacks the sharp "ring" of lead glass.
- A range of clear vases with floral engraving in an Art Nouveau style designed by Heywood Sumner in the 1890s.
- "Tear-drop" table wares, retailed by Liberty & Co from the late 19th century.

From the 1850s James Powell produced Anglo-Venetian glass, with delicate, gem-like patterns adapted from Venetian models. The decorative techniques were applied onto and inside the glass itself and included latticinio (lattice work), spiral threading in opaque white enamel, beading and diamond "air trap" designs.

Note On some of Powell's products, the pontil marks were deliberately left unpolished to suggest age, especially on reproductions of ancient Roman glass.

Marks The glass is unmarked but often the silver component of Powell's wares is stamped with the initials "J.P.S.", below.

Collecting Some of Powell's exhibition pieces are now extremely valuable, but the simpler wares, such as vases and goblets, have recently fallen in price and are relatively inexpensive.

PRESSED GLASS

A miniature Sowerby vase in gold vitro-porcelain glass 1879; ht 4¼in/10cm

Other makers In Britain, high quality pressed glass was also made by the Manchester firms of Molineaux, Webb & Co., and John Derbyshire. In the late 1860s and 1870s, these companies all issued designs in Greek key patterns, and star and leaf motifs with frosted effects that contrasted with the shiny body. John Derbyshire also manufactured lions after the painter Sir Edwin Landseer, as well as figures of Britannia and Punch and Judy.
• The best known maker in the United States was the Boston & Sandwich Glass Co. (1825-88) which specialized in the production of lacy glass.
• The most sought after American pressed glass is commemorative.
• Pressed glass is of uniform thickness with mould lines sometimes visible on the interior.

Press-moulding glass by mechanical means was one of the major achievements of Victorian glass makers. Most of the wares consist of domestic items such as drinking vessels, jugs, bowls, dishes, celery vases, salt cellars, and so on. These are usually made in clear, colourless "flint" glass. Coloured pieces, sometimes known as "slag-ware", tend to fetch higher prices.

Many of the designs imitated the fashionable and more expensive styles of cut glass. However, pressed glass motifs are regular but less sharp than in cut glass, and the seam lines made by joins in the moulds are often visible. Pieces have a novel and decorative form. The surface is glossy, the body almost opaque.

Pieces can be precisely identified as most carry a maker's mark or a Design Registration mark. The marks are sometimes difficult to see, but can usually be detected by running a finger over the surface of the glass.

SOWERBY (ENGLISH, 1847-1972)

Some of the best quality pressed glass, such as the piece pictured above, was made by Sowerby's Ellison Glassworks in Gateshead on Tyne. They registered their products with the Patent Office from 1872 and introduced their peacock's head trademark in 1876.

The most sought-after glass is made of vitro-porcelain, which looks like porcelain or bone china, and was produced from 1877. It was made in many colours, including cream (called "Patent Ivory Queen's Ware"), white, gold, pale turquiose and jet (appearing black, but usually deep purple). It was also available in marbled colours, such as purple, blue and green (malachite).

The Sowerby range consisted of vases, spill holders, small baskets, candlesticks, and other ornamental items, but also ribbon plates and stands for dessert services. The designs were mostly in the 1870s and 1880s "Aesthetic" style, some in imitation of carved ivory and showing a Japanese influence; others derived from children's book illustrations by Walter Crane (1845-1915).

HENERY GREENER (ENGLISH, 1858)

From the late 1850s, this Sunderland works manufactured good quality clear and coloured glass. Like Davidson's, below, they produced many items to commemorate Queen Victoria's Jubilee in 1887, and other royal and historic occasions. Their mark was a lion with a star, and after 1885, a lion with an axe.

DAVIDSON'S (ENGLISH, founded 1867)

Davidson's Teams Glass Works at Gateshead also produced a wide variety of useful and ornamental wares in clear and coloured glass. Their trademark was a lion above a crown within a circle, or from around 1880-90, a lion above a tower.

Lacy glass – inexpensive machine-pressed glass developed in the United States in the 1830s – is categorized by its intricate patterns. This bowl (**below**) was made to celebrate the Silver Wedding Anniversary of the Prince and Princess of Wales in 1888.

The beaded lettering is characteristic of Greener's wares. It was also used by Davidson and copied on the Continent. The Continental pieces, which are unmarked, are of inferior quality. Pieces made before 1840 are in great demand.

This jug and tumbler was made in Davidson's "Pearline". In blue or primrose, the patterns usually imitated the current fashion for "brilliant" cut glass.

GALLÉ AND FRENCH ART GLASS

An enamel, acid-etched and gilded jardinière by Emile Gallé c.1885/90; dia. 12in/31cm

French art glass designers provided a bridge between traditional, Renaissance and Venetian styles and the French interpretation of Art Nouveau. Their style is best typified by Emile Gallé, but others, particularly the Daum brothers, began to drift towards the naturalistic decoration and sculptural forms of the Nancy school and, together with Desiré Christian, Auguste Légras, the Muller Frères and Burgun, Schverer & Co., they pioneered a revival of cameo decoration, as well as popularizing enamelled glass. They abandoned the elaborate cutting of previous generations and concentrated on sculptural and surface possibilities. The skills of chemists and master glass blowers, combined with the fertile imagination of designers, resulted in some completely new and exciting forms. Improved methods of mass-production meant that designers could recreate the style of the expensive studio pieces very much in demand at the time at a much more affordable price.

EMILE GALLÉ (FRENCH, 1846-1904)

Emile Gallé was considered the greatest master-craftsman in glass, even within his own lifetime. He established his workshop in Nancy in 1874, and produced glass and ceramics using a wide variety of styles and techniques, and also furniture (see p.36). He made his initial foray into the world of glass with enamelled wares, mainly influenced by decoration from medieval France. He then moved towards a more sculptural style, capturing in glass the sense of movement advocated by exponents of Art Nouveau. He often included floral and naturalistic motifs, using insects and flowers peculiar to his home town of Nancy, such as cow parsley. Mushrooms were another recurring theme – some of his lamps imitate the fungus's entire shape. From around 1890 Gallé produced cameo glass, whilst still maintaining an interest in more exclusive studio ware.

Iznik-type ware was inspired by the brilliantly coloured pottery produced at Iznik in Turkey in the 15th and 16th centuries. This enamelled glass bowl illustrates Gallé's adaptation of an Iznik design to a form of Art Nouveau. Typical designs take the form of stylized flowers or arabesques, often with (genuine or fake) Koranic scripts woven into the decoration.

Early wares Initially, Gallé produced hand-finished and -decorated wares in green or brown tinted or clear glass, moulded into innovative forms, and carved, sometimes with an incised or sunken decoration called intaglio. Further decoration included gilding and acid etching, as in the enamelled jardinière at the top of the page. This added texture makes it more desirable than pieces that are only enamelled. Bases have a ground and polished pontil.

The brown-tinted glass body of this pitcher from 1890 is carved and enamelled with a dragonfly motif. Gallé has applied delicate brown and cream gilding, which is often used on his enamelled pieces. The black and silver enamelling on the foot is decorated with stylized flowers and leaves made from red sealing wax. The shape is characteristic of Gallé's early work.

Above The hand carving on this coupe is noticeably deeper than on machine-made pieces, adding a premium to its value. The design of the base – each prong set with a carved cicada – is highly innovative. The foil inclusions highlighting the wings and eyes of the cicadas would not be found on industrially carved pieces. Hand-carved pieces tend to be fire-polished. This coupe has been splashed with colour and then polished. The light amber mottling is particularly unusual.

From 1899 increased mechanization enabled Gallé to produce cameo glass on a commercial scale. These pieces are the most usual type of Gallé cameo glass found today as the sheer plasticity of the medium made it perfect for Art Nouveau designs.

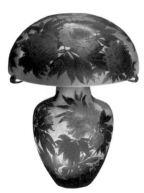

This lamp is one of Gallé's most collectable pieces. The vibrant peony decoration is intricately etched, and the detailing of the flowerheads give the lamp a strong sense of depth, particularly when illuminated from behind. The size and the "blowout" decoration enhance value.

Later studio glassware From 1889 Gallé concentrated on producing the innovative wares for which he is best known. These made greater use of mottled and striated glass, and of naturalistic decoration. Many pieces use Gallé's traditional *marquetrie de verre* process, whereby fragments of hot coloured glass are pressed into the hot and malleable body of a vessel and then rolled in. Once cool, the glass is then carved on a wheel.

Gallé's cameo glassware Cameo glasswares, using two or more layers of coloured glass from which decoration is cut or carved away, were the staple product of the Gallé glassworks. At first hand-made, cameo glass, after around 1904, was almost invariably industrially made.

•Much of Gallé's glassware has applied decoration, commonly floral. Crustacea, molluscs and mushrooms are also found, but are rare and hence particularly sought by collectors.

•Gallé's cameo landscape vases generally fetch higher prices than those with floral decoration. Other subjects include polar bears, elephants and fish.

Dating and marks Gallé's work is always signed. On enamelled pieces signatures are often in black enamel or gilt on the base, but the gilt may be worn away, making it necessary to hold the object to the light to see the trace of the original mark, which is relatively small. Occasionally the signature may be carved. Some earlier, historical pieces incorporate the cross of Lorraine in the mark. Cameo pieces generally have a cameo or incise-carved signature. For three years after Gallé's death a star was added slightly above the signature, which is held to represent the loss of France's shining star. After 1907 the firm reverted to using Gallé's signature.

Left Some Gallé pieces, like this intaglio-carved vase from c.1904, may bear an engraved verse, generally by Victor Prouvé, Mallarmé, Baudelaire or some other French giant of literature, and these are referred to as *verreries parlantes*, or speaking vases.

Above Electricity led to a large output of lamps. The functional aspect of this one enhances the decorative: the light illuminates the stem and the waterfall that runs its length. This lamp is three-coloured, but four- and five-layer examples exist.

Landscape vases are most popular today. Decoration is stiffer, with shallower carving, which lets the internal yellow mottling show through as a part of the design. Careful carving and the depth of the purple glass layer have allowed toning from light mauve to almost black.

PHILLIPE-JOSEPH BROCARD (FRENCH, ACTIVE 1867-90)

This enamelled opalescent glass vase by Brocard, although not wholly Iznik, nevertheless has certain Iznik characteristics, such as Persian-style carnations and foliage and gilded edging.

Phillipe-Joseph Brocard taught Gallé many of his enamelling techniques, and was himself an acclaimed glass maker. He started a revival of Islamic glass-enamelling. Inspired by 14th-century Syrian mosque lamps, he tried to rediscover the Syrian enamelling techniques and after much experimentation eventually mastered them to make many copies of these lamps as well as other vases and bowls.

•Brocard signed his wares "Brocard", sometimes with the address of the firm, or "Brocard et Fils". The vase on the left bears his signature on the base.

DAUM FRÈRES (FRENCH, 1875-Present)

The Daum brothers, Auguste (1835-1909) and Antonin (1864-1930), worked together with Emile Gallé before establishing their own glassworks in Nancy. No distinction has so far been made between their work. The firm, now operating as Cristallerie Daum, is still in business today.

Although Daum Frères produced some carved and enamelled pieces, most of their Art Nouveau wares are cameo glass or acid-cut and colour enamelled. A rare technique was *intercalaire*, where pieces would be cameo-carved – usually by laminating two layers of glass together – and then covered with a layer of carved or etched semi-transparent glass. Early Daum pieces tended to be enamelled.

Above Decoration is sometimes picked out with gilt, as in this four-handled vase. The vase has a mottled background, with carving applied over the top. Like all Daum pieces, it is hand-carved.
•Beware of cut-down vases with irregular rims, sharp edges and a polished appearance.

Above The *intercalaire* technique is apparent on this tall enamelled rainstorm vase, which also makes use of underlying mottling to provide toning. The factory produced a number of similar pieces with autumnal and winter scenes, and those displaying the rain-streaked effect evident on this piece are particularly sought-after. The firm was also adept at enamelling on top of carved decoration: the green on the base of this vase has been painted onto carving. The enamelled tree is typical of Daum decoration, in that it disappears over the edge of the vase.

Left Early work tended to be enamelled. Like other members of the Nancy School, the Daum Frères were inspired by the flora and fauna of their native Lorraine. This vase is a good example of their early work, with tinted glass lightly etched with a dragonfly, and richly enamelled with waterlillies and wild flowers around a lily pond.

Collecting point

Daum glass divides into the popular sculptural and other technically complicated studio work, and the industrially produced (although still hand-carved) pieces. All the pieces shown here are of high quality and would command high prices.

Marks Some pieces are signed in cameo; most feature the gilt signature, "DAUM, NANCY", on black enamel on the underside of the base, accompanied by the cross of Lorraine.

The Daum Frères produced technically competent and innovative decorative wares, although lamps, possibly intended for use, were also produced. This table lamp in overlaid and etched glass is typical of their Art Nouveau wares, most of which were produced before 1914. It also demonstrates the sculptural form, delicate carving and mottled decoration which were typical of the Daum brothers' designs. The applied glass snails on the base increase the desirability of the piece, and may add as much as 40 per cent to the value.

Above Some Daum pieces feature metal mounts by Louis Majorelle, as does this bronze-mounted double overlay and *martelé* glass table lamp.

The Daum brothers also produced mould-blown or "blowout" vases, where the glass was blown into a mould, as in this overlaid and engraved glass vase. Typically of such pieces, the design appears in relief over a mottled background. The mould lines are visible, but, as here, should not appear too pronounced. Use is made of familiar natural motifs in the delicately engraved village scene and trees.
•Vase bases are sometimes shallow and carved with stylized bands on a granular background.
•Figural decoration is rare.
•The firm later went on to produce heavy, acid cut pieces, often with geometric decoration.

This cameo vase typically features internal mottling and *martelé* (planished) surface decoration. The leaves and stems are gilded with gold. Pieces were fire-polished. Bases tend to be solid, and silver mounts were used on some examples. Other pieces were raised upon solid, circular feet.

BURGUN, SCHVERER & CO. (FRENCH, 1711-Present)

Following the Franco-Prussian War (1870-71), the previously French provinces of Alsace and Lorraine were annexed by Germany, and the long-established Lorraine glassmaking firm of Burgun, Schverer & Co. found itself in Germany. However, the firm maintained its contacts with France, and particularly with Emile Gallé who had served a three-year apprenticeship at the firm's factory at Meisenthal during the late 1860s. In 1885, Burgun, Schverer & Co. entered into a contract to produce glass for Gallé. Also in that year, the designer Desiré Christian joined the firm. The firm also designed a few one-off pieces to commission. Today Burgun, Schverer & Co. is back in France, operating as Verrerie de Meisanthal.

Marks Wares are marked with an etched gilt thistle and cross of Lorraine, accompanied by the words "VERRERIE D'ART DE LORRAINE BS AND CO", or a variation of these three elements. Some Burgun, Schverer & Co. wares from before around 1870 bear Gallé's signature as well.

Cameo Wares Burgun, Schverer & Co. were the only company in Germany to produce cameo glass during these early years. Forms tended to be conservative and included traditional Venetian and naturalistic-inspired examples. The emphasis was on decoration, which was influenced by local flora such as cowparsley, and the thistle (the emblem of Lorraine), visible on the vase on the left.

•Other decorative techniques used by Burgun, Schverer & Co included acid cutting, foil inclusions, gilding and the use of overlay. Some pieces, which are known as *vases parlantes*, had inscribed verses in French included in the decoration.

This enamelled coupe is typical of the firm's acid-cut pieces. A design was etched onto the glass, which was then coated with wax and dipped in acid to cut out the design. Craftsmen often applied gilding and enamelling in conjunction with cameo and internal decoration. Such pieces usually reflect styles and motifs from Ancient Egypt or, as in this case, Renaissance Venice, and as such cannot be called pure Art Nouveau.

DÉSIRÉ CHRISTIAN (FRENCH, 1846-1907)

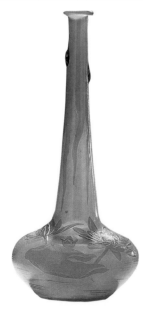

This etched, polished and applied green vase with teardrop *appliqués* around the neck, produced by Christian's firm, is very similar to the wares designed under Christian at Burgun, Schverer & Co.

•Christian's thick-walled vases often display isolated surface carving, with colourful internal and surface streaking.

Christian was Burgun, Schverer & Co.'s chief artistic designer until 1896, when he opened his own firm, initially called Christian Frères et Fils, with his brother François and son Armand. Christian excelled in vases with enamelled decoration encased with a further layer of clear glass. He often cut away the outer surface to reveal the layer of colour beneath.

Marks It is not known exactly which pieces were designed by Christian himself, and which were designed by his brother, his son, or one of the firm's other designers, although a small number are engraved with the monogram "D.Ch". In general, wares carry the signature of the firm "DESIRÉ CHRISTIAN".

AUGUSTE LÉGRAS (FRENCH, 1864-Present)

The work of Auguste Légras bears a strong resemblance to that of Gallé, Daum and Müller Frères, but generally commands lower prices. He made enamelled cameo vases and commercial glassware, including perfume bottles designed by René Lalique (see pp.90-1).
• Légras favoured internally mottled or streaked glass.
• His pieces are usually signed "LÉGRAS".

Légras preferred mainly floral and landscape decoration, as in this enamelled glass lamp, whose decoration resembles Daum's woodland scenes. The effect of fire-polishing is visible on relief areas.

MÜLLER FRÈRES (FRENCH, active 1895-1933)

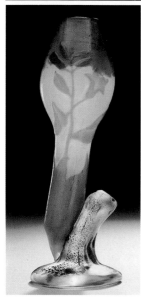

Henri and Désiré Müller worked initially with Emile Gallé. In 1895, Henri Müller set up a workshop in Lunéville, near Nancy, where he was later joined by Desiré and others. Their glasswares were blown at their Croismare factory before being sent to Lunéville for decoration. Except for a brief period of closure in 1914, the business prospered until it was disbanded. The Müller brothers worked in a variety of styles, but are best known for their industrially-produced cameo glassware.

Above Müller's rarest wares are the sculptural studio pieces, which tend to have overlaid, carved and internal decoration. This fire-polished lily vase is overlaid in lavender, white and lime green. The stem is decorated inside with foil.

Above Many of Muller Frères cameo designs ape those by Gallé. Forms were relatively standard, with vases often having a short, everted neck, as in this example. Particular proficiency was shown in their floral and landscape decoration applied to vases, ceiling bowls and table lamps. It was always well-carved, with attention given to depth and perspective. Often glass would be internally mottled or streaked. Some rarer pieces include Japanese-inspired decoration – this vase features stylized landscapes, figures and birds.

Marks Pieces are marked either "Müller Frères - Lunéville" or "Müller-Croismare", or simply "M.F". Most acid-etched glass was made at Lunéville, whilst wheel-carved pieces came from Croismare.

A word of advice about glass lamps

Any collar mounts should be removed and the neck beneath checked. If encased in metal, examine the glass carefully for signs of stress cracks. Lamps could be lit internally, with one light for the shade and one for the base. Avoid pieces where the base has been drilled to take a wire. Usually, the stems of such lamps were hollow, and the wire went under the lamp. A recess for the wire stopped the lamp wobbling.

AMERICAN GLASS PIONEERS

The American art glass industry developed along roughly parallel lines to the movement in Britain. By the mid-nineteenth century, glassmakers on both sides of the Atlantic shared an enthusiasm for the innovative techniques and materials used by Venetian craftsmen. American manufacturers were also inspired by ancient glass, and glass from the European Renaissance and the Near East. American manufacturers relied greatly on English technology, and often used immigrant employees.

A Crown Milano vase by the Mount Washington Glass Company c.1885-95; ht 13¾in/33cm

MOUNT WASHINGTON (AMERICAN, 1837-1958)

Like most early American glassworks, Mount Washington was established near Boston. In 1870, its owner, William L. Libbery, moved the firm to New Bedford, Massachusetts. Its manager from 1874 was Frederick S. Shirley, who was closely associated with the American Aesthetic Movement. The company's art glass boom followed the exhibition of contemporary glass at the 1876 Centennial show in Philadelphia. By 1880, the works were making a full range of glassware including chandeliers, tableware and paperweights. In 1894, the business merged with the Pairpoint Manufacturing Co. (see p.86), but the production of art glass, especially Burmese ware, continued into the 20th century.

Royal Flemish glass Mount Washington produced a range of enamelled art glass, patented as Royal Flemish Glass, which closely resembled ancient Islamic wares.

Crown Milano glass The vase at the top of the page is a fine example of Mount Washington's Crown Milano range. The pressed-milk glass is rough-finished with acid and lavishly enamelled, either in subdued colours, as here, or sometimes in vivid tones. Some pieces were further embellished with prunts or finials.

Burmese glass From 1885 Mount Washington patented its range of Burmese glass, which was moulded or free-blown into vases, ewers, bowls, candlesticks, perfume bottles, table and boudoir lamps and tablewares. It usually has a matt satin surface and is often finished with elaborate ornament including figural painting in polychrome and gold enamels. It is among the most highly valued of all American art glass. Some examples bear printed Burmese labels, and collectors also look for those signed with the designer's name, especially Albert Steffin, the company's Art Director.

This marine pitcher from around 1890 is typical of Mount Washington's range of Royal Flemish glass. The clearly visible raised enamel lines which divide the glass into segments give a similar effect to stained glass. The subdued colours of brown, beige and gold are characteristic, as is the fish motif.
•In some of Mount Washington's wares the maker reheated the top edge of the vessel a second time, turning it yellow above the pink rim. These pieces are highly collectable.

This Burmese lamp was made between 1885 and 1895. The fish motif was one of Mount Washington's most popular designs. Other popular motifs included flora and American fauna, as well as "Egyptian" imagery. Some Burmese vessels were "diamond quilted" with a moulded cross-hatch design, or blown into "ribbed" or "hobnail" patterns. The exterior decoration is typically skilfully applied.
•The most widely produced type of shaded glass at this time was "Amberina" glass, developed at the New England Glass Co. by Joseph Locke, an immigrant from England.

HOBBS, BROCKUNIER (AMERICAN, 1845-87)

This Virginian company, founded by James B. Barnes in Wheeling, is the best known exponent of the Peachblow technique. Peachblow, or Peachbloom, was a shaded glass with a cased, inner layer of opalescent glass which gave the finished ware the appearance of Chinese glazed porcelain. Other Hobbs wares included cameo and crackle glass, with applied decoration, and many pressed or blown novelty items.

This "Morgan" vase was one of many made at Hobbs. It is based on a Chinese Kangzi period porcelain vase belonging to the collection of Mary J. Morgan, and is made of Peachblow glass on cast, pale amber stands. Such pieces are extremely collectable, but the stands are often damaged.

THE STEUBEN GLASSWORKS (1903-Present)

Frederick Carder (British, 1864-1963)

Frederick Carder established his reputation at Stevens & Williams (see p.69) between 1881 and 1902, before serving as Art Director at Steuben for over 30 years.

The Steuben Glassworks was founded in 1903 in Corning, in New York State's Steuben County, by members of the local glassmaking Hawkes family and Frederick Carder. Unlike some competitors, such as Tiffany, who adhered to the artist-craftsman principle, Steuben pursued a policy of mass-production of ornamental and useful wares. This made their wares distinct from studio glass, because the forms were intended to appeal to conventional rather than avant garde taste.

The Steuben range of art glass Steuben produced over 20 distinct glass types, the best known of which is "Aurene" ware. Among the many other types are "Calcite", made from 1915, a plated (cased) glass used for decorative wares and lampshades, with an Aurene finish on an opaque, opalescent ground simulating ivory; "Clutha", a heavily bubbled and mottled glass comparable to the Scottish "Clutha" (see p.68) and "*Verre de Soie*" – a pale, iridescent glass commonly used for stemware in the Venetian style.

Among the most innovative glass types Carder introduced to Steuben was *millefiori* ("thousand flower") glass, of which this bowl is an example. Canes of coloured·glass were arranged in bundles so the cross-section created a pattern. Slices of *millefiori* canes could be used as decoration, or fused together to form hollow wares. Steuben's *millefiori* wares are among the rarest and most valuable of the firm's commercially produced art glass.
•Carder also produced Aurene wares and some striking Art Deco glass (see p. 98).
•Aurene ware is usually acid-stamped on the base with a fleur-de-lys and the word "Steuben" on a scroll. The more complex glasswares, such as the *millefiori* pieces, bear the signature of the craftsman and are therefore especially appealing to collectors today. Some signed by Carder are also dated.

Aurene wares, produced between 1904 and 1933, account for the bulk of Steuben's large output. Vases are most common, but dishes and table lamps were also produced. Scent bottles, which tend to be of slender baluster form, are particularly collectable, as are floriform vases, especially those decorated in the Tiffany manner with trailing leaves or pulled feather motifs. Decorated Aurene is considerably more valuable than plain. Most wares have blue or gold iridescent decoration similar to the finish popularized by Tiffany's Favrile glass (see pp.84-5), but always with a smooth, even surface. This vase combines both blue and gold iridescent decoration.

Among the more technically complex, rarer and more valuable wares produced by Steuben, are those with acid-cut decoration which is comparable in style and standard of manufacture to Peking glass (see p.241). This plum-coloured vase from around 1910 is a fine example.

IRIDESCENT GLASS

The use of iridescence in glass and pottery was very much an Art Nouveau phenomenon. The most popular decorative motif of the peacock feather was repeated in the textiles of Liberty (see p.235), the glassware of Tiffany (see pp.84-5) and the ceramics of Zsolnay (see p.134). Loetz iridescent wares were the most innovative, with its designers applying finely controlled iridescent decoration to often inventive sculptural forms. Bakalowits & Söhne and Palme-Konig tended to produce paler copies of their Loetz counterparts, with Bakalowits using lustrous surfaces as a secondary consideration to form.

A large Loetz vase c.1900; ht 10½in/26cm

LOETZ (AUSTRIAN, 1836-1939)

This glassmaking firm, founded at Klostermühle by Johann Loetz, specialized in high-quality art glass. After 1848, when Loetz died and his widow Suzanne took over direction, the firm became known as Glasfabrik Johann-Loetz Witwe. It was guided to success by Max von Spaun, the designer who introduced the iridescent glasswares that attracted attention during the 1880s and for which the firm won numerous awards. At the Vienna Jubilee Exhibition of 1898, Loetz showed a group of iridescent wares which soon rivalled the products of Louis Comfort Tiffany in popularity. Although many collectors view Loetz glass as the Austrian attempt to emulate Tiffany, it was actually Tiffany who was impressed by the Loetz wares shown at the various international exhibitions. In fact, many Loetz creations predate similar works by Tiffany. Loetz also produced cameo wares, but these are fairly rare.

Forms Loetz forms are very inventive, and may recall Persian or Roman models. Pieces often have applied slender handles trailing from or around the body.

Other wares Loetz also produced glass in contrasting primary colours, as well as a variety of lamp shades for Koloman Moser (see p.82). From around 1900, Loetz made large quantities of "Papillon" (Butterfly) glass, decorated with closely clustered iridescent peacock or kingfisher blue raindrop splashes.
•Another Loetz designer, Michael Powolny, used vibrant colours, such as orange and yellow combined, with applied black rims and decoration.

One of the most famous sculptors associated with the company, Gustav Gurschner (see p.161), produced the metal bases for a memorable series of table lamps. This example is very much in his style, although it is not signed.
•The feathering on the shade of this piece is typical.

This "goose-neck" vase is based on a Turkish rosewater sprinkler. Other vases have straight necks, without the swollen knop, or resemble the "Jack in the Pulpit" vases of the American art company, Quezal (see p.87). Pontils are ground, except on pieces with metal frames, which usually have moulded bases.

Decoration The thick, solid body of Loetz iridescent wares tends to be dark, with the finely controlled decoration displaying a spectrum of colours. Vessels with deep purple bodies, highlighted with silver and peacock blue iridescence, were very popular and are the most collectable today. Dark amber glass with green-gold iridescence was also popular. The colour of the vase in the main picture is unusual, but the controlled, feathered decoration, iridescent gold motifs and slender, sinuous handles are typical. Loetz also pioneered the use of electrolytic deposit techniques. The most desirable pieces are those with a distinctively Art Nouveau design. Pieces may also feature silver casing.

A distinctive feature of Palme-König wares is the use of the trailed spider's web-type decoration seen on this vase. Decoration typically uses light-coloured overlays against dark grounds, such as claret or green. On frosted pieces, the process was reversed.

PALME KÖNIG (BOHEMIAN, established 1786)

The Bohemian commercial glassmakers Palme-König produced good quality Art Nouveau iridescent glasswares and table glass. The firm employed forms pioneered by Loetz, with the result that its work is often seen as a less expensive imitation of Loetz.

Palme-König's iridescent pieces are often attributed to Loetz, but they are less controlled. The decoration of this vase from around 1900 has a random, splattered effect.

E. BAKALOWITS & SÖHNE (AUSTRIAN, established 1845)

One of the leading Austrian retailers of glassware at the start of the 20th century was the Viennese firm of Bakalowits. With the rise in popularity of iridescent glass, the firm commissioned a number of striking avant-garde pieces from such leading designers as Koloman Moser of the Wiener Werkstätte (see pp.82-3).

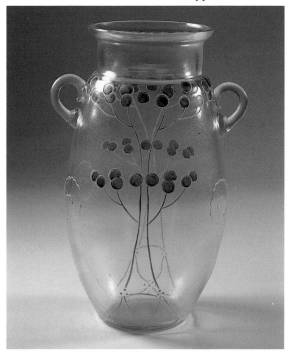

Left The pearlized, iridescent surface of wares such as this pale green vase has led many people to regard them as insubstantial competition for the bolder, more colourful designs of Loetz. Bakalowits products are sometimes wrongly catalogued as Loetz, although they are typically of thinner glass and are lighter in weight and less substantial, with less pronounced, paler iridescence. Unlike those of Loetz, Bakalowits wares tend to have moulded bases, without a visible pontil mark.
•Recently, Bakalowits wares have begun to be appreciated in their own right, but they will probably never achieve the desirability of Loetz.

This electroplate-mounted glass sherry jug, designed by Koloman Moser, shows Bakalowits producing to the order of a designer. It would probably fetch many times the price of the vase on the left by virtue of its association with Moser.

Identification and marks

Loetz items made for export are marked "LOETZ" or "LOETZ AUSTRIA". Others carry engraved crossed arrows, or are unmarked. Palme-König wares are not marked. The most common colours are green, amethyst and deep red. Bases are often moulded, but some may have a ground pontil mark. Beware of spurious Loetz marks. Bakalowits wares are unmarked, but documentation does exist for Moser's work.

THE WIENER WERKSTÄTTE

The members of the Wiener Werkstätte, or Vienna Workshops, produced glasswares in a variety of styles, concentrating on simple, functional shapes, with minimal ornament. The most important designs were by Josef Hoffmann and Koloman Moser (who also designed furniture, pp.42-3, and metalwork, pp.189-90), Dagobert Pèche and Otto Prutscher. Prominent glassmakers executed the Wiener Werkstätte designs. Many of Hoffmann's and Prutscher's designs were made by the firm of Meyr's Neffe. Often one artist would design the piece and another would decorate it – Pèche decorated many of Hoffmann's designs.
•For the collector, it is more important to know the designer of a particular piece, than which firm was responsible for its execution.

Right A Wiener Werkstätte glass table lamp designed by Otto Prutscher 1908; ht 15in/38cm

OTTO PRUTSCHER (AUSTRIAN, 1880-1949)

In addition to table lamps, Prutscher produced various suites of glassware flashed in a wide range of colours, including red, black, green and yellow: stronger colours are the most desirable. The chequered motif on the typically dangerously long thin stem of this rose-pink wine glass is almost Prutscher's trademark. Glass makers invariably prefer the foot to be wider than the rest of the piece, but Prutscher produced many pieces like this, where the bowl is as large as, or larger than, the foot.

Although best known for his jewelry and silver, Prutscher designed some of the Wiener Werkstätte's most distinctive glasswares. He used a traditional Austrian and Bohemian form of glass decoration in which glass was flashed with a single colour and then carved and polished to form a design pattern. Prutscher adapted this technique to produce unique pieces that were strongly geometric both in form and in decoration. The clear glass table lamp shown in the main picture is a typical example of his technique.
•Prutscher's designs are collectable singly and complete sets are unlikely to turn up.
•The condition of such delicate pieces is all-important.

KOLOMAN MOSER (AUSTRIAN, 1868-1918)

The designs of Koloman Moser were executed by Bakalowits (see p.81) and by Loetz (who also manufactured the glasswares of Michael Powolny, see p.80).

Moser's designs were revolutionary and differed radically from Loetz's more usual wares, which were often iridescent and more restrained. As shown by this bowl, many of his designs were acid-cut on overlay and embellished with enamelling. The use of ball feet is characteristic of his work.

Right This iridescent glass vase was designed by Kolomon Moser in 1899 and executed by the firm of Loetz in 1902. At 5½in (14cm), it is fairly small. The applied feet are a typical decorative motif,

as is the pod design set against a feathered background. The random element of the designs is unusual for Moser and it is difficult to tell how much was originally his intention.

JOSEPH HOFFMANN (AUSTRIAN, 1870-1956)

Left Hoffmann's undecorated glass was generally made by Meyr's Neff. Some designs were elaborate, but others, like this green bowl from c.1924, rely upon form and have no external decoration. The spreading base was applied to some of his silver designs.

Above Hoffmann produced a range of cameo glass, such as this vase from 1911. Many pieces had a vertical emphasis and shapes tended to be relatively simple. The motifs of the spade-shaped leaves and stylized bell-flowers are typically Viennese, as is the panel decoration. Similar pieces were made by other glassmakers.

Until the 1920s, Josef Hoffmann's glass designs concentrated on decorative form, with many pieces in single colour panel-cut glassware which echoed the form of the Biedermeier glass of the early 19th century.

Above Maria Kirschner designed vases of unusual shape, executed in iridescent glass by Loetz. This vase from around 1905, is only 4½in (11.5cm) high. The decoration is rather random and echoes many earlier producers of iridescent glass (see pp.80-81).

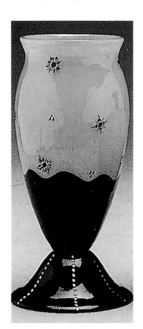

Dagobert Pèche was a member of the Wiener Werkstätte from 1915 until his death in 1923. This vase is characteristic of Pèche, with its relatively simple enamelled body and freely-placed graphic motifs. Other popular motifs included flowers or figures.

Above During the Art Nouveau period. some glassware was produced from designs by Austrian art students. Alternatively, the designs of a well-known member of the Wiener Werkstätte were executed by a *Fachschüle* (art college).

This bonbonnière, with alternating clear and enamelled bands, was produced by Fachschüle Haida to a design by Karl Pohl. Some of the pieces have a signature or maker's name inscribed in gilt on the base.

As well as furniture (see p.41) Olbrich designed glasswares such as this pewter-mounted glass vase from 1905; unlike the simple geometric forms used by Koloman and Hoffmann, it is a hybrid of the French and German treatment of Art Nouveau.

TIFFANY AND THE AMERICAN APPROACH

An Apple Blossom leaded glass and bronze Tiffany table lamp c.1910; ht 27in/68.5cm, shade dia. 18in/ 45.5cm

Louis Comfort Tiffany was considered the leading arbiter of taste in the New World and among the rich social élite in America. His influence was not restricted to glassware, but spread to the entire matter of interior decoration. He was fortunate to be living in a time when arts and sciences were being amalgamated and was particularly lucky to have been living in the age of the light bulb, which was developed by fellow American, Thomas Edison, in 1878, and of the filament lamp which followed in 1879. It was the marriage of the electric light with his colourful leaded lampshades that sealed Tiffany's success.

Tiffany's designs were emulated by several American companies, including Handel, the Pairpoint Corporation and Quezal. Whilst Handel and Pairpoint concentrated upon creating innovative lampshades, often, but not always, in the style of Tiffany, Quezal helped to satisfy the increasing demand for the iridescent glassware popularized by Tiffany in America.

This six-dragonfly lamp is the most common of several similar versions. Some include coloured glass cabochons, either pitted around the shade or used for eyes, as here. These insects' heads are contained by the shade, but some "drophead" dragonflies protrude beyond the rim. The wings are of pierced grille laid over the glass.
•Shades are sometimes crimped to resemble silk; others have pierced bronze bases with glass blown into the frames.
•Larger leaded shades may have supporting struts on the interior.

TIFFANY STUDIOS (AMERICAN, 1879-1936)

Louis Comfort Tiffany, son of the renowned American jeweler, Charles Tiffany, founded Louis C. Tiffany & Associated Artists which became Tiffany Studios. In 1900 the firm designed interiors for private and public buildings, such as the White House in Washington. Tiffany's unique style became a driving force behind the emergent Art Nouveau style. In 1880, he patented an iridescent glass called favrile (meaning hand-made), which became their staple material, and the type most often found today. Louis Comfort became art director of his father's company, Tiffany and Co., in 1902.

Tiffany's lamps Tiffany table lamps were made in two sections; the base and stem, and the shade. Shades consist of many pieces of favrile glass set in a bronze framework of irregular lozenge shapes, with decoration often inspired by organic and naturalistic motifs. Dragonflies are common, as are Renaissance, zodiacal, bamboo and medieval motifs. Bases are bronze or gilt bronze, and sometimes incorporate tile or mosaic work. The shade may reflect the design: the irregular border of the example at the top of the page enhances the organic effect of the tree-like base and floral motifs. Being hand-made, no two shades are identical.

Many of Tiffany's lamps have complementary bases and shades, but it is unusual for these elements to be integral, as they are in this Zinnia lamp, which is inlaid with leaded and mosaic glass to imitate zinnias. The base is designed as six trees supporting the shade.
•This piece was probably a one-off and is thus particularly desirable, as most Tiffany pieces were made in editions of more than one.
•If the integral elements are separated, a piece will lose value.

Towards the end of the 19th century, ancient glass was found around the Mediterranean. Generally of Roman origin, the glass had developed a beautiful iridescent surface, as the result of being buried. Tiffany's "Cypriote" wares, like this vase from around 1895, attempted to reproduce the iridescence and finely pitted surface of this glass.

Other Tiffany studio ware As well as table lamps and lampshades, Louis Comfort Tiffany also produced vases and scent bottles, tiles, lamps, stained-glass windows and glass mosaics and desk furniture. Some mosaics measure as much as 15 x 49ft (4.6 x 15m).

Tiffany developed and used innovative glassmaking methods. He avoided surface decoration, preferring to make ornament integral to the body of the piece. However, he was a designer of glassware rather than a glassmaker, and he paid little heed to the technical aspect of working in glass. The craftsmen employed at the factory to produce his designs frequently found them technically impossible. For every hundred or so attempts, only one design might prove practical. To achieve the natural agate effect on the vase pictured on the right requires great technical expertise.

The very accurate similarity of this favrile agate glass to the natural stone is achieved by blowing layer upon layer of multicoloured opaque glass, and then carving through the layered glass at an angle to create the effect of the striations of natural agate. The olive-green, ochre, moss-green and pale yellow coloration of this example, made around 1904, is typical of Tiffany's agate vases.

Tiffany's lava glasswares, such as this vase, took iridescence to new heights. Form and decoration are usually irregular, often with a dripping effect against an irregular iridescent ground. Lava glass resembles stone, and is produced by mixing volcanic slag with glass metal, a process first developed in late-18th century France. Lava glass is the most sought-after of Tiffany's glass today, and fetches several times the amount raised by comparable pieces in favrile or agate glass.

The flower form of this vase, with its flaring ruffled rim above a band of green striated petals is typical of the organic and naturalistic inspiration of Art Nouveau. The iridescent interior of this example is gold; others are gunmetal blue.

This glass vase is unusual in being one block of solid colour – a deep Chinese red. The form is traditional; some similar vases have necks banded in a contrasting colour with feathered decoration. This example is rare and desirable.

Marks and fakes All pieces are marked, usually with the initials "LCT", in small letters. Lamps and some larger pieces bear the full name, perhaps with a reference number. Some have original paper labels. On lamps, shades are also marked with a bronze pad. Fakes and copies abound; collectors should develop an eye for Tiffany's distinctive style. Faked signatures tend to be inept and, as Tiffany wares are well-documented, sequence numbers can be checked. Forgers often overlook the small pad found on most genuine shades.

This paperweight vase is so-called because the design is painstakingly embedded and manipulated within layers of clear glass, a process loosely akin to that used for paperweights. Design definition can vary from clear and sharp to softer and more abstract. Today, good paperweight glass with clear definition is amongst the most collectable and expensive of Tiffany's wares.

Above Value is largely determined by decoration. All-over floral decoration as on this example is common, as are autumnal landscapes, and these raise only moderate prices.

Above Handel also made exterior-painted and leaded glass shades, and a range of art glass, called "Handel Ware". Enamel-decorated, chipped glass was called "Teroma". This vase is an example. All the pieces in this range were inferior to contemporary European products but are avidly collected in the United States.

THE HANDEL COMPANY (AMERICAN, 1885-1936)

The Handel Company was established by Philip Handel (1867-1914) in Meriden, Connecticut, home to several lamp manufacturers. The success of the company was largely due to the rapid spread of domestic electricity in the United States. Before 1900, Handel decorated bought-in glass blanks for kerosene lighting. However, by the early years of the 20th century they were designing, making and decorating all types of lamps, including ambitious shade designs in leaded glass of Tiffany type, mounted on metal bases.

The company's most commercially successful products were their reverse-painted table lamps.

Reverse-painted lamps "Reverse-painting" refers to the American method of hand-painting the interior of glass lampshades with floral patterns or landscapes. Handel produced reverse-painted tables, boudoir, floor and hanging lamps.

Shades are either domed (as **above**), conical or hemispherical, finished on the exterior with a frosted crackle ("chipped glass") to diffuse the light. This base is bronze; most were white metal with a patina simulating bronze.

Above Venetian or tropical island scenes are more unusual than floral patterns, especially those decorated and signed by Henry Bedige. This shade, painted by Bedige, could fetch twice as much as the floral shade on the left.
•Often the lamps were weighted.
•The necks of the shades were fitted with a bronzed metal collar.

Marks and fakes of lamps Most Handel lamps bear a painted signature, a design number and perhaps the artist's name or initials on the shade rim interior. Metal bases have "Handel" either moulded or on a stitched tag fixed to the felt base. Fake shades exist: most are vertically ribbed and betrayed by poor standards of artistry.

THE PAIRPOINT CORPORATION (AMERICAN, 1880-1958)

Left Lamp bases vary: some simulate bronze; some resemble tree trunks, or are ribbed; others, like this one, are made from gilt metal. Figural designs are very collectable.

The Pairpoint Corporation of New Bedford, Massachusetts also made lamps in the Handel manner, together with a range of innovative reverse-painted, moulded table and boudoir lamps called "puffy" lamps, with uneven glass shades like the one on the left.

QUEZAL ART GLASS & DECORATING CO. (AMERICAN, 1901-25)

Quezal was established in Brooklyn by two former Tiffany Studio employees, using glass recipes and decorating techniques developed by Louis Comfort Tiffany. The company did little more than interpret Tiffany's popular favrile ware. Colours are generally striking and forms either asymmetrically or organically inspired.

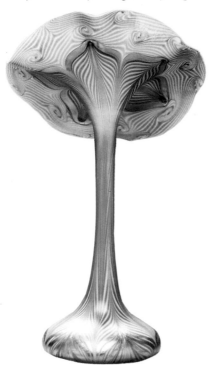

The most collectable wares today are those modelled as Jack-in-the-Pulpit flowers, as **above**, identified by a bulbous base, an extremely slender stem, and an open, spreading neck similar in form to a lily bloom. The best are made to standards of artist-craftsmanship which rival those of Tiffany Studios, and can command comparable prices.

Decoration The majority of Quezal glass is internally decorated, usually with striated colours forming a pulled feather type design, evident on the vase on the left. The better examples are also decorated on the rear of the bloom. Iridescence is usually the focus of decoration. Some simpler designs were painted just with gold lustre; these include vases of trumpet or egg shape designed to be mounted in metal stands.

Identification Some flower-form vases have ruffled rims: other American art glasswares generally have smooth, rounded rims. Quezal glass tends to be more heavily walled than Tiffany glass. Most Quezal pieces made after 1902 are engraved with the firm's name in large script. Some wares are also stamped with a quetzal, the exotic Central American bird-god of vivid plumage from which the company derived its name. Quezal signatures are sometimes faked on modern or inferior glass and some unsigned examples were later given spurious Tiffany marks.

Left This vase is highlighted with crackled gold iridescence. Some rarer examples have solely blue decoration. Quezal also made some desirable lampshades in gold or blue iridescence, or in gold, white and green.

VICTOR DURAND (AMERICAN, 1870-1931)

Victor Durand produced art glass at the Vineland Glass Manufacturing Co., New Jersey from 1897 until his death. Typical examples are vases of Neo-classical form in gold or blue iridescence. He employed Quezal artists, and many of his products resemble Quezal glass, but are generally less collectable than Quezal wares.

THE UNION GLASS CO. (AMERICAN, c.1893-1920s)

The Union Glass Co. of Sommerville, Massachusetts, made iridescent art glass in the Tiffany style from around 1893-1920s. Most Union glass reflects Quezal's coloration, scale and standard of manufacture, but is rarer and can command high prices.

•Other American art glassmakers include Duffner and Kimberly, and the Miller and Jefferson Companies.

Right Vases are often ovoid or of floral form with gold iridescence on the interior and an exterior of opaque white ground with mint green and iridescent feathering, as is the case here. This combination was used by Tiffany, then Quezal, and then copied by the

Union Glass Co.
•Any Art Nouveau pieces that are signed are engraved with the trademark "KEW BLAS".

PÂTE-DE-VERRE AND PÂTE-DE-CRISTAL

Pâte-de-verre was based on an ancient technique, whereby coloured glass or metallic oxides were added to a paste of powdered glass to give colour. Multi-coloured pieces were created by packing different pastes on top of one another. The mixture was fired in a re-usable mould to give shape and fired in a kiln at a critical temperature, so the mixture fused rather than melted. Internal mottling may occur as control over pigments is not as precise as with cameo works. The most successful pieces have a degree of translucency. *Pâte-de-cristal* is similar to *pâte-de-verre*, and is made by adding an aqueous adhesive before subjecting the mould to an extended firing at a lower temperature, making the colour easier to control and resulting in a translucent, richly coloured vessel.

A *pâte-de-verre* paperweight by Alméric Walter; 9¾in (24.8cm) long

Makers *Pâte-de-verre* was first exploited on a commercial basis by the Daum factory. Alméric Walter was a French master of the Art Nouveau period, along with Albert Damousse (1848-1926) and Henri Cros. Gabriel Argy-Rousseau and François-Émile Décorchement made pieces in *pâte-de-verre* and in *pâte-de-cristal*. Walter produced the work of other designers: Joseph Chéret, created the nude at the top of the page.

Condition Items should be examined carefully, as the media lend themselves well to skilful reductions of ears and other projections to remove signs of damage, seriously reducing value.

Cros figures, like this bust of a woman, may be modelled in high relief, or as profiles in low relief. His work tends to be fairly small-scale, and decorated with classical portraits.

ALMÉRIC WALTER (FRENCH, 1859-1942)

Initially a ceramist, Walter joined the Daum workshops in 1908 to make *pâte-de-verre* decorative wares. In 1919 he set up his own glassworks to produce mainly small, useful wares, covered boxes and some *pâte-de-verre* medallions, wall sconces and decorative panels. His work, influenced by Art Nouveau styles, featured naturalistic motifs including small reptiles and insects; nude studies were rarer. *Pâte-de-verre* pieces, relatively heavy and opaque, usually include more than one colour.

Marks Pieces before 1914 are marked "DAUM NANCY" with the cross of Lorraine. After 1919 Walter's work bears the moulded signature "AW" or "A. WALTER NANCY" and may include the impressed signature or monogram of the designer.

Daum sculptor, Henri Bergé, designed this 1920 *pâte de verre* chameleon. The sculptural design and contrasting blue and yellow are typical. The salamander is spotted for a more realistic effect.

HENRI CROS (FRENCH, 1840-1907)

From 1891 the Sèvres porcelain factory (see pp.122-3) put a workshop at the disposal of Henri Cros, one of the modern progenitors of the *pâte-de-verre* process. He designed a series of *pâte-de-verre* plaques with relief decoration, inspired by ancient wares exhibited in Paris in 1878. These plaques tend to have a strongly sculptural feel and a maquette-type appearance, which is also apparent in his other figures, such as the bust of a woman on the left. Some pieces are dated. Because the glass paste was not easily controlled, it can contain a multitude of internal fissures, and the surface may feel granular or sugary. Colour tends to be streaked and uneven.

GABRIEL ARGY-ROUSSEAU (FRENCH, 1885-1953)

Argy-Rousseau's pieces are usually richly-coloured and relatively opaque. He favoured white against tortoiseshell to simulate shell cameo, and also mottled pinks against frosted ice reserves. Green was also popular, and was used for this *pâte-de-cristal* figural lizard vase, made in around 1920.
•Pieces tend to be relatively small (under 9in/23cm, high) and are surprisingly light in weight.

Initially a maker of false teeth, Argy-Rousseau first exhibited his *pâte-de-verre* in 1914, and from 1919 onwards made a series of enamelled scent bottles. In 1921 he went into partnership with Gustave-Gaston Moser-Millot, who funded a workshop called Les Pâtes-de-verre d'Argy-Rousseau, where workers produced his designs, sold in Moser-Millot's shop. Argy-Rousseau also made table lamps, bowls, jars, pendants, brooches and perfume burners. In 1928 he produced a group of *pâte-de-cristal* sculptures designed by Marcel Bouraine.

After the glassworks closed in 1931, Argy-Rousseau worked alone, making commissioned religious plaques (not popular with collectors) and angular vessels in streaked, jewel-like colours.

Collecting Between 1921 and 1931 glasswares were produced in large quantities. Moulds were reusable, but pieces were coloured by hand and individually finished. Later work is rarer. His Classical vases of Egyptian inspiration and those depicting prowling wolves are considered the ultimate pieces among collectors, who have recently paid large sums for such items.

Marks All Argy-Rousseau's pieces are incised with his mark, which usually appears as his initials, or "G. ARGY-ROUSSEAU" in capital letters or in upper and lower case letters.

The Egyptian maidens on this vase from around 1925, were a common motif on Argy-Rousseau's wares. Figural decoration is popular, although his wide range of subjects includes stylized flowers, fruit, birds, animals, butterflies, and some rigidly geometric motifs. His *pâte-de-cristal* often features Neo-classical relief decoration.

Décorchement used bright, jewelled colours developed by using metallic oxides. Rather than creating tonal variations, he produced uniform colours, but he often marbled them with black or purple to simulate semi-precious stones.

FRANÇOIS-ÉMILE DÉCORCHEMENT (FRENCH, 1880-1971)

Initially a ceramist, Décorchement experimented with *pâte-de-verre* glass, and in 1910 turned to *pâte-de-cristal*, his predominant medium. From 1915 to 1926 he worked for René Lalique (see pp.90-91), before setting up the Cristalleries de Saint-Rémy. He concentrated on heavy forms, and internal colours, with decoration deeply moulded (or engraved) on the exterior. By the 1930s he had turned towards decorated window panels.

Left This *pâte-de-verre* vase of 1924 is typical of Décorchement's progression from Art Nouveau floral and symbolist themes towards a bolder, more stylized look that featured flowers, fruit, animals and masks. He particularly favoured this serpent motif. Repeat motifs are characteristic of Décorchement's work of this period, as is the shaping of the handles in the form of snakes' heads.
•Décorchement's pieces carry an incise-cast signature.

RENÉ LALIQUE (FRENCH, 1860-1945)

René Lalique was the foremost jeweler of the Art Nouveau period (see p.202) and became the leading glass designer of the Art Deco period, making a wide range of objects, including car mascots, perfume bottles, vases, tablewares and plates, clocks, jewelry, lighting and figurines. Some of his glass was incorporated into furniture. Most wares were machine-made for the mass-market, although his perfume bottles were relatively expensive in their day as they often carried fragrances by top parfumiers. Those pieces which incorporate figural subjects are the most popular, followed by insects, animals, geometric motifs, floral wares and fish. As in the clock, left, many of Lalique's figures are nude or semi-naked, and show precise attention to detail, especially in facial expressions.

A René Lalique glass clock entitled *Night and Day* c.1930; ht 14¾in/37.5cm

Perfume bottles Lalique made a large number of interesting perfume bottles. The earliest ones were commissioned by François Côty. These are usually in crisply moulded panel form, with the emphasis on the decorative stoppper. Later, Lalique produced perfume bottles for many of the top perfumiers, including Molinard and Roger & Gallet. Some bottles had more than one stopper design. The underside of the stopper should bear a number corresponding to that on the base of the bottle. Documentation can be found in the 1932 catalogue of Lalique's wares which carries almost the full range of items designed by Lalique, and their respective catalogue numbers and sizes. Quoted heights should not be regarded as definitive, as proportions do vary slightly between pieces.

Vases Lalique produced a number of decorative vases, which were designed as pieces of sculpture and never intended to hold flowers.

The most inventive perfume bottles are the most collectable. Bottles with a tiara stopper, like the one above, are very collectable, and like many of Lalique's designs, were made in a choice of colours. Bottles in solid colours are highly desirable, and sealed bottles with original contents and cartons are also at a premium.

The integration of form with decoration, evident in many of Lalique's pieces, is particularly striking in this famous serpent vase, which was issued in a range of colours besides this amber. Typically of Lalique vases, the design is in high relief.

Car mascots Lalique made car mascots in 29 different designs. Birds and animals are common subjects, showing either just the head, or the full creature.

This head of a horse, entitled *Longchamps* frequently comes up at auction. Mascots are usually in clear and frosted glass, which may be polished. A few are in clear tinted glass. Other Lalique car mascots which frequently come up at auction include *Victoire* (a female head), *St Christophe*, *Archer*, *Coq Nain* (a cockerel), *Perche* (a fish), *Grand Libellule* (a dragonfly), *Tête d'Aigle* (an eagle's head), *Sanglier* (a wild boar), *Tête de Paon* (a peacock's head) and *Cinq Chevaux* (five rearing horses).

Cire perdue The only wares made by Lalique rather than by the workshop to his designs were those made by the *cire perdue* ("lost wax") method (see p.240). This, together with the fact that the process results in unique casts (the mould was broken to retrieve the glass), makes such wares very desirable. As well as Lalique's wheelcut signature, these *cire perdue* wares often carry the last two numerals of the year preceded by a serial number.

This glass vase was made by Lalique using the *cire perdue* technique, and is consequently highly collectable.

Alterations Some pieces have been altered, but the changes are usually obvious. Vases may have had their handles removed, and some shell bowls were converted to ceiling bowls, often with non-Lalique frosted glass surrounds, by the Brèves Gallery, who retailed most of the Lalique glass sold in England.

Opalescent glass Most of Lalique's wares are in opalescent glass, produced by adding phosphates, fluorine and aluminium oxide to the glass to make it opaque, and then adding a minute amount of cobalt to give an internal blue tint. The French glassmakers, Sabino (see p.92) also made opalescent glass. This type of glass was made only during Lalique's lifetime and any modern reproductions tend to be in frosted clear glass or in solid colours.

Condition Unless the item is exceptionally rare, Lalique pieces must be in pristine condition to be of any great value. Chips can often be removed by grinding and polishing. The overall proportion of the piece may have been distorted as a result of smoothing out chipped areas. Bases and rims are the areas most liable to damage. Acid may have been used to disguise damage by re-frosting glass that was originally frosted.

Fakes Many of Lalique's pieces have been faked. Modern fakes are of a very poor standard; those from the 1920s and '30s are slightly better, but they can still be detected upon close examination. If in doubt, check the piece with the 1932 catalogue. Fakes tend to be fairly lightweight, and opalescence, where it is used, is often all-over, rather than controlled.

The rim on fake Lalique vases is often thicker than that on the original piece. Genuine pieces will exhibit a faint mould line extending from the rim to the base – beware of pieces where the base is so highly polished that the mould line is not apparent.

Some lamps, like the one above, contain figural decoration. Many are mounted on similar bronze bases.

As with this figure of *Thais* the high-relief areas on opalescent glass are always more opaque than the thin-walled parts. The distinct blue tint is also clearly visible.

Lamps Lalique made wall lights, chandeliers, ceiling bowls and table lamps. The table lamps are often highly inventive – for example, several have forms similar to that of the tiara stoppered perfume bottle on the opposite page.

Other wares Lalique made tablewares which, like the vases, are sculptural in appearance. He also made jewelry, which because of its fragility is rare today. Many pieces feature brightly coloured glass as an alternative to precious stones (see p.202).

ART DECO PRESSED GLASS

The 1920s and '30s saw a revival in decorative pressed glass after its decline at the end of the Art Nouveau era. Glass was taken to new extremes and used in new ways as a structural as well as a decorative medium. Although René Lalique was the leading artist in moulded opalescent glass, there were some other important designers. The French glassmaker Marius Ernest Sabino designed architectural glass fittings for prestigious exhibitions and liners such as the *Normandie*. Edmund Etling from France and the English firm Jobling and Co. produced fine pressed glasswares, as did Baccarat, French designers of perfume bottles and tablewares.

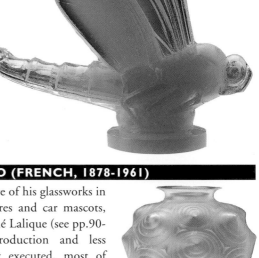

Sabino has been accused of borrowing images from other designers, especially Lalique, and rendering them in a clumsy way. Nevertheless, he occasionally achieved a pleasing synthesis of form and decoration. In this dragonfly vase from 1930 the dragonfly is delicate and well-proportioned.

Right A moulded glass dragonfly car mascot by Sabino c.1935; ht 5in/12.5cm

MARIUS-ERNEST SABINO (FRENCH, 1878-1961)

From around 1923 until the closure of his glassworks in 1939, Sabino made glass tablewares and car mascots, many in a style close to that of René Lalique (see pp.90-91), but intended for mass-production and less expensive. Although competently executed, most of Sabino's work is inferior to Lalique's, but some pieces withstand comparison and are worth collecting, especially figural wares and ceiling lights. He used moulded glass in blue, creamy white and pale amber. Tablewares and light fittings were opalescent throughout, whereas opalescence was localized in the figures. Female figures are stylized, with soft features and long legs.

Marks Early pieces usually had a moulded signature. Engraved signatures tend to appear on pieces from the 1930s. Many Sabino moulds were re-used when the factory reopened and pieces can be difficult to date, as none of Sabino's work is dated or numbered. Production ceased in 1975, but an American firm continued to make Sabino wares using the original moulds. These have a paper label, saying "Sabino, made in France", but if this is missing the only way to determine the date is to examine the piece for signs of ware.

This vase is amongst the least desirable of Sabino wares, as it is clumsy and ill-proportioned. As with his car mascots, draftsmanship is poor, especially in comparison with Lalique wares, and the mould lines are very evident.

Note Sabino is a minefield for collectors. Experience in observing and handling opalescent glass from the 1920s and '30s may help in detecting a modern piece.

EDMUND ETLING ET CIE (FRENCH, active 1920s and '30s)

Etling often alternated polished and matt sections in his work. This figure of c.1925 has a matt body and is cloaked in polished folds of a bluish tint.

Opalescent glass was also made by Etling. In addition to female nudes, the firm made models of animals and ships. Etling also commissioned and retailed bronze and ivory statuettes by a number of leading designers.

JOBLING AND CO. (ENGLISH, active 1930s)

The North-East England company Jobling and Co. produced machine-made pressed glass in a similar style to that of Sabino. In 1933 they introduced a range of collectable art glass, using French-inspired designs.

The high gloss surface of this Jobling opalescent vase is typical, but the design is not very successful, and the form is uninteresting.

BACCARAT (FRENCH, founded 1764)

Marks Bottles are marked with a small intaglio or relief-moulded butterfly, or a stencilled circle mark incorporating a central decanter and stopper flanked by a tumbler and wine glass. The firm's 19th century-style moulded lustre vases usually have "Baccarat" moulded in low relief. Wares do not carry names of designers. Fakes are not known, but the bottles were widely copied.

In the 1920s and '30s, under the influence of George Chevalier, the emphasis was on enamelling, and geometric motifs and panel forms with sharp edges. Design was restrained, with a Neo-classical influence, and decoration often confined to the stopper. Cut and moulded forms were also used. The butterfly motif was popular.

Baccarat designed bottles for a number of French parfumiers, including d'Orsay, Jean Patou, Rimmel, Yardley, Elizabeth Arden, Coty, Roger & Gallet, Lenthéric and Guerlain.

Beware Many stoppers had an integral dropper, which is often damaged or missing. A Baccarat stopper may have been matched up to the wrong bottle. Collectors of perfume bottles from any factory should examine the proportions and fit of the bottle and stopper and familiarize themselves with the types made by a given factory. Books are available that catalogue the output of specific firms.

CZECH PERFUME BOTTLES

This Czech bottle lacks the delicacy of the French pieces – compare the crisp edges of the Baccarat bottle with the relatively heavy edges of this example.

The new demand in the scent trade for inexpensive perfume bottles was mainly satisfied by Czech glassworks: there were over 50 during the 1920s and '30s, making mass-produced and relatively poorly-moulded glass perfume bottles. However, they are increasingly collectable and relatively inexpensive. The more inventive the design and the closer to the Art Deco style, the more desirable (and costly) they are. Seldom marked, and rarely individualistic, it is hard to distinguish between various makers and factories. Styles often echo the French, although the Czech designers did not copy them, as has been suggested. Tinted and enamelled bottles resemble those of Baccarat. This is evident in the use of black and clear enamel on the perfume bottle, **left**. Nevertheless, Czech pieces are attractive and collectable.

This Czech bottle is among the best produced and will command a relatively high price: its striking fan-shaped form, nicely complemented by the stopper, is characteristic of the period. It is well-moulded and attention has been paid to the intricate decoration.

STUDIO AND STUDIO-TYPE GLASS

Studio glass is the term given to one-off, highly individual hand-made pieces. The Frenchman Maurice Marinot was the chief designer of this type of glass: Henri Navarre and André Thuret adopted similar styles and techniques, although their work is less distinctive and consequently more easily affordable. The Daum factory produced very similar glass, but used machine methods to create the form, and achieved a studio effect by hand-finishing. The factory's acid-etched pieces, where the granular surface is used as a decorative feature, closely resemble the work of Marinot. Monart and Gray-Stan were the two most significant British producers of studio glass. Gray-Stan used surface enamel, whilst Monart followed the French taste for internal decoration with swirls. Other studio glass designers include Marcel Goupy and Jean Luce.

Right An internally decorated glass vase by Maurice Marinot 1926; ht 9in/22.5cm

MAURICE MARINOT (FRENCH, 1882-1960)

Even small pieces, like this scent bottle, are heavy in form. This example has Marinot's characteristic simple ball stopper; stoppers are nearly always in clear glass although they may be given a decorative surface treatment, as here.
•The majority of Marinot's work bears an engraved signature and is numbered on a paper label which is attached to the base.

A trained technician, chemist and painter, Marinot became fascinated with glass when he visited the glassworks of his friends, the Viard brothers, Eugène and Gabriel. At first he created designs which they executed but then took to glassmaking himself. He treated glass as a sculptural medium. All pieces were handmade; many have a clear-grey or pale yellow tint. Marinot also employed deep acid cutting, contrasting a polished upper surface and a granular or frosted lower surface. In the 1920s he shaped the glass at the furnace, using the hot technique to experiment more with form (for example, by the inclusion of metal oxides, such as tin foil), and dispensed altogether with surface decoration.

CHARLES SCHNEIDER (FRENCH, 1881-1962)

Although Schneider's glass does not compare well with Marinot's, it is attractive and collectable in its own right and is far more affordable. This vase shows Schneider's preference for heavily-walled moulded forms and for an irregular, trapped bubble effect. The decoration appears truly random, rather than intentionally so, and the decoration and form are not so well integrated. The control over tinting is somewhat loose and the form relatively conventional, without any sculptural quality.

Charles Schneider founded the Cristallerie Schneider in Epinay-sur-Seine, near Paris in 1913. He studied under Emile Gallé (see pp.72-3) and worked in the Gallé and Daum factories. Influenced by Marinot's highly individual style he produced a range of *intercalaires* (cameo-carved wares, created by laminating two layers of glass together, and then covering them with a layer of carved or etched semi-transparent glass). Schneider also made cameo glass and internally mottled opaque glass, lampshades and table lamps, some of which resemble the work of the Daum factory.
•Pieces are signed with the stencilled signature "SCHNEIDER" and many are signed "Le Verre Français", or "CHARDER".

MONART (SCOTTISH, 1924-39)

The British glassworks of John Moncrieff Ltd in Perth was founded by John Moncrieff in 1865 to make specialist glass products for the chemical and engineering industries. In 1924, together with Salvador Ysart, Moncrieff set up Monart (a combination of MONcrieff and YsART), expanding into art glass. When Ysart moved to set up Vasart in 1946 his son, Paul took over Monart.

•A paper label, always one inch (2.5cm) in diameter and using black on gold, was stuck over the pontil mark, bearing the shape, colour and size of the piece.

Monart glass was blown to specific shapes, recorded in a catalogue. Swirls often formed an integral part of the design, together with mottles, bubbles and stripes, as in this *Paisely Shawl* vase. Early pieces used subdued colours and textured surfaces, often resembling ceramics; this green glass, designed to resemble moss agate, is typical. Later, bright colours were used. Other pieces incorporated aventurine or silver flecks.

GRAY-STAN (ENGLISH, 1926-36)

Mrs Graydon Stannus established her glass-making studio in 1922 to make reproduction Irish lighting and table glass; from 1925 she expanded into the modern coloured art glass now synonymous with her name. Her chief designer was Noel Billinghurst, notable for his vases with deep figurative engraving. James Manning, an Irish artist and the chief glassmaker, was largely responsible for the company's striking colour effects.

•Many pieces were marked Gray Stan, with or without a hyphen. Later pieces have an additional "British" on the base.

Mrs Graydon Stannus experimented with colours to create different shades and pastels in her work. This vase from around 1930 has red, yellow and white enamels worked into streaks and swirls and has then been crystal-cased. Vases and bowls coated in enamel to give this cloudy and marble effect are the most distinctive. The colours used by Gray-stan were mainly amber, green and red.

MARCEL GOUPY (FRENCH, 1886-1954 retired)

Although Goupy used bright colours he managed to avoid the garishness that characterizes much glassware of the period. The colours of this "Jazz band" tumbler are subdued and the enamelled rim trim – a typical Goupy decoration – echoes the hues of the main design. The figures are characteristically stylized.

Marcel Goupy, artistic director at La Maison Geo. Rouard from 1909 until 1954, produced a wide range of hand-blown glassware. He designed both the form and the decoration but did not execute his designs. He also produced designs for ceramics, sometimes to complement his glasswares. Between 1919 and 1923 the enamelled decoration on many of his designs was executed by a young French glassworker, Auguste Heiligenstein. All these pieces bear Goupy's signature in enamel, but some Goupy items are unsigned.

Using mainly thick-walled glass Goupy concentrated on small, utilitarian, enamelled glasswares – this vase is only 7in (18cm) high. Some pieces from the end of the 1920s were engraved. This nude is a typical motif; others include flowers, birds, landscapes and mythological scenes.

ENA ROTTENBERG (AUSTRIAN, dates unknown)

Rottenberg's subjects are predominantly female, often semi-naked and depicted in a classical pose. They tend to have highly stylized faces with a pronounced nose, deep-set eyes and high cheek bones.
Typically, on this vase, the rim is untrimmed.
•A number of unsigned glasswares, similarly decorated but with skin tones, have also been attributed to Rottenberg.

A very distinctive type of enamelled glass was produced by Ena Rottenberg in Austria. Wares are invariably small — even vases are seldom taller than one foot (30cm). Light and shade are cleverly used to create a three-dimensional tableau effect. The glass, hand-blown, and usually thin-walled and relatively light, is not of high quality, and often shows a pontil mark on the underside. Bases are usually thick.
•Rottenberg's pieces are unsigned and do not carry the mark of the firm, Lobmeyr, which executed many of her designs.

THE DAUM FACTORY (FRENCH, established 1875)

As well as a wide range of Art Nouveau glass (pp.74-5), the Daum Factory made some important studio glassware in the 1920s and '30s. Closing down during the First World War, the Factory reopened in 1919 under Paul Daum to embrace Art Deco with enthusiasm, producing machine-made, but hand-finished wares.

Lamps Lamps were an important part of the factory's output during the 1920s and '30s. Daum made glass lamps and also supplied glass shades for other lamps, most notably for the wrought-iron bases produced by Edgar Brandt (see p.192). Heavyweight lead glass was used for hanging and standard lamps. These items were mass-produced, but copied the labour-intensive hand-decorated work of other studio glass producers, as well as of Décorchement and Argy-Rousseau, and from a distance could be taken for *pâte-de-cristal* (see pp.88-9).
•Some lamps have been copied using inferior glass.
•To examine lamps, if possible remove the metal mount and check the neck of the base under a strong light — when the lamp is lit, the heat can cause the glass to crack. Internal cracks may not be readily apparent.

Heavy acid-etched wares with deep decoration predominated, in colours of smokey grey, turquoise, yellow and sea green, and occasionally clear glass. Emphasis was on decorative ornament and irregular, frosted, light-diffusing granular surfaces which sometimes resembled the designs of Marinot. Alternatively, matt and polished surfaces were combined. Decoration is either geometric or floral, and tends to be freeform, although it may be more formalized, as in this bowl from around 1930.
•Most Daum glass of the period is thick-walled and heavy and has generally survived well. Rims are usually gently rounded — a sharp edge may mean a chip has been removed with a polishing wheel.

Marks and fakes Most vases are wheel-engraved with the words "Daum, Nancy" and the cross of Lorraine, but wares do not carry the name or initials of individual designers. Lamps also usually bear a wheel-or acid-cut signature.

Few fakes have appeared on the market so far, perhaps because the acid-cut wares have been regarded by collectors as less important than the firm's cameo wares (see pp.74-5).

This etched glass lamp with a frosted white ground and acid-etched geometric design, is typical of Daum's lamps. Many of them were mushroom-shaped in amber or amethyst with a mottled perimeter in contrasting colours. Surfaces were matt.

DESIGNS ON GLASS

The 1920s and '30s saw a revival in the engraved glass first popular at the end of the 19th century. Designers were employed within glassmaking factories to decorate existing forms. Scandinavian designers working at the Orrefors factory led this revival and influenced British and American glass designers – the American Steuben Glass works moved away from their former mass-produced ornamental wares of the Art Nouveau period (see p.79) to concentrate on engraved glass. Clyne Farquharson, working for the Birmingham glassworks John Walsh Walsh, and Keith Murray, working for Stevens and Williams, were probably the two most important contributors to British design during these decades. They introduced more modern decorative elements into the work of a range of factories that had been producing mainly fussy, opulent brilliant-cut lead crystal glassware in Victorian patterns, popular at the beginning of the century.

An Orrefors engraved vase and cover 1937; ht 17in/43.5cm

ORREFORS (SWEDISH, founded 1898)

Although the Orrefors factory also made utilitarian wares, it is the innovative engraved or internally decorated wares that are most collectable today. Inventive in both form and decoration, pieces were often decorated on both sides to give a three-dimensional effect. Popular motifs are engraved nudes, Neo-classical scenes, and legends. The clear delicate glasswares, with scant decoration, mostly belong to the 1920s.

Above Orrefors is best known for its Graal wares (from the Swedish for Holy Grail), developed by Simon Gate in 1916, and refined during the 1920s. They were made using a kind of cameo technique by which the design was etched onto the glass and then encased in a clear outer layer. Early Graal is often tinted, with orange-brown a particularly popular colour. This Graal glass vase, designed by Edvard Hald and executed by Knut Bergkvist in 1928, is typical in the way it incorporates colours into the decoration and in the impression it gives of fluidity and mobility.

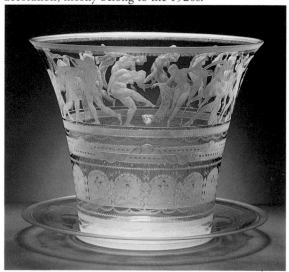

Orrefors glass of the 1930s was heavier than it had been in the 1920s, and designs became bolder and more emphatic, with a greater degree of stylization. Many of the mermaids and sub-aqua scenes, like that shown on this glass vase, engraved by Vicke Lindstrand, were produced in the 1930s.

Left The work of Simon Gate (1883-1945), leading designer at Orrefors from 1917, is distinguished from that of Orrefors' other engravers by its deep surface engraving, evident on this glass vase. The muscular stylized figures in athletic poses are typical, as is the Neo-classical style.

Lindstrand, who had a more Modernist approach than Gate, joined Orrefors in 1927/8. In the 1930s he developed "Ariel" glass, manipulating the glass to create unusual effects to complement the subject, for example to suggest the undulating surface of water for an underwater scene by trapping air bubbles between layers of clear glass and forming them into patterns. This Ariel vase was designed by Edvin Öhrström who, along with Hald, also produced Ariel glass for Orrefors.
•Much of Orrefors' glass, especially from the 1920s, has a subtle tint, sometimes visible only on the rim.

Marks and output Production was relatively limited. Until 1930 only about 1,500 pieces were produced and just over one third of these were made before the end of the First World War. There is a wealth of infomation on the base of pieces: usually they are engraved with "Orrefors" or "O.f.m", with the name of the designer and engraver, and often with a year code and shape number as well. The Graal vase on the previous page is engraved "Graal 1928 KB-EH" and numbered 3112.

Collecting Orrefors Although it has become more expensive in the last few years, Orrefors glass still represents a good investment. As the body of later pieces is usually relatively thick and robust, and the pieces were treated as decorative cabinet wares, they tend to be in good condition, with little sign of wear.

STEUBEN GLASSWORKS (AMERICAN, 1903-Present)

The Steuben Glassworks was founded in 1903 by members of the local glassmaking Hawkes family and the Englishman, Frederick Carder, and became a division of Corning in 1918. In the United States its work is regarded as the epitome of elegance in Art Deco glass. Before 1930 Carder designed many items himself, but from 1930 onwards the company employed a number of leading designers, inlcuding Sidney Waugh and Walter Dorwin Teague, who were to produce most of the recognizably Art Deco work of the 1930s. Carder's work tended to be the more traditional.

Since Carder's departure in 1934, the Steuben Glassworks has produced only items of particularly pure, clear cut and engraved crystal of a high standard, concentrating on massive vessels with swelling, fluid, and fairly restrained forms, complemented by fine engraved designs. It continues to prosper on a site adjacent to the Corning Museum of Glass.

FREDERICK CARDER (ENGLISH, 1863-1963)

Frederick Carder established his reputation at Stevens & Williams between 1881 and 1902. He served as Art Director at Steuben for over 30 years, and until he left in 1930 designed many of the firm's finest items himself. Initially his influences were strongly European and rooted in his 19th century training. His work remained relatively conservative although he adopted aspects of the new 1920s style, such as rhythmic curves and zig-zags, clearly influenced by French Art Deco designs, including the work of René Lalique. Between 1934, when he retired from Steuben, and 1959, Carder worked independently and concentrated on casting glass in the *cire perdue* technique ("lost wax"), a process that results in unique glass casts. Most of these pieces are signed.

•Aurene ware varied little during its 29 years of production and is thus difficult to date. Scent bottles, of slender baluster form, are particularly collectable, as are floriform vases, especially those decorated in the Tiffany manner with trailing leaves or feather motifs. Decorated Aurene is considerably more valuable than plain.

Carder's coloured glass continued European design traditions, and his work uses brilliant colours and organic shapes, typified by this 1920s bronze and acid-etched alabaster glass lamp.

Carder developed a number of styles, including Aurene iridescent wares in various colours, particularly gold and blue, made between 1904 and 1933: this Aurene vase is from c.1920. The range includes vases and candlesticks, with a classical or Art Nouveau influence.

SIDNEY WAUGH (AMERICAN, 1904-63)

In the 1930s Waugh developed a range of crystalware inspired by traditional, mythological themes, such as this zodiac glass platter, which clearly shows his use of elongated, highly stylized mythological figures and sleek animals, crisply engraved to give the impression of bas-relief.

•The influence of Scandinavian design is evident in the restrained style of much of Teague's and Waugh's work, especially the tablewares. Waugh in particular was influenced by the glassmasters of Orrefors.

•Many of Waugh's pieces were issued in limited editions and may bear engraved series numbers.

Sidney Waugh
was Chief Associate Designer for Steuben Glassworks from 1933 until his death.
Walter Dorwin Teague (1883-1960), also a designer for Steuben's, is best known for his industrial designs, which include cars, cameras and pens.

Steuben marks Beware of the various marks used by Stueben, as the firm still operates. Glass made between 1903-1932 is usually acid-stamped on the base with a fleur-de-lys and the word Steuben on a scroll. After 1932 Steuben or "S" was engraved with a diamond point. The name of the designer is not usually included.

Right This colourless blown and engraved ice tea glass from around 1932 is from the brief period during which Teague was employed by Steuben to create a range of five or so patterns of elegant, functional crystal stemware.

KEITH MURRAY (NEW ZEALAND, 1892-1981)

Keith Murray, primarily an architect, turned to glass design when he moved from his native New Zealand to England in the early 1930s. In around 1932 he became a prominent designer for Stourbridge-based Stevens and Williams, the company now known as Royal Brierley Crystal, where he produced engraved wares, known as "Keith Murray Glass" up until the beginning of World War Two. Later work for Brierley was influenced by Scandinavian and Austrian designers, whom he strongly admired, and included a range of fine engraved crystal with deep-slashed cactus motifs, marketed as Brierley Crystal. All his work is hand-made.

•Murray's glass has an etched or stamped signature, bearing his name over a fleur-de-lys and "Brierley".

Murray's primary concern was with form and he believed that decoration was often superfluous. The innovative body of this vase is engraved, but many of his other pieces have no decoration at all.

Farquharson produced limited editions of glassware under the name of "Clyne Farquharson Crystal". Ranges include Leaf, Kendal, Barry and Albany. The designs were initially created for large vases and bowls, but were later adapted to decorate decanters, tumblers and other smaller pieces.

CLYNE FARQUHARSON (ENGLISH, dates unknown)

Marks All Farquharson's glass is signed "Clyne Farquhsarson" in diamond point, followed by the date. NRD was added after 1939.

Another important British designer was Clyne Farquharson, who worked for the Birmingham glassworks, John Walsh Walsh, in the mid-1930s. He produced an elegant series of vases and tableware with cut decorations of formalized leaves and stems, exemplified by the vase on the right.

CERAMICS

Early Victorian ceramists in Britain produced mainly useful wares in bone china for a new nation of wealthy tea drinkers. The market was dominated by Minton and Coalport who often worked in the Sèvres style, and the later firm of Crown Derby which adopted Japanese-inspired themes. Ironstone china, made in Staffordshire predominantly by Masons and popular in the 1840s and '50s, was superseded by opaque earthenware, primarily for domestic pieces, but some Chinese-inspired enamelled and gilt vases and covers were made. Victorian over-embellishment peaked at the 1851 Exhibition, where pieces were smothered in beautifully-crafted floral swathes, figures, grotesques and animals. The Arts and Crafts movement turned to simpler and more practical pieces, often inspired by nature, where form and decoration were in harmony; and the end of the 19th century in Britain saw smaller art potteries like Elton, Martin and de Morgan making simple hand-made wares. In the 1880s and '90s factories such as Bretby and Linthorpe began to mass-produce ceramics, often slip-cast and with unusual glazes, some incise- or sgrafitto-decorated, or trailed in the same slip. The new Victorian middle classes also favoured sculpture, creating a market for small porcelain (or "Parian") copies of classical, military or political figures, which would fit into their homes. 19th-century American ceramics tended to imitate those in Europe, but sometimes with specifically local images for decoration.

Experimentation in Art Nouveau styles was led by the French and Americans, with Grueby's highly innovative glazes that imitated leaves and succulents in America, and the iridescent glazes of Clement Massier in France, copied by Zsolnay in Hungary and de Morgan in England. Many French ceramists preferred the clean white porcelain of Georges de Feure, retailed by Siegfried Bing. Forms were organic or symbolic, with transferred, hand-painted or slip-trailed decoration. The *École de Paris* in France decorated wares with stylized plant or figurative motifs and the Bohemian firm of Royal Dux produced a range of ornate shell bowls festooned with diaphanous-clad nymphs which were very popular in Europe and the United States. In England, naturalistic motifs of animals, birds, fish, owls and bats appeared on Bernard Moore's *flambé* wares, and William Moorcroft's Florian wares. The typical Scandinavian palette of pale blue, grey and pink was used by Rörstrand in Sweden for their relief decorated floral motifs. Other wares, like Rozenburg's teawares, were purely decorative. New technology enabled artwork of the period, such as lithographs, to be captured in glaze for decoration. Art Nouveau designs also appeared on domestic wares, including toilet pedestals and basins. Studio potters such as the German Max Läuger applied slip-trailed stylized grasses and flower heads to their wares. Also in Germany, Villeroy and Boch produced stoneware art pottery mechanically incised and colour enamelled as part of their extensive Mettlach range.

In the 20th century ceramists continued to experiment with decoration and glazes, but on fairly traditional forms. In England, the highly influential and often-imitated Clarice Cliff applied bright modern colours to simple tablewares, whilst Susie Cooper and Burleigh and Myott produced more original shapes. Wedgwood created highly emulated lustre wares and the Lancastrian Pottery adopted innovative decorative techniques for their Lapis wares, where glaze was fused into the body. In contrast, Shelley and Royal Doulton were known for their stark white bone china. There was also a trend for cheap ornaments sold in seaside shops, which, mass-produced and badly made, are not worth collecting today. In Italy, Gio Ponti and the Lenci factory produced stylish porcelain and earthenware pieces in which decoration complemented form, and in Germany bone china and porcelain manufacturers, such as Rosenthal, produced mainly tablewares in a clean, classical style. In Vienna, Anna Goebel and Hucenreuther made figurines and Kazhütte made earthenware. Even in France ceramics remained predominantly traditional, with Limoges at the centre for mass-produced ceramics. Scandinavia produced some of the most "modern" looking pieces including the interesting stoneware animal sculptures by Knud Khyn, covered in heavy celadon and orange-green glazes. The most collectable American Art Deco wares include the bright monochrome glazed Fiesta wares of the Hall China Company and the geometric designed "Futura" vases with matt, polychrome glazes of The Roseville pottery in Ohio.

The condition of ceramics is always important in valuation. Hand-painted and hand-made wares of the Victorian period are highly desirable, as are the moulded vases and figures of Worcester and James Hadley (discernible from mass-produced pieces by their uneven mould lines). In the Art Nouveau period, pieces by top designers are at a premium, and are usually marked. Mass-produced items tend to remain anonymous.

Above A plate by Susie Cooper, decorated with a stylized fox, c.1935
Right A Copeland Art Union of London stoneware jug, c.1870.

EARLY DECORATIVE PORCELAIN & TABLEWARES

The most significant development in Victorian ceramics was the transition from 18th century hard- and soft-paste to bone china – a mixture of hard-paste ingredients and large quantities of calcined animal bone. Bone china was especially popular because it was less expensive than previous recipes. Its main feature is a soft, translucent body covered by a glassy glaze prone to crazing. During the early 19th century porcelain wares tended to echo the Baroque and Rococo fantasies that had been revived when George IV and William IV were on the throne. These shapes provided a ready alternative to the well-tried and somewhat staid classical forms of earlier years.

Ironstone began to gain in popularity during the 1820s but reached a peak in around 1850. The principal manufacturer was Charles J. Mason, who patented the medium in 1813, although several other firms produced ironstone china wares, among them Spode, Ridgway, Folch and Hicks and Meigh. Most ironstone wares were decorated with *chinoiserie* or Japanese designs. Vases were of heavy form and again of pseudo-Chinese shape, often with gilt dragons and mythical beast handles and finials. Mazarin blue was a favourite reserve colour, combined with gilt floral and inset coloured enamel decoration.

An early Victorian teapot c.1840-50; ht 9-10in/21.5-24cm

The most sought-after early Victorian teawares were made by the Yorkshire factory of Rockingham, to which a large majority of this type of porcelain is often mistakenly ascribed: identification can be difficult because few pieces actually bear a factory mark. It is therefore essential to gain a knowledge of shapes and the various styles of pattern numbers used by the individual factories. Pattern numbers vary a great deal in style and format, but many are expressed as fractions. This tea cup and saucer by the Staffordshire firm of Samuel Alcock (established c.1826) illustrates the new shapes that became fashionable in the early Victorian period. The spur or protrusion at the base of the handle is typical. Many pieces had several such spurs.

Owing to its plasticity, bone china was suitable only for small-scale objects. Production of statuettes was concentrated in the Staffordshire area, and some of the best examples were by Minton (see p.106), whose wares do not usually carry a Minton mark, but can be identified by their impressed shape number. The same is true of Rockingham wares. Favourite subjects included personalities from literature, and famous people of the day. Many figures were made in unpainted, white biscuit (the forerunners of Parian ware, see p.105). This rare Ridgway and Robey figural group, made in around 1837, depicts characters from Charles Dickens's popular novel, *Nicholas Nickleby*. These and other Dickens characters are the only known marked pieces produced by the pottery. Unlike the slightly later flat-back figures (see p.105), they are painted in the round.

Decoration Apart from rare pieces such as commemorative items, hand-painted wares are more desirable than those that have been transfer-printed. The teapot in the main picture is decorated by transfer-printing, and embellished with onglaze enamels, but its unusual subject makes it collectable. These wares were sometimes given a pink lustre (often associated with the Sunderland area but not exclusive to it). Some early Victorian teapots are very inventive, with mythical animal terminals on the spouts and imaginatively treated finials. Many have ribbed or moulded bodies. Typical motifs include seaweed and fronded weeds; vermicular patterns were also favoured.

•Underglaze cobalt blue tends to have been favoured by many factories, especially Coalport and Minton, but a variety of other colours was used as well.

CHARLES JAMES MASON (ENGLISH, 1813-62)

Marks The most common early Mason's mark, used 1813-25, shows "Mason's Patent Ironstone China" impressed in a continuous line. During the Victorian period the printed crown and banner was used, with subtle variations on the shape of the crown indicating the date of manufacture. When unmarked, pieces that cannot be definitely attributed to Mason's are simply described as Staffordshire, as in the case of the pair of ironstone vases on the right.

Pieces after 1862 are marked, often with the impressed words "Ashworth Brothers", sometimes within a coat of arms.

Mason's concentrated on large and extensive dinner services decorated in underglaze blue and onglaze enamels with elaborate Imari-type patterns popularized earlier in the century by such manufacturers as Derby, Coalport and Spode. In 1862 they were taken over by Ashworth's and became Geo. Ashworth and Brothers. As well as designing new styles, they manufactured the shapes and patterns that had been popular during the 1850 period.

Alongside ironstone, another medium for producing very similar wares was the material referred to as opaque china, or semi-porcelain. This is lighter in weight than ironstone, and less sturdy. This dinner service was made in around 1862-80 by Ashworth's and carries the firm's marks and a pattern number. The Oriental-style decoration is typical of the period and is referred to as a Japan pattern.
•Opaque china was also produced by Minton's, Ridgway, Wedgwood and many others.
•Ashworth's also reproduced and adapted some Mason's ironstone designs in earthenware.

The Oriental decoration and the gilding on these vases from c.1835-50 are typical features of the ironstone china made in the Staffordshire area.

F. & R. PRATT & CO. (ENGLISH, 1840-c.1899)

Marks and identification Reissues of prattware are generally marked on the back with "F. & R. Pratt & Co.", and carry a statement of reissue from the makers, Royal Cauldon. Fakes tend to exhibit poor-quality printing and weak colours on a heavily crazed base, and are not usually signed.
•Some covers are signed on the reverse; many of those which were printed with Jesse Austin's engravings bear his signature.

The technique of multi-coloured printing on a white earthenware base was perfected by the firm of F. & R. Pratt & Co. Thus, these wares became known as prattware, although they were made by other firms as well. Pratt made a variety of wares in this medium, including decorative plates, mugs and loving cups, often with exotic borders and printed to simulate green malachite and seaweed. However, their staple products were their covers for jars intended to contain potted meat, fish paste or "bear's grease" – a gentleman's hairdressing preparation. Subjects include royalty (mostly executed by Jesse Austin), children, bears and fishing and village scenes, like that shown **right**. Although the covers are the focus of interest for collectors, pieces that retain their original jar command a premium.
•Covers pre-dating 1863 tend to be wiped free of glaze on the edges. Later examples, which are those that are most commonly found today, have a crazed, bluey-grey glaze.

Multi-coloured lids tend to be more desirable than those decorated only in black and white. This cover clearly shows the crazing typical of prattware. The small circles visible halfway down on the left and right of the cover were used to place the transfer print neatly in position. Not all examples exhibit these features.

THE SCULPTURAL INFLUENCE

Until the 19th century sculpture was purely the domain of the aristocracy: not only was it expensive, but because it was often life-size or even bigger it was better suited to the homes of the rich. However, in 1828 the sculptor Benjamin Cheverton invented a reduction machine which could produce small-scale replicas, in ceramic rather than bronze, with universal appeal. This led to the development of Parian, cheaper than biscuit but a very close replica of it, used to produce figures that would suit any modest middle-class home. Portrait figures were also popular, especially with the masses. These mirrored Victorian society and its various pastimes, pursuits and person-alities and cannot be bettered for sheer interest and variety. The relief-moulded jug was another ideal vehicle for sculptural carving.

A large Baggeley relief-mould-ed jug commemorating the 1855 Paris Exhibition c.1855; ht 15in/38cm

Many early Victorian jugs from the 1840s were Gothic in form or decoration, like this Apostle jug by Charles Meigh. These were perhaps the best-known and best-selling of all relief-moulded jugs, and are most common today. Biblical episodes were always popular, as were figures inspired by novels of the day, especially those of Sir Walter Scott. Classical subjects, especially Bacchus and the favourite Minton design of putti with grapes, were in steady demand.

RELIEF-MOULDED JUGS

Relief-moulded jugs had been produced during the late 18th and early 19th centuries, but in a very different style from those made later in the 19th century. Often decoration was applied in a contrasting colour onto a stoneware body to resemble Wedgwood's jasperware. Most relief-moulded jugs are slip cast in stoneware in various colours, including buff, dark green, pale green, white and grey. Interiors were usually smooth. Designs were mass-produced and were often graduated in size, sometimes in sets of three. Usually there is little surface decoration. The Baggeley jug **above** is unusually elabo-rate and because of this it would command a premium today.

Marks Many jugs are marked. Early marks were often impress-stamped against an ornate applied cartouche pad giving the maker's name and location and the date when the design was registered. Later, most makers impressed their name onto the base and sometimes included the diamond-shaped registration mark.
•Minton jugs usually have a script "M" hidden some-where in the cartouche.

Lids Some relief-moulded jugs were given Britannia metal mounts and hinged covers which are often mistaken for pewter. Covers are weighted so that they lift up when the jug is tilted for pouring. Many jugs which do not have a cover may nevertheless have two holes into which mounts for a lid could be fixed if required.

PARIAN WARE

During the Victorian period "statuary porcelain" was renamed Parian after the Greek island of Paros, where marble for statuary was quarried. The first examples were produced by the English firm of Copeland and Garrett in around 1842-4. Parian is noticeably finer and more highly vitrified than earlier porcelain clays, and it has a slight surface sheen. Statuettes predominate but Parian tablewares and wall fittings also exist. The medium lends itself to elaborate detail, and several manufacturers took advantage of this quality, notably Samuel Alcock, Minton, Coalport, Worcester and Belleek.

While most Parian wares have a white body and semi-matt glaze, some are wholly coloured and others have a high-gloss surface. Some firms used an iridescent glaze to simulate oyster shell. Glazed and unglazed areas could be combined in one piece. Some jugs were glazed inside to aid washing and general hygiene.

Portraits of famous royal, military or political figures were extremely popular. Many were based on maquettes by well-known contemporary animaliers and sculptors, such as John Bell and Raffael Monti.

Left Worcester Royal Porcelain Company produced Parian ware, including some very ornate tableware incorporating three-dimensional figures and groups. This delicate figure, *Watercarrier*, shows two common features of Parian – a smooth, matt surface and a white body (although here the statuette is highlighted in gilt).

Right Minton often made *risqué* figures like this one, which depicts a semi-naked woman. The cream of the drapery is characteristic of Minton's restrained colour scheme. The firm also made finely-detailed Parian tableware and wall brackets.

Left and above Robinson & Leadbetter (1856-1924) produced some very good Parian figures. Some were covered in a wash glaze to simulate ivory; most have matt surfaces. Victorian pieces are marked with an "RL" surrounded by an oval border, as are these busts.

PORTRAIT FIGURES

Some figures, such as this one of Prince Albert, c.1841, by John Lloyd of Shelton, display fine modelling and decoration. Early pieces tend to be hollow. The gilt lines of honey-coloured gold around the base typical. Figures after 1880 tend to use bright, distinctive gilding, called liquid gold.

Staffordshire and Scotland were the the major British centres for the production of portrait figures in the Victorian period, but some flatback figures (with flat, undecorated backs, designed to stand against a wall) were made in South Wales. All are generally called "Staffordshire Figures". The earliest (1830s-'40s) were in bone china or similar porcelaneous material and tended to be decorated in the round. Royal subjects are most collectable, followed by military figures and animals. Others included personalities of the day and murderers. By 1845 Staffordshire figures were being widely mass-produced. They are usually on plain bases, sometimes with a title; others are more ornate. Scottish figures tend to be slightly heavier than English ones and make more use of a blue-grey glaze. The distinctive palette includes claret, pine green, black and ochre.

Spaniels were popular subjects. Modern copies have blander expressions and duller colours and display less signs of attention to detail than originals.

THE MAJOLICA YEARS

Victorian majolica was a type of earthenware painted to resemble the colourful glazes of 16th century Italian *maiolica*. Wares are moulded in high relief with a palette of ochres, browns, whites, turquoises, pinks and greens, or are in buff-coloured earthenware, decorated in relief under translucent, coloured glazes. Majolica tablewares were made in greater numbers than the decorative figures, and include moulded jugs in the shape of animals or fish, vases and dessert services. Those moulded with Japanese-type decoration – for example, with fan-shaped panels or small birds in flight, moulded in low relief – are among the more sought-after. In Britain Minton dominated the market, but the wares of the smaller Staffordshire companies offer a reasonable, less costly alternative.

A massive Minton & Co. majolica urn 1865; dia. 33in/ 84cm

From 1870 Minton introduced majolica wares with a strong Japanese influence, such as this dazed-looking ape supporting a garden seat.
•All Minton figures are hollow. The bodies were slip cast separately before being joined together. Figures are very vulnerable, and a certain amount of sympathetic restoration is considered quite acceptable.

MINTON & CO. (1793-Present)

This Staffordshire pottery traded under the name of Minton & Co. from 1845 until 1873, when it used the name Mintons Ltd. The firm made high-quality earthenware and porcelain, and as well as majolica, produced art pottery (see p.108). Minton majolica from the early 1860s incorporates strong sculptural elements and inventive forms, often on a large scale, with hand-painted decoration inspired by classical and Renaissance elements. All Minton majolica employs high and full relief decoration. Handles are often embellished with lions' or rams' heads.

Marks Everything produced by the firm is marked "Minton" and has a shape and pattern number and date code. Individual years have special symbols. There are no known fakes or copies.

With its heavily sculpted appearance and figural decoration, this moulded plate depicting Venus is typical of Minton's majolica tablewares: it would probably have been decorative rather than functional.

GEORGE JONES (died 1893)

The fine modelling and clearly defined colour areas of this camel make it particularly desirable. Decoration is hand-painted in many colours. The camel is impressed with the title "Kumassie", the letters of the name forming a circle within a round panel. Simulated tortoiseshell glazes are often found on undersides with a small glaze-free area, usually with a mark.

George Jones worked at the Minton factory before founding the Trent Pottery in Staffordshire in 1861. He manufactured white and transfer-printed earthenware, majolica and the closely-related "Palissy" ware, some figural pieces and bird and animal statuettes.

Marks Jones's mark was usually an impressed or printed "GJ" monogram. Wares marked with a crescent bearing "& Sons" date from 1873 or later. "England" was added in 1891.

BROWN-WESTHEAD, MOORE & CO. (BRITISH, 1858-1904)

•A range of majolica wares was also produced by Wedgwood in the 19th century. The most popular pieces were oval game dishes ornamented with dead game animals in relief moulding and coloured in cobalt blue, mustard and leaf green.

This pottery produced figural and ornamental majolica wares in a similar style to those by George Jones. In 1878 they exhibited several majolica vases and plaques at the Paris Universal Exhibition. They were also noted for their flower-holders decorated with animals.

Marks Ornamental groups by Brown-Westhead are usually impressed with the maker's full name or the initials "B.W.M." within a shield, while the firm's tablewares usually have a printed mark.

This Brown-Westhead tiger statuette from around 1878, was made as an exhibition piece and can be expected to fetch considerably more than the smaller majolica wares of good quality.

CONTINENTAL MAJOLICA

Production of Victorian majolica ware on the Continent was less important than it was in Britain and America. The French and German makers – such as Sarreguemines and the Berlin State Porcelain Factory – were the most prolific. Rortstrand and Gustavberg manufactured majolica in Sweden as did Cantagalli and Doccia in Italy.

AMERICAN MAJOLICA

The production of American majolica only really began after the Centennial Exhibition in Philadelphia in 1876 where the enormous commercial success of European and Japanese ceramics provided the impetus for a massive expansion in the American ceramics industry which lasted until the First World War. The Phoenixville Pottery was its most important manufacturer.

THE PHOENIXVILLE POTTERY (c.1867-1902)

Above This begonia leaf dish, made by Griffen, Smith and Hill c.1880, is one of the designs for which the firm is best-known. Its colour scheme of yellow, pink or green is typically American, even though the palette was based on recipes developed for Staffordshire majolica in the 1850s and 1860s. Like all American majolica it was inexpensive.

Right The Etruscan range of mainly useful, glazed ware was heavily influenced by popular English designs. Many pieces had identifiably American uses such as this corn/maple syrup jug and incorporated American motifs – this sunflower pattern was especially popular in Kansas, the "Sunflower State". Pieces were more lightweight and far less ornamental than contemporary English majolica, with a crudely made body.

The Poenixville Pottery, established by Griffen, Smith and Hill in Pennsylvania in around 1867, produced a range of "Etruscan" majolica between the years 1879 and 1871.

Marks Etruscan wares are often marked, usually with an impressed monogram GSH (for Griffen, Smith and Hill), sometimes within a round border enclosing the name, Etruscan Majolica, and possibly including an impressed design number with the prefix E. These latter two marks may be the only ones present.

Above These butter pat dishes incorporate the fashionable Etruscan shell and seaweed design, reminiscent of early 19th century Wedgwood. The lustrous effect, achieved by a controlled reducing atmosphere in the kilns, was very unusual in American majolica. These dishes are extremely collectable today. Later wares were sparsely decorated or even undecorated.

THE RISE OF THE COMMERCIAL ART POTTER

The early Victorian period saw the production of mainly sculptural or functional pottery, which was often over-embellished and, to a large extent, mass-produced. However, following the teachings of John Ruskin (1819-1900), who was one of the greatest influences on Victorian English taste, commercial art potters began to employ artists in a quest to improve design and produce pottery that was aesthetically pleasing. Potteries such as Mintons and Doulton set up studios specifically to produce hand-crafted decorated wares and Linthorpe and Ault had the prestigious Christopher Dresser as their chief designer. William Moorcroft, working a little later, experimented with inventive forms and glazes to produce designs retailed and popularized by Liberty and Co. and inspired by William Morris. All these potters were amongst the pioneers of the Arts and Crafts movement, returning to values where form and ornament harmonize, and shapes are natural.

A Mintons jug in the Viennese Seccessionist style, 1904; ht approx 14in/35.5cm

Between 1900 and 1909, under the directorship of Leon Solon, Mintons produced a range of Secessionist-influenced earthenware which epitomized the Viennese Art Nouveau style, with flowing plant shapes and geometrical patterns. Many pieces are an unusual shape and are decorated using tube-lining, whereby lines of slip are piped on to a piece and fired, with glazes painted in between the lines. Glazes tend to be runny and uneven, often over-running the confines of their raised slip boundaries.

Mintons' "Secessionist" wares feature a striking palette – purple is common, often used to dramatic effect with ochre and white; tomato or blood-red are other colours, usually set against leaf green or turquoise. The vase above is typical of these pieces in its colour combination: many pieces were vibrant, almost shocking.

MINTONS LTD (1793-Present)

Mintons pottery was established at Staffordshire in 1793, since when it has remained at the forefront of the production of innovative art pottery, making a wide range of wares exhibiting a high level of craftsmanship. A separate studio was set up at Kensington Gore in 1870 to produce art pottery.

Left Mintons' Kensington Gore studio opened in around 1870 specifically for producing art pottery, and survived only three years before being burned down. W.S. Coleman, who painted this plaque, was the leading artist. His work frequently incorporates small naked or partially-clad children, often in classical settings, and recognizable by their flat bottoms. He also depicted fantastic or mythological worlds. Most of his work is in a typical palette of vivid enamels with subtle flesh tones. Pieces bear a printed circular mark for Mintons' Art Pottery Studio, Kensington Gore.
•Henry Stacy Marks, R.A, a leading designer at the Kensington Gore Studio, developed the *Seven Ages of Man* designs, depicting stylized medieval-type figures in gardens or interiors, which were mass-produced by the firm as a series of rectangular ceramic tiles and plaques. Individual pieces may turn up at auction.

THE TORQUAY POTTERIES

Out of a number of ceramics firms based in and around Torquay in Devon, most prolific were the Torquay Terracotta Company, the Watcombe Terracotta Company and the Aller Vale Potteries. In 1901, Aller Vale merged with Watcombe to become the Royal Aller Vale and Watcombe Pottery Company. They all used the local red clay, ideal for the manufacture of both their decorative and useful terracotta wares, which are all fairly unadventurous in design.

The most striking Torquay wares are those with a turquoise glaze, known as *celeste*, often applied in geometrical bands or motifs to a plain terracotta body. The design of this elegant water bottle has been attributed to Christopher Dresser, c.1870.

Marks A variety of marks was used. Aller Vale impressed their wares with the name of the pottery in capital letters. In the late Victorian period they also used a hand-written incised signature. Among the marks used by the Torquay Terracotta Company are the initials "T.T.C." or the name in full, usually surrounding an oval or circle. The mark above was a common Watcombe mark.

Staple Torquay wares consisted of pieces decorated with coloured slip representing floral studies, and small birds in bold designs that exhibit wide brush strokes, as in this urn, made by Watcombe in around 1900. Typically, the shape is of classical inspiration.
•The slip technique was used for the enormous number of motto wares for which Torquay is best known.
•Most desirable are the sculptural groups and large, slip-decorated vases. Least collectable are the small souvenirs, motto wares and nick-nacks that dominated the market at the end of the 19th century and in the early 20th century.

DELLA ROBBIA (ENGLISH, 1894-1906)

The Della Robbia Pottery, Birkenhead, was set up by designers, including Harold Rathbone and Conrad Dressler, to promote the ideals of "honest labour" and individualism held by the Arts and Crafts movement.

Left Pieces generally have a pale blue-green glaze on a cream earthenware body, are hand-thrown and have a rough surface. Colours tend to be harmonious, and washes uneven. The firm's most characteristic decorative technique was a variation of Italian majolica, with lead glazes, instead of tin, applied over a white slip. A sgraffito line was used to outline glazed areas. Other decorations include moulding, painting and applied relief. Designs, in at least two colours, always cover the entire surface.

Right Della Robbia employed many artists, including women; this Algerian vase was decorated by Liz Wilkins. For other pieces, Islamic, Celtic and heraldic inspired patterns were applied to Italianate and classical types of jugs, vases and chargers. From 1898, Carlo Manzoni, an Italian sculptor, popularized strongly geometric designs which later gave way to organic plant shapes. Other subjects include fish, animals and figures, often inspired by Renaissance, Medieval or Pre-Raphaelite portraits, some based on designs by Edward Burne-Jones.

Tiles Decorative tiles which borrowed heavily from Persian and Iznik originals for their design were a staple product of the de Morgan pottery. Those tiles which are decorated with ruby lustre glazes and small animals, birds or grotesques are particularly sought-after today.

•Several other English companies produced decorative tiles, including Maw & Co., who also manufactured de Morgan's tiles, Mintons, Wedgwood and Doulton.

•Tiles from the William de Morgan Pottery are usually marked, but not always with de Morgan's name or initials. Some of them may be impressed with "Carter", the name of the firm who provided the blanks for painting.

•Others tiles bear the de Morgan flame mark or a circular mark.

The Iznik-inspired emphasis on stylized trees, plants and flowers is evident in this detail from an extensive series of tile panels.

THE WILLIAM DE MORGAN POTTERY (ENGLISH, 1872-1907)

William Frend De Morgan (1839-1917) was the most significant potter to be connected with the English Arts and Crafts Movement. He worked with many different artists throughout his life and many of his designs were executed by others. He is best known for his decorative tiles, but also created numerous chargers, plates, dishes and vases, hand-painted in all-over decoration.

Phases of production in de Morgan's career

•Chelsea phase: 1872-82 Initially, de Morgan bought earthenware blanks from Staffordshire which he decorated, often in a single-colour lustre glaze. After 1875, he introduced Persian colours, notably vivid blues and greens. These wares tend to be the least collectable.

•Merton Abbey phase: 1882-87 The repertoire expanded to include dishes, vases, bowls, bottles, jugs and flowerpots, many with elaborate decoration, often enamelled.

•Fulham phase: 1888-1907 From 1888 de Morgan worked with Halsey Ricardo at the Sands End Pottery in the London suburb of Fulham. He then joined forces with the potters Frank Iles and Charles and Fred Passenger, until around 1905.

Motifs Favourite enamels include all-over patterns of fish, stylized flora, birds, animals and grotesques, and single-masted galleons, which were introduced in the Merton Abbey Period. At Chelsea and Merton, de Morgan tended to concentrate on ruby lustres, and his first two-colour lustre wares date from the Merton period, with ruby usually forming one of the colours. De Morgan's lustre-wares were always well-controlled and well-executed.

Marks Apart from the ready-made blanks bought from Staffordshire at the start of his career, all de Morgan's decorative and tablewares are signed. The several marks or stamps include "Merton Abbey" or "Sands End Pottery" for the Fulham phase, and "DM" or "W. De Morgan". From c.1880 pieces bear the initials of the decorators.

Most William de Morgan pieces found today belong to the Fulham phase, when the firm's Persian and Iznik-type wares were created. Like this Iznik vase which was painted by Charles Passenger in around 1900, these pieces show a greater integration of form and decoration than those from earlier periods.

This charger is typical of de Morgan's lustre wares, which date from his Merton Abbey period. This piece, with a shallow well and wide rim, incorporates the two lustre colours of puce and amber.

•While in Florence in 1892, de Morgan employed Italian painters to carry out his designs, and some of the lustre wares produced by the Florentine form of Cantagalli closely resemble his own.

LINTHORPE (ENGLISH, 1879-82)

Noted designer and aesthete, Christopher Dresser established the Linthorpe Pottery in Middlesborough, North Yorkshire, with local land owner and artist Henry Tooth as manager and himself as artistic creator. In the pottery he designed for Linthorpe, Dresser combined the Arts and Crafts Movement's belief that household objects should be functional with his mystical view of nature (see also p.70). He adapted many designs from Celtic, Egyptian, Ancient Greek and Roman, Islamic, pre-Columbian and Aztec originals. Later pieces are often painted in slip or underglaze colours, or sgraffito. The firm's wares were all made from local clay.

Glazes Early Linthorpe pottery is noted for Tooth's glazes, developed in two or more rich colours. His slips combined various metal oxides to create irregular flowing, swirling and dripping effects.

Dresser's glazes tended to be dark brown with green, or solid yellow, blue or green. The use of grotesque shapes is typical – Dresser's designs are always inventive.

Marks Linthorpe ware is marked with the pottery name, sometimes shown over an impressed outline of a squat vase. An incised facsimile of Dresser's signature appears on some of the firm's pieces alongside Tooth's monogram. Today, Dresser's ceramics are among the most highly sought-after of any 19th century English designer.

AULT (ENGLISH, 1887-1923)

William Ault worked in Staffordshire before joining Henry Tooth at Bretby. He opened an art pottery under his own name at Swadlincote, Derbyshire, producing ornamental earthenware and domestic objects, often designed by Dresser. His daughter, Clarissa, often painted butterflies and plants on his vases.
• The Ault pottery mark is a tall fluted vase over "Ault" on a ribbon or an "APL" monogram. Some pieces also bear Dresser's signature.

Many of Dresser's designs for Ault continued the Japanese, pre-Columbian themes initiated at Linthorpe. This vase has an onion-shaped cylindrical neck and a characteristic turquoise and brown streaked glaze. Some completely new forms by Dresser include a series of "egg vases". Pieces were sometimes coated with the shimmering aventurine glazes invented by Ault.

BRETBY ART POTTERY (ENGLISH, 1883-1920)

Bretby was established by Henry Tooth and William Ault in Derbyshire to produce mainly earthenware pieces, but also some amusing novelty objects, including realistically modelled biscuits and nuts on dishes. Most desirable are the anatomically correct figural subjects. Also popular are jardinières grasped by seated apes, and small black cats. Bretby wares are always marked.

Early wares favoured flowers, painted on slips in autumnal colours, foliage and insects, sometimes applied using light-coloured clay. Monochrome glazes included dark brown, a rich amber colour, *sang-de-boeuf* and dark green. They are marked with an impressed sunburst motif above the word, "Bretby".

These vases show the high-quality anatomical drawing of later Bretby ware (1895-1900). The birds' semi-matt glaze contrasts with the streaky glaze on the bamboo stalks. Typically, the pair is well-balanced but not identical. Japanese motifs in high or low relief appeared on many later pieces; bamboo was part of a range of realistic effects.

The most desirable wares are those which, like this vase, are decorated with an Iznik-type palette. Typically, the decoration features intricate scroll-work and stylized flowers.

BURMANTOFTS (ENGLISH, 1858-1904)

Burmantofts, founded by Messrs. Wilcox & Co., was based in Leeds, Yorkshire. At first it made architectural terracotta but from 1880 produced art pottery – made of earthenware from clay mined from the factory site and covered with feldspathic glazes and fired to high temperatures to make the body extremely hard.

Burmantofts produced decorative tiles, vases, bowls and some tableware. The most notable early pieces were bottles and jars resembling Japanese or African gourd water vessels, nests of small jars fastened together, and "pilgrim" bottles. Later wares were retailed under the name of the Leeds Fireclay Company.
•Pieces are marked on the base with the pottery's name in full or the monogram BF.

Glazes Pottery was covered in multiple streaked or monochrome glazes in *sang-de-bouef*, orange, lime-green, yellow, or turquoise. Other glazes include copper or silver lustre over a dark red or blue ground. Some objects were hand-painted; these usually have smooth surfaces.

ELTON WARE (ENGLISH, 1881-1920)

Sir Edmund Elton (1846-1920), an English baronet, devoted his later life to making hand-made art pottery. With the help of an under gardener, George F. Masters, later his chief assistant, Elton set up his workshop and kiln on his estate at Clevedon, Somerset, trading as the Sunflower Pottery until December 1882. Elton, entirely self-taught, concentrated on purely decorative art pottery. He was more interested in creating new and challenging forms than in repeating designs he was sure of and thus the quality of his output always fluctuated.

Collecting and marks Marks were painted or impressed, and vary from "E" for Elton, to "E. H. Elton", or "Elton Clevedon" with or without a date mark. George Masters sometimes marked pieces he decorated himself with his initials, "GFM". After Elton's death in 1920 a painted "X" was added.
•The fish-headed jug (**left**) was made by several other small West Country firms.

Elton sometimes created different versions of the same idea. This fish-headed jug was transformed later with a coating of one of the crackled lustre glazes for which Elton became famous after 1902.
•Gold and silver lustre wares are the mot collectable of all Elton's products.
•White Oriental-type prunus flowers were popular.
•Other inspiration was derived from Japanese metal-work and anient Romano-British pottery.

MARTIN BROTHERS (ENGLISH, 1873-1914)

Marks All Martin wares are hand-incised on the underside with the name and address of the maker and the date of production. The most sought-after pieces, made before 1873, are marked "Fulham". Later pieces are marked "London & Southall". "Bros." or "Brothers" was added in 1882. No fakes or reproductions are known.

The Martin brothers (Robert Wallace, Charles Douglas, Walter Frazer and Edwin Bruce) set up their first art pottery studio in Fulham, London, under the leadership of Robert, but their work was collaborative. At the Lambeth School of Art, Robert learned the method of salt-glazing stoneware which became the Martin Brothers hallmark. The firm produced mainly hand-thrown jugs and vases with an Arts and Crafts feel, some in organic pod forms and some of grotesque form.

This grotesque and pensive bird tobacco jar is a favourite design. The firm also produced face jugs and chess pieces.
•Decoration tends to be painted or sgraffito, in a palette of subdued blues, greens, browns and greys. Painted decoration tends to be naturalistic.

WILLIAM MOORCROFT (ENGLISH, 1872-1945)

Marks Moorcroft signed all Florian wares, usually "W. MOORCROFT des", sometimes with "JAMES MACINTYRE & CO. FLORIAN WARE" printed in brown in a cartouche, or "WM des". Pieces marked "MOORCROFT BURSLEM" are post-1913. Patterns commissioned by Liberty include the printed mark "made for Liberty & Co."

From 1898 Moorcroft headed the Art Pottery department of Macintyre & Co., the Staffordshire pottery firm established around 1847 at Burslem, where he produced designs for both utilitarian wares and the now more collectable art pottery. His inventive forms, applied with original designs, echoed the fabric designs of William Morris and those popularized by Liberty & Co.

Moorcroft's "Florian ware" was possibly the greatest British contribution to Art Nouveau ceramics. Designs, which were often symmetrical, depicted flora, usually applied to slender vases or ewers, such as this "Iris" vase from around 1900. Others incorporated peacock feathers. Decoration tends to cover the whole surface. Interiors are usually glazed and interior decoration may creep over the rim. Wares with a cream or near-ivory body are more sparsely decorated and also make use of gilding.

DOULTON & CO. (ENGLISH, 1815-Present)

Doulton was founded in the early 19th century to produce saltglaze sewage pipes and sanitary wares. In 1871 Henry Doulton opened a studio at his Lambeth Pottery, eventually employing many artists from the nearby Lambeth Art School. Several became pre-eminent in their field, especially the Barlow sisters and their brother Arthur, as well as George Tinworth, Frank Butler, Mark V. Marshall and Eliza Simmance. The Pottery concentrated on ornamental wares in sombre colours, such as dark green, brown, blue and grey, but the decoration was often lively, spirited and inventive. Doulton set up a factory in Burslem, Staffordshire in 1881 to produce earthenware and bone china (see p.116).

Doulton faïence Notable for their well-executed decoration, these pieces feature mainly English flowers set against toned reserves, often ochre toning to yellow-green or green toning to pale blue. Faïence with figural decoration is scarce and desirable, especially if children are the subjects. Faïence is currently undervalued and prices are bound to rise.

Other designers Doulton's many designers each had a distinctive style. Frank Butler, a deaf and dumb artist who worked at Doulton between 1872 and 1911, produced carved and modelled designs bearing relief patterns set against grounds decorated with circles, dots or lines, which were generally better executed than those of Marshall (see right). Margaret Thompson, an illustrator, specialized in tiles and vases painted with mainly sylph-like fairy figures with delicate wings, often in striking purple, green and white, with features outlined in black.

Florence Barlow's wares favour *sgrafitto* decoration over a coloured slip, and show a preference for small English birds, both features of this vase from c.1885. The border is typically elaborate.
• Hannah Barlow's earlier incise-decoration tends to be quite bold, with scant attention paid to background but after an accident in 1876 which left her without the use of her right hand, her work became more detailed. She frequently depicted animals, often sandwiched between elaborate borders.

The work of the outstanding modeller, George Tinworth, included architectural commissions and endearing small models of mice and frogs, often in humorous situations, with incised titles. This stoneware tankard is typical of his ornamental wares. He was the only artist at Doulton allowed to put his monogram on the piece itself (rather than underneath).
• Mark Villiers Marshall was one of Doulton's leading designers in the Art Nouveau period, best known for his grotesque animal subjects in salt-glazed stoneware with low relief and rich ornament, similar to those produced by the Martin Brothers.

THE TRIUMPH OF BONE CHINA

A pair of Coalport vases and covers c.1870-73; ht 17in/43cm.

Bone china was an excellent medium for a vast array of ornamental wares, as the body was ideal for the modelling of finely applied detail, such as flower heads. Unlike soft paste, it was easily mass-produced and soon a number of potteries, including Coalport, Minton, Worcester and Royal Crown Derby, were producing decorative wares and tablewares on a fairly large scale. Several companies were able to produce less expensive wares by using slightly inferior bone china and transfer printing techniques rather than hand painting. The Irish pottery, Belleek, produced extremely fine, thin bodied porcelain teaware which appears to be too fragile to use. At a time when French designs were in vogue, many designers, including Coalport and Minton, produced close copies of Sèvres to satisfy the demands of the rich in Britain. The early Rococo style soon gave way to Neo-classical themes.

COALPORT (ENGLISH, 1796-Present)

This fine Coalport dessert service was painted mainly by F. Howard in the early 20th century. All the pieces are signed. The green ground and the pink and yellow tones of the cabbage roses are typical, as is the gilding.

Note Many of the English factories mentioned in these pages also made miniature porcelain for children. Wares included tea services, ornamental vases, coal scuttles and watering cans. These tea wares are often more valuable than their large counterparts.

Marks Wares are often marked "Coalport AD 1750", the date the firm claimed to have been founded, and not the date of the piece's production. Various marks were used by Coalport, including an "ampersand" mark, with the initials C, S or N in the loops, which represent Caughley, Swansea, and Nantgarw.
• Artists at Coalport did not sign their wares until the later years of the 19th century.

This Shropshire factory was founded in the 1790s by John Rose, who later bought Caughley and Nantgarw. Now housed at Stoke-on-Trent, the factory is still in production. The firm began to produce excellent tablewares in fine quality white bone china from around 1820, using Sèvres-type ground colours which included *bleu du roi*, a brilliant dark blue, as well as beige and the apple-green of the dessert service on the left. Coalport also made ornamental wares such as flower-encrusted "Coalbrookdale" pieces, parian figures and copies of Chelsea, Meissen and Sèvres. Later wares are sometimes "jewelled" with drops of enamel in a Rococo style.

Decoration Coalport employed some accomplished artists to paint in the Sèvres style, including John Randall, who was famous for his bird paintings, and who designed the pair of vases at the top of the page. These vases are made in modified bone china which the firm produced from around 1870, enabling wares to be made on a larger scale. Earlier examples of Randall's work incorporated birds which tended to be much more exotic than the rather more naturalistic apporoach which is evident here. As well as birds, figures after the French painter J. A. Watteau also feature on Coalport pieces of this period.
•Some of the earlier wares produced at Coalport are almost identical to Sèvres originals, and sometimes can only be told apart by scrutinizing the porcelain body.

WORCESTER ROYAL PORCELAIN CO. (ENGLISH, 1783-1902)

Figural wares Figural wares, particularly those modelled by James Hadley, proved more popular than any of the sculptural pieces. They are usually functional, incorporating a vase, a bowl or a candlestick. Figures inspired by the drawings of children by the English illustrator Kate Greenaway were the most popular, both then and now.

The original company, Chamberlain & Co. was established in 1783 by Robert Chamberlain. It was revived in 1852 under the direction of Kerr and Binns (by which it became known) and became the Worcester Royal Porcelain Company in 1862, producing a wide variety of fine porcelain wares as well as their staple tablewares, the quality of which was never sacrificed for the sake of increased output. Victorian designers included James Hadley and Thomas Bott, whose dramatic wares in the manner of 16th and 17th century Limoges enamels, are now extremely rare.

Wares produced by the company reflected the changes in popular taste. The Aesthetic Movement inspired majolica wares and Japanese-type pieces, which, produced in a blush ivory porcelain and often incorporating hand-coloured enamels on transfer-printed outlines, were the staple products of the late Victorian period. These have survived in some quantity and in good condition.

This pair of candlesticks shows the late-Georgian dress typical of Royal Worcester's figures. The design was influenced by the contemporary illustrations of Kate Greenaway. Other subjects were inspired variously by Japan, India and Classical Greece; humorous pieces, such as nuns, monks, and owls with nightcaps, were also popular.

Left The popularity of Persian-type Iznik wares during the 1880s inspired a range of vases. Those produced by Worcester, like this example, attempted to simulate the precious jewelling of the original Moghul vases, using colourful enamels. The form of this piece, with its slender neck and flange handles, is also typically Persian.

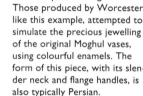

Left This unusual game service from around 1889-90, printed with pheasants, woodcocks, and other game birds, may well have been painted by C. H. C. Baldwin, who was employed by the company to decorate many of its tablewares.

GEORGE OWEN (ENGLISH, died 1917)

George Owen specialized in the production of reticulated or pierced wares for the Worcester Royal Porcelain Company during the latter half of the 19th century. His pieces are solely decorative and display an amazing combination of ornate form and dexterity of execution, evident in the vase and cover on the right. The porcelain is usually ivory-coloured and applied with elaborate pierced openwork. (This was not innovative – in earlier years Worcester had produced a series of cups and saucers displaying pierced decoration and enamelling.) Decoration tends to be a combination of enamelling and painting, using a predominantly soft palette.

Marks and availability Owen was one of the few designers allowed by Worcester to sign their wares. Most have "G. Owen" incised into the clay along with the Worcester stamp – a crowned circle, either impressed or printed.

•George Owen's reticulated wares surface in small quantities at most of the London and good provincial auction houses, and in the United States.

The pale blue, pink and pale green of this vase are all characteristic of Owen's wares; turquoise was also favoured. Soft gilding is typically used to highlight decoration and is applied to rims, bases, handles and often the main body of pieces. Demand for all Victorian Worcester is high.

This Crown Derby vase and cover was painted in the Sèvres style in around 1878-90, and strongly echoes the work of the French artist Jean August Dominque Ingres (1780-1867). The combination of gilt relief work and translucent enamel beading was popularized to a state of excess by the premier Victorian French makers.

The shape of this tureen, made for the Paris Exhibition of 1900, echoes the French Empire style, and the floral design and the palette resemble pieces produced by French factories such as Sèvres. However, the style is distinctly Art Nouveau.

ROYAL CROWN DERBY (ENGLISH, 1811-Present)

In 1811 Robert Blooor acquired the Chelsea-Derby factory from its successors, John Heath and William Duesbury, and managed it until its closure in 1848. In 1876 a new factory was established in Derby, initially trading as Derby Crown Porcelain Company, but changing to Royal Crown Derby Co. in 1890. It continued traditional Derby designs and produced a lot of Japanese-inspired Imari patterns, with underglaze blue and onglaze red and gold decoration as well as pieces with outstanding strong ground colours and additional gilding and jewelling, often in the Sèvres style. Among its chief designers was the painter Albert Gregory.

DOULTON & CO. (ENGLISH, 1815-Present)

Alongside the Doulton Lambeth factory, in operation between 1820 and 1956 (see p.113), a second Doulton factory opened in 1883 at Burslem, Staffordshire which concentrated on the manufacture of earthenware and bone china, especially dinner and tea sets.

MINTON & CO. (ENGLISH, 1793-Present)

Minton produced extensive tea and dinner services; these dessert plates date from 1855. Bird designs were popular with Joseph Wareham who worked for the company c.1838-1860; and it is possible he decorated these plates. He also painted flowers and fruit in the Sèvres style.

Minton & Co. was founded in 1793 by Thomas Minton, who is said to have invented the "Willow Pattern", and traded as Mintons Ltd from 1873. The factory has always maintained a consistently high quality and has been one of the most innovative in Britain, producing a wide range of pottery (see p.106 and p.108).

Earlier Victorian products of the Minton factory were made to reflect tastes of that period. The popularity of French Louis XIV and later 18th century pottery and porcelain resulted in Minton's producing large quantities of Sèvres-style porcelain. This was often so accurate in its rendition that it even confuses experts today. Minton made use of all the typical Sèvres palettes, which included *bleu celeste* and *rose pompadour*.

The nautilus shell enjoyed a special popularity, both at Belleek, where this porcelain vase was produced, and at Royal Worcester and Moore Brothers. Belleek also employed shell motifs in their tea wares.
•Belleek is famous for its iridescent glazes, which were applied to their parian paste, and used to produce their tablewares. Other Belleek wares include centrepieces and ice pails. Many of their models are still being produced today.

BELLEEK (IRISH, 1863-Present)

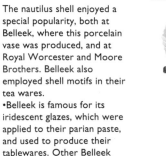

Belleek, who operate from County Fermanagh, specialized in producing openwork baskets applied with finely executed flowerheads. The earliest, three-stranded baskets with densely encrusted rims are the finest.

Marks Pieces are often simply impressed with a single pad on the underside saying "Belleek". From 1863 to around 1880 wares also carried a printed black mark of a seated Irish wolfhound, harp and round tower. After 1880, "County Fermanagh" was usually impressed upon several slender applied pads. The more pad marks, the later the piece.

AMERICAN EXPERIMENTATION

Rookwood was the first American art pottery to receive international acclaim when it exhibited at the Paris Exposition of 1900. With its excellent-quality painted decoration it quickly established an all-American identity, especially for its Matthew Daly American Indian vases. Experimentation lead to the use of silver deposit overlays, and various glazes, such as vellum for landscapes. The Grueby Faïence Co. produced naturalistic forms complemented by interesting glazes. Similarly, the Gates Potteries applied glazes to create textured vases for their Teco range.

A Rookwood vase, decorated by Matthew Daly c.1900

ROOKWOOD (AMERICAN, 1880-1960)

Maria Longworth Nichols founded this Cincinnati pottery to produce wares that combined Japanese ideals of craftsmanship and aesthetics with naturalistic imagery. Decorative motifs include indigenous American flora, fauna and landscapes, which often show the influence of the Nancy School (see pp.34-5).

Identification Rookwood's wares have not been faked, but several potteries, such as the Roseville Co., produced items similar to Rookwood's Standard glaze wares. Many are marked, but unmarked examples are distinguished by signs of inferior manufacture, such as visible seams and crudely executed decoration.

Most of the firm's wares are impressed "ROOKWOOD" and are dated, with perhaps an artist's monogram.

From 1886, "RP" was used (**above left**). A flame device was added – one flame for each year between 1887 and 1900 (**above centre**). From 1900 the last two digits of the year were impressed in roman numerals below the monogram (**above right**).

Right Standard glaze wares, first made in 1883, tend to be heavily potted, slip cast and painted in coloured slips under a clear, high glaze. The ground often tones from one shade to another – this vase, decorated by Matthew Daly in c.1886, shades from a rich amber to umber. Other standard colours include "Sea green", "Iris", a pale, muted grey, and the mottled "Gold-stone" or "Tiger-eye". Sunflowers are a recurrent Art Nouveau motif.
•Wares bearing portraits of American Indians, particularly those decorated between 1897 and 1903 by Matthew Daly (see above) or by William McDonald, are particularly sought after.
•In 1904, Rookwood patented a matt glaze called "Vellum". Vellum-glazed wares tend to bear stylized flora or landscapes similar to some contemporary French overlay glass.

THE GRUEBY FAÏENCE CO. (AMERICAN, 1894-1930)

William Grueby (1867-1925) trained at the Low Art Tile Works in Boston, Massachusetts, which produced tin-glazed earthenware, architectural faïence and press-moulded, glazed tiling in the English taste. He founded his own firm in East Boston where he continued to use processes learned at Low Art, such as the application of thick opaque glazes. He produced mainly architectural faïence, tiles and sanitary wares with simple, often Japanese-inspired forms, with any decoration being minimal and of vertical emphasis.

Forms and motifs often combine to create an organic effect; the bulbous shape and stylized leaf and flower decoration of this vase reflect the naturalistic preoccupation of Arts and Crafts. Decoration is in relief with an outline in thin trails of slip. Broad leaf motifs, including lotus, acanthus and tulips are often used to create vertical ribbing, as on the lower section of this vase.

Grueby tiles tend to be thickly slab moulded in porous, pale buff earthenware; the most desirable are glazed in a muted palette with a matt finish. Decoration is usually stylized and is often tube-lined. Some tiles were designed as part of a landscape series. These seven tiles are part of a set of 14 depicting a landscape of sky and palm trees. Naturalistic designs are very collectable, as are medieval designs which echo the work of the British ceramist, William de Morgan (see p.110). Other common motifs include turtles, illustrations from Lewis Carroll's non-sense poetry and prose or images from the works of Rudyard Kipling. Some examples are deeply relief moulded.
•Grueby tiles are generally unsigned, although some tile backs do bear an impressed company name and lotus blossom trademark.

Marks Fully marked wares, bearing the firm's name, sometimes in a roundel with a lotus leaf trademark and an artist's monogram, are very collectable. Particularly desirable artists' marks are those of Ruth Erickson, George P. Kendrick and Wilhemina Post.

Grueby won international acclaim at the Paris Exposition of 1900 for their thickly potted vases, with matt, monochrome glazes thickly applied to give a textured and pitted effect similar to that of cucumber or watermelon skin and hence called "watermelon". This effect was compounded by the firm's favourite glaze, a rich organic, moss green. Their most collectable wares also take the form of a melon; this example was designed by Ruth Erickson, one of Grueby's finest artists. Pieces decorated in more than one colour are particularly popular.

GEORGE E. OHR (AMERICAN, 1857-1918)

Marks and copies

Most of Ohr's pottery is signed, usually impressed "G E OHR Biloxi Miss". Later examples bear an incised facsimile script signature. A number of forgeries bear convincing marks and can be difficult to distinguish from the originals. Copies are commonly small-scale with a very red body and a mirror-black lustrous glaze.

Another American potter who experimented with unusual shapes and glazes was George Ohr, a great virtuoso art potter, who never achieved huge commercial success. He opened a makeshift studio in the artist's colony of Biloxi, Mississippi in 1885, working alone but for a brief association with Newcomb College Pottery in the mid-1890s. His eccentric lifestyle and appearance (he looked like Salvador Dali) earned him the nickname "the mad potter of Biloxi". He made both useful and decorative wares. His work is particularly popular with American collectors and museums.

Above Ohr's favourite modelling technique was to pinch and fold vessels into unusual, even bizarre, shapes prior to firing. The extreme irregularity of this vase is characteristic of such pieces.

Left Ohr used a wheel and a wood-burning kiln to produce unique, hand-thrown pieces which resemble amateur-made studio pottery. He worked almost exclusively in red earthenware and pieces tend to be thinly-walled with the lightweight and brittle, eggshell-like appearance evident on the rim of this vase from around 1895. Glazes tend to be mottled and lustrous and of a deep colour. More rarely he used bronze or rich black glazes, or more striking glazes such as the unusual salmon and orange glaze on the vase on the right. Pieces with applied ornament, such as the handles on this vase, are likely to raise higher prices.

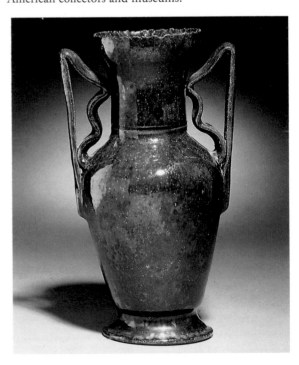

NEWCOMB COLLEGE POTTERY (AMERICAN, c.1895-1945)

Founded at Newcomb College, New Orleans, this pottery produced some of the rarest, most valuable American art pottery. Operated mainly by women, it developed a distinctive style of hand-thrown wares hand-decorated with incised patterns of local flora highlighted in polychrome slip. Examples from before 1910 have a high glaze, whilst later wares tend to have a semi-matt finish. The range included small, ovoid or globular vases, drinking mugs and teawares. Most collectable are the larger wares and those featuring landscape decoration, or those by the better artists, such as Mary Sheerer or the founder Joseph Meyer.

Newcomb Pottery's palette usually combined blue with green, yellow or white. This typical colouration is evident on this high-glazed vase decorated with stylized irises, produced at the pottery c.1905 by Sabina Elliot Wells.
•Pieces are all fully signed with "NEWCOMB COLLEGE", or an "NC" monogram incised or impressed, a body letter (Q or W) and an artist's monogram or cipher.

TECO (AMERICAN, 1902-c.1923)

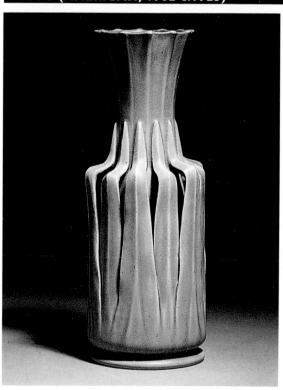

William Day Gates established Gates Potteries at Terra Cotta, Illinois, in 1881, to make architectural terracotta, tiles and bricks. He introduced his "Teco" stoneware in 1902 which, unlike other American pottery of the period, was mass-produced in large industrial kilns using sophisticated slip-casting and glazing methods.

Teco's wares, which include garden ornaments, pots and vases designed by local architects, have an architectural feel and tend to be heavily walled, with good, crisp outlining. This vase, like many Teco examples, reflects the "Prairie" style advocated by Frank Lloyd Wright (see p.46), and is highly attractive to collectors today. Some pieces display complex moulding. The designer, William J. Dodd, favoured reticulated patterning. The organic form was also common. Wares often had a metallic, evenly textured, pale green, matt glaze resembling oxidized copper. Other glazes include deep blue, plum, yellow and brown.

Availability Pieces by the firm's more sought-after designers, such as Fritz Albert, William Dodd and William Day Gates, are rare and highly collectable, particularly in the United States. Pieces bear a design number, usually 3 digits, with one of two possible marks in vertical print.

ARTUS VAN BRIGGLE (AMERICAN, 1869-1904)

Artus van Briggle began his career at Rookwood (see previous page) and opened a studio in Colorado Springs in 1901, to produce fine interpretations of French Art Nouveau, such as vases with floral or figural relief decoration.

Van Briggle's pieces have matt glazes – the bluish-green featured on the vase on the left was the most common colour; others include deep and pale blue, plum, brown and off-white.

This vase, which is entitled *Lorelei*, is moulded as a female figure whose arms, head and hair form the rim. The most collectable wares, produced before van Briggle's death in 1904, bear an incised date. Later undated examples are common and of little collectable value.

NEW ERA POTTERS

In Britain, late-Victorian and Edwardian art potters sought to produce entirely hand-painted wares with tasteful forms and graceful decoration. Several potters, including Pilkington's, Bernard Moore and Maw and Co., produced an exciting range of lustre-decorated wares and flambé glazes. North of the border, the Wemyss pottery, under the guidance of Karel Nekola, produced their distinctive range of wares, all with hand-painted decoration. The designer Walter Crane was particularly popular, and both Pilkington's and Maw and Co. decorated their wares with his designs.

A Wemyss pig decorated with cabbage roses by Karel Nekola c.1899-1914; ht 12½in/32cm

This two-handled cup was made to a design by Karel Nekola between c.1899 and 1914. Examples with decoration of cocks and hens are especially desirable, as are those depicting ducks in a landscape of reeds.
•Handles and rims are sometimes patterned or twisted and often have single-colour borders.

WEMYSS (SCOTTISH, 1817-1930)

Wemyss ware, named after Wemyss Castle in Fife, Scotland, was made at the Fife Pottery from 1880. In 1883 the owner brought in Karel Nekola, a Bohemian artist who quickly applied his personal style to the wares, giving them simple, solid forms but highly distinctive decoration. Commissions came via Thomas Goode & Co., sole agents for Wemyss pottery, who retailed the wares from their prestigious shop in Mayfair, London.

The Wemyss range covers both useful and ornamental wares, from buttons to garden seats. From 1897-1911, Nekola made commemorative souvenirs – starting with a range of tablewares celebrating Queen Victoria's Diamond Jubilee and ending with pieces made for George V's coronation – and these are very collectable. Perhaps most charming are the moulded pigs (see above), together with cats and rabbits, all in different sizes for use as door stops or ornaments on nursery shelves. Decoration is always hand-painted by Nekola and his assistants; the background is often in white. Motifs vary, but sprays of brightly-painted and realistic fruits and flowers, animals, birds and insects, and fishing fleets are most typical. Colours tend to be restricted to pinks, greens, blacks, browns and purples. The pig is decorated with one of Nekola's most popular themes – large, pink cabbage roses.

Common 19thC Wemyss marks

Authentic Wemyss ware bears a maker's mark or "Thomas Goode and Co." Some pieces show the initials "RH" for Fife's owner, Robert Heron, as well as "Wemyss". On pieces executed by Karel Nekola, the "y" of the word Wemyss is elongated. Karel's son, Joseph, marked his best pieces with "Nekola pinxt".

MAW & CO. (ENGLISH, 1850-67)

This decorative vase, like many of Maw & Co.'s ceramics, was designed by Walter Crane, and uses the familiar ruby lustre glaze set against a pale buff earthenware body. The shape and movement preempt the more curvilinear extravagances of continental Art Nouveau wares.

Maw and Co. took over the former premises of the Flight, Barr and Barr Worcester porcelain factory in 1850, then moved to Shropshire in 1852, from where they became one of the world's largest producers of ceramic tiles and architectural faïence. In the 1870s they began to produce tesserae (small tiles) for decorative mosaics and in the 1880s produced a series of ornamental wares decorated with primarily ruby and yellow

PILKINGTON'S TILE & POTTERY CO. (ENGLISH, 1892-1937)

This vase was painted by William Salter Mycock, a senior decorator, who produced a large number of lustre wares at Pilkington's.
•In 1928 the company introduced its Lapis ware which had a slightly blurred appearance. Many of these pieces were decorated by Gladys Rodgers; some exist with the incised initials of the thrower, Edward T. Radford.

Pilkington's Pottery rose to prominence after the introduction of William Burton from Wedgwood in 1897, and achieved international acclaim when they exhibited at the Paris Exhibition of 1900. Although the company produced a large and extensive range of monochrome glazes they are best-known for their lustre-decorated wares of mainly decorative vases, wall plaques, bowls and candlesticks. Artist decorators included Gordon Forsyth, Charles Cundall, William Salter Mycock, Richard Joyce and Gladys Rodgers.

Marks The early mark includes a large "P", upon which perch two little bees, representing William Burton, and his brother, Joseph Burton, who also joined the factory. Underneath appears the year mark in Roman numerals. In 1913, when the company became Pilkington's Royal Lancastrian, the Tudor Rose replaced the bees as their mark. Commissioned artists all signed their work with their monograms and some artists had individual year symbols and motifs.
•Forsyth uses a rebus for his mark – four scythes forming a circle.

This lustre vase, painted by Gordon Forsyth, commemorates the fire at the Brussels International Exhibition of 1910, where both the British and Belgian displays were destroyed. It makes excellent use of iridescent glazes, and gives the impression that everything is set against swirling flames. It is relatively large for Lancastrian pottery, at 20in/51cm high.

BERNARD MOORE (ENGLISH, 1853-1935)

Bernard Moore and his brother, Samuel, succeeded their father in his porcelain factory at St Mary's Works, Longton, and began trading as Moore Brothers. From 1905, at Wolfe Street, Stoke-on-Trent, Moore specialized in producing art pottery which made strong use of flambé glazes in deep red, decorated in black or grey. His work uses strong, good shapes, often of Oriental inspiration. The quality of his draughtsmanship was always high. Common motifs include nocturnal animals and birds – bats and owls often appear silhouetted against a moonlit yet blood-red sky.

Right The Oriental influence is evident in this flambé glazed vase, dated 1909, not only in the shape, but in the decoration, which features a phoenix flying above a pine tree. Typically, the piece is signed on the base with "BERNARD MOORE", and the number 09, for the date. Other decorators working for Moore were allowed to sign their work, but always on the base of the piece, never on the decoration.

RUSKIN POTTERY (ENGLISH, 1898-1933)

William Howson Taylor, an English art potter, set up his art pottery in West Smethwick, Birmingham and began commercial production in 1901, under the trade name of Ruskin Pottery. For an initial three year period Taylor produced a lot of experimental pieces and it was not until 1909 that he was officially allowed to trade as Ruskin. His range of wares includes his "soufflé" pieces in a mottled, monochrome glaze, and lustre-decorated wares (both in earthenware) as well as an eggshell thin bone china in crystalline glaze, and his keenly sought after high-fired stonewares. Other wares include bowls, candlesticks and jars and small items such as buttons.

Left Shapes often followed popular Oriental designs. This flambé vase rests on a flared foot. The veridian spots over the mottled white ground were achieved by using copper salts.

SÈVRES

The Sèvres factory was founded under royal patronage at Vincennes, France, in 1750 and from 1756 operated from the Hauts-de-Seine factory at Sèvres. It attracted the most talented French designers and artists, adapting to current trends right through to the 20th century, producing outstanding work which consisted mainly of hand-painted large decorative wares for the new rich *élite*. Early pieces were in a Rococo style. 19th century wares kept the neo-classical forms popular during the 18th century, with decoration featuring their celebrated reserve colours, such as *bleu céleste* and *rose pompadour*. From around 1900 Sèvres produced Art Nouveau pieces, now seen as some of the finest of the period, and from around 1920 it moved on to Art Deco wares, initially regarded as the poor relations of their other wares, but now receiving much more interest than before.

A Sèvres vase decorated by Henri-Joseph Lasserre c.1912; ht 9in/22.5cm

Early Sèvres The sculptor Albert Carrier-Belleuse became director of Sèvres in 1876 and employed other sculptors, including Auguste Rodin, to create innovative designs. At the end of the 19th century he introduced new decoration with imitations of Chinese celadon, *flambé* and *sang-de-boeuf* glazes.

Art Nouveau wares Sèvres' Art Nouveau wares were slip-cast and purely decorative, the decoration achieving a harmony with the form. Shapes were more sculptural. The *vase d'Ormesson* shown above echoes a popular Chinese form. Typically, the motifs are floral and hand-painted in underglaze against a pure white ground. The Sèvres palette of soft mauve, pink, green and yellow is reminiscent of the colours used at Royal Copenhagen (see p.135). The fine gilding is typical of Sèvres' high-quality wares.

Most early Sèvres wares were traditional and ornate, with vases decorated in narrative panels of classical scenes, courting lovers and idyllic country pursuits, as seen in this vase, decorated in around 1840. The exuberant gilding is characteristic of Sèvres.

TAXILE DOAT (FRENCH, born 1851)

Taxile Doat, a porcelain decorator and designer, worked at Sèvres between 1875 and 1905 and advocated a more avant-garde approach to design. He often used the *pâte-sur-pâte* technique of decoration. The medallions on the gourd on the right are white *pâte-sur-pâte* on green.

The innovative form of this Sèvres Art Nouveau *vase de Chévilly* is known as *à pans*, meaning that the vase is rectangular or square when seen in cross section.

Right Some vases take unusual shapes of organic inspiration; this bottle is designed as a gourd with the flower as the stopper. Doat's work has a strong neo-classical element; he avoided the common Art Nouveau wispy maidens.

Right This porcelain *jardinière* made in 1924, characterizes much of the output of the factory in the Art Deco period. Egyptian motifs such as the pillars, the pose of the woman and the chevron and gold patterns, were very popular during this time. Geometric decoration was also frequently used. The central female nude, simplistically represented and with no painted embellishment, was also very common.
•As on earlier pieces, the matt glaze is heightened by gilt.

This Sèvres vase, designed by Jacques Emile Ruhlmann (see p.57) in 1932, is unusual in its ornate, even avant-garde form. However, the use of gilt, is characteristic of Sèvres wares, as is the harmony achieved between form and decoration: the large expanse of ivory porcelain is juxtaposed with the busy design of overlapping, pale blue, lilac and grey panels.
•Other leading Sèvres designers and decorators include: Robert Bonfils, Emile Decoeur, Jean Dupas, Anne Marie Fontaine, Suzanne Lalique and François Pompon.

Henri Rapin, one of Sèvres' leading designers, created the form of this massive vase and cover in 1925, but the decoration (called *Tropiques*) was not added until 1939 – by Anne-Marie Fontaine, a designer who worked at Sèvres. Typically of Sèvres designers, her mark appears on the footrim.
•The same vase and cover was also made in plain dark cobalt blue.

Marks Sèvres' wares were signed between 1738 and 1954, but signatures should be regarded with caution. At least 80% of 18th and early 19th century porcelain with the Sèvres mark was not made at the factory – many factories producing wares at the same time freely copied the mark. However, from 1900 a new system was introduced at Sèvres which showed the letter "S" or "Sèvres" with the date underneath, contained in a triangle, either impressed or printed in green.
•Individual decorators sometimes added their own mark. Taxile Doat incised his entwined initials.
•Collectors should particularly beware the Sèvres mark that shows two interlaced "L"s (the royal cipher) as this is the most commonly faked one. It was introduced in 1739 and a date coding mark was added in 1753.

Art Deco wares

Georges LeChevallier-Chévignard took direction of the Sèvres factory in 1920 and because of the high reputation of the firm was able to call upon the top designers of the day. The designs from this period are so individual that it is impossible to cover the whole range here.

MINTON'S SÈVRES-STYLE WARES

Influenced by Sèvres designer, Marc Louis Solon, Minton

The Minton pottery studio in Staffordshire (see p.106) produced a large quantity of Sèvres-style porcelain which is often so accurate in its rendition that it even confuses experts today.

produced *pâte-sur-pâte* pieces. The drawing and craftsmanship of this category of wares were extraordinarily accurate, as seen in this group of three vases by Solon from c. 1875.

Minton made use of all the typical Sèvres palettes, including the *bleu celeste* in the decoration on this Sèvres-style vase of 1840, which is a direct copy of an 18th century shape.

DUTCH AND GERMAN CERAMICS

A Rozenburg eggshell pitcher and pair of vases
c.1910; ht 11in/29cm

Two distinct types of ceramics were produced by Dutch potters during the Art Nouveau period. The first of these was the traditional blue and white wares for which the town of Delft is world famous. The second was the art pottery of the 1880s. This came from the Hague School, which preferred floral motifs, sinuous curves and both symmetrical and asymmetrical decoration (probably best exemplified by Rozenburg's wares); and from the Amsterdam School, which concentrated on simpler forms and formalized, sometimes geometric decoration (as produced by the Amstelhoek Factory). In Germany the Art Nouveau style found expression through the studio potters: Max Läuger applied slip-trailed, stylized grasses and flowerheads to hand-made pots, and Villeroy and Boch produced stoneware art pottery mechanically incised and colour enamelled.

Some of the firm's earlier "Arab" wares emulated Iznik and Persian earthenware in both form and decoration. The pottery also produced landscape tiles. Most are decorated with standard Dutch landscapes with figures in interior settings. Rozenburg's earliest wares tend to be decorated using the darker, more subdued palette evident on this earthenware plaque. Motifs were fairly stylized, and used forms of relatively traditional type. Decoration was often allover.

•In 1906, the company introduced their range of "Inkrustierte Fayence". These wares are sparsely decorated with colour enamels enclosed within deep incise-moulded outlines. "Juliana Fayence", introduced in 1910, used busy decoration in a colourful palette on a cream earthenware body.

ROZENBURG (DUTCH, 1883-1916)

The Rozenburg pottery concentrated initially on simple earthenware. However, in the late 1880s and '90s the firm led a revival of Dutch ceramics, and its eggshell earthenware is now considered to be among the finest earthenware ever produced. During this period, decoration became more obviously influenced by both Art Nouveau and Japanese art. Leading designers included Theodorus A.C. Colenbrander, Sam Schellink and J. Juriaan Kok, artistic director from 1895.

Under Kok's directorship, Rozenburg won fame for its "eggshell porcelain" – lightweight, extremely thin, delicate earthenware of pale ivory colour, introduced in 1889, and used for elegant vases, ewers and tea wares, usually in exotic and innovative shapes. Designs were often elongated, as in the "iris" pitcher in the centre of the picture at the top of the page. The square base is also typical: the factory's eggshell wares were often designed in square section, visible on the "chrysanthemum" vases flanking the pitcher. All three pieces were decorated by Sam Schellink who, together with W.P. Hartgring, was among Rozenburg's finest decorators. It can be difficult to tell their work apart but both are collectable. Birds were a popular motif with both of them.

Marks Rozenburg's wares typically bear one of two marks: "ROZENBURG DEN HAAG", printed with a stork, **right**; after 1900, this was surmounted by a crown device or a painted monogram and year symbol. Decorators had their own monogram.

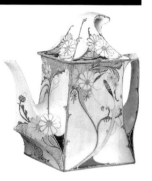

Rozenburg's wares often have elongated loop handles which emanate from rims or lips or, as in this eggshell teapot, evolve from the shoulders or sides, to give an organic feel. Bases are slightly concave, apart from a rim of approximately ½in (1.5cm). Because Rozenburg's wares are slipcast, the joints are not visible.

WEDUWE N.S.A. BRANTJES & CO. (DUTCH, 1895-1904)

This short-lived factory, although based in Purmerend, had some affinities with the Hague School. Some designs may have been inspired by the pattern books of the French potter, Maurice Pillard Veneuil. The firm merged with the Haga factory of the Hague (established 1903), and its name changed to N.V. Haga. The name was changed again in 1905, to Plateel Bakkerij.

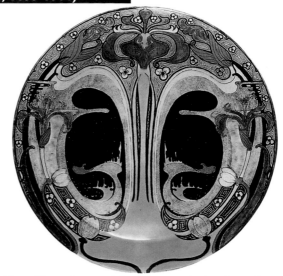

Brantjes concentrated on decorative earthenwares, usually with strong forms and bright, floral decoration. He was not afraid of experimenting with novel forms, as this two-handled vase shows. Shapes were often symmetrical. As with the dish, decoration on this piece is all over and very brightly coloured.
•Pieces were usually signed.

Above This earthenware dish from around 1900 displays typical characteristics, including very bright colours, all-over symmetrical decoration and black outlining.

AMSTELHOEK (DUTCH, 1894-1910)

This factory was founded by the goldsmith W. Hoeker as a ceramics workshop for the sculptors Lambertus Zijl and Christian Johannes van de Hoef, who produced earthenwares decorated with inlaid designs in coloured clays on ochre or brick red grounds. In 1896 a metalware department was opened.

Amstelhoek's main ceramics designer, van de Hoef, designed this Egyptianesque *jardinière*. Typically, this is slip cast, but has a hand-crafted appearance. In 1903/4 van de Hoef moved to Haga.

DISTEL (DUTCH, established 1895)

Distel's main designer between 1895 and 1896 was Bert Nienhuis, a well-known painter and designer. The arrival of Theodorus A.C. Colenbrander led to a more colourful interpretation of floral and other designs. Colenbrander advocated the use of bold abstract designs with large areas of reserve, repeating some of the shapes he had used while at the Rozenburg factory.

Other Dutch factories
•Zuid Holland, 1898-1964. This Gouda-based factory is best known for its use of relatively dark, sombre palettes and stylized floral and fruit decoration with semi-matt glazes. The firm also produced some wares inspired by the Rozenburg pottery, produced under Colenbrander.
•Arnhem Fayencefabrik, 1907-1928. This firm concentrated on symmetrical stylized flower-and-leaf decoration.
•Ram Factory, 1920-28. This short-lived factory was founded by Colenbrander in Arnhem.

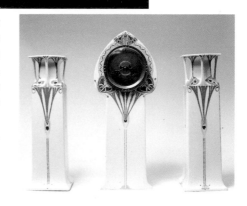

Nienhuis used mainly white glazes with restrained decoration often applied in soft pastel colours. As in this clock set, designs were symmetrical. Nienhuis moved to Hagen in Germany in 1912, but returned to Holland in 1917 and worked as a studio potter producing mostly undecorated pieces and using a variety of glaze techniques.

Meissen wares bear the factory's mark of blue painted crossed swords (**above left**). On wares produced between 1860 and 1924 the swords may include a curved guard. Pieces made in 1910, the firm's jubilee year, bear the dates "1710, 1910". Some may have an artist's mark – for example, the work of van de Velde may bear his monogram (**above right**).

MEISSEN (GERMAN, c.1710-Present)

By 1910, some Meissen designs began to show the influence of the Vienna Secessionists; this vase and cover, made in around 1912, borrows a Secessionist form and palette. As on earlier Meissen wares, the porcelain itself is the main feature, rather than simply providing a canvas for the decoration.

In the early 20th century, Meissen used mainly raised *pâte-sur-pâte* decoration and trailing flowers. This vase and cover, designed by Julius Konrad Hertschel in 1905, features a clematis and has a typical toned ground. Despite its organic nature, the design is symmetrical – Meissen's Art Nouveau designs tend to be more symmetrical than other European ceramics. The majority of these wares are purely decorative.

•Meissen also produced wares decorated with crystalline glazes inspired by the works of Royal Copenhagen (see p.135) which were exhibited at the Paris Exhibition of 1900.

•Amongst the most reputable designers commissioned by Meissen were Henri van de Velde (see p.39), Richard Riermerschmid and Paul Scheurich. Otherwise, despite their reputation, Meissen produced few great names during the period and little is known of most of their artists and designers.

Founded at Meissen, near Dresden, this firm was the first to produce true porcelain as developed by the Chinese. The soft paste porcelain of Sèvres from the mid-18th century was the first real competition: otherwise, Meissen has kept its reputation as Europe's premier producer of tablewares and figures. During the 19th century, the firm rested on its 18th century laurels, adapting traditional forms to suit modern tastes, with the emphasis on technique and decoration rather than novel shapes. Its Art Nouveau wares were applied with contemporary designs in under-glaze decoration and matt or semi-matt glazes similar to those used on Rookwood wares of the same period (see p.117).

MAX LÄUGER (GERMAN, 1864-1952)

Max Läuger was an architect, engineer and sculptor who began experimenting with ceramics at the end of the 19th century. He was one of the very few potters working in Germany to be influenced by the activities of his French contemporaries, and the decoration of his pieces almost invariably takes French-style floral or organic forms. His work is robust, often with strongly innovative elements.

The painted decoration featured on this vase, of stylized, honesty-type circular flowers hanging from trailing stems, is typical of Max Läuger's work, which generally has a naturalistic or organic appearance. The slightly irregular glaze – in this case cobalt blue – is another common characteristic of Läuger's ceramics.

Läuger's ceramic designs were produced at the Tonwerke Kandern in Baden, where Läuger was artistic director from 1895 to 1913. Most wares bear the Kandern mark (**above left**) and Läuger's monogram (**above right**).

Läuger's distinctive decorative style involves naturalistic motifs — usually long, slender-stemmed flowers and grasses — painted in trailed slip on a stoneware body, which is often of a slender, tapering form, coated with a one-colour reserve. Läuger attempted to integrate form and decoration. This is clearly evident in this earthenware double gourd vase. The applied handles continue to the bottom of the vase, giving it an organic feel.
•Läuger also designed decorative tiles in an Art Nouveau style, as well as some ceramic sculpture.

ALBIN MÜLLER (GERMAN, 1871-1941)

The work of Albin Müller, a fellow German architect and designer, is in stark contrast to that of Läuger. In Germany in the late 17th century there was a vogue for grey stoneware with a blue glaze. Although sometimes referred to as *gres des Flanders*, most of these wares were in fact produced by potters in the Westerwald region of Germany. During the late 19th century and early 20th century, several designers in the region, including Müller, were inspired to produce similar wares with a peculiar Teutonic emphasis. The style was referred to as Jugendstil, meaning "youthful style" – the German equivalent of the term "Art Nouveau".

Marks Müller's ceramic wares may bear a printed mark similar to that, **right**. They were manufactured by the Burgau porcelain factory and by Ernst Wahliss.

This stoneware pitcher is typical of Müller's Jugendstil wares: the frieze decoration involves stylized flower, bead or pod forms, historically popular in the Westerwald region. The piece has a hinged pewter cover in the 18th century manner – the German metalwork industry worked together with the pottery industry.
•Müller also produced pewter wares for Eduard Hueck, a German metalworking firm.
•Most pieces are salt glazed.

VILLEROY AND BOCH (GERMAN, 1836-Present)

The two separate firms of Villeroy and Boch merged in 1836 to produce earthenware and stoneware, and are particularly famous for their Mettlach art pottery, produced from the 1880s, and decorated with inlaid clays in contrasting colours. This involved incising leather-hard clay, which was then fired and hand-enamelled. The firm initially concentrated on a range of highly decorative and colourful beer *steins*, which were highly popular, especially in Germany and America.

Marks Pieces are marked with the Mettlach castle and the monogram VB and may be accompanied by the word *schutz* (copyright), a four-figure number, indicating the shape, and a two-figure number for the date. Many are signed by the artist as "decorated by".

Principal motifs used by Villeroy and Boch include medieval tavern scenes, scenes from classical antiquity, and occasional Rhineland views and fairytale lands. Most dramatic are probably their large circular wall plaques with profile portraits of Mucha-esque maidens, elaborately attired and bejewelled with exotic headresses. The decoration on this Mettlach ceramic charger is very like the hand-painted designs found on Rozenburg's wares. Here the design was incised before being hand-painted, and depicts two owls in a fantasy landscape.

FIGURAL CERAMICS

An earthenware "Amphora" portrait vase made by R.S.K. c.1900; ht 9in/24.25cm

The "Amphora" range consisted of mass-produced vases decorated with incise-moulded outlines upon thick onglaze enamels. The more exciting examples bear portraits of mystical, regal women, face-on and usually with a gilded, halo-like surround to the head. Most subjects, like the woman at the top of the page, are shown in a woodland setting. Vessels were often of exotic form, like this tulip vase, perhaps with moulded decoration in the shape of leaves, berries and stems, with branch or whiplash handles, possibly terminating in a number of tendrils, often edged with gilding.

Bohemian and Austrian potters started to produce figural ceramics in the late 19th century, adopting new slip-moulded techniques to mass-produce easily affordable figural wares on a hitherto unprecedented scale. Early factories, such as R.S.K and Royal Dux, seized upon the Art Nouveau style, with its organic and symbolic forms, to produce maidens and nymphs in various symbolist and amorphic forms, using a palette of subdued tones of green, ochre and ivory, sometimes heightened with gilt dusting. Often vases were simply used as a vehicle for these designs. In the 20th century, pieces became more sculptural and more purely decorative and moved away from figural vases to the ceramic sculptures in Continental Europe by Goldscheider, Michael Powolny at Wiener Keramik, and Lenci. Designs and colours were bolder and reflected contemporary trends. In England, John Skeaping and the Doulton pottery produced similar wares but in a much more reserved style.

REISSNER, STELLMACHER & KESSEL (AUSTRIAN, established 1892)

This porcelain manufactory, established at Turn-Teplitz in Bohemia (now Austria) is best known for its "Amphora" porcelain from the 20th century.

Other wares Although "Amphora" vases represented the best of R.S.K.'s designs, the firm's other wares reflected a similar high standard and repeated many of their Art Nouveau themes and motifs. A series of wall-hung masks depict other figures, such as wood nymphs. These are fairly small (about 9in/22.8cm in diameter) and relatively rare. They tend to be marked "Amphora", which suggests that R.S.K. attempted to capitalize on the success of their premier vase range by adopting the term generally. R.S.K. produced a number of pieces with ivory glazes decorated with matt greens and sometimes dusted with gilt. A series of extremely ornamental dishes was produced in this style, with all-over decoration.

Marks Vases are marked with the word "Amphora" and "R.S.K.", sometimes accompanied by a mark containing three stars within a burst of sun rays (see **above**). The vase in the main picture is printed on the underside with the starburst mark and the extended legend, "Turn Teplitz Bohemia R. St K. Made in Austria" accompanied by an impressed trademark "Amphora".

ERNST WAHLISS (AUSTRIAN, 1863-1930)

As a ceramics retailer, Wahliss acted as an agent for such companies as R.S.K. and Zsolnay. In around 1880, he established the Alexandria porcelain works at Turn-Teplitz, home of R.S.K. It was under that firm's influence that he began to produce figural moulded vases, although his examples tend to be more sculptural and with less emphasis on decoration, than other designers. His figures often have an ivory glaze washed with sepia tones.

ROYAL DUX (AUSTRIAN, 1860-mid-20thC)

Royal Dux was the most prolific of the three Bohemian firms. They followed a safe path with a range of wares depicting animals, German Goths and classically-attired maidens.

Marks The firm's mark is a salmon pink triangular pad mark impressed with "Royal Dux" in arch form. "Bohemia" appears on wares made before 1918. In 1918 the firm found itself in the new Czechoslovakia; pieces made after this date bear the word "Czech". Some wares carry both marks and were probably made in around 1918 or held, undecorated, in stock.

The colouring, matt glaze and fussy style of this bust is typical of Royal Dux porcelain.

A few Royal Dux examples were quite risqué, with leggy women and nudes. These two exotic dancers were made in 1930 after a model by Schall.

GOLDSCHEIDER (AUSTRIAN, 1885-1953)

Another Viennese firm, Goldscheider, was founded for the manufacture of porcelain, faïence and terracotta. The firm was very prolific and mass-produced a whole range of figures in mainstream Art Nouveau style. Some figures were classically-inspired; others were more generic, depicting goose girls and sea nymphs.

Above Goldscheider designed figures as electrical fittings for table and hall lamps. This terracotta lamp, entitled *Chère*, is typical. The three light bulbs are located in the cloak held above the woman's head. Goldscheider tended to use surface enamels that emulated bronze patination; this is clearly seen on the lamp. Other wares include novelty objects, such as fish tanks decorated with pottery figures, and large earthenware sculptures and figures.
•Some Goldscheider pieces were made for export to the United States.

Above Typical of later pieces is the lithe, rather idealized figure of this dancer in period attire, designed by Joseph Lorenzl c.1930; others featured couples dancing. Many figures were in cream earthenware, with a vivid underglaze. The firm also made ceramic versions of the bronzes of Lorenzl (p.167) and Bruno Zach (p.168), among others.

Left Wall masks, popular in the Art Deco period, were made by many companies. Those by Goldscheider are the most desirable. They made a series of six or more designs, all the same size, hand-painted and with a sculptural look. This one (c.1930) is typical, with its serene, stylized facial expression and downcast, half-closed eyes, and bright colours. Hair, also bright, was often in ringlets.

Marks Pieces after 1918 have a transfer-printed mark on the back plate, "Goldscheider Wien. Made in Austria", which superseded the earlier, pre-war mark of an embossed rectangular

pad of a kneeling figure from Greek pottery. Commissioned wares sometimes carry the name of the designer as well, and a serial number. A few are still have their original paper label.

Staffordshire Goldscheider In the late 1930s the rights to produce Goldscheider figures were taken up by the Staffordshire company Myott, Son & Co. Ltd. Their wares, marked

"Goldscheider made in England", are not as sought-after as the Austrian versions. Goldscheider set up its own British pottery in 1946, and pieces made there have a signature mark.

MICHAEL POWOLNY (AUSTRIAN 1871-1954)

Powolny, a ceramics decorator, co-founded Wiener Keramik in 1905, together with Bertold Löffler. The firm employed some Wiener Werkstätte designers.

Michael Powolny worked mainly in earthenware, which he preferred to porcelain. He produced several distinctive series of solid, figural, purely decorative pieces, the most notable of which was his line of small, cherubic boys, some shown grasping bouquets of stylized flowers, like this figure from around 1910. Other examples in the series show the boy sitting upon an enormous snail. Invariably of white earthenware, these figures are detailed in black. Despite the Teutonic appearance of the child, the flowers signify a sympathy with French figures in their use of similar decorative details to those found on some French furniture designs. The base is typical in its restraint and chevron-type design.
•Powolny's wares are rare and not usually signed, although the characteristic style should be proof enough of their having been designed by him.

Above Powolny produced some bas relief wares, of which this plaque is a typical example, with its central figure of an elegant young woman, cherubic in appearance, and surrounded by flowers that are integral to the design. The figure has a distinctly Neo-classical feel; other examples exhibit a more modern, geometric influence. These bas relief wares employ the coloured majolica-type glazes favoured by Wiener Werkstätte designers, such as Josef Hoffmann and Dagobert Pèche.

ROSENTHAL (BAVARIA, 1879-Present)

Rosenthal is best known for his sculptural figures – many of which feature groups of fawns or nymphs in underglaze pale blue, grey, brown and skin tones, similar to those of this single figure. Other earlier popular figural subjects include mythological characters, and occasionally, small boys.

Philip Rosenthal, a German potter, established his porcelain factory in 1879, to produce a range of high quality wares, which were simple and restrained in both form and embellishment. Early products included tablewares decorated using a blue and white palette similar to that found on Japanese Makuzu wares. Some of his vases have *pâte-sur-pâte* decoration. Favoured motifs include landscapes and exotic birds.

Figures Rosenthal, always noted for his responsiveness to contemporary tastes, set up an art department to produce fine-quality ceramic figures, with inventive shapes and ornate forms or patterns. Many of the figures were attired in contemporary dress, such as bathing suits. Others were figures taken from the theatre at the time, and included Pierrot the clown.

Rosenthal also produced a range of cabinet objects, including animals and stylized figures, which were modelled exclusively in white.

Collecting Rosenthal's work is relatively underrated. It is in fact probably the nearest equivalent to the fine-quality work of Meissen (see p.126), but is far more affordable. The figures he produced are more desirable than the tablewares, which are not really worth collecting at all, unless decorated or designed by a leading artist.

Marks Rosenthal's pieces are incise-marked with the designer's name on the side of the base, and have printed green crossed roses and crown marks underneath.

Rosenthal figures have an individual, sculptural quality which can be seen clearly in this piece from 1927. Although this quality is always evident in the firm's work, pieces gradually became more stylized throughout the 1920s and '30s.

Later subjects included dancers wearing colourful, exotic or futuristic costumes. This sculpture of a "Korean Dancer", which was executed by Rosenthal in 1919, and designed by C. Holzer-Defanti, is a typical example of the firm's work .

THE LENCI WORKSHOPS (ITALIAN, established 1919)

The Lenci workshops in Turin produced a mixture of stylish and kitsch glazed earthenware and porcelain figures in the 1920s and '30s. Most are single subjects; groups are less common. Lenci also made a number of wall masks, and in the 1930s produced a series of highly colourful characters.

Lenci figures are all hand-painted and usually depict women with serene, coy or coquettish expressions and exaggerated painted eyebrows. Even those that do not display recognizably period features still manage to show a combination of naïveté and sophistication that is characteristic of the period.

Collecting and marks Some of the less successful Lenci figures, including some nudes, border on the kitsch. These are generally less sought-after by collectors than the more sophisticated pieces and those that depict contemporary figures or situations. A feature of Lenci figures is the use of combined glazes on a single piece. Many have matt subjects on a shiny gloss base. The body is usually in a smooth semi-matt finish in white or flesh tones.

The prominence given to the hat in this group of two women from around 1937 is typical of Lenci's sculptural studies. Usually in straw, the hats are often highly exaggerated, as in the cornucopia of fruit worn here.

Marks Lenci figures sometimes have paper labels attached identifying the factory; individual designers usually remained anonymous. There are various marks for the Lenci workshops. Sometimes the single word "Lenci" or "Lenci Made in Italy Torino" is painted on the figure. Collectors should note that on some pieces, the word Lenci reads backwards – the result of having been set in positive rather than reverse in the mould.

Note Lenci took some artistic license with their portrayal of the human form. This is clearly evident in the impossible length of the girl's arms on the right, and in the blue star-spangled hair of the woman featured on the previous page. The Royal Dux factory in Bohemia produced some figures which featured similarly lean and leggy women (see p.129).

Hair is often very blond, sometimes unrealistically yellow, as in both the women featured on this page. Many Lenci figures are very modern for their period: to show a langorous woman reclining in an armchair would have been highly innovative. Typically for Lenci's clothed women, this figure is depicted in relatively chic, accurate contemporary dress.

The imagery of some Lenci figures is emphatically that of the 1920s or '30s. This is evident in this lady in a polka dot dress, who is portrayed standing on high-rise apartment blocks while powdering her nose.

JOHN RATTENBURY SKEAPING (ENGLISH, dates unknown)

Skeaping worked for Wedgwood from 1926, specializing in animal figures, but also producing some birds. He created 14 designs for Wedgwood, 10 of which were in production through the 1930s. They are somewhat reminiscent of the work of George Sandoz (see p.170).

Marks The J. Skeaping mark is usually incise-cast into the side of the piece, together with the impressed Wedgwood mark.

Note Some pieces have fitted wooden stands. If the object is a very tight fit the stand should be profesionally removed, because the figures are prone to cracking.

This seated deer was designed by John Skeaping for Wedgwood in around 1935 and its passive stance is typical.

Pieces are usually in matt or semi-matt glaze in cream, celadon green moonstone, or black basalt, as here.

DOULTON & CO. (ENGLISH, 1815-Present)

Most Doulton figures feature women shown in the context of their new-found freedom. This is often reflected by the costumes – for example, elegant evening gowns such as the one shown here, *negligés* (see opposite page), or the dress of a gala ball poppet. Others wear carnival costume, which is particularly evocative of the 1920s.

During the 1920s and '30s Doulton produced a range of white porcelain figural wares very much in the Art Deco style. These represent a departure from the Victorian style crinolined ladies, and the nymphs and sirens so beloved in the early 20th century. Produced primarily for the British market, most have a characteristic "English Rose" look.

During the 1930s the firm of Beswick and Wade produced some figurines, but these were not as popular as those produced by Doulton.

Condition The exposed limbs of figurines are especially susceptible to being chipped or broken and are therefore the parts most likely to have been restored: look for very subtle changes in skin tone and surface glazes, where retouching may have occurred. Enamels, particularly the blacks, were unstable and prone to flaking, and should be examined for signs of overpainting.

The bases, which were mass-produced, sometimes show stress cracks. This need not unduly trouble the prospective purchaser as long as they don't extend more than an inch (2.5cm) from the hole underneath the base, or extend to the visible areas of the piece.

Figures were often mounted on table lamp bases; these bases are not especially desirable and may be removed. However, this should always be done professionally, as the rubber retainer has a tendency to vulcanize.

Marks The figures are usually painted on the base with the words "Potted by Royal Doulton", and those from the 1920s and '30s have a hand-painted title (as opposed to the printed mark used in the post-war period). They also carry an "HN" number – the factory reference number which gives the title and records when the piece was introduced and when it was withdrawn. Reprints of contemporary Doulton catalogues provide valuable information on individual items.

MINOR CERAMICS

There are many figural ceramics available today which are relatively inexpensive because they are either unmarked, not by major craftsmen, or not quite as finely executed as those by the top artists. Any contemporary-looking figure is worth looking at as they are all collectable.

Above This figure, entitled *Négligé*, was designed by Lesley Harradine for Doulton in around 1927. The woman's complexion is charact- eristically fair and she has a healthy-looking rounded face and rosy cheeks, synonymous with the "English Rose" look frequently featured in Doulton's work. Here, pale flesh tones are set against the vivid primary colours of the hat and cushion; on other figures the flesh tones are set against pastel colours, as in the bust, pictured below.
•Doulton figurines are often clothed in costumes of one bold principal colour – as are all those featued on these pages.

Dressing table wares with figural tops were popular in the 1920s and '30s. There are many types, varying in size from ½in (1.2cm) to around 4in (10cm). This unmarked porcelain powder puff is probably German or Austrian. The subject is unusual: most are either Louis XV Pompadour types with bouffant hair, or naked wanton women. This piece retains its original powder base, a nice but not essential feature – most collectors are interested in the porcelain top, which must be in good condition. Figures are hollow, and pierced to enable the powder puff to be attached.

Above *The Bather* is one of the most famous figures of the period; as well as this nude, risqué version, there was also a more modest one, clothed in a black painted swimsuit. Both convey a mood of joyous abandon and escapism found in some of Doulton's figures.

Above Although most Doulton figurines of the period are depicted full length, the firm did make some head and shoulder busts, like this one, which still bear the Doulton characteristics – the casual pose is especially typical and would have been considered avant-garde in its day.

THE CHALLENGE OF IRIDESCENCE

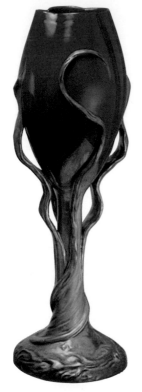

The application of iridescent glazes to ceramics was pioneered by William de Morgan in England (see p.110) and Cantagalli in Italy in the late 19th century and coincided with the rise of iridescent glass in Austria. The shimmering glaze readily complemented the organic, naturalistic and stylized forms of Art Nouveau, capturing, for example, the colours of peacock feathers or butterfly wings. The controlled iridescent glazes used by Clement Massier in France on his range of ceramics were emulated by such firms as Zsolnay in Hungary and Samuel Weller and Pearsons in America who adapted the glazes to suit their own style. In England, Wedgwood and Carlton both produced a range of lustre wares in the 1920s and '30s, with a high-gloss, pearlized glaze which gave a richly coloured, jewel-like appearance.

Left This tulip-shaped Zsolnay vase from 1900 relies on a pod-like naturalistic form, with moulded leaves and branches picked out in contrasting iridescent colours. The glaze on the tulip head, known as Eosin, was developed in 1894 by Vilmos Zsolnay and Vinsce Wartha, and was used until well into the 1920s.

ZSOLNAY (HUNGARIAN, established 1862)

Until the 1890s, Zsolnay (pronounced "Jerni") produced ornate, Islamic-inspired pierced wares. Under the directorship of Vincse Wartha in 1893 the firm started to make decorative wares using relatively simple, organic forms and iridescent glazes, particularly inspired by the ceramics of Clement Massier. Vases, often thickly-potted, were sometimes decorated with low relief-moulded detail. Motifs included female figures, tree silhouettes and dark ruby skies, with lustrous surfaces, often with a multi-coloured iridescent glaze.

CLEMENT MASSIER (FRENCH, 1845-1917)

This plate was designed and decorated by Lucien Levy Dhurmer, one of Massier's leading designers. Typically, the decoration is applied over an opaque underlying glaze.
•Factory signatures are either painted or impress-marked.

Clement Massier took over his father's pottery workshop in 1883 to produce mainly earthenware vases and plaques – primarily a canvas for the subtle iridescent or lustre decoration which often gave his pieces the appearance of iridescent glass.

JOSIAH WEDGWOOD & SONS (BRITISH, founded 1759)

The pixies and goblins featured on this *Fairyland* bowl were unusual for the 1920s and hark back more to 1900. However, the modern shapes and bright colours made them popular.

During the Art Deco period Wedgwood produced a range of lustre wares which included *Chinese* and *Butterfly* lustre, and the *Fairyland* series illustrated by the bowl on the left, featuring underglaze enamels to create a smooth surface.

CARLTON (BRITISH, 1890-1957)

Carlton produced lustre wares, inspired by Wedgwood's *Fairyland* range. This vase is typical, with its bright and delicate design, hand-enamelled on a printed outline. The enamels, applied over the glaze, are slightly raised. The interior has a slightly iridescent, pearlized effect not found on Wedgwood's wares.

Carlton's lustre is generally on a cobalt blue ground (as were Wedgwood's), sometimes allied with a mottled tangerine-coloured matt glaze. Decorative features include butterflies, chinoiserie and naturalistic flora. For their lustre wares Carlton used as many as twelve colours, many of which were dark. Prices for Carlton's lustre range have increased dramatically in recent years, although they are still lower than for the more desirable lustre wares of Wedgwood.

SCANDINAVIAN STYLE

Scandinavia was at the vanguard of Art Nouveau design, with Bing and Grondahl's "Heron" service achieving great international acclaim and setting a precedent for other factories to use naturalistic motifs and organic forms. The Danish firm of Royal Copenhagen imitated this style with its simple shapes, clean lines and sensible decoration; and Arabia, the Helsinki based subsidiary of Rörstrand in Sweden, also produced some notable Art Nouveau designs. Only wares from the Rosenthal factory in Germany bore any real comparison at this time.

A Rörstrand tea service c.1900

BING & GRONDAHL (DANISH, 1853-Present)

This Copenhagen firm produced Art Nouveau-inspired pieces in stoneware and earthenware. Their best-known designer, F. August Hallin, had previously worked at Royal Copenhagen.

This tuilp vase echoes the pre-occupation with naturalism of Royal Copenhagen's director, Krog, for whom the designer of this piece, Effie Hegermann-Lindencrone, also worked. The Japanese-inspired pierced decoration and carving which give the piece an almost three-dimensional effect are typical.
•In 1888 the firm introduced its internationally acclaimed "Heron" service, designed by Pietro Krohn.

RÖRSTRAND (SWEDISH, 1726-Present)

Rörstrand, near Stockholm, was the premier Swedish porcelain factory at the turn of the century. It produced faïence, initially English in style, but later adopting European Art Nouveau designs. Wares have simple and balanced forms with relief-moulded decoration and colour-enamelling in a subdued palette of blue, grey and pink against an overall white reserve. Usefulness is combined with decoration. The handles and saucers of the tea set in the picture above are shaped like dragonflies, a typical Art Nouveau motif. Americans prefer the more avant-garde designs of Rörstrand, whereas the British prefer the more sudued designs of Royal Copenhagen.

Marks 19th century wares were printed with "R" or "Rörstrand". From 1884 a printed mark was used incorporating the three crowns of Marieberg.

ROYAL COPENHAGEN (DANISH 1775-Present)

Royal Copenhagen was established and run under royal auspices until 1883, when Arnold Krog, architect and ceramist, became art director and introduced his innovative glazing and decorative techniques which revolutionized output. The firm produced dishes and plaques painted mainly in soft blues, greys and pinks, with misty Danish scenes of birds, figures, landscapes and seascapes, as well as tablewares in novel, naturalistic forms, including teapots with dragonfly-shaped handles.

This classic Danish porcelain figure was designed by Professor Theodor Lundberg in 1899. Slip-cast, and hollow inside, it would have been mass-produced and hand-painted. Extremely well-controlled flesh tone glazes and dramatic postures produce a style unsurpassed in Lundberg's time. The symbolism, composition and the woman's flowing tresses are strongly Art Nouveau in style and the sense of movement is apparent in many Royal Copenhagen pieces.

Marks Marks can aid dating. The mark near right was used from 1894 to 1900, the central mark between 1894 and 1922, and the mark, far right, from 1905. Parian wares are marked "ENERET" meaning "copyright'. *The Rock and the Wave* is still produced today, so collectors should pay careful attention to marks.

THE AVANT-GARDE STYLE

In the 1920s and '30s a number of designers created some very original pottery with avant-garde forms, and with decoration that took inspiration from contemporary fashions and lifestyles for its themes and colours. In France, René Buthaud made hand-painted vases featuring African figures and dancers, many of which were reminiscent of the American dancer, Josephine Baker, and her performances in *La Revue Nègre*, and Primavera frequently used the female dancer as a decorative motif in its wares. In Belgium, Boch Frères echoed the vivid colours of the *Ballet Russe* in its enamel, floral decorated vases. The Cowan Pottery in America recreated the jazz age with its large bright bowls. More reserved was Keith Murray, working a little later in England, who created innovative geometric and mechanical forms for his pottery, which was rather severe and spartan.

An earthenware vase by René Buthaud, 1920s; ht 13in/33cm

RENÉ BUTHAUD (FRENCH, 1886-1986)

Buthaud initially trained as a silver decorator before going on to study art in Paris. As well as the pottery for which he is most remembered, he also produced graphics, watercolours and some stained-glass windows designs. The vase in the picture above is typical of his work with its central figure of an idealized female with a firm brown painted outline. Similar outlined women are used in his poster designs. The influence of other painters, especially Jean Dupas (see p.222) and Eugène Robert Pougheon, is often evident in his work. Other pieces had Neo-classical imagery.

Buthaud started to work in ceramics after the First World War, and his vases were first exhibited in 1920. He also produced faïence vases with hand-painted figural decoration similar to that used on his painted wares and again, often with brown or green outlines. Buthaud's ceramics consisted mainly of vases of simple, conventional form, either painted, crackle-glazed or *sgrafitto*, and usually with a stone or cream ground. Often they featured a painted rim.

•Buthaud was one of the first and most successful artists to incorporate African motifs into his work after the *Revue Nègre* performed in Paris.

This earthenware vase from the 1920s, incised with highly stylized mermaids, is typical of Buthaud's *sgrafitto* work, with its dark, chocolate-brown tones and paler underlying earthenware body. Other colours include blue-greys and iron-reds. Female subjects often have elongated forms and very stylized faces. Hair is usually rendered in waves giving a crimped effect, as in the vase at the top of the page.

Geometric designs often feature in Buthaud's decoration. Like this earthenware vase, geometric wares usually have a brown palette and are decorated in various tones of one main colour. Typically, the interlocked curves accentuate the almost spherical form.

Sgraffito Buthaud was a principal exponent of *sgrafitto*, Italian for "scratched". This is the technique by which a pottery body is dipped in a slip of another colour, through which the decoration is then carved.

Crackle-glazed vases Buthaud made a number of crackle-glazed earthenware vases. These bear either the painted mark "R. Buthaud", or the incised or painted monogram, "RB". Some have quasi-mythical figures, such as mermaids and fauns; others are decorated with pastoral elements or landscapes.

• The crackled glaze was also used by other potters, including Boch Frères (see over) and Royal Copenhagen (see p.135).

Availability Buthaud's work is much collected in Paris and New York and to a lesser extent in Britain. He was not prolific, and prices tend to be high. Fakes are not known, perhaps because of the difficulty of reproducing true signs of age.

PRIMAVERA (FRENCH, 1920s and '30s)

Primavera was the design studio of the Parisian department store *Au Printemps* and was one of the leading salons of the Art Deco period. The firm produced a range of ceramic wares, including figures and simple monochrome animal studies. Well-known Primavera designers include Jean Jacques Adnet, René Buthaud, Marcel Renard and Leon Zack.

Glazes Primavera earthenware tends to have a reddish tone, often with evidence of some gentle crazing, usually apparent from the inside, as is the case with the two pieces shown here. In the 1920s crackled glazes were made in electric kilns and were sometimes used as a ground for painting and other decoration – they were often used by René Buthaud. Crackle-glazed wares produced for Primavera were made by the Longwy factory and bear that name.

Condition The figure on the right has suffered some damage, notably on the shoulder, knee and drape. Although some blemishes can be disguised, the value is inevitably affected. However, as items are bought as much for their academic or scarcity value as for their decorative value, the fall in price is minimal.

Marks Hand-made Primavera wares are invariably signed on the base, usually by the potter/modeller and the decorator, and in addition always carry the Primavera mark. Signatures are either hand-painted or are impressed in block capitals. Moulded wares carry an incise-moulded signature.

This vase from 1925 is typical of Primavera's designs, with its stylized, almost unreadable, female figure. Like the designs of Buthaud, it incorporates a Negro motif, which appears on the reverse. The form is relatively simple but original, with a sculptural quality. The most desirable Primavera wares are the hand-made artist-decorated ones, although those made in a mould are also collectable.

Right This hand-painted signature from the base of the figurine, is Claude Levy's, one of Primavera's main decorators.

Primavera figures often convey a strong sense of movement. This female is unusual in not having the lithe figure commonly associated with Art Deco ladies. In particular, the legs are somewhat thick and unshapely. Nonetheless, the piece is recognizably of its period, with its stylized face, serpentine-like drape and the contrast between black and mottled ochre.

Left Madeleine Saugez, whose signature appears on the base of the vase, **above left**, was another important Primavera decorator.

Signatures A number of marks were used on Keramis wares: some pieces are stamped "KERAMIS MADE IN BELGIUM" with a painted design number. Others may be stamped "BOCH FES LA LOU-VIERE, FABRICATION BELGE". These may also have a style and pattern number. Others may bear the painted initials "B.F.K.", and a style number. Some pieces also bear the name of the designer: the elephant vase is inscribed "Keramis" with the painted mark "Ch. Catteau D.1082. B.F.K.

BOCH FRÈRES, KERAMIS (BELGIAN, mid-19thC)

The Belgian firm, Boch Frères, was founded in 1767 at Sept Fontaines in the Saarland, but by the mid-19th century, following a split, part of the firm established the manufactory, Boch Frères, Keramis, in Belgium to produce earthenware vases, tablewares, and candlesticks. Their wares of the mid-20s to the '40s represent the most important Belgian contribution to Art Deco. Some stonewares were also produced. All their pieces from this period are white-bodied.

The English artist Arthur Finch worked for Boch Frères as a decorator until 1930. His vases employ the large, swollen shape typical of the factory, but he used a red background in slip and glazed ochre to the dark green and blue motifs.

•Wares produced by Boch Frères are similar to Czech Amphora wares (see p.128), which are also heavily enamelled with incised, deeply moulded outlines.

Charles Catteau was the leading Art Deco Keramis designer. Characteristic motifs include animals in naturalized settings, such as penguins or leaping gazelles. This elephant vase also typifies his work in its monumental size (it is 4ft/1.2m high). It is decorated with thickly applied enamel motifs which stand out in relief from the background, which characteristically is of a thickly glazed ivory with a *craquelure* (crackled) effect.

Right This monumental earthenware vase from around 1925 features another typical Catteau motif of incised stylized flowers pendant from the rim. Favourite colours were deep green, blue, black and brown. The form, with its simple ovoid shape, little or no base and a narrow rim, is also typical. Later Catteau designs were more geometrically elaborate – for example, the ovoid form might be extended at the base, as in the elephant vase.

KEITH MURRAY (NEW ZEALANDER, 1892-1981)

Murray used a distinct range of glazes of matt, semi-matt or celadon satin, first developed in the Art Deco period. Some have names. The blue of this bowl is duck-egg blue, a popular clear pre-war glaze. Other colours include matt straw, matt green and matt grey.

Keith Murray spent most of his working life in England. A trained architect, his background is evident in the architectural, Modernist ceramic wares he produced in the 1930s and '40s. From the late 1930s he also made glass for the Staffordshire firm of Stevens & Williams (see p.68) and was one of the few designers in England to actively promote Modernist principles in his designs.

Right With its simple geometric form and lack of surface embellishment, this vase from c.1935 is instantly recognizable as Murray's work. Form and decoration are nearly always integral, as here. He specialized in vases, which are often ribbed and fluted, with narrow circular footrims. He also produced inkstands, bowls, candlesticks, tablewares and litho-printed commemorative wares celebrating Edward VIII. His slip wares were introduced after 1936 and continued in production until the mid-1950s. His simple functional designs continued to be popular during the 1940s.

Authenticity Murray's work, especially his vases and bowls, is much reproduced today. However, these modern wares, not intended to deceive, have a mass-produced, Constructivist look that distinguishes them from the originals, and they do not bear Murray's signature. If a piece is not marked, it is not Murray. Deliberate fakes have not so far appeared.

On items made after 1941 the initials "KM" and the Barlaston mark, **above**, are usually used. •Murray's black basalt wares, the rarest of all his products, are signed in red on the base.

The full script signature like this one, from the underside of the vase shown above left appears on pre-war items.

Annular *shape tea wares*

iris *pattern*   green tree *pattern*   lotus *pattern*

Wedgwood From 1933 Murray worked part-time for Wedgwood, designing several ranges of hand-thrown and hand-turned tablewares and other functional but ornamental items. He initially worked on the new Annular service, see **right**, which had two versions; one with a matt glaze, the other with painted decoration.
•Murray also designed patterns for tableware (bottom right). The most popular, designed from 1934, were *Lotus*, *Weeping Willow* (also known as *Green Tree*), *Iris*, *Pink Flower*, and *Pink and Red Flower*, as well as the border patterns *Lotus* and *Radio*.
•Pre-war pieces invariably have a smooth finish; post-war pieces are sometimes crazed.

COWAN POTTERY (AMERICAN, 1913-31)

Viktor Schreckengost specialized in ceramic decoration in a sophisticated modern style of uniquely American taste. His best-known work for Cowan Pottery is his design for the *Jazz* punchbowl (1930) made in an edition of 50, each slightly different, using *sgraffito* decoration, with images symbolic of the jazz age in New York.

This works, founded by Reginald Guy Cowan, produced mainly decorative vases and figurines. Most early designs were by Cowan himself. In 1927 the works included the Cowan Pottery Studio Inc. and over the next four years produced its most impressive and advanced designs, employing outside designers, including Waylande Gregory, Edward and Thelma Frazier Winter and Paul Manship. The "studio" lines issued in limited editions are highly collectable. Wares are usually slip-cast, with any painted decoration applied by hand and highly stylized, with minimal use of colour, although some polychrome statuettes in a bright, unnaturalistic palette are found. Statuettes, typically quite large, are slip-cast, and thus lightweight. Glazes are well applied and modelling well-executed.

Marks Pieces designed by Guy Cowan are marked with "Cowan" moulded in relief, sometimes with a monogram "R.G." below. Most Cowan products bear impressed, relief-moulded or printed marks, sometimes with the artist's name or monogram. "Lakeware" appears on some inexpensive flower vases (made for florists) between 1927 and 1931.

CLARICE CLIFF (BRITISH, 1899-1972)

Clarice Cliff dominated the British pottery scene during the late 1920s and '30s. She joined A.J. Wilkinson's Royal Staffordshire Pottery in Burslem in 1916, where she learned all aspects of pottery-making. In 1927 the firm recognized her talent and enthusiasm and set her up in a studio in their nearby Newport Pottery with a team of paintresses. The first pieces were very successful and she became a household name, continuing to produce a wide range of wares until the outbreak of the Second World War.

A Clarice Cliff teapot c.1935;
ht 4½in/11.5cm

Tablewares dominate the range but Cliff also designed book ends, candlesticks, figurines and masks. A distinctive and very extensive range of shapes and patterns was used. Many forms are highly innovative – exemplified by this cone-shaped sugar sifter, beehive honey pot and futuristic bowl, but Cliff also produced more traditional wares that represented an economically safe compromise. Her first successful range was *Bizarre Ware,* launched in 1928. Others followed soon after, with patterns gradually becoming more elaborate, although Cliff took care to ensure that each design was fully applicable to a full range of shapes and sizes.

Cliff designed all her own wares, which were then hand-painted, sometimes by a number of people in production-line fashion. The various ranges are named, as are some glaze techniques. Early geometric patterns are regular in design, and employ wide bands of colour. Later patterns are more abstract and use finer banding, sometimes to provide a textured background to floral or landscape motifs. Typically, both here and on the teapot above decoration is outlined in black. Many wares depict highly stylized landscapes. Cliff's pieces are earthenware, with a distinctive "honey glaze", warm and yellow-tinted, which gives an ivory colour. Glazing is not rigidly controlled. Enamels are usually laid on relatively thickly so that the brush strokes are visible.

•Lines were exclusive and were sold in many top department stores. As a result, there were many less expensive imitations on the market.
•Wares decorated with the *Inspiration* design and executed in the characteristic blue and lilac colour are particularly sought-after.

Right Many wares show cottages, especially with a red roof, in country gardens, or a house at the side of a hill. Trees are often drawn with long, spindly trunks surmounted by clouds of foliage. Whatever the motif, it is usually bold and decisive with bright, almost garish colours.

Left Cliff produced a series of masks, which includes some wall pockets, which are very collectable today – the geometric types are the most desirable. Cliff designed some of these pieces herself; others bear the incise-cast initials of the designer. The moulded floral garland seen here is popular: other Cliff masks also tended to feature various types of floral head-dresses. In Cliff masks the subject is shown face-on: on masks by rival firms they tend to be in profile.

Collecting Cliff pieces are usually collected by pattern or object, rather than in sets. *Crocus*, the earliest floral design, is the least collectable range because it was so popular at the time and, therefore, produced in large quantities. Similarly, the more traditional shapes are less desirable. Rare shapes, usually those with unusual rims or flanges, or those made in several sections joined together, are also desirable. Collectors like the strong geometric forms; floral moulded pieces tend to be ignored, as do the flower vases in water lily form. The rarest range is *Inspiration*, followed by others that use experimental techniques. Cliff's extensive range included many small objects, providing an opportunity for the collector of miniatures or for those with limited space or budget.

• Not all novelty items are as highly collectable – for example, Cliff toby jugs have never been in strong demand.

• Other leading Clarice Cliff designers included Dod Proctor, who designed a dinner service decorated with a lively horse motif, Graham Sutherland, and Frank Brangwyn, who designed large circular plaques decorated with figural subjects, originally intended for the House of Lords.

Marks and identification Pieces are marked in a variety of different ways. They often carry impressed dates, although these may indicate the date of production rather than of design or decoration. The pattern name was often given alongside the Clarice Cliff signature. Pattern names and signatures were initially hand-written; later they were stamped and eventually were lithographed. Pieces also carry the factory name, which was printed. Marked fakes exist but can usually be identified as such.

The pottery was produced by Wilkinson's at their Newport works in Stoke on Trent and their pattern books and contemporary advertisements can be used to identify patterns. Sometimes different names were used for the different colours in which patterns appeared.

 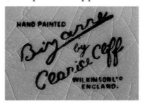

On genuine pieces the mark is usually smooth, like the *Fantasque* signature, **left**. A crackle effect like the one of the faked *Bizarre* signature, **right**, may be cause for suspicion (although a few genuine pieces have appeared with such crazing).

• On flatware, three circles or stilt marks around the signature where the pot stood in the kiln are a sign of authenticity.

• There are some genuine Clarice Cliff reproductions, but these are clearly dated.

• Hand-painted signatures and marks were phased out from around 1931.

Age of Jazz figures like these dancing couples are much sought after. They have a three-dimensional effect but are in fact free-standing plaques.

Above This plate was one of a set, designed in around 1934 by Laura Knight as part of her *Circus* series for Clarice Cliff, which although now very collectable was not a great commercial success in the 1930s. The borders and faces are printed, while the rest is hand-painted in stencil, then gilded.

Genuine Cliff can usually be distinguished from the many reproductions and fakes on the market, such as this fake jug. The standard of painting on fakes is usually poor and the colour enamels washed out. The honey glaze is often murky, and unevenly applied. This piece is relatively competent but lacks the definition of genuine pieces. Also, the handle is a little thin, and the unglazed footrim somewhat narrow and irregular. It shares with other fakes the tendency toward pronounced ribbing.

ENGLISH TABLEWARE—THE NEW APPROACH

A Susie Cooper tea set c.1935

After the first World War the major English potteries centred around Stoke on Trent, with the exception of Poole Pottery in Dorset. They all responded to a growth in demand for tea and tablewares and introduced new, relatively simple forms, complemented by stylized and innovative decoration. Bone china was most popular – nearly every English household possessed a china tea or dinner service. Earthenware was also used, especially by Susie Cooper for her tablewares, and the Poole Pottery, for mainly colourful ornamental products. Shelley catered for the mass market, producing bone china wares in geometric forms similar to those of Clarice Cliff's earthenware, but more conservative, and thus more acceptable to the English market. Noritake, although Japanese, created forms closely modelled on English designs, especially those of Royal Worcester, and employed such major designers as Frank Lloyd Wright (p.41) to produce hand-painted, table and ornamental wares.

THE SUSIE COOPER POTTERY (ENGLISH, 1929-42)

Marks Some of the Grays wares decorated by Susie Cooper have a printed back stamp and her initials SV (for Vera), C or SC. Cooper's designs were still used after she left the firm, although not always on the shapes she created them for. Pattern numbers during her time at Grays are from the late 2000s to the mid-8000s.

Decorative techniques Susie Cooper used a variety of techniques, including under- and over glazed decoration and experimented with new decorative methods, such as *sgrafitto*, crayons, and tube-lining. In the 1930s she produced a series of incised stonewares, decorated with leaves, flowers, dots or dashes.

Between 1922 and 1929 Susie Cooper worked for A.E. Grays & Co. Ltd in Staffordshire, initially as Assistant Designer, but soon making her own contribution to the company's style. She decorated a variety of wares in floral, abstract or, more rarely, geometric designs, buying in blanks from other factories. In 1929 she set up her own pottery in Staffordshire. From the mid-30s some designs were lithographed or transfer-printed, but retained a hand-finished feel. Colours became more subtle, favouring autumnal shades. The range included vases, jugs and tea and dinner sets. Clean, traditional designs were treated innovatively – tureens often had a self-supporting lid that could be turned upside down and used as a serving dish. The factory reopened in 1946 and continued in production until 1987, although Susie Cooper is still designing wares today.

Shapes and Patterns Most Susie Cooper wares have shape and pattern names and numbers. The teapot at the top of the page is in the *Kestrel* shape, introduced in 1932, and in production until the 1950s. Other shapes were *Curlew* (1933), *Wren* (1935), *Jay* (1935), *Falcon* (1937) and *Spiral* (1938) (see **left**). The pattern on the set above, *Dresden Spray*, has been transfer-printed. It was first used in around 1935 and was one of her most popular. Others include *Tadpoles, Scarlet Runner Beans, Nosegay* and *Polka Dots*. Patterns may appear on any number of forms.

Collecting The most collectable wares are those made before 1939. After the Second World War bone china replaced earthenware. Collectors of Susie Cooper will find a catalogue of her wares very helpful in distinguishing between pre- and post-War designs, especially as some designs from the 1920s and '30s have been reproduced since the war.

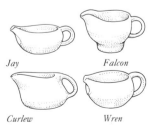

Jay

Falcon

Curlew

Wren

SHELLEY (ENGLISH, 1872-1966)

Designs were hand-painted in enamels and have a transfer-printed outline. Trees, flowers and the sun were popular motifs, and geometric designs were often used. Striking colour combinations include yellow and black and mauve and green. This tea set, in the *Queen Anne* shape, uses a *Blue Iris* pattern. Wares in jade green with a silver lustre trim are especially desirable. Colours became progressively more subdued and florals less stylized during the 1930s.

The factory, originally known as Wileman & Co., and later trading under the name "Foley", changed its name to Shelley in 1925, although the Shelley stamp had been used as early as 1910. During the 1920s and '30s the firm tempered more avant-garde lines with commercially safe classic shapes and designs. Many tea and dinner sets were made. Today complete sets are at a premium, especially those designed by Mabel Lucie Attwell. No fakes are known, although there are many contemporary look-alikes, as the firm set a standard for bone china in the 1920s and '30s.

Marks All genuine Shelley wares are marked, usually with a script signature inside a cartouche. Anything marked "Fine Bone China" is post-1945. Pattern numbers progressed from around 11,000 in the mid-1920s to around 13,000 in 1939. The serial number for seconds begins with a 2.

The most successful designs are simple. More innovative ones were often impractical: *Vogue*, above, and *Mode*, had solid handles.

Shelley used the talents of two illustrators, Mabel Lucie Attwell and Hilda Cowham, for its highly sucessful range of nursery wares. Some were decorated with characters from Attwell's own stories.

Shelley wares from the Art Deco period are very desirable, especially the shape *Eve*, shown left, which combines innovative design with practicality. The clean overlapping geometrics and iron-red and black trim are typical of the best Shelley. Rims often have a silver lustre or coloured bands.

ERIC RAVILIOUS (ENGLISH, 1903-1942)

Eric Ravilious produced attractive utility wares for Wedgwood during the late 1930s, which although not a huge commercial success at the time, are very popular with collectors today. He applied his decoration to traditional plain ceramic shapes and created tablewares deliberately designed to be mass-produced. Pieces tended to be printed in one colour and then tinted by hand with one or more colours. Shapes tended to be those of the firm's standard current tableware. Although Ravilious' wares were designed earlier, most were not executed until the 1950s. Some reissued by Wedgwood in 1987 in response to the recent increase in demand lack the originals' charactristic signs of wear.

This *Travel* teaset (1937) shows Ravilious' fascination with technology, with its motifs of boats, planes and trains in action. All ranges are still quite widely available.
•Pieces are signed in a small rectangular panel "designed by Eric Ravilious" and carry an imprinted Wedgwood mark.

This plate was part of a set of *Alphabet* nursery ware designed in 1937. Ravilious repeated his many designs on specific ranges of pottery, including *Persephone* (1938), with motifs of fish, fruit and other produce, *Afternoon Tea* (1937) and *Garden Implements* (1938), applied to outdoor earthenware.

Ranges Tableware shapes were introduced in larger ranges in 1933, but only in 1936 was the first competitive standard machine-made tableware, *Streamline*, produced. Pieces are collected by design rather than artist. The pottery's collectable ranges include:

•1933 *Studland*, a plain body with angular handles, in dark green, or blue with a mottled finish, or with modern leaf and floral patterns.

•c.1933 *Picotee*, rounded shapes, and *Everest*, ribbed, with solid diamond-shaped handles, both decorated in plain glaze colours.

•1936 *Streamline*, simplified traditional shapes, with two-colour glazes in subdued autumnal colours, known after 1945 as *Twintone*.

Marks Usually the base is impressed "Carter, Stabler, Adams Ltd" or "C.S.A.", and includes the decorator's monogram. If the base is unmarked, the piece is almost certainly not Poole. Some pieces have pattern codes, few are dated. Pieces after 1963 carry just the Poole mark.

This vase from around 1930 is typical of Carlton's geometric decorative wares – the firm's rarest and most collectable range of pottery. The form is simple. Dramatic effect is achieved through the juxtaposition of bright colours in motifs of formalized flower heads or brocades.

CARTER, STABLER & ADAMS (ENGLISH, established 1873)

This English firm operated from the Poole Pottery in Dorset and was established as Carter and Co. in 1873. In 1921 it expanded and became Carter, Stabler and Adams. It was an unusual and successful hybrid of an art and a commercial pottery, although it became increasingly commercial throughout the 1930s. The pottery produced some tablewares in the 1920s, but specialized in small, decorative, functional wares, such as vases, preserve jars and ashtrays. It also made some portrait plates depicting stylish faces, and a series of ship plates.

•Although not officially known by this name until 1963, the firm's early wares are sometimes known as, and described in auction house catalogues as, Poole.

Small morning tea and coffee sets were produced during the 1920s, but these were decorative rather than utilitarian. In this terracotta coffee set decoration is restrained when compared with Poole's ornamental wares.

The pottery is particularly associated with floral and bird patterns, usually in harmonious blends of deep, subtle colours under a matt glaze. Many pieces have a characteristic dentil rim or trim, usually picking up a colour from the decoration, as in this vase from around 1930. The predominance of blue in the painted decoration is typical.

• Hand-thrown pieces have irregular ribbing on the inside and a less clinical appearance than is usual with moulded wares.

CARLTON (ENGLISH, 1890-1957)

Another Stoke-based pottery producing tablewares during the 1920s and '30s was the Carlton Works, renamed Carltonware Ltd in 1958. They produced innovative matt-glazed ceramics in a variety of styles, which included geometric design work, exotically-coloured lustre art pottery and moulded tablewares, and small novelty items, such as dishes in the form of leaves. They were one of the first companies to produce oven-to-tablewares, but these pieces have yet to become popular with collectors.

Marks Individual designers are not identified; pieces carry the word "Carlton Ware" in script.

Shapes and decoration The firm's wide range of forms included some very popular inventive Modernist shapes as well as more traditional items. Colours tend to be bright, and decoration is hand-painted, often featuring stylized flowers.

This service shows the firm's later tendency to use pastel colours. The shape is typically inventive, and the decoration features characteristic gilding and geometric motifs.

NORITAKE (JAPANESE, established 1904)

The Japanese company, Noritake, produced hand-painted porcelain tablewares on a similar scale to the printed designs of the English potteries. From 1914 they made mostly tea and dinner wares, matching accessoreis and novelty pieces and figures. During the 1920s and '30s the design team was based in New York. Designs were executed in Japan and reimported to the United States, the major market for their more adventurous, and now most collectable, designs. They also designed wares for the British market, including hand-painted designs of Arab encampments, still fairly readily available in Britain, and French-type tea and decorative wares reminiscent of 18th century styles. Wares made for Europe are often lavish, many with gilt decoration.

Noritake executed wares by a number of top designers. This six-piece porcelain place setting designed by Frank Lloyd Wright in 1922 displays Noritake's typically modernistic decoration, which tended to use geometric or cubist motifs, often outlined in black. The ground of fine white porcelain is usually relatively free of any imperfections.
•Wares are marked on the base, usually with the words "Noritake" and "MADE IN JAPAN". Pieces are not dated, so collectors should try to check the date of the design with contemporary catalogues or specialist books. Later marks include "Noritake Nippon Tokikaisha Japan".
•Copies of Noritake's less adventurous wares exist, usually executed by smaller Japanese factories for export, mostly to Europe, bearing a variety of marks on the base, such as "Nippon" and "Samurai".

STUDIO POTTERS

A Pilgrim stoneware dish
by Bernard Leach c.1930

From the late 1920s a number of potters began to concentrate on producing hand-made and hand-decorated art pottery. Bernard Leach set up his St. Ives pottery after a visit to Japan and became the first British potter to demonstrate a true understanding of Oriental ideas about art, with the Japanese potter, Shoji Hamada becoming a lifelong friend of his. Many students, including Michael Cardew, flocked to Leach's pottery to further their knowledge of both pottery and Oriental decorative techniques. Working at the same time as Leach was William Staite-Murray, who although less emulated, was commercially better-known, his work being collected by the London cognoscenti and also widely exhibited in numerous West End galleries.

BERNARD HOWELL LEACH (HONG KONG, 1887-1979)

Bernard Leach came to London from Hong Kong and attended the Slade and the London School of Art, where he studied etching under Frank Brangwyn. On his return to Japan in 1909 he met the potter, Tomi Moto, together with whom he was honoured with the title of "seventh Kenzan" after a family of great Japanese potters. In 1920 he returned to England with Shoji Hamada to establish his pottery at St. Ives and they held their first joint exhibition in London in 1923, and another alongside Staite-Murray in Japan in 1926.

Leach's pottery is particularly well-known for its harmony between body and glaze, and for the use of a wide range of decorative techniques, such as brushwork, stencils, slip decoration and stamped relief motifs. The fine stoneware dish above is decorated with a pilgrim, a recurrent and highly sought-after motif in Leach's work, created here using his wax-resist technique of glazing.

During his time at St. Ives Bernard Leach made a number of slab bottles with a complicated panel form, raised upon a narrow, near-oval foot. On this bottle a mushroom glaze has been applied and the front and back have been quartered with two panels washed in blue, each panel with an Oriental-inspired iron-red decoration. This example bears the BL impressed mark and the pottery seal, but as

often occurs, the mark has been obscured by the glaze.
•These slab vases were the subject of a forgery scandal in England in 1980/1, when a number of deliberate fakes were produced by inmates in an open prison during their pottery recreational periods. These are often identifiable by their strange glazes and unusual proportions. Most were recovered by investigating police.

This stoneware vase is of a characteristically strong, robust form. The upper section has an irregular olive-green and brown glaze band and has been decorated with another popular Leach motif of stylized willow leaves. Like the pilgrim dish above, this vase also employs the wax-resist technique. The lower body, which has been wiped free of glaze to leave the seal mark uncovered, is impressed with the BL and St. Ives seals.

Marks Most pieces bear the impressed BL monogram within a rectangle and the seal of the St. Ives Pottery, plus the letters S and I, crossed with two dots within a square or circle. Alternatively, the mark may be painted.

This stoneware "fish" vase was a popular design during Leach's St. Ives years. The mushroom glaze with iron-brown brush-work depicting two bands of leaping salmon is similar to decoration on Chinese Tzu-Chou wares, made from the Ming Dynasty to the present.

SHOJI HAMADA (JAPANESE, 1894-1978)

The Japanese art potter Shoji Hamada studied the glazes of early Chinese wares and his initial work was strongly influenced by the Korean ceramics of the Yi dynasty. Hamada concentrated on producing stoneware vases and useful wares in strong simple shapes and soft colours, often of brown, olive, grey and black, and incorporating free brushwork decoration frequently with abstract or naturalistic motifs. He travelled to England with Bernard Leach in 1920, giving him advice and support in setting up the St. Ives pottery, and it is Hamada's work at this pottery which is his most rare and collectable today. Hamada returned to Japan in 1923, where he spent the rest of his working life.

On this cut-sided stoneware bottle Hamada has used a *ten-moku* glaze over a red body. This is the only real decoration, and although the design is seemingly random, it is in fact controlled. The form, like those used by Leach, is strong and robust.
•Many pieces are illustrated in one of the first definitive works on Leach and his contemporaries, Muriel Rose's *Artist-Potters in England*, which gives such pieces added status.

Marks Early pieces from the St. Ives pottery are signed with an impressed signature alongside the name of the pottery. From then on pieces are unsigned, but many, like the three examples featured here, are in fitted wooden boxes that bear his signature. Other marks include a Japanese seal within a rectangle.

Right The wax-resist technique employed for the decoration on this fine stoneware dish gives a very controlled effect. The plant design seems relatively spontaneous, and as on many of Hamada's pieces appears to be more relaxed than the designs found on Leach's pieces, where decoration is more controlled, and often features repeat motifs. Hamada is also more likely to allow his glazes to run, although this is not true of the piece here.

Above This pot is very close in form to a late 16th century *alberello* (drug jar). Once again, Hamada makes use of the *ten-moku* glaze, which in this case is further decorated with a three finger-wipe design. The collar neck is decorated with a textured green glaze which has run and pacified in certain areas.

CHARLES VYSE (ENGLISH, 1882-1971)

Unlike the other studio potters mentioned here, Charles Vyse grew up in the Potteries. He was apprenticed to Doulton & Co. as a modeller in 1896. His talent won him a five-year scholarship to the Royal College of Art in 1905, which included a travelling scholarship to Italy. By 1911 he had become a member of the Royal Society of British Sculptors.

In 1919 Vyse set up his studio with his wife, Nell, in Cheney Walk, which was essentially a commercial venture, employing several workers. They made a series of cast pottery figures depicting local characters of the area, such as *Punch and Judy*, *Daffodil Woman* and *Madonna of the World's End*, as well as high-fired Chinese and Japanese-inspired vases and bowls. In 1940 the studio was bombed and Vyse became a modelling and pottery instructor at the Farnham School of Art, whilst at the same time continuing to make his own wares.

Marks Pieces are either marked with Vyse's painted or incised initials or his signature in varying forms, together with the date. His figures and groups also incorporate the word Chelsea in the mark.
Glazes Vyse made frequent use of Oriental glazes, including the *chün* glaze on the vase featured here. Other glazes used by Vyse include *tenmoku* and *celadon* (see opposite).
Collecting Vyse is sometimes accused of being rather tame, as his pieces are often very close to their Oriental inspiration and may show a lack of originality.
However, his work is always of very high quality, and is therefore collectable in its own right.

This attractive grey glazed vase is of a gently lobed form and is decorated with a finely crazed Oriental *chün*-type glaze, which can be identified by the slightly reddy-pink tinge around the neck.

•Original examples of Chinese pottery with *chün* glazes are keenly sought after and very expensive – they tend to have more definite splashes of the pink colour than in Vyse's pieces.

WILLIAM STAITE-MURRAY (ENGLISH, 1881-1962)

This vase from around 1924 is typical of Staite-Murray's attempt to combine finishes – in this case an irregular and pitted grey-green glaze streaked in pale blue is combined with a foot rim which has been wiped clear of any glaze.
• Staite Murray's decorative techniques show an obvious similarity to those of Hamada, whom he greatly admired.

William Staite-Murray experimented with pottery and bronze casting between the years 1912 and 1915, setting up his Yeoman Pottery in Kensington with Cuthbert Hamilton. He opened a second pottery in Rotherhide in 1919, and in 1926 he was appointed the Head of the Pottery Department at the Royal College of Art. As well as visiting Leach at his St. Ives pottery, Murray was in contact with, and strongly influenced by, Hamada.

Staite-Murray was regarded in his day as the most famous and successful potter of the pre-war years, with much of his work exhibited in London galleries for quite large sums, but although a leading figure, he was not as influential as Leach in the art schools of Britain.

Oriental glazes

Tenmoku Originally used on Chinese Chien ware, this is a black or brownish-black glaze, sometimes with a silvery iridescence, which may form rings, or have blue or grey streaks.

Chün Named after kilns founded in the Sung period at Chün Chous, this is an opalescent blue, thick glaze, with purple or crimson *flambé* which varies according to the degree of oxidation of copper in the glaze.

Celadon A translucent glaze applied to Japanese pottery, in varying shades of green, which changes depending on the amount of copper present. The original glaze from the early Sung dynasty has a jade-like quality.

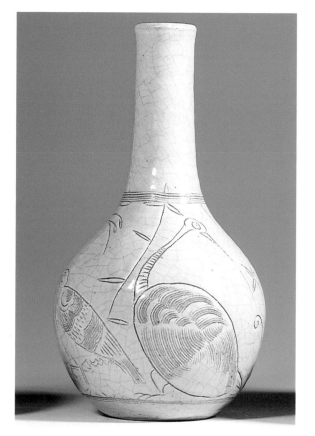

Marks Pieces are incised with the WS monogram, within a pentagram, dated, with a model number and the pottery, the piece on the left being stamped "London" to indicate the Rotherhide pottery.

Staite-Murray tended to use strong and often large forms complemented by interesting glazes and decorated in vibrant brush strokes. His work was often inspired by the Orient, as can be seen in the form of this bottle vase. The cream crazed glaze has been incised through to the underlying dark body with a highly individual design of birds, fish and plants.

MICHAL CARDEW (ENGLISH, 1901-83)

Cardew's enthusiasm for pottery led him to visit Bernard Leach's St. Ives pottery in 1923. He became apprenticed to Leach the following year, staying there until 1926, when he set up his own pottery near Winchcombe, Gloucestershire, to make domestic wares which concentrated on slip-trailed decoration, popular during the late 17th and early 18th century in Britain. In 1939 he set up a second pottery at Whenford Bridge.

Marks Pieces are impressed with the MC monogram and the pottery seal mark.

Cider jugs, typical of Cardew's useful wares, were always popular. The upper section of this jug is painted with green slip, which has been drawn through the brown background to give a continuous serpentine band, which, like the bird motif, has become synonymous with Cardew's pottery.

These two plates feature a simplified bird design, which was commonly used by Cardew on his stoneware. On the plate on the left he has used slip-trailed decoration, whilst the plate on the right, although incorporating the same stylized bird motif, has been painted in blue upon an irregular grey-glazed surface. Both these pieces were made at the Winchcombe pottery.

SCULPTURE

Early Victorian sculpture continued to be strongly influenced by the Neo-classical tastes popular during the reigns of William IV and George IV. The work of the foremost classical-style sculptors, such as John Gibson and Sir Matthew Digby Wyatt, continued to reflect that of the Roman artist Canova and the Englishman, John Flaxman. Early 19th century sculpture, life-size and in marble, was the preserve of the rich and aristocratic. However, Cheverton's reduction machine facilitated small-scale and identically proportioned copies of existing sculptures, and its presence at the 1851 Great Exhibition led to an increase in demand for small sculpture. Queen Victoria's taste ensured the popularity of romantic and sentimental sculpture – she particularly favoured Sir Edgar Boehm (1834-1890), and Sir Edwin Landseer, whose work was transformed into sculptures. A group of "New Sculptors", headed by Frederick, Lord Leighton, attempted to capture more daring, unrecorded moments and postures in their work. Invariably in bronze, these sculptures have a dark patination and are mounted on plain plinths, usually of the waisted socle (circular) type. The same passion for realism and adherence to classical proportions, techniques and materials inspired American sculptors of the period, notably Hiram Powers. In France and Britain the work of the animaliers predominated.

The most popular methods of casting during the Victorian period were *cire perdue* ("lost wax", solid casting, see p.240); sand-casting, where the piece is cast in sections, joined and patinated; and electrotype, not generally sought after today. *Cire perdue* pieces command a premium.

By the early 20th century sculpture became much more widespread. Form and decoration became increasingly interdependent and sculptural elements were used to decorate useful objects – Raoul-François Larche and Leo Laporte-Blairsy were the first sculptors to apply their sculptural forms to the newly-invented electric light. The female form was the central decorative element, usually with an ethereal, dreamlike expression and flowing hair. Forms and motifs from nature were also important. British sculptors continued to rely on the ethics of the "New Sculptors", and rather than the symbolistic approach of the Continent, concentrated on more impressionistic elements.

Much Art Nouveau sculpture was mass-produced in Germany, largely based on French examples. The work of the Viennese Gustav Gurschner is highly collectable, but has only recently been fully appreciated, particularly his figural table lamps with iridescent glass shades by Loetz. Little fine Art Nouveau sculpture was produced in the United States, except by Whitney Frishumth (1880-1980) and Frederick MacMonnies (1863-1937). Sand-casting was the most popular method of production at this time.

The Art Deco years saw a revival of sculpture as an art form for the masses, replacing the expensive one-off art objects made before the First World War. France was the main centre of production, followed by Germany and Austria. German figures tend towards athletic, modernistic types; French figures are evocative of the frivolous jazz age.

Common subjects include athletic and Amazonian women, as in the work of the Frenchman, Marcel Bouraine; futuristic or theatrical studies, exemplified by the Romanian, Demètre Chiparus; and figures performing modern activities. Erotic subjects, such as those of the Austrian, Bruno Zach, are especially collectable; historical figures are less keenly sought-after. Sporting subjects are popular, as are pierrots and pierrettes, children, and exotic animals, especially those of a sleek and speedy nature, often pursued by Diana-type figures. Most were of bronze, or chryselephantine – a combination of bronze and ivory which was popular in the 1920s and today commands a premium. Gilt and silver patination were often applied. Bases became important features – green Brazilian onyx, black slate and cream-striated marble were popular materials.

Victorian sculpture was rarely faked, except the work of the French animaliers, particularly P. J. Mêne. Faking abounded in the Art Nouveau period, even though most pieces are signed and many bear a foundry mark. A Larche lamp with the right foundry mark may be a copy – many have been made in Paris in the last 15 years. There are many Art Deco fakes on the market. Simulated chryselephantine of bronzed spelter combined with plastic ("ivorene") can be hard to identify as the bronze patination can be quite thick – genuine pieces have a yellow base metal. Most fakes are inferior, with suspicious, unconvincing patination, often excessively worn in the wrong places – dirt is sometimes forced into crevices to falsify signs of age. There should be no mould lines. Fakes are usually applied to very heavy bases, often marble, to make the overall piece seem heavier and therefore more authentic.

Above *A Lorenzl gilt-bronze figure of an exotic dancer, c.1930.*
Right *A Hagenauer silvered metal and wood figure, c.1920*

THE NEO-CLASSICISTS

Sculpture in the Neo-classical style was already popular in Britain when Queen Victoria's reign began. Pieces were mainly in marble, large-scale and figural, and because of their size and high price were primarily for aristocracy and monied people. Themes were historical or classical and many of the subjects were of an Anglo Saxon or Northern European origin. As Queen Victoria's reign progressed, the figures gradually adopted Victorian faces and features, even though they were still dressed classically. Many pieces were exhibited at the Great Exhibition of 1851, where the biggest attraction was *The Greek Slave* by Hiram Powers. Often naked or semi-naked, these figures were in complete contrast to the styles generally accepted by the puritanical Victorians who insisted upon propriety of dress and manners.

Tinted Venus, a wax-tinted marble sculpture by John Gibson c.1862; ht 69in/175cm

JOHN GIBSON (ENGLISH, 1790-1866)

John Gibson attempted to imitate precisely the subjects and methods of the Greek sculptors. The sculpting of his celebrated *Tinted Venus*, pictured left, involved the Ancient Greek practice of covering the piece with a flesh-coloured wax overlay in an attempt to add a realistic skin-tone. His subjects are almost always classical or sentimental. The execution of his pieces tends to be stiff and lifeless, resulting in a contrived posture and stance. Faces are generally bland with a characterless expression. Typical to the Neo-classicists, the figure is partially clad, with drapery used primarily for modesty.

EDWARD HODGES BAILY (ENGLISH, 1788-1867)

A prolific artist and sculptor, Baily was responsible for many prestigious public commissions. His idealized subjects are often perfect embodiments of physique and youth. Baily's sculptures are often smaller than those of his contemporaries and tend to be more affordable.

The young, athletic subject of *The Tired Hunter* is typical. The proportions of the piece and the muscularity of the subject are classical, but the facial detail, hairstyle and the contrived positioning of the drapery are obviously Victorian.

JAMES WYATT II (ENGLISH, 1808-1893)

In *Lila Asleep*, a portrait of the artist's daughter, the realistic and detailed face contrasts with the relative blandness of many Neo-classical subjects.

A member of the hugely talented Wyatt dynasty, James Wyatt II began his career executing his father's sculptural designs, especially those with an equestrian aspect. His work tends to be more sentimental than austerely classical as seen in *Lila Asleep*, on the left.

•Cushion bases were a popular feature of pre-Victorian sculpture. Fellow designer, John Bell, produced several studies of children at prayer on similar cushion bases.

JOHN HENRY FOLEY (ENGLISH, 1818-1874)

Although it was produced in marble, this version of *The Norseman* is innovative in its use of bronze, a material rarely used during the early 19th century, but which became very popular as the century progressed.

Often referred to as the last of the Neo-classicists, Foley's work hints at the New Sculpture to come (see pp.156-7). There are still strongly Neo-classical elements – for example, the convenient drapery and the rather stilted pose of *The Norseman*, yet a sense of drama and a meaningful gesture save it from being lifeless.

THE ANIMALIERS

During the Italian Renaissance animaliers from Padua produced wonderful animal bronzes of bulls and horses which were full of life. Since that time there had been few animal figures of any merit produced until the 19th century when a group of French sculptors emerged who concentrated on producing animal and bird figures on a scale unprecedented since the Egyptian times. Pierre Jules Mêne was probably at the forefront, producing bronzes that were full of drama, movement and fine detail and were often humorous (for example, in his piece called *Monkey Derby*). Sculptors responded to various inventions, such as the reducing machine, developed by Benjamin Cheverton in 1828 (see also p.104), to make small affordable pieces for the newly wealthy Victorians, who liked to surround themselves with nature, often in the form of stuffed birds.

Le Prise du Renard-chasse en Ecosse (After the Hunt in Scotland) by P. J. Mêne, 1861; ht 21¼in/54cm

•Animal sculptures enjoyed a revival in the 1920s and '30s, but in more streamlined and simplified forms. They were designed to complement the furniture of the time and tended to be panthers, antelopes, bears, sea birds, monkeys and dolphins – wild animals juxtaposed against very modernist interiors and furnishings (see p.170).

PIERRE JULES MÊNE (FRENCH, 1810-1979)

Mêne invariably demonstrates very precise detailing and an excellent sense of balance in his sculptures. These vary in size, although figural groups rarely exceed two feet (61cm) in height. The smallest works can be as little as 6 or 7in (15-17cm) high. Bases, which are usually elongated, are of uniform casting, and they often act as a naturalistic setting for the piece.

Many of Mêne's groups incorporate whippets, such as those featured in this piece. Both dogs are in the rich dark brown favoured by the animaliers in general and Mêne in particular. Check that the piece is complete. Sometimes the ball the animals are playing with is missing.

Mêne's best-known works are the groups. Scottish subjects, such as *Le Prise du Renard-chasse en Ecosse*, were popular during the Victorian period, largely due to the enthusiasm of Prince Albert for the Scottish Highlands. Many other works of the period show idealized Scottish scenes or characters. Another version of the group above exists in silver.

Fakes and copies After his death a number of Mêne's sculptures were cast in bronze by A. N. Cain, Susse Frères and Ferdinand Barbedienne. These bear Mêne's signature and foundry mark, usually cast into the base. Some copies were made by Coalbrookdale and bear that name.

Horses Mêne's horse studies are very popular, especially those that incorporate a jockey, particularly if the subject is depicted high in the saddle, or "with jockey up". The horses invariably have a rectangular outline on the underside of the belly. This is because in the casting the piece is filled with fireclay which is subsequently emptied out, the hole then being covered with a plate. Occasionally, fragments of the fireclay get trapped inside, causing the piece to rattle when shaken.

Condition Animal sculptures tend to be extremely vulnerable, especially around any tails, ears or hooves. They should never be lifted by their legs as these are prone to snapping.

As well as some stylized pieces of stately animals bearing noble subjects, Barye also sculpted naturalistically rendered, humbler creatures, such this *Half-bred Horse*.

Later pieces often use a combination of patinations to achieve a lively effect. This bronze reading bear from around 1850 employs rich red and brown. The "FRATIN" signature is visible on the front of the base.

This *Cockerel and Stoat* shows Moigniez's accurate understanding of anatomy and plumage and his attention to detail – the feathers are ruffled and hair carefully delineated. Some sculptures appear as embellishments to other items.

ANTOINE-LOUIS BARYE (FRENCH, 1796-1875)

Barye was among the first of the animaliers and exhibited as early as the 1830s. Less prolific than Mêne, he used the *cire perdue* method to cast bronzes, resulting in unique casts (see p.240). His subjects tend to be spirited and shown in dramatic situations.

Marks Most of Barye's sculptures bear an incise-cast signature, usually in capital letters, and are numbered. In the late 1840s and '50s, some less successful castings were produced by Barye's creditor E. Martin. These are generally signed by Martin and not numbered. After Barye's death, some of his casts were edited by the Barbediènne foundry. These bear Barye's signature and the foundry mark but are not numbered.

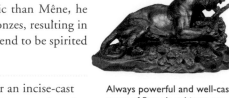

Always powerful and well-cast, many of Barye's subjects are shown hunting other animals – for example, a hound chasing a stag, a tiger leaping on an antelope, or, as in this example, a lion about to devour an owl.

CHRISTOPHE FRATIN (GERMAN, 1800-1864)

Although born in Germany, Fratin worked in France. He is remembered for his highly individual treatment of animals, especially bears, in human situations and postures. The quality of casting and chiselling, and the attention to detail are excellent. His work was produced by such founders as Susse Frères and E. Quesnel.

As well as bears, both anthropomorphic and naturalistic, Fratin depicted other animals, such as monkeys and retrievers, some of which are thought to be parodies of notable people of the period. Many are humorous – the bear, **left**, is smoking a pipe. Others show violent scenes – for example, horses being attacked by wolves.

Characteristics Many of the sculptures are quite small – some as little as 5in (14cm) high.
• Early bronzes had an irregular matt black patination; on these some of the yellow metal beneath is evident and the recesses are very black.
• Some pieces are gilded over the bronze.

JULES MOIGNIEZ (FRENCH, 1835-94)

Moigniez is best known for his sculptures of birds, but he also produced animals, some in a style similar to that of Mêne. However, his work is often more detailed than Mêne's with less emphasis on the patination. Moigniez favoured brown patination, sometimes with gilt highlights. Bases are usually shallow and plinths waisted. Moigniez produced a series of caskets which incorporate birds and are also very collectable. All his work is signed.

Note Even fairly tame birds convey an element of ferocity – they are often open-mouthed or poised to pounce and represent a departure from the gentle love birds of earlier sculptors.

EMANUEL FREMIET (FRENCH, 1824-1910)

Unlike Moigniez, Fremiet, although a keen observer of animals and birds, concentrated on these creatures' more endearing and sympathetic qualities, which perhaps explains why he was one of the most popular sculptors of his day. He also depicted equestrian groups, and some wilder animals, such as gorillas. These pieces are generally later than the domestic sculptures, dating from the 1860s or later. Fremiet's work is not as easily found as the work of the other sculptors featured in this section.

Friendly domestic groups form the bulk of Fremiet's output. This *Kitten and a Chick*, with dark brown patination and careful detail on the coat and feathers, is typical.

THE BONHEURS (FRENCH, ROSA, 1822-99; ISIDORE, 1827-1901)

During the 19th century Rosa Bonheur was the better known of these two artists, although she produced fewer sculptures. A celebrated painter, her works were a favourite with Queen Victoria and Napoleon III. Her pieces are still more collectable than her brother's, although often it is hard to distinguish between her work and Isidore's.

Rosa Bonheur designed a number of farm animals, including several bull studies. This *Walking Bull* admirably captures the strength and power of the animal. The dark brown patination and waisted base are typical of her sculptures.

Note Isidore Bonheur's most sought-after works today are his horse and jockey groups, some as high as 2ft (61cm). A number of fakes have been offered for sale. The bases on these are usually uneven and imprecise.

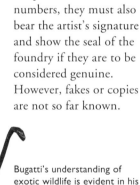

Like Rosa, Isidore concentrated on strong or powerful studies of bulls, often in more dramatic postures than those depicted by his sister. This prancing bull is one of a pair with a standing bull, cast in three sizes. Isidore's subjects usually stand on a naturalistically rendered base, which bears his incise-cast signature and the stamp of the founder Hippolyte Peyrol. Patination is almost invariably brown.

REMBRANDT BUGATTI (ITALIAN, 1885-1916)

As the son of Carlo Bugatti (see p.42), and younger brother of Ettore, the automobile designer, Rembrandt Bugatti came from a truly remarkable family. Although his career spanned a mere 15 years, Bugatti created some of the finest animal sculptures ever produced.

Unlike earlier 19th century animaliers, Bugatti attempted to capture the personality or the spirit of the animal in his work. The modelling of his 150 bronze sculptures shows an acute understanding of natural forms. Bugatti concentrated on exotic wildlife, and created few studies of domestic animals. From 1907, he worked in Antwerp, home at that time of Europe's finest zoo, which provided both inspiration and the models for his pieces. He was awarded the Legion d'Honneur in 1911.

Above This elephant illustrates many characteristic features of Bugatti's work. The impressionistic form coveys the character of the elephant, while the sculpted, uneven surface suggests the texture of the animal's skin. The size (22in/57cm) is typical. The surface colour of the bronze is a rich, dark brown. On many other Bugatti pieces the patina is nearly black.
•Nearly all of Bugatti's pieces were cast by the Hébrard foundry, using the *cire perdue* ("lost wax") method, where a hollow wax mould is first made of the artist's original clay model which is then encased in plaster. When molten bronze is poured in, the wax melts and flows away and is "lost".

Marks Although some of Rembrandt Bugatti's sculptures have edition numbers, they must also bear the artist's signature and show the seal of the foundry if they are to be considered genuine. However, fakes or copies are not so far known.

Bugatti's understanding of exotic wildlife is evident in his pieces, although the figures often seem posed. In this pair of leopards it is the stance rather than the detail of the modelling that evokes the animals' spirit and personality. The wooden plinth is uncommon, and may have been attached to the original thin bronze base some time after manufacture.

Animal sculpture fakes In recent years there have been a massive number of fakes appearing on the market, most emanating from France and Canada, and many complete with fake signatures as well. These lack the precision of detail of the originals and many have a waxy type of patination which seems to attract and accumulate dirt, especially in the crevices and incise-cast detail. On originals dust tends to be less apparent. Often the bases lack signs of wear and the underside is likely to appear unnaturally bright. Also, any screws and bolts may be overbright if they are new, or they may be artificially rusted to suggest age.

NEW SCULPTURE

The Sluggard, a bronze sculpture by Lord Leighton c.1890; ht 20¾in/53cm

Availability Leighton also produced a number of larger sculptures, which are often marble. Such pieces were comparatively expensive, and tended to be bought only by the more wealthy. They are relatively scarce today, perhaps because many have been kept in the family of the original owner.

Several like-minded sculptors, headed by Frederick, Lord Leighton, were working during the last quarter of the 19th century and the early 20th century, to produce what is referred to as New Sculpture. With their more expressive and impressionistic approach they strove to throw off the shackles of the Neo-classicists and breathe new life into figures taken from classical, contemporary and medieval times. Their emphasis on realistic detail and experimentation with unusual postures is exemplified by the highly original stance of *The Sluggard* by Leighton on the left.

FREDERICK, LORD LEIGHTON (ENGLISH, 1830-96)

Primarily a painter, Leighton was seen as the pioneer of the New Sculpture movement. He made clay models of his subjects to help in picture composition, and a casting in bronze of his *Athlete Wrestling with a Python* led to a marble version which, reduced in size, became the cast for his first commercially produced statuette.

Sculpted from a series of relaxed sittings by an artist's model, *The Sluggard* represents a complete departure from the Neo-classical subjects of the earlier Victorians. It displays a true sense of movement, despite a lethargic facial expression. The rich chocolate brown patination is typical, as is the simple, square undecorated base. Like most of Leighton's pieces, it bears the publisher's details: it is signed, entitled and inscribed "Published by Arthur Leslie Collie, 39B Old Bond Street, London May 1st 1890"

Note The popularity of the bronze statuette led to the establishment of several foundries in England, including the London-based Collie Foundry, which published some of Leighton's and Thornycroft's pieces.
Methods All of Leighton's work uses the sand-casting method (see p.241). This creates the superbly light and thin casting that is characteristic of his work.

Some of Leighton's subjects are given a humorous treatment, such as this girl taking fright from a toad. Typically, this piece is simplified almost to the point of being impressionistic, with an emphasis on posture and the drama of the situation. Leighton generally preferred simple bases.

SIR ALFRED GILBERT (ENGLISH, 1854-1934)

This sculpture of *Perseus Arming*, from around 1882, uses the *cire perdue* (lost wax) casting method (see p.240), which gives it a solid, seamless appearance. Gilbert tended to subtly alter re-casts or copies of his originals – examples of *Perseus Arming* exist with horizontal, forward-pointing helmet wings, unwinged sandals (or no sandals at all) and straight-bladed swords.
•Gilbert's civic sculpture includes the famous Shaftesbury memorial surmounted by the statue of *Eros* at Piccadilly Circus in London.

Gilbert was one of the most public sculptors of the late Victorian era, receiving many public commissions, including several for the Royal Family. He worked mainly in bronze, although occasionally in aluminium, to produce sculptures, with fine muscular detail and natural, even casual, poses, which foreshadow the later Art Nouveau style. Subjects include mythical and allegorical figures and saints or realistically conveyed well-known contemporary figures.

Gilbert tended to make several smaller, often miniature versions of his monumental or commissioned pieces and it is these that are generally found today. He later included enamel, or relief panels and plinths, occasionally executed using copper electrotyping.

SIR EDGAR BERTRAM MACKENNAL (AUSTRALIAN, 1863-1931)

Mackennal came to Europe in 1882, working mainly in Paris, but also in London, in a style influenced by French Symbolism and Romanticism. A popular craftsman, he was commissioned to design George V's coronation medal, the obverse of the new coinage, and postage stamps. His bases and plinths are unusual and inventive, often decorated with figures or motifs that reflect the theme of the piece. Mackennal was also commissioned to do some maquettes for memorials, including some mother and child groups and bas-reliefs, which are less sought-after.

Many of Mackennal's pieces, like this bronze figure of *Circe* (c.1893) exist in a life-size version as well as in the form of small statuettes. Mainly in bronze, a few marble works also exist. The life-size *Circe* is mounted on a base depicting a *mêlée* of naked figures, which caused so much outrage when exhibited at the Royal Academy in London in 1894 that it had to be covered so as not to "corrupt" the public.

SIR W. H. THORNYCROFT (ENGLISH, 1850-1925)

Also working in a realistic style was Thornycroft, who created a series of life-size plaster statues of subjects drawn from Greek mythology. Many of his pieces break from tradition by depicting figures in everyday poses – for example, he produced a sculpture, entitled *The Mower*. Thornycroft also made smaller copies of his figures in bronze, issued as limited editions, as well as replicas in plaster. Patination was dark, and was usually either brown or green.

Marks Most of Thornycroft's models are signed, dated and numbered and they are not known to have been faked.

Exhibited in 1880 at the Royal Academy as a life-size plaster cast, *Artemis and her Hound* was so well received that a marble version was commissioned for the Duke of Westminster's home. The novel arrangement of Artemis' gown and the revealing of her breast lend this figure an originality symptomatic of the new movement in English sculpture.

ALBERT TOFT (ENGLISH, 1862-1949)

Toft learned sculpture at Wedgwood and Elkington and Co., and opened his own studio in London to produce bronze figural pieces, usually with a rich brown patination. His work often shows the influence of Bertram Mackennal. His female figures have more of an ethereal feel to them than the sculpture of Gilbert.

The arms of this bronze figure of *Peace* are typically expressive and gesturing. The figure here holds a winged tribute; others hold a casket. Bases are simple – this example is cast with masks and foliage. Pieces bear an incise-cast signature.

CHARLES DE SOUSY RICKETTS (ENGLISH, 1866-1930)

Collecting point

Orpheus and Eurydice has been repatinated, but this should not lessen its value. Repatination can reduce the value of some sculptures by as much as 20 percent, but the rarity of this piece ensures that it will still command a high price.

Of all the British sculpture produced in the early 20th century, the work of Ricketts is most representative of the Art Nouveau style. Ricketts claimed to be the only man to understand Rodin, and the influence of the French sculptor is clearly evident in all his work.
• All Ricketts' sculptures bear the monogram "CR".

Ricketts had a good understanding of the human form, and his figures convey a strong sense of emotion. In *Orpheus and Eurydice* the subjects typi-cally appear to be emerging from the base. The sculpted surface and lack of detail were intentional, and do not indicate a poor quality casting.

THE CULT OF THE WOMAN

As in other media, Art Nouveau sculpture took inspiration primarily from nature and the female figure. Forms were flowing and robes diaphanous, and subjects included dream-like and metamorphic wood and sea nymphs, which were mostly naked. Loïe Fuller, the American actress considered by many to be the embodiment of Art Nouveau, was a popular subject for European sculptors such as Raoul Larche. In many pieces, such as those by Gustav Gurschner where women seem to evolve out of the bases of candlesticks, there is even a certain surrealism.

A pair of Bouval gilt-bronze lamps c.1900; ht 20in/50.5cm

MAURICE BOUVAL (FRENCH, died 1920)

Right Bouval was not prolific and, of his relatively few larger pieces, it is versions of this bust that turn up most frequently at auction. The subject's serene downcast gaze and aura of mystic symbolism reflect the preoccupation of many Art Nouveau designers with mysterious, melancholy women. The entwined leaves and flowers are typical. A high-quality plinth (here of dark red marble) generally indicates a high-quality piece – as do the green onyx bases on the lamps above. Bouval's most famous bust, *Ophelia*, is similar in style and form to this example.

A chief exponent of the Art Nouveau style, Maurice Bouval is best known for his lamps and busts of female figures that give the impression of merging with nature, and which are often entwined or draped in leaves and foliage. In the pair of bronze lamps at the top of the page, the naked figures seem to grow out of the swirling base and are entwined in the iris-shaped stems (which conceal light fittings). Both women have their eyes closed, a common feature of Bouval's subjects. Bouval's other work includes inkwells, covered boxes, pin-trays and useful objects, usually in bronze.

The strong similarity between Bouval's bronzes and those of Alphonse Mucha meant that for many years Bouval's work was considered a poor imitation of Mucha. However, Bouval's style is now appreciated and demand for his work has increased significantly in the last ten years.

LOUIS CHALON (FRENCH, dates unknown)

Chalon often combined metal in his work; in another version of the gilt bronze lamp, *Cleo de Merode*, featured here, he combined gilt-bronze and silvered bronze. This lamp anticipates the work of the Art Deco sculptors through its strong geometry and the dramatic, confident stance of the woman. It combines decorative and useful functions very well. The woman's stance and her sunburst ornament suggest illumination, and the electrical fittings seem to grow out of the outstretched branches.

The work of Louis Chalon resembles that of Bouval in many ways. He also produced lamps and busts, and his mantel clocks, vases and dishes usually feature a female figure emerging from a flower. However, Chalon's female studies lack the dreamy quality of Bouval's maidens and tend to be more powerful and vital. The dancer Cleo de Merode, hailed by Chalon as the embodiment of the new optimistic spirit ushered in by the 1900 Paris Exhibition, was one of his favourite subjects.

Marks Chalon used an engraved signature and monogram. The lamp, **left**, is marked "CHALON" and bears the seal of the founder, E. Colin & Cie of Paris.

RAOUL-FRANÇOIS LARCHE (FRENCH, 1860-1912)

Marks and identification Very good fakes of Larche's work abound. It is important to compare a piece with one known to be genuine. Be suspicious of a lack of wear on the base, or an excessive amount of wear on areas not usually susceptible. A new light fitting does not necessarily indicate a fake: many genuine pieces will have received updated fittings over the years. Larche sculptures always bear an incise-cased signature as well as the seal of the Paris founder, Siot Décauville. This may appear as "SIOT FONDEUR". The seal features as a small circular medallion on the base of the piece (though not on the underside).

Raoul-François Larche is particularly famous for his series of bronzes of the American actress, Loïe Fuller. His work invariably involves women, whether in the form of a nymph appearing from a seashell, a dancer or a symbolic or allegorical figure such as Diana (Wisdom), of whom he made great play, both naked and sheathed in diaphanous drapery.

This figure of *Wisdom*, from c.1902, conceals a hinged inkwell and demonstrates how some Art Nouveau sculptors moved away from pure fine art towards a more functional, decorative art. The meaningful facial expression, with its erotic undertone, is typical of Larche's work, as is the base of the piece, which is integral to the figure.

Loïe Fuller is the subject of this figural lamp, which exists in two versions. Although the facial detail of this piece is less precise than on the figure of *Wisdom*, the strong sense of swirling movement inherent in Larche's Fuller bronzes has led to their being considered among the finest Art Nouveau bronzes ever produced.
•Most of Larche's work is gilt-bronze and was made using the sand-casting method, by which pieces were cast in sections, and then joined and patinated. The surface should be intact. Some pieces have been erroneously polished until the bright surface underneath is revealed, which reduces value.

AGATHON LÉONARD (FRENCH, born 1841)

Marks Pieces are marked "A. LÉONARD SCLP, M" and also bear the seal of the casting foundry, "SUSSE FRÈRES EDITEURS".

Léonard worked for Sèvres, producing Art Nouveau-style biscuit figures for table decoration. One series of at least six dancers, *Le Jeu de l'Echarpe*, was used as the model for the gilt-bronze statuettes for which he is best known. Léonard often combined a number of media – for example, bronze and marble.

This figure is based on the dancers from the *Jeu de l'Echarpe* series and is typically realistic, although rather stereotyped. The dancers invariably wear high-waisted, pleated gowns, the wide sleeves of which almost form flower heads. Facial detail tends to be quite severe, and hair is arranged *en chignon* (in a roll at the back of the head).

Some of Léonard's pieces, like this bronze *Femme Chauve-Souris* (*Bat Woman*) show the high symbolism of Art Nouveau. The figure's partial nudity and zoomorphic features, such as the batwings, give it a sensual, decadent expression.

LEO LAPORTE-BLAIRSY (FRENCH, 1865-1923)

Like Maurice Bouval, Laporte-Blairsy studied sculpture under Falguière and exhibited his quality silver and jewelry designs at the 1900 Exhibition in Paris. He favoured the flowing, sensuous lines used by Larche and Léonard for his female and organically-inspired subjects.

Marks The incised mark "LEO LAPORTE-BLAIRSY" appears, usually with the foundry seal "SUSSE FRÈRES EDITEURS PARIS".

Laporte-Blairsy's designs successfully integrate form and function. Lighting fixtures generally incorporate novel construction elements. In this silvered bronze and glass lamp, from around 1900 the globe held by the figure, symbolizing light at night, is engraved with the same star-shaped motif which appears elsewhere on the piece in pierced and stamped form. The piece demonstrates Laporte-Blairsy's characteristic fine casting and great concern for detail, such as the hair and facial features.
• Laporte-Blairsy also produced bronze sculptures, many with marine motifs.

This gilt and patinated bronze bust, entitled *La Nature*, designed by Mucha in 1900, is very similar to the exotic ethereal dream maidens he popularized in poster form. The long flowing hair cascading over the woman's body to form the stylized base, and the elaborate head-dress, are typical of Mucha's graphic style. This bust appeared in several versions, including one with softer features.

ALPHONSE MUCHA (CZECH, 1860-1939)

Alphonse Mucha, painter, designer and decorative artist, studied in Paris, Vienna and Munich. Although most famous for his poster designs for Sarah Bernhardt (see p. 216), between 1899 and 1903, with the help of fellow-sculptor Auguste Seysses, he produced a very limited number of decorative sculptures which represent some of the most impressive of the Art Nouveau period.
• Mucha signed his work "MUCHA", or "M".

EMMANUELE VILLANIS (FRENCH, dates unknown)

Like his contemporary, Korschann, Emmanuele Villanis was a successful Paris-based commercial sculptor best known for his extensive range of bronze sculptures depicting maidens in a typical Art Nouveau style. Unlike Korschann's, most of Villanis's work is purely decorative, apart from a few sculptural lamps.

This bust of *Silvia* shows Villanis' preference for portraits of head and shoulders only, although he did make a few full-length works. He concentrated on facial expressions, which as here, are usually soulful and dreamlike.

Most pieces tend to be patinated in dark brown or dark green.
• Sculptures stand on relatively simple, pyramidal bases. These bear the title of the work modelled in low relief in distinctive lettering.

CHARLES KORSCHANN (BOHEMIAN, born 1872

Charles Korschann achieved considerable commercial success with his sculptures, but produced few exclusive commissions. His work, which includes inkwells, lamps, bronzes and vases, usually contains typically Art Nouveau elements, often women, combined with naturalistic and organic motifs.

Marks Korschann's signature appears as "CH KORSCHANN". Pieces also usually bear the mark of the Paris founder, Loucet.

Above Like many of his contemporaries, Korschann showed a fondness for naked, half-naked or diaphanously-clad maidens, typically with slender figures and coiffured hair and possibly adorned with flowers. Korschann often used cold-painting or enamelling to produce variously coloured patination – the decoration of this vase, from around 1900, contrasts gilding with cobalt blue enamel, for a jewel-like effect.

Right This gilt-bronze piece shows Korschann's preference for placing figures upon floral or organic-type bases. He generally makes strong use of whiplash motifs, as well as natural motifs such as cow parsley, both of which are found on this base. The subject's slender figure is typical of Korschann, as is the particularly detailed treatment of the facial features. The casting is of characteristically high quality.

Gurschner employed a variety of media besides bronze. Some of his lampshades were made from nautilus shells; others from iridescent glass, much of which, like in this example, was produced by Loetz (see p.80). The strong use of figural forms is typical, as are the sinuous style and elegant subject .

GUSTAV GURSCHNER (BAVARIAN, born 1873)

Until recently, Gurschner was regarded by many as a commercial artist working in a debased French style, but his work is now being taken more seriously. Although associated with the Viennese Secession, he worked in a fluid style that has more in common with French Art Nouveau. Typically, his work concentrates on human forms, most often applied to sculptural lamps. At the 1900 Paris Exhibition Bakalowits & Söhne (see p.81) exhibited iridescent glass lamps in metal mounts by Gurschner.

THEODORE RIVIÈRE (FRENCH, dates unknown)

Rivière had a good understanding of the human form and his bronze figures tend to be anatomically accurate. His subjects were mainly theatrical and usually symbolic. Several popular figures by Rivière commemorate the role of leading ladies of the stage. The sculpture of *Carthage* on the right, depicts a scene from the play *Salammbo*, in which the title role was played by the actress, Sarah Bernhardt. Rivière's inscribed signature is prominent on the base of the piece.

In this mildly erotic bronze group, entitled *Carthage*, the posture, expression and headdress of the goddess-type figure of Salammbo are strongly theatrical; a further sense of drama is added by the figure clinging to her waist.
•Unusually for Rivière's sculptures, decoration extends over the base.

DANCERS AND RECREATIONAL FIGURES

Many Art Deco sculptors reflected the increased involvement of women in sporting and recreational pursuits. Particularly inspired by the *Ballet Russe* and the *Folies Bergères*, sculptors favoured dancers as a subject, together with golf and tennis players, and snake charmers and acrobats. Some pieces, those by Ferdinand Preiss for example, depicted real people. Most of the sculptors employed the new luxurious and expensive chryselephantine – a combination of bronze and ivory, which was often chased and gilded, silvered or patinated, and frequently cold-painted.

Right *The Girls*, a gilt and cold-painted bronze and ivory group, by Chiparus c.1930.

Preiss made a few all-ivory figures, often small classical female nudes. This rare piece, from around 1930, depicts a sea siren standing before a rising wave. Preiss also made some ivory child sculptures but these are not as desirable as the chryselephantine or female studies, and are generally regarded as small cabinet-fillers.
•Most of Preiss's figures are made up of parts which were carved separately and screwed to the bronze. They were then individually finished.

FERDINAND PREISS (GERMAN, 1882-1943)

Most of Preiss's figures are made from chryselephantine. The quality of his carving was usually very high and he took pains to render anatomically correct figures. Many are teutonic, Aryan types with tinted naturalistic faces (often wearing rouge) and stained hair. Like other Art Deco sculptors, Preiss concentrated on sporting figures and dancers, as well as actresses. Most Preiss figures are quite small, at less than 14 inches (35cm) high.

Preiss formed the Preiss-Kassler Foundry in Berlin in 1906, designing most of the models himself, although by 1914 there were about six designers working for him including Rudolf Belling, Dorothea Charol, Walter Kassler, R. W. Lange, Philip Lenz, Paul Philippe, Otto Poertzel and Ludwig Walter. The factory closed during the First World War, but reopened in 1919. In 1929 Preiss-Kassler took over the firm and the sculptors of Rosenthal und Maeder (RuM).

Marks Preiss's pieces usually bear the "PK" monogram, for the Preiss-Kassler foundry, and the signature "E. Preiss".
Value Preiss figures featured on ashtrays or ones that are dish-mounted tend to be less desirable than those figures mounted on blocks.
Beware As with the work of the other top sculptors of the period, copies of Preiss's work exist. These often use a softer type of stone which resembles onyx. Be suspicious of any figures attributed to Preiss that have a very elaborate base.

Most Preiss bases are made of green or brown Brazilia onyx, or as in this *Javelin Thrower*, a combination of the two. Other pieces are banded with black Belgian slate.

The Golfer, a bronze and ivory figure, was created by Preiss in the 1930's and is typical of his work, both in its choice of subject and the medium used.

The naturalistic features of the girl and the metallic finish on her dress are characteristic. Many figures were based on contemporary sportsmen.

OTTO POERTZEL (GERMAN, born 1876)

For many years controversy has surrounded some figures emanating from the P. K. factory which are marked "Prof Poertzel". They bear such a resemblance to the work of Preiss that it was suggested Preiss used the name Poertzel as a pseudonym. However, it is now believed that Poertzel worked at Preiss's foundry. Poertzel figures are usually chryselephantine and, unlike some by Preiss, seldom appear in all-ivory.

Some figures emanating from the Preiss-Kassler foundry bear both Preiss's and Poertzel's signature. Although the figure here, known as *The Twins* or *Butterfly Dancers*, is signed by Poertzel, an almost identical example bears Preiss's signature, and another version bears both names.

DEMETRE CHIPARUS (ROMANIAN, dates unknown)

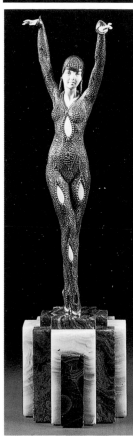

Above The elaborate and tight-fitting costume of this female dancer is typical of many featured on Chiparus' sculptures – his women often wear the catsuits and skull caps featured in the group on the previous page. Pieces also tend to have an exotic or science fiction appearance. The pose of this figure is characteristically theatrical.
•Some pieces were made in more than one size or in both bronze and chryselephantine.

Although born in Romania, Chiparus worked in Paris. Many of his early figures were produced by the Parisian company, Etling (see p.92). Some later works were produced by the LN & JL foundry. Chiparus was the chief exponent of chryselephantine.

Left Chiparus specialized in depicting exotic women, like this bronze and ivory figure of a dancer from 1920. Many were inspired by the *Ballet Russe*, popular in Paris between around 1917 and 1920, but inspiration was also provided by other contemporary figures and shows. Many of his sculptures exhibit Mexican, Inca, Aztec or Mayan influences. Nudes are uncommon.

Bases The bases of Chiparus's pieces are usually elaborate, with a sculptural quality, as seen in the pieces featured here. The plinths are often architectural and of marble or onyx. Many sculptures also have inset plaques whose motifs echo the theme of the subejct.
Marks Chiparus nearly always signed his work on the base. The group on the previous page is signed "DH. Chiparus" and inscribed "ETLING PARIS", while the dancer on the left bears the signature "D. Chiparus".

Most dancers in the dancers of the world series have a specially tailored base. The bas relief on the base often reflects the nationality of the dancer. Dancers often hold an emblem typical of the country they represent, such as the sombrero brandished by this Mexican dancer. Other figures in the series include the Hindu dancer, Theban (Egyptian) dancer and Ankara dancer (Turkey).

Marks Signatures vary – for example, the *Ankara Dancer* is inscribed simply "CL. J R. Colinet 13". A different edition, 24 inches (61cm) high with a green marble base and no brass leggings, and bearing the inscription "C.J.R. Colinet", is stamped "42 Made in France", and impressed with the LN & JL foundry seal, with a separate brass tag inscribed "DANSEUSE D'ANKARA Par Cl. J. R. COLINET.

CLARE-JEANNE-ROBERTE COLINET (BELGIAN, dates unknown)

Colinet is mainly known for her series of dancers, including a series of dancers of the World. Several versions were made of the same figures. She also depicted a number of mythical and historic figures, such as Narcissus, Cupid, Joan of Arc, and a crusader. These are less collectable and therefore less expensive.

Left Many of Colinet's dancers are of chryselephantine, with a gilt or cold-painted surface, or a combination of the two. Bases are onyx or marble or, very occasionally, alabaster. This *Theban Dancer* on a marble base is unusual in being of patinated bronze, although there is a more expensive version in chryselephantine. Fakes are known.
• It is not known precisely how many dancers were in the series, as new ones are still being identified.

Above Colinet also produced some useful figural wares. This bronze lamp from around 1925, modelled as a semi-naked dancing figure, makes use of the extended arms of the dancer to support light fittings. The costume is patinated and decorated.

Left This *Ankara Dancer* (a snake dancer) in cold-painted bronze and ivory, designed by Colinet in around 1925 is 13 inches (25.5cm) high. Typically, the figure, in flowing and elaborate costume, embodies a strong sense of movement. Many of his pieces have an Eastern flavour and his women, usually well-proportioned, in contrast to the streamlined figures of Chiparus (see over), often convey a sense of the *femme fatale* of the 1920s.

Condition and Value Condition is crucial to the value of all Art Deco figures: the extremities of many figures have suffered from knocks and chips. Ivory is especially susceptible to being damaged and is also prone to cracking, which is particularly detrimental to value when the cracks extend down the face, giving the piece a disfiguring black-veined appearance. It has often been assumed that the dull surface of patinated figures, such as those by Lorenzl, is caused by dirt. Consequently, many of them have been polished to such an extent that their patinated top surface has been rubbed away. This is very detrimental to their value.

JOSEPH LORENZL (AUSTRIAN, dates unknown)

One of the leading sculptors of the Art Deco period, Lorenzl produced a range of figures in bronze, ivory, and occasionally chryselephantine, usually single white females, often dancers or women in acrobatic or athletic poses. Unusually for sculptors of the period, he seldom depicted figures from antiquity or the theatre. However, his females have the 1920s and '30s look, with bobbed or cropped hair. Lorenzl's women tend to be very slim, with streamlined figures and small breasts and are usually idealized, although the facial features are realistic, with a serene, calm expression. Like both the pieces featured here, the women tend to be nude, although versions do exist in a skin-tight mini-dress.

The bases of Lorenzl's sculptures are usually faceted and of plain onyx, although black slate and marble were occasionally used. As with the work of some other sculptors featured in this section, figures were often produced in a range of sizes. Plaster and ceramic versions of Lorenzl bronzes, and also those of other important sculptors of the day, including Bruno Zach (see p.168), were produced by the Austrian-based firm of Friedrich Goldscheider (see p.129).

Marks Lorenzl used a variety of signatures, which were usually permutations of his name. Script lettering is commonly used on taller pieces, generally on the domed base. Capital letters, usually on smaller pieces, are found on the perimeter of the flat base. Some of Lorenzl's sculptures are numbered, but the numbers are not considered significant by collectors. Lorenzl's work is not believed to have been faked. The most commonly found signatures include:
•"Lorenzl" in full, which is the most common of his signatures.
•"Lor", on small pieces, when it is usually found under the skirt or under the foot.
•"Renzl".

This typical bronze figure of a naked woman shows Lorenzl's preference for a patinated silver or gilt finish which gives his figures their characteristic metallic look. Scarves, hair and so on are often given additional enamel colouring. The green onyx base of this piece bears the signature "Lorenzl".

This polychrome bronze figure of a dancer from around 1928 is unusually large for Lorenzl at 28½ inches (72.5 cm), as most tend to be no higher than 12 inches (30.5 cm) without the pedestal. The unusual and somewhat unrealistic length of the dancers' limbs, intended to convey elegance, are typical of Lorenzl's work, as is the dramatic posture – standing on one leg, with outstretched arms. The nude here is holding a scarf. Others may hold a fan or other accessory.

Copies and fakes of chryselephantine figures

Fakes of chryselephantine figures have appeared on the market, including some made of plastic. Examine the following carefully:
•The quality of casting and carving, and the subtlety of joints.
•The graining of any ivory (although recently fakes made from artificially grained plastic or "ivorene" have appeared).
•The facial tint. This should be subtle, possibly showing signs of age. Be suspicious of pieces with garish, modern-looking paint, but don't rule them out altogether as it is possible that the sculpture may have been retouched.
•The gilt surface, which should display a patination which is very difficult to reproduce identically.
•The base joints. The original figures were sometimes secured to the base by wing nuts; the fakes invariably use an ordinary screw and nut and these often display excessive rusting and corrosion.

THE ART DECO WOMAN

The revolutionary emancipation of women that resulted from the Great War was immediately reflected in the sculpture of the time. Poses became ever more confident and assertive, and showed a definite move away from the serene and demure women depticed in Victorian sculpture (see pp.152-3). In France, Marcel Bouraine produced a large number of rather forbidding athletic and Amazonian women, while Pierre Le Faguays drew on contemporary dancers for his subjects. At the same time in Berlin, Bruno Zach presented mainly erotic women involved in a number of modern activites, such as smoking and taking part in sports. Many of his figures are reminiscent of the Berlin cabaret.

A bronze female figure by
Pierre Le Faguays, c.1925
24in/61cm

PIERRE LE FAGUAYS (FRENCH, born 1892)

A leading sculptor in the 1920s, Le Faguays produced work for Arthur Goldscheider's Parisian foundry (which outlasted its Austrian parent company), and exhibited under Goldscheider's "La Stele" label at the Paris Exhibition in 1925. He also worked for the house of Le Verrier, making decorative items for sale through Max Le Verrier's shop in Paris.

Le Faguays worked in three distinct idioms. The most successful and desirable of these is his female studies with a strong element of stylization. In the bronze figure pictured, above left, the hair is represented as a skullcap, the features are prominent and simplified, and the pose is serene. These sculptures convey a distinct feeling of stillness, with the arms and legs usually held close to the body – a style very different from that of many other craftsmen working in this period. Another group is that depicting idealized mythological or allegorical figures which show high-quality draughtsmanship and attention to anatomical accuracy. The third group is his women in conventional Art Deco poses.

Marks and availability Sculptures are usually signed "Le Faguays". Signatures may be carved or incise-cast into the base. Some bear the foundry mark "LNJL Paris", and may carry a design number. Pieces displayed at the 1925 Paris Exhibition carry the "La Stele" foundry seal as well as Le Faguays' name.

Although relatively prolific, Le Faguays' work seldom comes up for sale, and is most readily available in France. Some pieces incorporate jardinières or are fitted with electricity for lighting; these command a premium. The largest group, the dancers and harem figures, represents Le Faguays' more commercial side – and are perhaps slightly less sought-after.

In strong contrast to the female study at the top of the page is this 1930s *Dancer with Thyrsus*, in a conventional Art Deco pose – sculptures were often nude or scantily clad, and shown dancing or as a harem girl or warrior. Many are given formal draperies, or something to hold: garlands of flowers, as here, or musical instruments. Others may incorporate cold-painted colours, for example, one entitled *Dancer with Floral Skirt*, or incorporate slightly unusual materials, such as alabaster.

Many of Le Faguays' sculptures, and most of the larger ones, are in bronze; smaller pieces may include ivory. He also worked in wood, stone and silvered bronze. All-ivory figures, like this small (37.25cm) *Water Carrier* from around 1925, are rare.

MARCEL BOURAINE (FRENCH, dates unknown)

Marks and authenticity Bouraine sculptures are usually marked. Much of his work was commissioned and distributed by the Parisian firm Etling (see p.92) whose marks often accompany the sculptor's signature. The Harlequin is stamped "BRONZE FRANCE", signed "BOURAINE", and inscribed "ETLING PARIS". The underside is inscribed "MADE IN FRANCE".

The French glass artist and ceramist Gabriel Argy-Rousseau (see p.88) created statuettes in *pâte-de-verre* during the 1930s which were based on Bouraine's designs. These have the incised signature of G. Argy-Rousseau on the base.

•Some figures were made in more than one size and with minor variations to decorative details.

•No fakes of Bouraine's work are known to exist.

Bouraine is best-known for his chryselephantine figures, made during the inter-war years, and for his groups fully cast in bronze. His subjects are usually women, taken from history or mythology, or portrayed as a dancer or clown. Some wear two-dimensional formalized draperies, and many others are nude. As well as human figures, groups may contain an animal, especially hunting dogs, swans or other birds.

Above Bouraine's sculptures are distinctive for their use of a variety of media in one piece. This *Harlequin* lamp (c.1925) combines bronze, ivory and glass. Patinas of gold were also used; some pieces have silvered surfaces.

Above Many Bouraine figures, like those of Lorenzl (p.165), are portrayed with outstretched arms and holding some kind of prop, such as a hoop, bow, spear or, as with this bronze dancer of the 1920s, a fan. The pose is often exaggerated and dramatic, and the subject is often depicted balanced on one leg.
•The complicated, partially stepped, yellow-veined marble plinth supporting the fan dancer is typical, as is the use of several media and colours. The fan is cold-painted in silver, gold, blue and white.

Left A recurring subject in Bouraine's work was the streamlined, naked Amazonian figure of a Diana-like huntress, with windswept hair, frozen in the motion of running, hunting or throwing a spear. These women are invariably powerful, detailed and realistic.

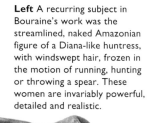

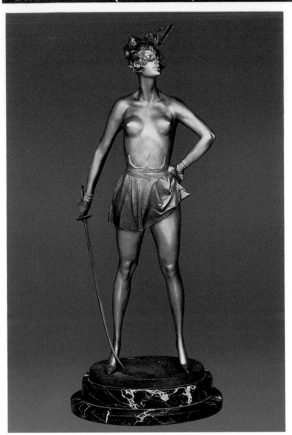

Zach's work is nearly always boldly signed. Some unsigned pieces have been attributed to him, but unless marke pieces should not be accepted as Zach without contemporary documentation. Copies abound, distinguished by their poor-quality casting and patination, apparent in this pseudo-Zach figure which has an ungraceful, almost dumpy figure, and is neither sensual nor erotic. The proportions of the body are wrong – there is even the suggestion of a paunch! – and no suggestion of Zach's idealized figures. The posture is a little awkward and unflattering and the costume is static – there is usually a sense of movement in Zach's clothes which adds to the provocative feel of his pieces. The base is thinner than in genuine Zach figures, and the pedestal, although striated, is green onyx, which was rarely used by Zach – he preferred black or grey marble with fine cream striations.

Zach's subjects are nearly always female. Multiple figures are rare, but pairs exist, usually of dancers or lovers. Women often hold riding crops or whips or, as here, a sword. Most stand with their legs slightly apart in an affirmative stance, rather than in the lady-like pose typical of many figures of the period. They are in contrast to the jewel-adorned playthings often depicted in the 1920s and '30s, by such sculptors as Demetre Chiparus (see p.63), and have an uncharacteristic severity. It is not uncommon for Zach's dancing figures to be poised on one leg.

Zach accurately depicted the costume of the period, which is helpful for dating, as some items, such as pyjama suits and camisoles, were not introduced until 1920. Hair is often bobbed or tied with a bow. The costumes also contribute to the sensual impression given by the figures – for example, garters, and full-length gloves. Some figures wear leather clothing and most have shoes or boots – even if they are otherwise naked or scantily clad.

Little is known of the life of this sculptor, famous for his erotic, slight prurient portraits of the Berlin *demi-monde*. He also produced some lesser works including sporting figures and skiers which are not as collectable as the erotic subjects.

Cold painting The

Austrian, Franz Bergman, popularized cold painting, which was used by Zach for some of his figures. Whereas most Art Deco figures were finished with a metallic patination, obtained by exposing the metal to the fumes of various chemicals, Bergman used coloured enamels, which were annealed or painted on to the figure.

Zach worked mostly in bronze or chryselephantine. He favoured gilt patination, and very occasionally used patinated bronze. Ivory was often contrasted with black patination. He also made a few cold-painted pieces. Well-known Zach figures include *The Riding Crop* (in bronze and bronze ivory), featured here, and *The Cigarette Girl*.
•Although Zach's erotic figures might seem threatening, many are softened by humorous touches.

STYLIZED SIMPLICITY

HAGENAUER (AUSTRIAN, est. 1898)

The Hagenauer Workshop was founded in Vienna in 1898 by Carl Hagenauer (1872-1928). It represented a move away from the intricate, naturalistic approach of 19th century sculptors toward a radical, simplifed and often streamlined approach. Initially Hagenauer specialized in practical and ornamental artefacts – metal tablewares, lamps, mirrors and vases – but became famous for the metal figurines and groups of the 1910-30 period, which were exhibited throughout Europe. Carl Hagenauer's eldest son, Karl, joined the firm in 1919 and, together with his brother Franz, took over in 1928. In the 1930s their designs were at the forefront of the New Realism. The movement of Hagenauer's pieces, whether a dancer, gymnast, horse or panther, is conveyed by a simple unbroken design pared of superfluous detail, as seen in the kneeling woman on the right. Her face is typically mask-like and reflects the influence of Brancusi's head of a sleeping muse.

Collecting Hagenauer It is difficult to distinguish between the work of the three Hagenauers. Carl and Karl were largely responsible for the utilitarian wares, while Franz specialized in decorative sculptures.
•Hagenauer's masks are particularly sought after, as well as those figures with a Modigliani or Brancusi influence. Usually, the more decorative and stylish the piece, the more collectable it is.
Marks Pieces are usually stamped on the base with the Hagenauer monogram "wHw", sometimes with the designer's name, the date and place of origin. If there is no base, it appears in another unobtrusive position.

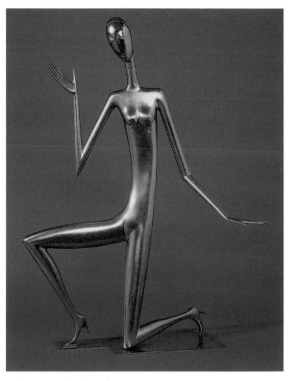

A chromium-plated metal Hagenauer sculpture of a kneeling woman c.1928; ht 35½in/90.5cm

Even if the main subject is not figural, figures usually feature somewhere on the piece. On this brass candelabrum from the 1930s the open friezework of the base incorporates a stylized cat and two horses.
•Hagenauer figures are very often self-supporting; others, as with the sculpture of the dog pictured on the right, are mounted on a minimal thin metal base.

This brass figure of a dog, from the 1930s, demonstrates Hagenauer's stylized and streamlined style, combining flowing curves with clean angles and elongated tapering limbs. Surfaces are smooth, without decoration, carving or other embellishment.

Form often merges into function, with horse-riders made into lamp-stands, arms and hands into brackets for candelabra and bodies made into bowls, as in the case of this

1930s bird, designed by Franz Hagenauer. Sculptures are usually of bronze, copper, chrome or brass, or a combination of metal and wood (often ebony).

ART DECO ANIMALS

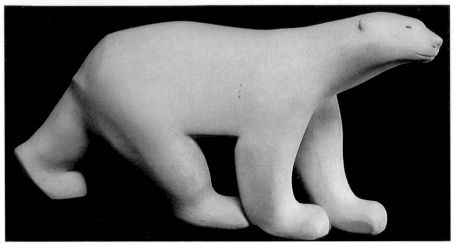

A white stone polar bear by François Pompon c.1930; ht 10in/25.5cm, lgth 18in/45.7cm

With the exception of some imported Japanese bronze animals at the end of the 19th century, animal sculpture tends to have been relatively ignored from the days of the top French animaliers (see pp.153-6), until after the Second World War. A renewed interest, again led by the French sculptors, and in particular, François Pompon, was prompted by a revival of African and Negro art, popularized by Josephine Baker and her performances in *la Revue Nègre*. The most popular animal was the panther, followed by the gazelle, often depicted with Diana the huntress, or with seabirds, especially albatrosses and gulls. Other animals include birds and cats. Bookends often took the form of pairs of animals, such as pelicans, unicorns and seals.

FRONÇOIS POMPON (FRENCH, 1855-1933)

Pompon was one of the leading animaliers of the period. Inspired by the impressionistic work of Rembrandt Bugatti, and the bird and animal etchings of Paul Jouve, both of whom worked in the early years of the 20th century, Pompon created a number of important animal sculptures. The white stone polar bear at the top of the page is Pompon's most famous sculpture, and was exhibited at the Paris Exhibition when Pompon was 67. Like all his work, the piece is highly stylized, with particular attention paid to the finish – the colour of the stone is used to maximum effect. Although his figures are very stylized, Pompon nevertheless manages to suggest a strong sense of movement. Here the bear is free-standing, adding to the mobile effect.

This bronze figure of a bull terrier from around 1920 is highly polished and has the mirror-black finish typical of Pompon's bronzes. Although mounted on a base there is still a sense of vitality about this piece.
•Pompon worked on a few model portraits and on outdoor sculpture, but collectors today are primarily interested in his animals. His work is usually signed underneath with the word "POMPON". Few fakes are known.
•Dogs were a common subject, especially borzois, which are sleek and fast.

EDOUARD MARCEL SANDOZ (SWISS, 1881-1971)

After Pompon, Sandoz is probably the most important animalier of the period. He also produced monuments and portraits of lesser importance. He broke away both from the highly naturalistic presentation of many of the French animaliers, and from the impressionistic work of Bugatti. His approach is more formalized. Many of his animals have expressions, sometimes humorous and many resemble those of Bouraine (see p.167).
•Other animal sculptors include Alex Kélety, G. H. Laurent, Max Le Verrier and Cornelia Chapin.

This black marble seated monkey is typical of Sandoz in its still, brooding attitude, and almost human expression. The somewhat static posture is even more pronounced in his bookends. Some of Sandoz's work is unusually small, less than 1½in (3.8cm) tall, and appears in glazed porcelain and biscuit, as well as marble. His animals are usually mounted on marble bases.

PAUL HOWARD MANSHIP

PAUL MANSHIP (AMERICAN, 1885-1966)

Manship studied art at some of the major colleges of the early 20th century including New York, Pennsylvania, and Rome. He was very impressed by the work of the French sculptor Auguste Rodin and his followers, and by classical sculpture, which was to prove influential in his later work. By 1912 Manship had developed a style and standard of modelling which combined the new thought of the Rodin school with classical principles of realism and scale, and which became associated with an entire movement of American sculpture in the 1920s and '30s. Manship's first exhibition in New York brought him instant acclaim, and he went on to enjoy a level of commercial success extraordinary for a 20th century sculptor.

Manship's work is characterized by its repeat-pattern techniques and use of flat, controlled drapery. The *Indian Hunter and his Dog* pictured left has a fluid and lively form and displays precise modelling with emphasis on sharp features. The quality of casting and patination is always of the highest standard. Bases are comparatively simple.

•Much of Manship's small sculpture was produced commercially in limited editions as reductions of large-scale works, many of which had been public commissions. The *Indian Hunter and His Dog* was originally cast as a life-size fountain of the same title in 1925.

•Most pieces were cast by American foundries, notably the Roman Bronze Works, in New York.

•The most famous of Manship's mythological sculptures is *Prometheus*, installed as a centrepiece in the Rockerfeller Centre in New York in 1934.

•In Manship's work there is an emphasis on linear elegance, with stylized hair and draperies and clarity of contour. Later works are more streamlined.

A bronze sculpture by Paul Manship entitled *Indian Hunter and his Dog* 1926; ht 21¾in/55.25cm

Marks
All Manship's pieces are inscribed with his signature, usually together with a copyright mark and the date.

Several sculptures by Manship take mythological characters as their subject: this bronze group from 1925, entitled *Acteon*, was designed to accompany another dramatic bronze group, *Diana*.

Manship's bronze sculpture was not limited to statuary. He produced a number of medals and medallions and, during the 1920s, cast a menagerie of animal sculpture, much of it stylized in the subtly geometric, Cubist-inspired fashion favoured by French sculptors such as Edouard Sandoz (see p.170). The range, commissioned by the Bronx Zoo, includes a collection of ten exotic birds, among them this crowned crane and concave-caked hornbill, as well as a number of other animals.

SILVER AND METALWORK

Rococo-style silverware peaked at the time of the Great Exhibition in 1851, but was popular well into the 20th century. Ornate designs continued into the 1850s, with a revival of French-inspired Renaissance silverware, which was often large-scale and expensive. The Victorian fondness for Japanese-style art is evident in the motifs that decorate much silver and silver plate after 1870. The simplification of design and the integration of form and function are typified by the work of Christopher Dresser in England. The Japanese influence was also strong in America, especially after the Philadelphia Centennial Exhibition of 1876. Some American factories made silver which was equally desirable, if not preferable to, European wares. Towards the end of the century, the Crafts Guilds produced prohibitively expensive hand-made silver, using traditional techniques. However, the development of electroplating – the application of silver over a copper or nickel alloy – brought silver plate, if not solid silver, within the range of far more people. Much electroplating used Britannia metal (an alloy of tin, antimony and copper) as the base. This resembles pewter, but was more durable and less valuable.

Apart from Liberty's Celtic-inspired Cymric range and some original designs by William Connell, and Kate Harris of Huttons, most British Art Nouveau silverware continued in a traditional Regency and Georgian style. The French largely produced enamelled *objets de vertu*, as well as a few fluid domestic wares. Enamelling was also popular in Vienna. In Scandinavia, Georg Jensen produced organic-inspired silver forms; and Bindersbøll designed some signifcant silver and metalwork. In Germany, Art Nouveau forms and motifs reached the masses through the pewter and silver plate wares of Kayser Sohn and W.M.F. Distinguished by entwined abstract symbols, these pieces inspired Liberty's Tudric pewter range in Britain.

The most important silverwares of the Art Deco period were streamlined tablewares with little or no decoration. The French led design, headed by Jean Puiforcat. Organic designs were produced by Georg Jensen in Denmark and the Wiener Werkstätte in Austria. In the United States the Bauhaus designers were influential, and Norman Bel Geddes's perpendicular forms, inspired by the skyscraper, were also important. British silverware remained traditional, but some silversmiths adopted new ideas, creating engine-turned geometric designs, especially for smaller items. Apart from the hand-made wares of some guilds, British silverware was largely mass-produced. Other Art

Deco wares include trophies and clocks in numerous forms, which were more Modernist and sculptural than hitherto. Translucent guilloche enamel was popular. It was often the only decoration applied to dressing table sets, which tended to be engine-turned designs in silver covered in a monochrome enamel.

In the Victorian period British wares in other metals were made by various guilds, such as Edward Spencer's Artificer's Guild, which worked in copper and silver. Wrought iron was used for garden furniture and, for the first time, for domestic wares. Brass and copper factories began to make larger items of furniture, such as beds. The American Tiffany Studios produced sheet bronze desk sets and other small objects; Gorham made interesting mixed metal wares, Roycrofters specialized in copperwork, and Dirk Van Erp produced Arts and Crafts style wares.

Wrought iron saw a revival in the 1920s and 1930s. Craftsman-metalworkers became popular, especially the Frenchmen, Edgar Brandt, Paul Kiss and Louis Majorelle. They often worked in conjunction with other manufacturers – Majorelle made mounts for Daum's glasswares.

Armand Albert Rateau, took metalwork to its height with his exotic bronze furniture, cast in a higly individualistic style. In Germany, W.M.F. continued its simple forms, often with geometric simulated bronze patination and silvering. Metal was also put to new uses – as mounts for light fixtures and screens, and, with plate glass, for tables. Dinanderie – the application of patinated enamel to non-precious metals such as copper and steel – was popularized by Claudius Linossier and Jean Dunand. Britain produced little of significance in this period apart from Liberty's modernized Tudric range, but American artists, initially influenced by the French, began to develop their own styles, in stainless steel, aluminium and chrome.

Not all metalwork is marked, but many pieces carry the name of the maker, and few pieces are faked. By law all British silver must be hallmarked, and similar constraints apply in Europe and America. The most collectable Victorian silverwares are the smaller, affordable pieces which can be displayed effectively in most homes. Ornate fire surrounds, attractive light fittings and unusual domestic wares of the Victorian period, and table and domestic wares from the Art Deco period are also collectable.

Above *A Georg Jensen silver and amethyst cup and cover, c.1922*
Right *A Wiener Werkstätte silvered metal basket, c.1905*

VICTORIAN ELECTROPLATE AND SILVER

In the early Victorian years great advances were made in silver and metalwork, with Elkington and Co. perfecting a technique for electroplating that was to replace Sheffield plate. New methods of mass-production and a growing public awareness of fine art fuelled by the Great Exhibition of 1851 led to an increase in demand, which Elkington and Co. were able to satisfy. Design at this time, largely based upon Renaissance and early French styles, incorporated naturalistic or realistic motifs. There were also some novelty designs, sometimes excessive, although many were elaborate and often spectacular. Ironically, the leading British silversmiths often employed French designers, but by the mid-1870s the combination of a general trade slump and strict hallmarking laws forced all these companies to make economies.

The "Milton Shield" designed for Elkington by Morel-Ladeuil 1867; lgth 33½in/85cm

ELKINGTON & CO. (ENGLISH, c.1829–1963)

By buying out their competitors and employing scientists as well as top designers, Elkington & Co. were able to offer high quality goods at lower prices than the other leading makers. Between 1840 and 1860, traditional, fused silver-plate was still often used for the main body of larger wares, but by the early 1860s, electroplate was respectable enough to be used on its own. An even more refined technique called electrotyping was employed to make exact copies of originals.

Elkington's earliest wares include small items such as snuff boxes, but during the 1840s, their range expanded to include tablewares, such as candelabra, chargers, tea urns and coffee pots, most of them highly ostentatious and always profusely decorated. They also made decorative wares and even pieces of furniture.

Elkington designers Many of the firm's early pieces were designed by a London silversmith, Benjamin Smith, who specialized in strikingly naturalistic motifs. Another of Elkington's notable assistants was the Danish architect, Benjamin Schlick, who used moulds from classical and Renaissance antiquites for his wares, and two Continental artist-craftsmen, Leonard Morel-Ladeuil and A. A. Willums, both inspired by Renaissance art. Their painstaking designs were mass-produced through a combination of electrotyping techniques which included gilding and damascening. Morel-Ladeuil's work was especially fine, and includes display pieces such as the "Milton Shield" above.

This oval mark (from the back of the "Milton Shield") certifies that the object was an approved copy of an original belonging to the Department of Science and Art (now the Victoria & Albert Museum in London). In 1853, the director, Henry Cole, allowed Elkington to reproduce antiquities and contemporary wares in the national collection, many of them exhibition pieces. Some, such as the shield, were copied by Elkington on a huge scale. The firm also reproduced some pieces unofficially; these carry just the Elkington mark.

This early pitcher is largely inspired by French designs. It was made with a combination of plating and gilding. Often if several techniques are involved, small nuts are visible on the reverse of the piece, where separate components have been joined.

• Elkington used nickel as the base metal for ordinary pieces, but preferred copper for special wares.
• Electroplated items are often marked "EPNS" for electroplated nickel silver. An electroplated item is worth three to four times less than the same piece in silver.

Marks The earliest wares were marked "E & Co" crowned in a shield and the word "ELEC TRO PLATE" in three sections.

Above In 1841 and 1842 the mark was changed and a date number added. The series ran from 1-8.

Left From 1843, "E M & Co" was added in three separate shields.

Above From 1849, the date was shown by letters, beginning with K, and the alphabet started again in 1865, 1886 and 1912. Not all the letters were used.

•Wares between 1842 and 1883, carry a diamond mark which shows the date when the design was registered.

RUNDELL, BRIDGE & RUNDELL

Founded in 1804, this London firm boasted the title of Royal Goldsmiths until 1843, although their wares were mainly silver or silver-gilt. Rundell's used the services of various designers including the English artist, John Flaxman, and outworkers such as Paul Storr – and Edward Barnard & Sons, one of the most important silver makers of the Victorian period.

STORR & MORTIMER (1822-c.1842)

Paul Storr was the most celebrated silversmith working in England during the 19th century, but his best-known pieces were large, Neo-classical silver-gilt wares produced for the Prince Regent before Victoria acceded to the throne. In partnership with John Mortimer until he retired in 1839, Storr signed his creations with his initials.

R. & S. GARRARD (ENGLISH, 1819-Present)

Garrard's inherited Rundell, Bridge & Rundell's royal patronage in 1843, but preferred to be known as the Crown Jewellers, a title they hold to this day. The firm's 19th century wares are marked "RG". Like the work of the other leading silversmiths, although functional, pieces are also highly decorative.

This silver-gilt sweetmeat bowl and cover, made in 1839, is among the first examples of naturalism in silver. Although the composition is slightly unbalanced, the exuberance and inventiveness of the design make it highly desirable.

HUNT & ROSKILL (ENGLISH, 1843-c.1939)

A successor to the firm of Storr & Mortimer, this company was headed by Storr's nephew, the silversmith, John Samuel Hunt. He recruited a French artist-craftsman, Antoine Vechte (1799-1868), whose forté was intricate embossing (or repoussé work) in imitation of elaborate Renaissance designs.

Hunt's best pieces incorporated highly-detailed relief and three-dimensional figural compositions in oxidized silver to ornament large, presentation wares. Hunt also borrowed heavily from ancient Italian motifs for this silver-gilt ewer from 1853.

This christening set – a very popular 19th century item – shows how Victorian decoration could smother form: the ornament just stops short of covering the functional areas. Hunt & Roskill made many fine, decorative wares and exhibition pieces such as this.

CHARLES AND GEORGE FOX (ENGLISH, 1849-1921)

George Fox, probably the son of George Fox of Rundell, Bridge and Rundell, worked in partnership with Charles to produce individual, high quality silverwares which were functional as well as decorative. They both worked for Lambert and Rawlings.

This wandering minstrel salt cellar, which was one of a pair, was made by T. & G. Fox in 1872. It clearly demonstrates the firm's preference for novelty forms.

THE GUILD OF HANDICRAFT

Established by C. R. Ashbee, the Guild of Handicraft consisted of artist-craftsmen who sought to perpetuate the pursuit of beauty in hand-crafting, in accordance with the ideals of medieval craft guilds. They worked mainly in wood and metal, to produce wares that were functional as well as decorative; these included silverware, jewelry, furniture, leatherwork, and later, books. The Guild aimed to design and produce wares for the people, but in practice their pieces were exclusive, being hand-crafted. The ideals of the Guild failed as a result of competition from the imported jewelry made by the German firm, Murrle Bennet (p.207), amongst others, and by the silver and pewter wares retailed by Liberty & Co., (see pp.182-3), which despite being machine-made, appeared hand-crafted.

A silver cup and cover
designed by C. R. Ashbee
1900; ht; 8½in/21cm

Guild pieces often incorporate semi-precious stones. This buckle, designed by Ashbee for his wife, Janet, is set with four turquoises. Other stones used include chrysoprase (as in the handle of the silver dish at the top of the opposite page), abalone, moonstone and pearl clusters. Enamelling is a common alternative to stones.

THE GUILD OF HANDICRAFT (BRITISH, 1888-1908)

Other guilds The guild system was developed in England during the later years of Queen Vicoria's reign. The guilds brought togther designers and craftsmen who were determined to produce beautiful objects using handcrafting processes that dated back to medieval times. Other guilds included the Artificer's Guild, founded by Nelson Dawson and Edward Spencer; the Century Guild, one of whose founders was Arthur H. Mackmurdo; and the Birmingham Guild of Handicraft, which Alexander Fisher (see right) helped to found.

The Guild of Handicraft was notable for its production of superb silverware fashioned by craftsmen who, until the Guild's formation, had not worked in this medium. Ashbee himself was the Guild's most fertile and influential designer – Lewis Foreman Day was the Guild's other main designer. Pieces featured naturalistic decoration, which was often in the form of embossed or pierced friezes of flowers and leaves; any figural decoration was restricted to terminals or finials. Enamelling was often used as an alternative to precious jewels.

With the exception of Ashbee, none of the Guildsmen had any experience of silversmithing, and Ashbee had no formal training. This is hard to believe when considering the competence displayed by the Guildsmen. Early Guild silverware is regarded as pioneering; therefore, the earlier a piece the more desirable it is. Shapes are simple and have a hand-made appearance, with finely beaten surfaces. This is clearly visible on the base of the cup and cover at the top of the page. Clear or tinted glass linings are often incorporated into pieces. The green lining of the cup and cover was provided by the London glassworks of James Powell and Sons (see p.70), which supplied most of the glass used in the Guild's silverware.

CHARLES ROBERT ASHBEE (ENGLISH 1863-1942)

A leading figure in the Arts and Crafts movement, Ashbee was initially more an architect and designer than a craftsman, but appointed himself chief designer when he set up the Guild of Handicraft in 1888. He designed silver, jewelry and some furniture, which was functional as well as decorative.

Marks Early pieces are unmarked The initials "C.R.A." were used occasionally from 1896, when Ashbee registered his mark. Most pieces after 1896 are marked "G of H Ltd', but some of the guildsmen may have refused to submit their work for assay for fear of damaging their creations.

This cloak clasp from around 1902, designed by Ashbee, features amethyst and turquoise cabochons (smoothly polished, unfaceted gems) as well as enamelling.

Roped or beaded rims, like the one featured on this silver dish, are common Ashbee features. This example also has a characteristic wirework loop handle, here set with a chryso-prase. The piece displays the shallowness typical of much of the Guild's silverware.
•Many of Ashbee's designs were repeated, but because they were all hand-made, no two versions are identical.

The wirework on the handle of this dish was used by many workshops, but none to such an extent as the Guild silver-smiths. Close inspection reveals the finely beaten sur-face typical of hand-worked sil-ver. The *repoussé* decoration depicts the stylized foliage often seen on Guild pieces.

This hammered silver cup and cover, designed by Ashbee, takes the medieval-inspired form of a chalice. However, the decoration is typically Art Nouveau, and incorporates a chased band of leaves around the rim. The frieze, embossed with pierced flowers, was often incorporated into the Guild's wares. This piece has certain features which suggest that it was hand-crafted: the mother-of-pearl cabochon on top of the openwork finial lies at an angle, indicating that it was not mechanically set, and the lid does not fit exactly.

ALEXANDER FISHER (ENGLISH, 1864-1936)

Alexander Fisher is regarded as the greatest British enameller, and was responsible for taking enamelling to the heights it achieved at Limoges during the Renaissance. He founded his own London workshop, where he established an enamelling school in 1904. He also helped to found the Birmingham Guild of Handicraft and inspired contemporaries such as Nelson and Edith Dawson and Phoebe Traquair.

Fisher's silverware, which consists mainly of plaques, often depicts Celtic-inspired entrelac motifs, and also shows the strong influence of Liberty's Cymric range of silverware (see p.182).

Marks Most of Fisher's designs bear his stamped ini-tials. The silver cross and panel featured here is dated (1899) and bears the remains of an exhibition label inscribed "The Countess Grey, Howick Lebury Northumberland, Enamel by Alexander Fisher, 1899", indicating that it was designed by Fisher to a commis-sion from Earl or Countess Grey.

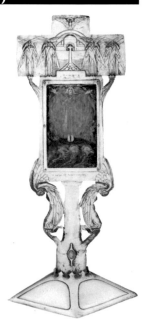

Fisher's plaques were often set into elaborate mounts or frames, as is this silver cross. Many had a religious subject: this piece depicts Christ rising above three sleeping mortals. The frame is supported by two kneeling angels, while another four rise above the scene.

AMERICAN MASTER METALWORKERS

A Gorham ice bowl with polar bears 1870; ht 6¾in/17cm; lgth 10¾in/27.5cm

Americans were very receptive to Japanese art, especially to their metalwork designs on sword furniture. A 19th century edict banning the Samurai from wearing swords led many Japanese craftsmen to turn to ornamental and useful wares. In America, the Gorham Corporation produced Japanese-inspired wares, differing only in their identifiably Western form. Tiffany & Co. adopted similar designs and techniques for their silverwares and, like Gorham, often made use of planished and hammered surfaces. Dirk Van Erp and the Roycrofters adopted a diametrically opposed stance, preferring a more arts and crafts-inspired approach and concentrating on an aesthetically pleasing combination of form and function.

GORHAM CORPORATION (AMERICAN 1813-Present)

So realistic is the modelling on this mixed metal tazza from 1881 that it even shows "worm holes".

Above In this martelé vase, c.1910, the fluid form is typically Art Nouveau, as are the floral motifs. Decoration is not as heavily *repoussé* as on the vase on the right.

This Rhode Island firm, the largest manufacturer of American silver in the 19th century, owed its success to its innovative and mechanical methods and high design standards. In 1868 Gorham adopted the Sterling standard for silver (925 parts of silver per 1000) and by 1891 was using the Britannia standard (950 parts per 1000). Gorham made mainly large-scale useful and decorative tablewares. The firm's more progressive styles often relied on American motifs, notably those connected with the nationalist movement following the Civil War. The ice bowl at the top of the page was made to commemorate the Alaska purchase of 1867.

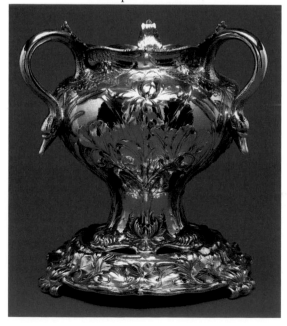

The distinctive anchor mark appears on most Gorham wares, with perhaps a serial number and a stamp confirming the silver standard. Earlier wares are often marked with a psuedo-English hallmark of a lion, an anchor and a Gothic "G". Hollow ware was marked with year letters starting with a capital "A" from 1868, and the sequence was followed with ciphers from 1885.

Between 1891 and 1910 Gorham produced their "martelé" silverwares – hand-made to the Britannia standard, and the most collectable of American Art Nouveau silverware. They tend to be thick and heavily gauged compared to Continental silver, with smooth contours and a lightly hammered (planished) surface. Many pieces feature *repoussé* or chased decoration.

TIFFANY & CO (AMERICAN, 1837-Present)

Marks Almost all Tiffany's silverware bears impressed marks including the word "STERLING" (or "English Sterling"). A capital "M" for the designer, Edward C. Moore, was used until c.1891.
•Tiffany adopted the English Sterling standard in 1852.
•Most Tiffany mixed metal wares were produced between 1878 and 1888.

Tiffany (see also p.84) was largely responsible for the popularity of American silver and plated wares on the domestic market. They used more advanced techniques and higher quality silver than Gorham. Early Tiffany silver is mainly conventional, or Rococo-revival flatware or useful hollow ware. Throughout the second half of the 19th century the firm covered a more adventurous, revivalist repertoire of Pharaonic, Louis XIV, French Second Empire, Etruscan and Renaissance styles. Islamic and Moorish designs were also copied, and typically American motifs such as American Indians were used as well. Surfaces were often chased, engraved or inlaid, and highly realistic three-dimensional depictions of flora and fauna were common.
•Other extremely active Tiffany collecting areas include flatware (especially serving pieces) and *objets de vertu*, such as match safes.

Some of Tiffany's finest wares are those in "mixed metal", such as this vase, which shows the firm's interest in Japanese metal-smithing techniques: each of the applied panels is an example of a Japanese alloy coloured by patination.

DIRK VAN ERP (DUTCH, 1860-1953)

The son of a Dutch coppersmith, Van Erp moved to California in 1886 and in 1908 opened The Copper Shop in Oakland, where he made decorative copper wares with hammered surfaces and a rich reddish brown patina. He moved to San Francisco in 1910, and expanded his range to include vases and desk items, including table lamps. His work is scarce, and almost unknown outside the United States and Canada, where the value of his wares has recently soared.

Van Erp worked in the "Mission Style", which had its roots in the Prairie School (see p.46). Pieces were simple in form and design and hand-made using traditional methods and tools, and were often of Japanese inspiration. His standards of design and production are comparable to the best medieval examples. Rivets and seams tend to be visible, or integral to the design. On this table lamp the trumpet-shaped battens of the shade echo the style of the base, and the rivets on the battens and the arms act as decoration on an otherwise simple piece. Van Erp's table lamps are among his most collectable pieces. Most are in the same hammered reddish-brown copper with shades panelled in mottled amber-coloured mica sheets. Forms vary; other bases may represent mushrooms, milk churns or bullets.

THE ROYCROFTERS (AMERICAN, 1895-1938)

Founded in East Aurora by Elbert Hubbard (1856-1917), this community produced simple, well-made mahogany and fumed oak furniture in the "Mission style", as well as textiles, hammered metalwork, books and lighting. Although based on the English Arts and Crafts style, their work was distinctively American and became known as Aurora Colonial furniture.

Wrought-iron wares, first produced in 1899, included andirons (rests for burning logs in a fireplace) such as these shaped like seahorses, designed by William Walter Denislow.
•The metalwork of Karl Kipp, director of the workshops from 1908, is very collectable.

DOMESTIC LIGHTING & METALWORK

A Benson brass wall light with vaseline shade c.1890; lgth 14in/35.5cm

The Victorian age saw a transition from candlelight to gas mantles, to the electric light bulb, and lighting became an increasingly important feature in the home. William Arthur Smith Benson was one of the most successful manufacturers, working in brass and copper sheet, with copper and brass fittings, often using art glass shades. Less avant-garde tastes were catered for by the traditional oil lamp with its standard cistern, chimney and globe shade. Metal was used for other wares. Cast-iron began to be used architecturally, initially by Coalbrookdale, for fireplaces and surrounds, hall stands and garden furniture. The brass bed, hygienically preferable to its wooden counterpart, gradually gained in popularity.

Light fixtures The wall light in the main picture is an excellent example of Benson's preference for shapes which were both functional and elegant. Characteristically spare, ornamentation is practical and decorative. The vaseline glass shade was probably made by his chief supplier, James Powell (see p.70). The design also shows Benson's liking for thin metal structures screwed together through a central axis. Benson's range of light fittings includes candlesticks, chandeliers and lanterns, many of which were intended for mass-production.

WILLIAM ARTHUR SMITH BENSON (ENGLISH, 1854-1924)

William Arthur Smith Benson was a champion of industrial design. Inspired by William Morris, he opened a metalwork shop in Hammersmith in 1880 and moved to Chiswick in 1882. He is best known for his light fittings and tablewares, often novel or futuristic in design, but he also designed wallpaper and furniture for Morris, and other architectural fittings. In 1887, Benson opened a shop in London's Bond Street, and his light fixtures were also on sale in Paris at the *Maison de l'Art Nouveau*. He became Managing Director of Morris's firm in 1896 while his own company was still in production.

Tablewares Many of Benson's tea and coffee pots were made of brass combined with copper, although he also used plain and silver-plated nickel. Sometimes a decorative pattern was embossed onto the metal; knobs and handles were of wood and/or cane.

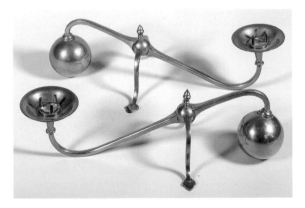

The most popular of Benson's candlesticks were those of Neo-gothic design and multiple construction. Balance was always an important consideration. Typically, the ball weights of these candlesticks are not disguised, but have become integrated into the design.
•Pieces are usually stamped with a shield trademark inside which are the letters WHSB.

Christopher Dresser designed this copper and brass kettle for Benham & Froud in 1885. It demonstrates Dresser's extraordinary ability to make a useful object beautiful without the addition of any unnecessary ornament.

BENHAM & FROUD (ENGLISH, 1873-93)

Another English firm, Benham & Froud, concentrated on household utility and kitchen wares. Most of their products are of little artistic merit and are not collectable, with the exception of those few designed by Christopher Dresser (see p.70), immediately identifiable by their original forms.

PERRY, SON & CO. (ENGLISH, 1876-83)

Dresser also designed household metalwares for the firm of Perry, Son & Co., one of several lighting manufacturers operating in and around Birmingham and Wolverhampton in the second half of the 19th century.
•Fakes of Perry wares are virtually unknown.

This brass chamberstick is stamped with Dresser's name and the firm's entwined rope mark and also bears a registration lozenge dating it to 1883.

COALBROOKDALE (ENGLISH, 1709-Present)

This leading British manufacturer of cast-iron wares, based in Shropshire, enjoyed a revival in the 1830s, when Abraham and Alfred Darby took over the running of the firm. The firm was innovative in its use of iron to produce beds (which had previously been made in wood) – at first camouflaging the iron to look like brass by covering it in brass foil and varnishing it. This successful use of iron for beds led to a greater awareness of the potential for using the medium in other ways and soon a variety of iron objects was available – iron furniture for indoor and outdoor use was particularly sought-after following the new popularity of the conservatory. It was often ornately cast, even fanciful, and sometimes decorated in relief with trailing ivy leaves. Seating often took the form of wooden splats (or, alternatively, thin iron straps).

Coalbrookdale also made pub or inn tables, usually round with central pedestal supports, and a number of small useful wares, including circular dishes, cast and pierced with Renaissance-type grotesques and arabesques. Most pieces were made in moulds on a commercial basis.
•Many of Coalbrookdale's pieces were exported to the United States and Europe.
•Garden furniture has increased dramatically in value in the last five years. There are now special sales devoted to garden furniture and statuary.

Marks Many wares bear the name Coalbrookdale on a pad applied to the underside of the piece at the centre. The patent mark was also used after 1849. Some very similar decorative and sculptural ironwork was made in Russia. Although the marks are in Russian, they are very similar to those used by Coalbrookdale.

Condition Most cast-iron pieces found today are likely to have been repainted several times. Multiple layers of paint can dull definition. Occasionally, some original paint, probably black or white, may show through. Any rust will also be visible through the paint and is usually impossible to disguise completely. Pieces that appear to be in their original state command a premium, although these can be very difficult to identify.

This cast-iron fire surround (c.1857) was designed by Alfred Stevens, whose work is much sought-after today. The pronounced sculptural quality of his work is evident. Cast-iron fire surrounds proved popular in the Victorian period. At first cast-iron was restricted to the surround, but later was an integral part of the fireplace.

This cast-iron hallstand was designed by Dresser in 1867. His designs are the most collectable of Coalbrookdale's wares. The typically ornate decoration includes piercing in the casting. Forms, as here, are often symmetrical. Dresser designed a number of hallstands for Coalbrookdale in the same general style as this one, but with variations on the back supports: this one is unusual in having a mirror.

METALWORK FOR THE MASSES

Innovations in mass-production techniques were taken full advantage of by Arthur Lasenby of Liberty, who adapted the machines so hated by many Arts and Crafts metalworkers to produce wares that simulated hand-made products. His Cymric range of silver paved the way for other designers to produce silver on a large scale – for example, Kate Harris at William Hutton and Sons produced predominantly Art Nouveau-inspired wares. On the Continent, most prolific was W.M.F. in Germany, who worked mainly in continental pewter, and Kayser Söhn, also German, whose art pewter prompted Liberty to produce its own range of "Tudric" pewter.

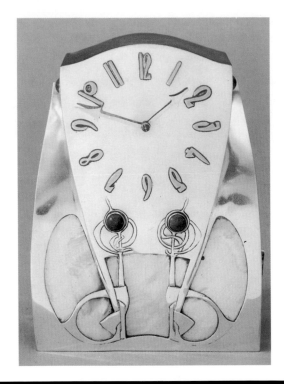

Right A Liberty & Co. "Cymric" clock 1903, ht 10in/24.5cm

Knox was particularly adept at adapting conventional forms. The novel thumb rest and hinged handle on this tankard enliven an otherwise standard form. He often uses enamels to highlight the entrelac, with this peacock blue-green colour most commonly used.

The relatively traditional form of this enamel vase was common throughout the early 19th century, but the decoration is highly individual. Knox managed to balance design and form and his work was always well-proportioned.

LIBERTY & CO. (ENGLISH, 1875-Present)

Arthur Lasenby Liberty founded this famous London retail firm in 1875, initially for the sale of British-made goods and imported Oriental art and fabrics. In the 1880s the firm began to commission art fabric designs and to produce Arts and Crafts-style furniture (see p.31), and by 1900 Liberty was widely regarded as the arbiter of taste in interior decoration. In 1899 it launched its Cymric silverware range and in 1901 Liberty & Co. (Cymric) Ltd was formed, in conjunction with the Birmingham silver firm of W.H. Haseler.

Archibald Knox (English, 1864-1933) Archibald Knox, one of the most important designers for Liberty, produced over 400 designs for their Cymric range, as well as some Tudric pewter. He was born and educated on the Isle of Man, and his observation of Celtic remains there was the underlying influence on his choice of decoration. His ornate elements, easily recognizable, often incorporate spear-headed entrelac symbols, a form of interlaced decoration drawn from ancient jewelry. Such motifs are clearly visible on the mantel clock at the top of the page. Design is enhanced by the use of enamels and applied cabochons (polished, unfaceted stones) or semi-precious stones such as turquoise and lapis lazuli, features associated with medieval Limoges enamel work.

Clocks Knox's clock forms were usually highly original and architectural, often with a tapering body and perhaps an overhanging pediment. The mantel clock at the top of the page is attributed to Knox and is one of the most innovative of his many designs. The copper numerals were not peculiar to Liberty, but the combination of copper and silver was uncommon. Copper was more usually set against gold.
•Clock mechanisms should preferably be in working order. However, it is unwise to replace movements, even when they are not working.

Knox's chalices did not feature religious motifs and were probably made for domestic use or as presentation cups. Some, like the one featured here, had multiple supports entwined with tendril-type wirework. They usually stand on a disc-shaped base, sometimes with a slightly raised centre. The decoration on this piece is typical in being limited to the support.

Liberty's designers did not sign their work and Knox is the only one whose pieces can be attributed with any certainty, as many of his original designs survive. Reginald (Rex) Silver (1897-1965) was another fine designer of Cymric wares. The lack of Celtic-derived motifs, the untypical combination of stones and the too delicate fluid style of this silver chalice suggest it is more likely to be by Silver than by Knox.

Marks Some Tudric wares may be stamped "ENGLISH PEWTER" and "MADE BY LIBERTY & CO." Others include a stock or shape number; earlier pieces have a three-figure or lower number, usually preceded by a "0". Most are stamped "TUDRIC".

Tudric wares Until 1902, Liberty retailed Kayser-Zinn wares (see overleaf) and other German art pewter. Following the success of these ranges and of the Cymric silver range, Arthur Liberty saw the opportunity to produce similar wares in the less expensive pewter. In so doing, he helped to revive the pewter industry, which had declined as pewter tavern wares were largely replaced by mass-produced glassware. The first Tudric wares were made in 1903 by W. H. Haseler & Co., who were already making the Cymric range.

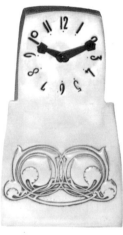

Although some Tudric forms were borrowed from the Cymric wares, others, like this inkstand, were unique. Enamelled wares command a premium, although small losses of enamelling, such as that on the circular decoration in the front right hand corner of this piece will slightly reduce value.
•After 1918 the range declined in quality; emphasis changed to simulated hammered surfaces and little, if any enamelwork. Production ceased c.1938.
•The Tudric range includes some rare cigarette boxes decorated with inset rectangular panels enamelled with landscapes, signed by Fleetwood Charles Varley, one of the few artists to sign his work.

Pieces were mainly decorative and many incorporated colourful enamelwork. Many Cymric designers also worked on the Tudric designs so they show similar inspiration. The tapering sides and overhanging

top of this clock from around 1905 are consistent with the traditional, architectural form of many of the Tudric wares. Other pieces were more innovative, with decoration verging on the avant-garde.

Some early Tudric clocks, such as this one, designed by Archibald Knox c.1902, have a distinctive enamelled dial, created by using a quick process whereby a shape was impressed into the metal and the sunken area then flooded with enamel. Small areas could also be enamelled in this way. Knox's entrelac motifs are typically more complex than on his earlier Cymric wares.
•As on Cymric clocks, hands should be original. They are often distinctive and are sometimes enamelled.
•Archibald Knox was the most prominent designer of Tudric wares, as he had been with the Cymric range. Other designers of Tudric wares include Oliver Baker (1856-1919) and Bernard Cuzner (1877-1956).
•Few competitors are worthy of mention. Most products tended to have hammered surfaces and simple forms, often with wooden handles.

The design of this blue glass bottle is strong and the decoration of trailing ivy leaves typically Art Nouveau. The glass lining, probably by the London glasshouse, James Powell and Sons (see p.70), is original, which will increase the value.
•Handles are an important feature of many of Harris's pieces: a coffee set of 1902 exhibits accentuated loop and wrapover handles. A sporting cup by her has elaborately pierced handles and the sinuous whiplash handles on one silver bowl liner extend from the rim to the base.

WILLIAM HUTTON AND SONS (ENGLISH, 1800-1923)

Founded in Birmingham by William Hutton, this firm produced both useful and ornamental wares in fine quality silver, silver plate, Britannia metal, pewter and copper. From 1887 to 1914, under the directorship of Thomas Swaffield-Brown, Hutton mass-produced some influential Art Nouveau wares in enamelled copper and silver. Much of their silverware of this period was made to the designs of Kate Harris. Most other designers are so far anonymous.

Kate Harris (English, active c.1890-1910)
Kate Harris began designing for Huttons in 1901, and fast became their foremost designer. She made useful and decorative wares in a distinctive style that displayed her individual interpretation of Art Nouveau. Her best work strikes a balance between decoration and form, achieved by combining inventive shapes with stylized figurative work. She mainly produced lady's dressing table objects, some of which were exhibited at the Paris Exposition in 1900.

Collecting
The value of Hutton's wares varies considerably. The work of Kate Harris commands a premium. There are no known fakes or imitations.

This casket is not definitely by Harris, but has been attributed to her on the basis of the honesty flower decoration and the renaissance-type scroll for the cartouche – both of which were typical of her work. The casket is basically of traditional form, but with innovative embossing. It will be lined with velvet inside and was probably used for jewelry.
•Harris designed several photograph frames, one of which incorporates colour enamelled stylized flower and stem decoration about a heart motif.

Marks Harris was purely a designer and consequently did not sign her wares. All her designs were made by William Hutton and Sons and bear the Hutton's mark and a London hallmark.

Harris's figurative subjects are generally female with a distinctive, Quaker-like appearance, suggested by a close-fitting Dutch-style hat. Most have a curl protruding from beneath the cap, and are shown in profile against a halo-like medallion, such as the example on this mirrorback, designed by Harris in 1902. The religious significance of this particular piece is heightened by the two lilies that flank the figure, a symbolic allusion to the Virgin Mary. Harris often gave the reserve areas within her designs an almost granular, finely pitted orange peel texture. On the mirror the effect is to make the subject appear in relief. This texture was achieved by machine, treating the silver as a plastic material or fabric.

W.M.F. (GERMAN, established 1880)

Reproductions and fakes Fakes of W.M.F.'s work are not known to exist. Reproductions are suspiciously bright, with artificial black patination in crannies. Backstands on picture frames will be clearly modern and probably covered in velour, whereas originals have wooden backs and a plate and metal easel support.

Marks W.M.F. wares made before 1914 are marked with a stork within a lozenge shape. Later wares bear just the initials "W.M.F."

•W.M.F.'s full name is Wüttembergische Metallwarenfabrik.

This metal foundry was the most successful German art pewterer of the Art Nouveau period. Designers such as Wilhelm Wagenfeld adapted classic Art Nouveau elements to commercial forms which were mass-produced in Continental pewter, an electroplated metal alloy more similar to Britannia metal than British pewter.

Other wares W.M.F. wares include vases, trophies, rose bowls and a large number of picture frames. They also produced glass claret jugs encased in pierced silver-plated decoration. In 1921 they opened a studio specifically to produce glass liners in clear, green or ruby red glass.

•During the Art Deco period W.M.F. also produced copper dinanderie vases (see p.194).

In this picture frame from around 1900 the form is engraved with typical Art Nouveau motifs of stylized flowers, trailing foliage and a woman with flowing hair and garments.

Wares tend to be purely decorative rather then useful, like this pair of electroplated plaques. The *repoussé* decoration shows a typical female figure with long flowing hair, surrounded by stylized poppies.

KAYSER & SÖHN (GERMAN 1885-c.1904)

J. P. Kayser & Söhn, established at Krefeld-Bochum, near Düsseldorf, was one of the first German foundries to produce art pewter, manufactured under the name Kayserzinn (Kayser pewter) from 1896. Unlike W.M.F., Kayser did not electroplate their wares, and so they were more akin to ordinary pewter. High standards of casting were achieved using a strong, malleable alloy of tin, copper, and antimony, which gave a fine silvery shine when polished.

The majority of wares, which included ashtrays, dishes and vases, were in the Jugendstil style (see pp.38-9), although some wares show a French influence. In turn, Kayserzinn was the inspiration for Liberty's "Tudric" range.

Designers included Hugo Leven, Karl Geyer and Karl Berghoff. Forms were flowing and organic with great use of naturalistic elements.

Most Kayserzinn wares were purely decorative, although some were designed with a practical function. These candelabrum have been adapted to receive electric light fittings.

FRENCH GRACE AND LUXURY

In the years that followed the Great War of 1914-18 French decorative arts underwent a dramatic transformation. The premier French manufacturers of silver and electroplate, Puiforcat and Christofle, launched a distinctly "Modern" range of tea and coffee services and other tablewares. The flowing, fluid excesses of Art Nouveau, still prevalent prior to 1914, were replaced by severe geometric forms which sometimes incorporated new materials, such as plate glass or exotic macassar ebony for handles. Ivory was also frequently used, primarily due to its insulation properties. Shapes based on traditional Empire forms were popular, sometimes "modernized" to suit contemporary styles.

A Jean Puiforcat silver and parcel-gilt covered tureen c.1935; ht 9in/24cm

JEAN PUIFORCAT (FRENCH, 1897-1945)

Jean Puiforcat joined the successful family firm after the First World War. He concentrated on graceful shapes and rejected traditional embellishments without sacrificing either beauty or luxury. Surfaces are usually left plain. Even the hammer marks – traditionally the sign of a hand-made object – are absent. Instead, the surface is enlivened by the way in which the large, perfectly smooth areas catch, reflect and distort light. All Puiforcat pieces show a very high standard of craftsmanship and minute attention to detail. Straightforward silversmithing techniques are used.

In the 1920s Puiforcat made functional rather than decorative pieces. During this period he produced tea and coffee sets, dishes and bowls in solid silver in simple cylindrical or rectangular forms. Rosewood handles are a common feature as seen on this four-piece tea and coffee service from 1925. Other sets were offset by knobs and handles of ivory, jade and lapis lazuli or other hardwoods.

Marks All Puiforcat pieces are stamped "Puiforcat" on the base and carry a French hallmark.
Clocks Puiforcat also made silver clocks during the Art Deco period. These often have unusual designs, sometimes with an open dial.

Collecting point
Incomplete sets suffer a disproportionate drop in value, and are probably not worth collecting at all unless very inexpensive. Some wares, although functioning perfectly as coffee pots or jugs, also appear as pieces of abstract, Cubist sculpture.

In the 1930s Puiforcat's style gave way to purer, sleeker shapes which were bold statements of form. He sometimes included touches of ice-green or salmon-pink glass in his pieces, or applied high-quality wood or crystal. This tureen from the late 1930s incorporates a rose quartz finial. These later objects sometimes appear futuristic, as do both the tureen here and the one at the top of the page.

Puiforcat's tea and coffee sets were mass-produced and consequently survive in large numbers. Many have ivory knobs and handles, as does this tea service from around 1930. While the handles are primarily functional, acting as insulators, they are often the only decorative elements in a piece. This service is unusually ornate – for example, the banding around the base of the pieces is made of amber bakelite.
•The tray is an integral part of the set, and has decorative ribbing and scalloped borders to match.

CHRISTOFLE (FRENCH, 1839-Present)

Although Christofle had been cautious in taking up the Art Nouveau style, this family firm was more receptive than Puiforcat to the simplicity and geometric shapes of Art Deco. The firm produced all kinds of utilitarian and decorative silverplate. In the 1920s they commissioned pieces from a number of notable designers, including Gio Ponti, Maurice Daurat, Luc Lanel, Süe et Mare, Paul Follot and Christian Fjerdinsgstäd. Christofle's pieces were mass-produced, many in electroplate, which was perfected by the firm in the mid-19th century.

The electroplating process was used by Christofle for their tablewares. This included some pieces produced for the *Normandie* liner in 1935, such as this silver-plated covered vegetable dish. Typically, the surfaces are virtually plain, and any decoration is incorporated into the plating.

This electroplated tea-service, entitled "Como", was designed by Lino Sabattini and demonstrates Christofle's typically clean and geometric shapes and spindly handles. The only decoration is in the form of the cream plastic applied to the handles; the service relies upon the shiny surface of the silver for any decorative effect.
•Bases are stamped "Christofle" and indicate the grade of silver used.

MARCEL WOLFERS (FRENCH, dates unknown)

The decorative elements of this tea set from around 1930 are restricted to narrow ribbing on the bodies, and the ivory handles, which also have a function as an insulating medium. This set displays the characteristic Modernist appearance of Wolfers' work, as well as his preference for combining different materials in one piece.

Marcel Wolfers concentrated on producing luxury items with simple, solid forms and very little decoration, in a style similar to that of the Danish goldsmith Georg Jensen (see p.188). Much of his silver has a pronounced Modernist appearance, which is often emphasized by geometric motifs.
•Wolfers' silver is always signed; indeed its affinities with the work of Puiforcat and Christofle are so pronounced that the marks might be regarded as the only distinguishing features.
•Ivory appears frequently on Wolfers' pieces – there was a ready supply from the Belgian Congo in the 1920s and '30s.
•Marcel Wolfers should not be confused with his father Philippe, the Art Nouveau jeweler and silversmith.

DANISH STYLE

Danish designs in metalwork were very distinctive, with clean lines and naturalistic motifs. Georg Jensen, at the forefront of Danish silver and metalwork design throughout the 20th century, developed a style that became synonymous with the decorative and applied arts in Denmark. His early silver was embellished with Art Nouveau organic motifs, but in a far more restrained style than many other designers working at this time. Later decoration became more simplified, moving closer to the stark designs of today. Among other metalwork designers working in Denmark were Thorvald Bindesbøll (1846-1908), and the firm of Just, which worked in copper dinanderie, producing simpler forms in a typical Danish style.

A silver caviar bowl on pine cone feet by Georg Jensen 1930; ht 14in/35.5cm

GEORG JENSEN (DANISH, 1866-1935)

From 1880 Jensen worked as a goldsmith in Copenhagen, gradually moving into silverwork. He opened his first shop in 1904 and soon had branches in Paris, London, New York and other major cities. Together with his partner Johan Rohde, he designed much of the firm's output, but also employed several artists, notably Harald Nielsen from 1909 and, in the 1930s, Sigvard Bernadotte; the latter was responsible for many of the firm's linear incised engraved bodies. The Jensen workshops made high quality tea and coffee sets, candlesticks, cocktail shakers, tureens, cigar boxes, jewelry and other, often modern items obviously intended for a luxury market. Many designs, particularly the very extensive ranges of cutlery, were revolutionary. Most of the firm's products combined hand and machine production. All Jensen's silverwares, even his later pieces, have some affinities with Arts and Crafts and Art Nouveau work, especially in the use of organic pod and tendril motifs and shapes, as seen in the caviar bowl at the top of the page.

Marks Jensen's pieces bear a variety of marks – usually, the guarantee of silver, the Jensen manufactory mark and maker's initials, and a shape number. Some pieces bear an importer's mark enabling them to be sold as silver outside Denmark. In Britain, pieces that do not bear this mark are designated "silver-coloured".

The main body is seldom embellished – the emphasis is almost entirely on form, as is the case with this cocktail shaker with its plain surface and characteristic highly-polished surface. Geometric forms and motifs are stringently avoided. Inset semi-precious stones are sometimes used.

Jensen's designs from the early 20th century have a timeless quality, and remain in production even today. Pieces feature finely sculpted decorative motifs drawn from nature, generally applied to a fairly simply shaped vessel. This would have been unusual for a period when the majority of designers attempted to integrate form and decoration. Typically, in this coffee service in Jensen's popular *Blossom Pattern*, designed in 1905, ornamentation is restricted to the knops, feet and handles. Ivory has been used as a decorative feature on the handles, as well as adding insulation.

• Jensen favoured *repoussé* decoration for his silverware, which was produced in relief by hammering the reverse side of the metal.

THE WIENER WERKSTÄTTE

A silver pierced vase designed by Josef Hoffmann c.1905; ht 9in/24cm

This group of artists and craftsmen designed furniture (see pp.42-3), glass (see pp.52-3) and a number of other household objects, and the silver and metalwork designed by its leading members – Josef Hoffmann, Josef Maria Olbrich, and Koloman Moser – bears obvious similarities to the workshop's other designs. They concentrated on clear lines and pure, abstract forms, and were committed to the functionalism of what became the future Art Deco style. After the First World War a more spontaneous style developed, and by the late 1920s and early '30s pieces became more ornamental and decorative, especially those by Dagobert Pêche.

THE WIENER WERSTATTE (1903-32)

Joseph Hoffmann (1870-1956) Although much of Hoffmann's work is in the severe style of the early 20th century, he produced pieces for the Wiener Werkstätte until the 1930s. His metalwork, characterized by smooth metal surfaces, is either pierced or beaten. His pierced wares , in silver or painted metal and purely geometric in form, include desk stands, vases, baskets and candlesticks, all with pierced fretwork and no surface decoration. Like the slender silver vase on the left, many were designed to hold glass liners.

Josef Maria Olbrich (1867-1908) Olbrich's style is more fluid than that of Hoffmann. His slender, tapering forms, popular in Germany, were much emulated by German manufacturers.

Koloman Moser (1868-1918) Like Hoffmann, Moser was influenced by Mackintosh and the English Arts and Crafts designers. His inventive metalwork designs used planished silver, or incorporated formalized friezes or panels into the decoration. Typical characteristics include ball or semi-spherical feet, embossed or applied wood beading and combinations of metals and variously coloured woods.

Dagobert Pêche (1887-1923) Pêche, a designer working in all fields of the decorative arts, joined the Wiener Werkstätte in 1915. (See also p.53.)

Marks The rose mark was registered as a trademark in 1903, when the Wiener Werkstätte monogram within an oval was registered as a hallmark. "Wiener Werkstätte" was registered in 1913 and the "WW" monogram in 1914. Individual artists and craftsmen all have their own monograms, but beware, as the form and decoration were not necessarily designed by the same person.

Although this candelabrum is in pewter, Olbrich also worked in silver. The curved, organic forms in low relief, are typical of his work.

Hoffmann's later beaten wares were made in silver or brass; often simple ribbed vases or dishes, with a planished (hammered) surface. This silver baluster vase, designed in around 1910, is hammered throughout, with deep, chased flutes forming the ribs. Embossed decoration often includes a stylized rose. Feet and base, as here, are usually spreading. Vases are often constructed in two sections, such as a bowl and foot.

Characteristically of Pêche's work, this silver centrepiece from c.1920 has a strong organic emphasis. The decorated centre panel is relatively ornate compared with other silverware decoration of the 1920s. Pêche also used flowering plant motifs. The eight claw supports are reminiscent of traditional claw-and-ball feet, but the style is highly individual, with each claw grasping a fluted melon ball. Pêche also used ivory in his silverware.

AMERICAN MODERNISM

The New World cities of America provided the perfect environment for both American born and European emigré designers and architects to fulfil their Modernist ideals. Many Bauhaus designers fled from Germany to a safer haven in America where they could implement their Modernist designs. The New York skyline of the 1930s was the embodiment of the Art Deco city, with skyscrapers such as the Empire State building standing as immovable monuments to the Modern Age. This new streamlined approach was applied to all manner of decorative arts, and is particularly evident in the metalwork of the time. Norman Bel Geddes was one of a number of industrial deisgners who created a range of streamlined tablewares which fully complemented the "Skyscraper" designs of the 1930s, and which were a direct reflection of the new American architecture.

A tea and coffee service by K. E. M. Weber c.1930; ht 10in/25.4cm

KARL EMMANUEL MARTIN WEBER (AMERICAN, 1889-1963)

Weber was regarded in the United States as a champion of Modernism. He produced designs for industry, domestic interiors and Hollywood film sets, as well as individually commissioned and mass-produced furniture, ranging from ornately decorative items to comfortably upholstered tubular metal and sprung steel chairs. His most important work is from after 1927.

The service above was designed for the Porter Blanchard company. He also designed for the International Silver Company. All Weber's silver and plate designs are sleekly modern yet wholly functional, many showing the influence of the German Bauhaus. There is very little surface embellishment; any decoration appears discreetly on bases or covers.

THE INTERNATIONAL SILVER CO. (AMERICAN, 1898-1984)

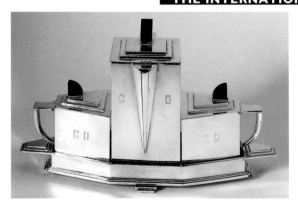

This silver-plated metal tea service from around 1928, was commissioned from the American designer, Gilbert Rohde.

•Rohde was a highly prolific designer, best known for his furniture, which was produced by the Herman Miller Company and others.

In 1898 a consortium of more than 30 small manufacturers of silver and plate combined to form one organization, the International Silver Company. Much of their commercial success was generated by the "Hotel Division", which specialized in flatware and hollow ware for use in hotels, institutions and, during the 1930s, steamships. Most of these wares are of little or no collectable interest, but in the 1920s and '30s the company employed a number of outside designers, notably Donald Deskey, Karl Weber and Gilbert Rohde, to design useful and decorative wares in silver, plate and pewter which are considerably more collectable.
•Rohde also designed Modernist chromium cocktail and smoking accessories for the Chase Brass & Copper Company. In the 1930s Chase published an extensive catalogue of its wares. Good examples are collectable.

Manufacturers Many International Silver pieces were produced through divisions which used older, prestigious trade marks – for example, the Wilcox Silver Plate Company, whose trademark was used for the tea service on the previous page; other names include Rogers, and Miller.

•All International Silver Company pieces bear the mark of the manufacturing company and many also bear the signature of the designer.

The International Silver Company's later 1920s designs include a series of four-part tea services such as this one

designed by Gene Theobald. In electroplated nickel silver with bakelite handles, they are designed to sit snugly in the fitted tray. Pieces such as these are clearly machine-made, although hand-finished, and are representative of American silver of the time, which was heading away from the European tradition of hand-crafting towards mass-produced industrial design.

NORMAN BEL GEDDES (AMERICAN, 1893-1958)

Bel Geddes produced metalwares for several manufacturers. Designs are mostly functional. Some are marked with his facsimile signature. This cocktail shaker, like the cocktail service on the right, is in chromium-plated metal and was commissioned by the Revere Copper and Brass Company in 1935. It shows a characteristic restrained, linear style that complements the streamlined and "Skyscraper" styles of the 1930s American Art Deco.

•Cocktail wares were popular throughout the 1930s, reflecting the new trends in lifestyle, where drinking and cocktail parties played an important part in leisure activities.

Bel Geddes was prominent among a group of talented and highly qualified designers, notably Russell Wright, Raymond Loewy, Henry Dreyfuss and Walter Dorwin Teague, who were all drawn to industrial design for its artistic and creative potential. Bel Geddes trained as a theatre and set designer before setting himself up as an industrial designer in 1927. His early commissions, before 1932, were largely for domestic products, such as gas stoves.

Bel Geddes produced designs for a wide variety of American corporations, such as IBM and General Motors. He also designed furniture, including some for the Simmons Co., which celebrated metal, rather than attempting to use it to simulate wood.

Some small streamlined wares were very successful – this chromed-metal soda bottle with a brightly coloured cover and a chromed metal conical body, was produced in great numbers by the Walter Kidd Sales Co. Inc., which patented the design. They were made in different colours and were originally sold at very low prices. They are of limited interest to collectors today, but may become more popular.

This Skyscraper cocktail service and Manhattan tray from 1937 typify Bel Geddes's Modern designs. He can be largely credited with creating the streamlined style which he declared a treatment suitable for virtually any product. Although some of his more outlandish suggestions for futuristic steam locomotives, transatlantic airliners and so on were not realized, he did produce designs for airplane interiors in the streamlined style which were used. His approach to industrial design followed closely the principles of the Bauhaus in its attempt to integrate form with function.

WALTER DORWIN TEAGUE (AMERICAN, 1883-1960)

Another industrial designer, Teague is mainly remembered for the service stations he designed for Texaco in the United States in the mid-30s. He was retained by Kodak for about 30 years to design some of their cameras and packaging. All his work is characterized by a readiness to harmonize function with bold design. In his metalwares he often contrasted chrome metal with black lacquered metal in a streamlined form. He also incorporated new materials.

THE UNEXPECTED BEAUTY OF IRON & COPPER

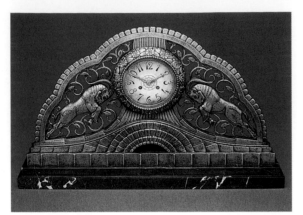

A silvered bronze mantel clock by Edgar Brandt c.1925; ht 15½in/39.5cm

The 1920s saw a revival in both decorative wrought-iron work and copperware. The French master ferriers injected new life into the medium with their often inventive and highly sculptural designs. Edgar Brandt in particular attracted international acclaim and his work was heavily featured in several pavilions at the 1925 Paris exhibition. The work of Raymond Subes follows a distinctive Modernist ideal, with his preference for strong, yet simple supports for often stark marble tabletops. There was also a revival of decorative copperware (dinanderie) which was prompted by the highly talented craftsman, Jean Dunand, and his Swiss contemporary, Claudius Linossier, both of whom produced strong, often Classical forms embellished with geometric inlay and subtle patination that closely followed the ideals of Japanese metalwork popularized earlier in the century. The work of all these designers was almost entirely hand-crafted and therefore for many people was prohibitively expensive. However, the German firm of W.M.F., recognizing the increasing demand for dinanderie, produced a series of vases which emulated these French masterworks but used mass-production techniques to make them available to a much wider public (see p.185 for W.M.F.'s silverwares).

EDGAR BRANDT (FRENCH, 1880-1960)

Brandt began working in iron at an early age. He made mostly jewelry and wrought-iron work until 1919, when he opened his atelier in Paris, producing his own designs and those of others. His work was acclaimed in 1925, when he co-designed the *Porte d'Honneur* for the Paris Exhibition, and exhibited his famous five-panel wrought-iron and brass screen, *Oasis*. With its stylized central fountain and French Art Deco-type scrolls, the screen was typical of much of the work Brandt produced during the 1920s. Brandt was the leading metalworker of the Art Deco period, both in Paris and New York, where he opened Ferrobrandt Inc., a company that executed commissions for several buildings and produced a range of domestic wares.

This marble, wrought-iron and bronze table, from around 1929, demonstrates Brandt's great use of the decorative elements of wrought iron. Joints, screws and bolts are subtle or, as here, concealed. Ornate decorative elements appear in the form of repeated scrolling devices and two bronze fans. Other popular motifs used by Brandt include animals, evident in the mantel clock above. Much of Brandt's work exhibits a symmetry which seems natural rather than mechanical and rigid.
• Brandt produced a range of highly collectable domestic items, including radiator covers, screens, umbrella stands, tables and fireplace accessories as well as small decorative wares such as jewelry, trays, vases and paper knives.
• Pieces are usually stamped "E. Brandt" often on the footrim.

Brandt is probably best known for his bronze serpent lamp, *La Tentation*, made as a table lamp, a standard lamp and in an intermediate size. The glass shade was by Daum. Fakes abound. These can usually be detected by the poor-quality patination and the lack of definition in the casting of the snake and the shades, which are usually of lightweight glass, inferior to the Daum originals.

On originals the shade and support meet perfectly, whereas on fakes they are a poor fit. Before buying, compare the article with one known to be genuine. Beware of lamps with old wirings and fixtures, as these may have been taken from another old lamp to create an impression of age. Similarly, a perfectly genuine old lamp may well have new wires and fixtures.

RAYMOND SUBES (FRENCH, 1893-1970)

Next to Brandt, Subes is probably the most renowned French metalworker of the Deco period. In 1919 he became director of the metal workshop of Broderel and Robert, a major architectural construction company. Most of his work was on government commissions, notably the *Normandie* and other important liners of the period, to which he contributed wall decorations as well as gilded metalwork. Like Brandt, Subes initially worked in wrought iron, sometimes gilded, and occasionally in bronze and copper. By the 1930s he was working in aluminium and oxidised or lacquered steel. His output was prodigious: despite their hand-finished look, his tables, mirrors, lamps and radiator cases were mainly mass-produced using industrial methods. Early motifs tend towards the naturalistic and slightly florid.

Identification Much of Subes' work is difficult to identify as it is incorporated into fixtures, such as building façades, balustrades and furniture mounts. Pieces rarely come onto the market, and are often unsigned.

By the end of the 1920s decoration had become minimal and was often restricted to the supports – for example, the S-shaped straps of this table. Here the iron has been finely bent into ribbon-like curls; in other cases he uses octopus-like curls or stylized flowers. Table tops are usually marble, as here, or granite.

During the 1930s Subes' work became much heavier in appearance, distinguishing it from that of Brandt. Often of bronze or aluminium in simple and bold forms it features architectural shapes, fluted columns and fans, or rectangular stepped or panelled plinths. The overall impression is of massive size and strength.

PAUL KISS (RUMANIAN BORN, dates unknown)

Kiss was another important metalworker of the Art Deco period, and was working in France at the same time as Subes. Like Brandt, he preferred ornate designs and motifs and his work displays keen attention to detail. As well as wrought iron, Kiss also worked in silvered bronze.

Marks Kiss's work usually has a stamped signature "P. KISS PARIS", or "P. KISS"

Kiss is particularly known for his mirrors, which tend to have an elongated form and may include decorative tassels. This mirror is supported by silk cords. It also shows Kiss's tendency to create a textured look. Pieces are often mounted, or enhanced by marble, alabaster or engraved glass. He also made table lamps and ceiling fixtures.

JEAN DUNAND (SWISS, 1877-1942)

Dunand, who moved to Paris in 1896, was a prolific metalworker, lacquerist and furniture designer who produced expensive high-quality pieces for the most exclusive end of the market. His work was all hand-made and specially commissioned.

Marks Not all of Dunand's work is signed, but some pieces are marked "JEAN DUNAND", sometimes with a serial number. Others have "JEAN DUNAND 72 RUE HALLE PARIS MADE IN FRANCE".

Left Dunand was particularly interested in dinanderie – a technique of applying patinated enamelling over a non-precious metal, such as copper or steel. His vases often feature sharp angular lines and have a geometrical bias, evident in this lacquered dinanderie vase. Red and black was a favourite combination on Dunand's vases, possibly reflecting the Oriental influence behind much of his work.

CLAUDIUS LINOSSIER (FRENCH, 1893-1955)

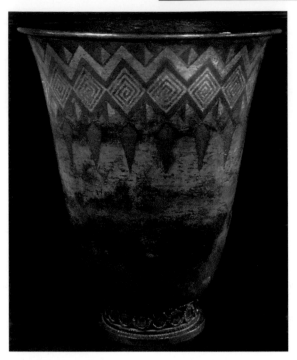

Linossier is chiefly noted for the elegant design and textured surfaces of his vases, bowls and plates, which were produced by his workshop in Lyon. He worked in copper, brass and occasionally silver. Surfaces retain a hammered texture, and are often chased, encrusted in metal (usually silver) to contrast with the patinated background, or inlaid with fired designs in which adjacent metals are finely fused. Surfaces are often patinated in black and russet, or dappled polychrome. Colours tend to be muted and autmnal.

Right As well as everted bell shapes, Linossier also used a baluster form, like that shown here. The bands of diamonds and chevrons are characteristic of his designs, as is their position near the top of the piece and pendant from the rim. Spiral motifs sometimes appear, especially on more rounded or pumpkin-shaped forms.
•Linossier was apprenticed to Jean Dunand, and his geometric, deliberately primitive designs, produced during the 1920s, reveal Dunand's influence (see previous page).
•Lipped rims appear on many of his everted vases.

This dinanderie copper vase from the 1920s looks typically hand-made, and is taken from a single, seamless sheet of copper to which inlays have been added. The shape is characteristically tall and elegant, tapering towards the narrow footrim which has latticed decoration.

W.M.F. (GERMAN, established 1880)

W.M.F.'s wares are usually smaller than Linossier's. This vase is 8in/20.5cm high. Although clearly not hand-made, it is nevertheless well-proportioned and has an attractive finish – and is likely to be within the budget of most collectors.
•W.M.F. also made a range of mass-produced German art pewter wares in a classically Art Nouveau style (see. p.185)

Linossier's influence is evident in the work of W.M.F., who managed to mass-produce its wares, using an electrolytic process. W.M.F. applied metallic deposits in various colours to its vases, which were made up of seamed pieces. Surfaces were not textured, but patinated, which gives a slightly rigid appearance. Although less desirable than Linossier's, W.M.F.'s wares are nevertheless collectable.

Beware A number of highly polished examples of W.M.F.'s work have appeared on the market, the patination having been stripped, often out of ignorance. These should be avoided.

ARMAND-ALBERT RATEAU (FRENCH, 1882-1938)

This rare bronze, marble and ivory dressing table by Rateau, from c.1920, has a simple form, embellished with strong decorative elements. The stylized birds supporting the mirror are a recurrent theme in his work.

Rateau, a French Art Deco interior decorator and furniture designer, is particularly recognized for his use of patinated bronze, usually in antique green, and his lacquering. His work is inspired by the Orient and antiquity, with butterflies, gazelles and acanthus being other common motifs.

OTHER ART DECO METALWORK

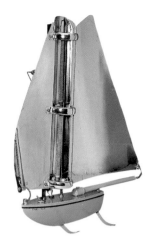

In addition to the products of the major metalworkers of the Art Deco period, there were a number of other pieces which are collectable today. Novelty items were popular, such as lamps and electrical fixtures in unusual forms. Other pieces emulated the work of the masters, such as Edgar Brandt and Raymond Subes (see p.192). Chrome came into its own and was used for a number of wares, including black-lacquered streamlined products, some in novelty forms, and for many of the fixtures in the Odeon cinemas in Britain, both for the interiors and for small accoutrements such as lighters and radios. Architectural fixtures, especially those in chrome, tend to surface with great regularity in street markets in England and elsewhere. The plating of these is often worn or flaking but can be restored.

An electrical heater; ht 2½ft (75cm)

TABLE LIGHTERS

Table lighters are probably the area that offers the greatest scope for collectors today, as there are plenty of chromed, lacquered, streamlined examples available. Many were a feature of fashionable homes and public buildings of the 1930s, especially in the United States.

This lighter is typical of those produced during the Art Deco years. Such lighters tended to feature strong primary colours, often with contrasting appliqués in either silvered or gilt metal. This particular example is very inventive as it incorporates a clock.

UNSIGNED ITEMS

A lot of decorative metalware displays high-quality craftsmanship and is close to the work of the top designers featured in this section. However, because such pieces are unattributed, they do not command very high prices today.

The quality of casting of the brooch below is quite good, but the lack of a signature means that the value of the piece will be considerably reduced.

This brooch, fashioned in the manner of Edgar Brandt, is an archetypal Art Deco piece in that it uses bronze with steel or hammered ironwork and shows a typically stylized women of the period, with bobbed hair, and an elongated face. Her earrings impart an African flavour, and suggest a date for the piece of c.1930.

ELECTRICAL ITEMS

The boat, above left, is an ingeniously designed electric heater: the element is in the mast, and the metal sails act as radiators. Electric heaters were a relatively new phenomenon in the 1930s, and only a few have so far appeared on the market. It is preferable, but not essential, that any electrical items are in working order.

The two-dimensional figure supporting this light fixture is made from cut-out chromed sheet metal. It is highly stylized, and shows the inspiration of the Amazonian images popular during the Art Deco period. It is not signed. Items such as this were mass-produced, but have not so far appeared on the market in any quantity: as period pieces, they are likely to become increasingly collectable.

RADIOS

Radios were also treated as both functional and decorative items during this period, and were often highly stylized. Many were produced in bakelite. Some were by top designers, including the British industrial designer Wells Coates.

JEWELRY & PRECIOUS OBJECTS

In the Victorian period jewelry became increasingly ostentatious. Britain borrowed designs from Europe, but adapted them to suit the British taste for heavier forms. Mourning jewelry was particularly popular, following the death of Prince Albert. As the century progressed styles became much lighter and more open, and often showed the influence of the Orient, and were sometimes more angular. The Continental influence was also important in the United States, especially in the second half of the 19th century, where forms were ornate and often heavily jewelled. Until around 1850 most jewelry was hand-made, but after that date increasing use was made of machines. Hand-made pieces are particularly sought-after. Materials included gold of different carats – the yellower the gold, the higher the carat and the greater the proportion of gold to metal (9 carat gold is one part gold to two parts metal). Most 19th century gold is 15 carat. Other pieces were gilded with a thin gold coating over a base metal. Difficult for the untrained eye to discern, gilded pieces can sometimes be identified by a patch of a different colour where the gilding has worn off and exposed the metal beneath. Sometimes a jeweller has to scrape an unobtrusive area with acid, and sadly, good pieces have been ruined by being scraped in an obvious place. Sets of jewelry were popular, and those that survive intact and in their original boxes command a premium. Marks on the boxes may be those of the retailer, rather than the maker. Watches were worn on gold pendants, sometimes enamelled, engraved or embellished with diamonds. Diamond watches are collectable, but others are sought-after only if by top makers. Men wore little jewelry during this period, apart from cravat pins, rings and watch chains.

Jewelry in the Art Nouveau period moved away from over-embellishment with ornate stones towards a more sculptural style, and materials were chosen for their function rather than any intrinsic value. The carving of jewels also underwent a renaissance. Subjects were naturalistic and, as in other media, included insects and flowers. The female form was also featured, often in a symbolic form. French designers dominated the field, with René Lalique demonstrating outstanding artistry in carving and composition. French designs were more fluid than those of the Germans, who preferred more abstract forms, and of the Viennese, who used simple, highly stylized motifs. Secessionist and Wiener Werkstätte designers produced some very strong designs. Viennese jewelry is compara-

tively rare today. In England Liberty sold Cymric jewelry designed mostly by Archibald Knox; Charles Horner produced a similar range. Enamelwork was revived by Alexander Fisher.

In the Art Deco period luxury jewelry was in vogue, with Cartier, Gerard Sandoz and Georges Fouquet all using Modernist forms as well as working in more traditional styles. Exotic jewels were often incorporated, and novelty forms were sometimes used. Chinoiserie was popular, especially in the 1920s, and coral and jade, often carved, became fashionable on a scale not seen before. Glass jewelry was promoted by Lalique, but its fragility means it is now rather scarce and therefore sought after. At the other end of the market, there was a quantity of mass-produced costume dress jewelry and metalwork. Techniques were evolved to simulate crushed eggshell, and some designs were painted on a base metal to simulate enamel inlay or more precious metals. Designs also used new plastics. Diamanté and marcasite were frequently used, especially in sunburst or fountain motifs. Changes in fashion in the 1920s and '30s demanded new forms of jewelry – for example, earrings became longer as women wore their hair shorter. Brooches became fashionable, and were worn on outdoor clothing, especially coat collars, not just on evening wear as before. The lady's wristwatch proved popular, the best examples being French. Watch faces were often silver or platinum inset with geometric initials or paste stones. Utility items, such as powder compacts, cigarette cases, evening bags and clasps for bags were also in demand, as were enamelled dressing table sets.

Condition is important when collecting jewelry. Avoid pieces that have been repaired with lead solder rather than gold, as lead looks ugly and untidy around the damaged area. On flexible (articulated) pieces examine wear at the links, especially at the joints of curved bracelets. Victorian jewelry can be a minefield for the inexperienced collector, especially as, apart from the work of the top makers, very few pieces are marked. Collectors should seek expert advice, especially in identifying stones as there are many excellent copies and fakes. Any marks are usually in a very obscure place – for example, on a hook or fitting, so it is also important to determine that such fittings are original to the piece. Evidence of provenance will increase value and is usually a sign of quality.

Above *A carved ivory pendant by Henri Vever, c.1900*
Right *A powder compact, attributed to Van Cleef and Arpels, c.1920*

VICTORIAN OPULENCE

Victorian jewelers, in revolt against the plainness of the jewelry of the George III period, created increasingly elaborate designs as the century progressed. Diamonds came into their own, jewelers taking advantage of better lighting and improved cutting and mounting techniques. Cameos came back into fashion, in keeping with the interest in all things Renaissance. Pendants and earrings were long. Fringed necklaces were popular, and wrists were adorned with bracelets, or later, bangles. Jewelry was worn in the hair as tiaras or on strings of pearls.

Right A foiled rock crystal and chrysolite openwork locket back brooch c.1840

PENDANTS AND BROOCHES

Most pendants and brooches of the Victorian era have small lockets in the back for a memento such as a lock of hair or a photograph. The symbolic padlock suspended from the example above would have contained the locket. Pieces were in 15 carat gold. Less exclusive versions were made for the masses in gilt metal, with coloured glass replacing the semi-precious stones. Although less expensive, these are still collectable.

Glass or semi-precious stones? Although it is difficult for the untrained eye to determine whether a jewel is precious, glass can often be identified by gas bubbles, visible under a magnifying glass.

Condition Pendants and brooches are susceptible to wear, especially on the high spots. One way to repair damaged or worn areas is to flood the whole piece with gold, but the colour match will not be perfect.

Collecting points

• Most lockets are backed with a piece of glass inside to protect the insert. Closed lockets have a hinged lid at the front; open lockets have a glass front and no cover.

• Most pieces are dual purpose: a small hinged ring at the back of the brooch flicks up to form the loop for a chain. The brooch fitting, screwed into the centre of the back, can be removed when not in use.

• English pieces are generally heavier in style than the Continental pieces that inspired them.

• Earrings were also made in stud form for pierced ears, many with pearls or garnets, or in the form of circles of turquoise. The pendant is more popular today.

• Garnets, popular during the Victorian period, although only semi-precious, fetch high prices.

Many Victorian pieces have hanging tassels, as in this oval locket pendant. It is crucial that all the tassels be intact, as they are easily damaged. Often, they were trapped between the lid and the box while being stored.

Spare fittings were kept beneath the silk cover of the box, so it is important to have the original fittings and preferably the original box as well.

Archaeological discoveries were an important source of inspiration for brooch and pendant designs. The simulated wire and beadwork of the ancient Etruscans is shown to good effect in this bulla and locket with the cruciform motif.

Frosted and gilded finishes are closely associated with the Victorian period. The frosted matt appearance of this gold locket complements the diamond star motif. Frosted gilding is sometimes replaced by a polished surface, which will cause a drop in value.

CAMEOS

Cameos regained popularity in the 19th century with the revival of interest in the early Roman art of gem cutting. The best cameo-cutters were in Italy, and most worked in shell rather than hardstone, paring away the layers to form a picture, each layer revealing a different colour. Many Italian cameos were imported loose (unmounted) to England, where they were mounted. A few cameos are made from more obscure materials, including moonstones, chalcedony and moulded glass. Lava cameos are probably the least popular, because of their usually murky colours, but the carvings are often delightful. Usually in very high relief they are also prone to wear.

Many early cameos, were inspired by early Roman examples of emperors and gods. This shell cameo of c.1840 shows the head of Jupiter above an eagle.
•Although often hand-finished, most 20th century cameos and reproductions are machine-cut, giving them a mechanical appearance. They often have clearly modern subjects.

Good quality cameos are usually in good surrounds. The best are gold or diamond. Most are ornate with good quality workmanship: this hardstone cameo has an elaborate gold surround with pierced decoration. The pendant loop of dual purpose cameos should match the rest of the mount.
•Cameo pendant earrings are sought after today. Pairs do not necessarily belong together – in genuine pieces the pair will face each other.

Hardstone cameos (made from onyx or agate) are the most desirable, being harder than shell and more difficult to work with. With the best examples several differently coloured layers can be achieved. In this cameo of a female head from around 1880, several layers of agate have been pared away to form the flower for the hair. To determine whether a cameo is

shell or hardstone, scratch the back of the piece – if shell, the scratch mark will be apparent, if hardstone, the cameo will be unaffected. Hardstone also has a higher gloss than shell. Shell cameos should be examined carefully for evidence of cracks, visible when held up to the light. High spots are also prone, and detail, such as strands of hair, may blur in time as the edges soften.

DIAMOND JEWELRY

Jewelry with diamonds, occasionally combined with other stones, was popular in the 19th century. Value is determined as much by the overall decorative effect as by the quality of the individual diamonds. The quality of modern fakes is such that even experts have difficulty in recognizing them. However, paste stones, which were not necessarily intended to deceive, are gilded at the back (or backed with glass) to brighten the stones.

The type and method of mounting aid dating. All closed setting 19th century diamonds are mounted in either silver, gold, or more often, silver on gold. Platinum was not used until the 20th century. Silver, softer than platinum, will not stand as much wear on the claws holding the diamonds in place.

These diamonds are set into an obviously more modern 1920s platinum surround. White metal mounts with a hard polished finish will either be platinum or rhodium-plated (both 20th century) to give a modern appearance. Such alteration will detract from the value.

Individual stones show up better against silver because it darkens naturally with age, as in this brooch. This dark patina should not be cleaned, as the character of the piece would be destroyed – although in time the silver would darken again.

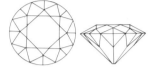

Cushion-shaped

Old (Victorian) brilliant-cut

Modern brilliant cut

Symbolism featured strongly in diamond jewelry. Necklaces in the form of a snake swallowing its own tail (symbolizing unity and eternity) abound. This example has rose-diamond and blue enamel decoration.

Diamonds were in open (**left top**) or closed (**left bottom**) settings. Closed settings, from the late 18th and early 19th century usually contain foil to add to the brilliance.

Cuts Diamond jewelry can be dated by the cut of the stones, which is particularly important as some Victorian diamonds have been reset into modern platinum mounts. The principal forms of cutting used in the Victorian period were rose-cutting, brilliant-cutting and cushion or table-cutting (**top left**). Rose-cut diamonds are chips from a larger diamond, flat at the back and faceted at the front. Modern diamonds are brilliant-cut (**bottom left**), but with more facets than Victorian brilliant-cut diamonds (**centre left**), which have a visible spot in the centre.

Messages in stone A popular Victorian practice was to spell out words using the initial letter of the colours chosen. The most common was R.E.G.A.R.D., made up of a ruby, emerald, garnet, amethyst, another ruby and a diamond. Other pieces incorporate a bar with the initials in stones of the owner or recipient; because they bear a name, these are of more limited appeal.

Motifs The butterfly is an ancient good luck symbol; wings were a popular Pre-Raphelite motif. Stars, also popular, were often used to adorn a tiara or hair comb. Other motifs include jockeys and horseshoes.

MOURNING JEWELRY

Mourning or memorial jewelry was as prolific during the Victorian era as in the 17th and 18th centuries but in a more subtle form than the skulls and crossbones previously favoured. Unfashionable for a time, it is now very sought-after and can command high prices. It is characterized by its use of dark grounds and stones, especially jet, black or very dark blue enamel, and agate and onyx. Unlike enamel, onyx has a lustre. Black glass (French jet) has a glassier texture than real jet.

Rings Initialled mourning rings were sometimes commissioned by a dying person to be given to friends and family after their death. Thus, identical rings are not necessarily copies or reproductions.

Flowers were used to good decorative effect against the dark enamelled background popular with mourning jewelry. Forget-me-nots, as in this bangle, were very common.

Hair jewelry includes necklaces and earrings and must be in good condition to have any value at all. It is mostly bought for its academic interest. Sprays of hair also appear in lockets. In time, photographs replaced hair as a memory of the loved one.

Pearls are symbolic of tears and were employed in many pieces of mourning jewelry. The pearls in these pieces have been cut in half and cemented or "pinch set" into position, allowing for a closer fit to the mount. Occasionally, mixed items are offered as sets which do not always belong together. These pieces are clearly a set as they employ the same materials and style of decoration.

TIFFANY AND CO. (AMERICAN, 1837-Present)

Although several American companies sold jewelry in the 19th century, none could compare with Tiffany for the quality and range of their products. Founded by Charles Louis Tiffany (1812-1902) and John B. Mill Young, the firm started as a modest New York store that sold small, decorative objects imported from Europe and the Far East, but within a few years had gained a reputation for supplying its customers with high quality gemstones and ornate, modern jewelry comissioned from German and French goldsmiths.

By the early 1850s, the company, then known as Tiffany & Co., had moved to showrooms on Broadway, and during the last half of the century, it offered fashionable accessories, silverware (see p.179) and many other desirable wares as well as jewelry. In 1868, the company opened branches in Paris, Geneva and London. It established its standards of excellence by commissioning designs in the form of working drawings from top American and foreign craftsmen as well as its own staff.

A Tiffany enamelled brooch set with two natural pearls c.1885

Jewelry ranges Tiffany's jewelry struck a balance between the demand for luxury, intrinsic value and modern design, but also offered a range of multi-cultural styles which looked to the past as well as at the present. The range included:
•Gothic, Rococo, Louis XVI and Renaissance designs, seen in watches as well as jewelry. The brooch at the top of the page is based on a drawing by Holbein.
•Classical antiquity, including Greek, Roman, Pharaonic and Etruscan models.
•Persian and Moorish-influenced designs.
•European Art Nouveau-inspired designs, quickly adopted after the Paris Exposition Universelle of 1889.
•American motifs, particularly by the 1890s.
•Realistically modelled flowers, insects and animals.

From around 1860 the firm exploited the contemporary taste for verisimilitude, making brooches and clips on gold frames, set with small diamonds or coloured gemstones against a polychrome, vitreous enamel. The diamonds were often in foliate settings on floral gold mounts.

In the Art Deco period Tiffany continued to create pieces for an elitist market. Their clocks in particular exemplified the new stylistic trends, demonstrating a Chinese influence and using precious stones, especially diamonds.

This small Tiffany clock, only 5in (12.7cm) high, combines a relatively plain, modernistic cabinet and support with a jewelled opulence, while the green jade elephant and pseudo-Chinese characters for numerals show an obvious Oriental influence. The bold colours are characteristic of those used by Tiffany.

Stars were popular on both sides of the Atlantic in the 19th century. This diamond starburst brooch with its densely-packed stones is a typical Tiffany design, and was made in around 1885. The centre stone is of Tiffany's typically generous size, and the diamonds are set in silver mounts with a gold back.

Marks Most pieces made by Tiffany since 1868 are impressed with the firm's stamp and relevant metal marks.

LALIQUE AND FRENCH EXPERIMENTATION

A blond horn and enamel butterfly stomacher 1900; ht 4-5in/10-12.7cm

The standard of craftsmanship and variety of invention in French jewelry was unrivalled in the Art Nouveau period. René Lalique was the leading influence, constantly experimenting with new materials, techniques and designs and introducing many motifs which are now synonymous with Art Nouveau style. Henri Vever and Georges Fouquet followed Lalique's ideas and their work was of an equally high standard. Also producing high-quality jewelry were Lucien Gaillard, whose designs were strongly influenced by the Japanese, and Eugène Feuillâtre, who intially worked for Lalique. Alphonse Mucha designed a limited range of theatrical jewelry.

This pendant displays several features typical of Lalique's work: the multiple form is common to his pendant designs and the neckchain is interspersed with opal beads. Chains are often innovative and integral to the design of the piece. They may consist of bar links or beads of precious stones.

Signatures Most early examples of Lalique's jewelry are engraved "R Lalique" perhaps accompanied by "France" and a model number in matching script.

RENÉ LALIQUE (FRENCH, 1860-1945)

René Lalique (see also pp.90-1) revolutionized the art of jewelry by emphasizing the sculptural quality of jewels. Fitness for purpose was an important factor and, although he made use of precious materials, he would only do so if they contributed to aesthetic quality. It was for aesthetic reasons that he combined materials of different intrinsic values. Tortoiseshell, horn or glass might be set within a frame of precious metal, or studded with precious and semi-precious stones such as pearls, opals or moonstones. Lalique's jewelry ranges from hat pins to the massive corsages designed for Sarah Bernhardt (one of his most important patrons) which included chokers, bracelets, pendants, stomachers (worn over a bodice), brooches and hair combs. Few of his designs were executed by himself, but were handmade by other craftsmen.

Decorative techniques Lalique used several decorative techniques; the butterfly stomacher at the top of the page, carved from one piece of blonde horn, is enamelled in various tones of brown. Other decorative methods include *pâte-sur-pâte*, *champlevé* enamelling and *plique-à-jour* enamelling (see next page), usually found on the wings of his insects. He also used oxidized silver and carved gemstones. Decorative techniques are often used to constructive effect: the strong colouring and definition of the larger butterfly here, set against smaller, paler butterflies, suggest a three-dimensional effect.
•Lalique started to experiment with glass in 1902 and some of his later Art Nouveau jewelry incorporates moulded glass, sometimes with glaze effects.

Lalique's pieces are famous for their inspired composition. His designs are typically symmetrical. The symmetrical enamelled peacocks in this pendant provide a balanced frame for the central triangular opal; in their beaks they hold the pearl terminal of the neck chain and from their tails hangs a decorative pearl drop.

Fakes A number of recent discoveries have been considered to be extremely dubious, because although of good quality, they often fall short of the superb craftsmanship of known Lalique pieces.

LUCIEN GAILLARD (FRENCH, born 1861)

Gaillard initially made his name as a silversmith in around 1889, but was persuaded by René Lalique to design jewelry, and his work owes much to Lalique. He is best known for his hair slides or combs in tortoiseshell, ivory or horn, and it is these that appear most frequently at auction. Like Lalique's, Gaillard's designs were always innovative and often used a combination of mundane and more precious materials.

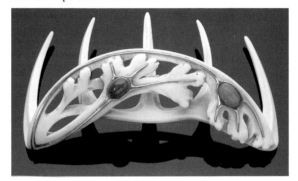

Gaillard favoured naturalistic motifs, such as the stylized fronds set with two oval chalcedonies on this ivory hair comb. Unlike the tortoiseshell comb on the right, here the form and decoration are integral. Sepia staining adds depth.

•Many of Gaillard's pieces are accompanied by their original presentation box; such examples are often preserved in their original condition.
•Gaillard signed his work "L GAILLARD" or "LUCIEN GAILLARD".

This hair ornament from around 1901 features a standard tortoiseshell hair comb, with enamel and diamond decoration added almost as an appendage. In spite of the high degree of craftsmanship evident in this piece, particularly in the enamel work, the swallows are slightly stiff in comparison with the work of Lalique. However, the piece has a striking three-dimensional quality.

EUGÈNE FEUILLÂTRE (FRENCH, 1870-1916)

After leaving Lalique's workshop in 1899, Eugene Feuillâtre set up his own business. He continued the tradition of enamelling established at Limoges in France during the 12th century, and often worked in *plique-à-jour* (see below). He produced mainly *objets de vertu* – often of quite substantial size – as well as jewelry similar to that of Lalique, using glass, gold and silver. Feuillâtre also perfected a technique of applying enamel to platinum jewelry.

Feuillâtre's designs tend to have a strong symmetrical element: the silver snakes supporting the ring tray of this spectacular piece are symmetrically arranged, although the decoration of the tray itself displays an asymmetrical *plique-à-jour* fish motif.

The quality of casting on this mounted and enamelled gilt-bronze vase is characteristically high. The use of enamelling against a toned silver background is unusual, as is the perspective of the piece. Again, the form involves a combination of symmetrical and asymmetrical elements.
•Most pieces bear an engraved signature, "FEUILLATRE". Any jewlery simply attributed to Feuillâtre, and without a supporting signature, should be treated with suspicion.

Plique-à-jour This is an open-braid method of enamelling whereby a structure of metal strips laid on a metal background form enclosed areas that are then filled with translucent enamels. When the backing is removed, a transparent "stained glass" effect is achieved. Developed in Russia during the 17th century this method was adopted by French and English Art Nouveau jewelers for pendants and brooches. Feuillâtre was perhaps the greatest exponent of the *plique-à-jour* method. Probably his nearest rival in quality was Carl Fabergé, the Russian jeweler and silversmith.

VEVER (FRENCH, 1821-1982)

This gold and enamel buckle from c.1900 depicts the typical Art Nouveau motifs of a higly stylized female in flowing robes and a cock pheasant, together with trailing vines. The symbolism is uncertain, although cockerels are a common symbol for France, and the woman may represent Liberty. The piece is characteristically well-chased, with good strong facial detail. The drapery is well cast and the enamelling on the cockerel is excellent. Most of Vever's pieces appeared in limited editions, and were never mass-produced.

Pierre Vever founded this retail and manufacturing jewelers in Metz in 1821. His son, Ernest, joined the company in 1848. The business moved to Paris following the German annexation of Alsace-Lorraine in 1871 and in 1881 Ernest handed over control to his sons Paul (1851-1915) and Henri (1854-1942), under whose guidance Vever became the leading Art Nouveau jewelers in Paris.

The Vever brothers combined fine technique, good form and semi-precious and precious stones to create jewelry which has an unprecedented sculptural quality. Their work is often compared to that of René Lalique, although it tends to lack Lalique's inventiveness. Vever favoured natural forms and took inspiration from botanical themes.

Vever commissioned several important designers, including the posterist, Eugène Grasset (see p.217), Lucien Gautrait, Henri Vollet and René Rozet. Grasset's designs display a strong element of symbolism.

The similarity of Vever's work to that of René Lalique can be seen in this plaque from a *collier de chien* (worn on a soft velvet collar), designed by Paul and Henri Vever in collaboration. The very fine openwork cast design is set with rose-cut diamonds and light blue *plique-à-jour* and green and orange enamelling. Interestingly, the decoration is not constrained by the design – one of the flowerheads overreaches the buckle on the left hand side of the picture. This technique tends to give perspective and a sense of depth.

Marks Most Vever jewelry is marked, usually with the firm's name and a serial number. The gold and enamel *collier de chien* plaque bears the legend "Vever Paris no. 1256", engraved. Alternatively, the mark could be stamped.
•Some items are offered for sale in their original box and these can provide valuable information as to provenance.

This fuchsia pendant, designed by Henri Vever in 1889, shows the company's preoccupation with the organic. The flowerhead is articulated – an example of the minute attention to detail typical of Vever's work. Characteristically, the design is symmetrical. Like other jewelers of the period, Vever used a wide variety of materials in its work: the pendant combines gold, opals, diamonds and enamelwork.
•This pendant still retains its original box bearing the inscripton "Ane Mon Marret & Baugrand, Vever 19 rue de la Paix 19 Paris Grand Prix Expon Univle Paris 1889", indicating that the piece was made for the Paris exhibition.

GEORGES FOUQUET (FRENCH, 1862-1957)

Gges Fouquet
G. FOUQUET

Also bearing close comparison with the jewelry of René Lalique was that of Georges Fouquet, the son of Alphonse Fouquet, a Parisian jeweller known for his enamelled renaissance revival pieces.

As well as his jewelry in the Art Nouveau style, he also made the transition to Art Deco (see p.209).
•Fouquet's work was designed to be exclusive.

Marks Most of Fouquet's work is well documented; many of his original drawings and designs are held at the *Musée des Art Decoratifs* in Paris. Pieces are signed, usually with the letter "G" or his signature, stamped (below left), and most also bear a reference number.

Georges Fouquet's sources of inspiration were diverse. As well as using motifs popular during the Art Nouveau period, he also experimented with more unusual forms. This ornamental hair comb, constructed from carved horn, opal, enamel and gold, is based on an Egyptian palmette-type pierced decoration, and the palm tree motifs and central fan motif give the comb an Egyptian feel.

Fouquet's work tends to be extremely well controlled. His designs are generally asymmetrical, but this does not detract from an overall sense of balance, apparent in all the pieces shown here. His jewelry is intricate; the exceptionally fine working of the delicate wings of this dragonfly demonstrate his great control and skill.

This diamond and pearl pendant in the shape of a stylized wing, has been enamelled in lavender and light blue using the *plique-a-jour* method. The form, a cluster of flowers with pearl blooms, reflects the popularity of the floral motif in Art Nouveau design.

Fouquet experimented with a number of different styles, although he appears to have preferred a purist interpretation of Art Nouveau. His forms were innovative and tended to combine a variety of media, often of differing intrinsic values – for example, this brooch is made of gold, with pierced arabesques studded with rubies and a pendant sapphire, but the central motif of a woman's head is carved from semi-precious stone. Fouquet was fond of the pendant jewel form exemplified by this brooch.

ALPHONSE MUCHA (FRENCH, 1860-1939)

Mucha is best known for his poster designs for Sarah Bernhardt (see p.216). However, he also designed some notable sculpture (see p.160) and jewelry. Many of his jewelry designs for Sarah Bernhardt were executed by Georges Fouquet, as was the snake bracelet, on the right.

The Spanish Masriera Brothers (1872-1958)

established a firm in Barcelona to produce jewelry which showed a strong French influence, with many pieces in particular reflecting the influence of René Lalique. Use was made of *plique-a-jour* enamelwork, in which figural subjects in gold were set against shaped panels outlined with rubies on a diamanté reserve.

This snake bracelet, designed by Mucha for Sarah Bernhardt and executed by Georges Fouquet in 1899, is considered to be one of the most important pieces of Art Nouveau jewelry. It is composed of gold, enamel and diamonds in the form of a bangle which is joined to a ring by a fine gold chain. Opal, much admired for its translucence and changeable colours, was often used during this period. The serpent, symbolic of sensuality and femininity, appealed to the new image of the liberated female.

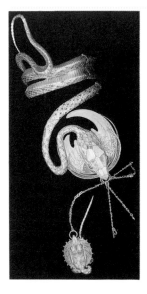

JEWELRY FOR THE MASSES

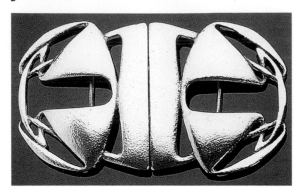

A Liberty & Co. "Cymric" silver buckle, designed by Archibald Knox, 1901; max diam 3¾in/9.75cm

Arthur Liberty was an important arbiter of taste during the late 19th century. One of his chief designers of the "Cymric" range of silver, Archibald Knox (see pp.182-3), also turned his talents towards jewelry design, producing a popular range of Celtic-inspired jewelry which, because it was largely made using mass-production methods, was relatively affordable. Other designers employed by Liberty & Co. include Jesse M. King and Frank Partridge (neither of whom, unlike Knox, were allowed to sign their work).

Charles Horner used similar techniques and, like Liberty's designers, made use of turquoise enamel decoration, although he concentrated more on Germanic themes, such as the naturalistic pod form. The Anglo-German firm, Murrle Bennet and Co., also produced a very successful range of inexpensive and widely available art jewelry for the British public, and created several designs that were very close to those designed by Knox for Liberty.

This Fred Partridge *plique-à-jour* necklace was retailed by Liberty in around 1900. It features moonstones and dragonflies along the chain (which also feature on jewelry designed by René Lalique, see p. 202).
•Partridge also produced a large number of items carved from horn, including hair slides. Those pieces that were not produced for Liberty are marked "PARTRIDGE".
•Pendants were very popular during the Art Nouveau period, and tended to be particularly sculptural in form, with the emphasis on design rather than value. Jessie King favoured pendants of an elaborate, multiple-type construction.

LIBERTY AND CO. (ENGLISH, 1785-Present)

Before Liberty introduced its own jewelry in the Arts and Crafts style, the firm sold reproductions from the Near and Far East and Europe. It was only in around 1899 that it began to develop its own range, when Arthur Liberty revolutionized silver and jewelry production by mass-producing pieces that emulated the hand finishes achieved by the craftsmen of the various guilds. Archibald Knox was a prolific jeweler and metalworker (see p.182). The surface of the Knox brooch at the top of the page has been "distressed" (artificially aged), a common effect on Knox's jewelry. Other examples have colour enamelling, which gives a jewel-like appearance.

This enamelled buckle displays King's preference for symmetry and planished (finely hammered) surfaces. The swallows around the edges of the buck-le are evidence of King's fondness for stylized bird motifs. Also typical is the bright, peacock blue-green enamelwork on the stylized flowerheads.

Jessie M. King (Scottish, 1876-1949)
A prominent member of the Glasgow School (see p.46), Jessie King produced some of the most exciting jewelry in the "Cymric" range for Liberty. Her designs tend to be more delicate and more feminine than those of Knox. Enamelwork features on many of her designs, notably in the form of peacock blue and green enamelled flowerheads, particularly rosebuds.

Fred Partridge (English, 1877-1942)
Fred Partridge previously worked for the Guild of Handicraft (see pp.176-9) before producing a number of pieces of jewelry for Liberty, many of which display a French influence.

MURRLE, BENNET & CO. (ANGLO-GERMAN 1884-1914)

Ernst Murrle, a German jeweler, and Mr Bennet, established this Anglo-German agency in London to retail low-priced jewelry in gold and silver, including many designs produced in Pforzheim, Germany, by Theodor Fahrner, a school friend of Murrle's.

Theodor Fahrner (German, 1868-1928)

Considered the most original jeweler in Pforzheim, Fahrner produced probably the first art jewelry on a mass-produced scale. As pieces did not incorporate real gems, they did not need to be inspected and could be ordered by catalogue.

Fahrner's work tends to be figurative, abstract or semi-organic in form, with highly-stylized decoration. He was fond of bird motifs, as well as geometric motifs and stylized animals or plants; this silver and enamel pin is typical. Webbed wing motifs often appear on Fahrner's pieces.

Fahrner's firm made inexpensive pieces in silver or low-carat gold, set with enamel-work, semi-precious stones, mother-of-pearl or glass. Pieces made from silver-coloured metal and enamel, such as this pendant, have little intrinsic value. Patriz Huber, who designed this pendant, was the most prolific of Fahrner's designers. Despite the attachments to this piece, most of Huber's work is simple, with dull surfaces and subdued stones or enamelling. Fahrner's jewelry appears hand-made, but was in fact made using Liberty's methods of mass-production. Some pieces have simulated rivets to add to this effect as well as providing decoration.

Identification and marks

Fahrner's work was similar to Liberty's "Cymric" range. Liberty sold some Fahrner jewelry and a few recorded Liberty designs also appear in Murrle Bennet's catalogues. It was always assumed that Murrle Bennet copied Liberty, but it now seems likely that Murrle Bennet produced modern jewelry first, and may have supplied Liberty with designs.

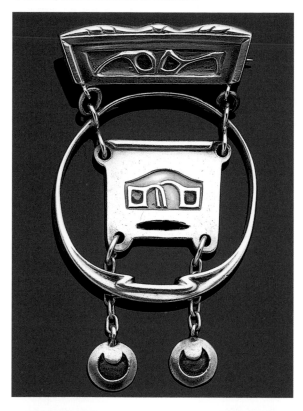

Several designers worked for Fahrner in the same abstract, organic style. This pendant designed by Franz Bohres, is in the Secessionist style, probably influenced by Joseph Maria Olbrich, who worked for Fahrner, among others. The geometric feel, the openwork and the simple form are typical, as is the enamel, often blue as here, but also in peacock green.

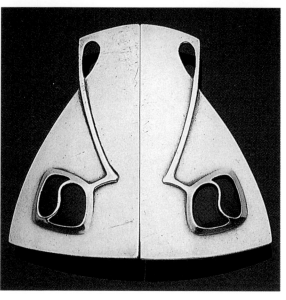

Most pieces bear a stamped mark, either "MB", or "MB & Co.". Of all the jewelry shown in these pages, only the Bohres pendant does not have a designer's monogram. Most also have the collaborator's mark. This silver-coloured metal and enamel buckle, designed by Albrecht Holbein for Fahrner in around 1900, is stamped with Holbein's mark and the word "Geschutzt" (meaning "copyright"); each element is numbered "VII".
•Some enamelled silver pendants designed by Archibald Knox were also made by Murrle Bennet and bear that factory's mark.
•Some of Bennet's pieces were designed as part of a set.
•Attribution to a designer will increase value.

LUXURY AND EXOTICISM

After the war years of 1914-18 there emerged a second nouveau riche, with new demands for luxurious jewelry that would create an appearance of wealth and complement the fashions of the day. The French firms of Cartier and Van Cleef and Arpels were eager to adapt to the demands of their new clientele, and used a variety of precious and non-precious metals and stones to produce exquisite accessories for the well-dressed women of the period. Their designs were strongly influenced by Chinese, Japanese, Persian and medieval art and by the exotic costume designs of Léon Bakst for the *Ballet Russe*. Often design was secondary to the decoration, the form acting purely as a canvas for expensive jewels. Base materials were gold, silver and platinum, rather than the stainless steel of the new world.

A Cartier clock c.1930 6 x 5½in/15.5 x 14cm

In the Art Deco period Cartier followed the fashion for contemporary shapes, which it adopted and then embellished with large and colourful gemstones. Jewels were always used to dramatic effect; often red or white was contrasted against black, as in this rock crystal, ruby and enamel brooch from around 1925. This piece is typical in its bold use of colour and shape.
•Cartier produced a wide range of jewelled luxury items, which included powder compacts and cigarette cases.

CARTIER (FRENCH, 1898-Present)

Collecting Clocks can be dated by their serial number, which can be checked with Cartier, who keep a record of everything they make.
•Any pieces that come from Cartier in Paris carry more of a premium than those from Cartier in either New York or London.

These French court jewelers, founded by Louis-François Cartier in 1857, opened a London branch in New Bond Street in 1909, and London workshops in 1921.

Clocks Cartier made a variety of timepieces, usually desk and carriage clocks or the new wristwatches. The firm treated the clock almost as a sculpture, and it is not always immediately apparent what the piece's function is. Designs are often exotic or Oriental. Chinoiserie forms, and decorative motifs with a Chinese influence are common. Semi-precious stones are often embellished with fine-quality gems. The clock above is one of Cartier's most popular designs. A roundel is mounted on a pediment, harking back to the classical shapes of the early 19th century, but the overall appearance is still "modern".

VAN CLEEF AND ARPELS (FRENCH, 1906-Present)

Van Cleef was happy to adopt the new design principles of geometric shapes and contrasting colours. However, unlike Cartier, who usually used enamels and semi-preious stones for decoration, Van Cleef tended to use more precious gemstones, as in this coral, enamel and diamond powder compact from c.1925.

Together with that of Cartier and Tiffany, jewelry produced by Van Cleef and Arpels epitomized the most opulent Art Deco designs. The firm acquired a reputation for inventive luxury items, including a vanity case known as a *minaudière* ("simperer"), and a wide range of accessories influenced by Persian, Oriental and medieval art, using coloured gemstones, enamels and lacquer.
•Van Cleef and Arpels pieces can be dated by their serial number.

GEOMETRICAL AND ORIENTAL INFLUENCES

The work of the French designers, Raymond Templier, Jean Desprès and the later work of Georges Fouquet illustrates well the spread of Modernist disciplines in jewelry design. All three designers produced highly original works of art; Templier and Desprès concentrated upon very individual abstract yet futuristic jewlery, while Fouquet preferred Oriental-inspired pieces that made good use of fine-quality jades and corals; his pendants in particular make strong use of interesting symmetrical and geometric forms and the finest materials available, and are often embellished with diamond-encrusted mounts. Gerard Sandoz and Jean Goulden also used geometric or Cubist elements in their work, often contrasting metals and surface finishes for decorative impact.

GEORGES FOUQUET (FRENCH, 1862-1957)

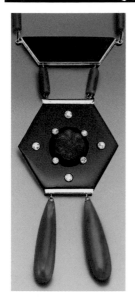

This pendant from c.1920 is typical of Fouquet's designs with its reliance on a variety of colours for decoration, and the insertion of tiny brilliants.

Fouquet took charge of the high-class Parisian jewellers, La Maison Fouquet, from his father, Alphonse, in 1895. He designed both Art Nouveau and traditional jewelry (see p.204) before taking up the Art Deco style in the 1920s. He continued to work on individual commissions after the house closed in 1936.

Materials Fouquet's jewelry from the 1920s and '30s is characterized by its use of combined precious and semi-precious materials and enamels, which became known as *mille-neuf-cent*. In the early 1920s he made mainly high-quality pieces in the Parisian tradition, using diamonds and often exploiting the conflict of black and white. Later he became interested in hardstone, juxtaposed with more transparent precious stones, and he began to use semi-precious stones, such as rock crystal, in significant proportions.

Pendants Fouquet's pendants are often multiple and use linked sections. Even his brooches have a pendant theme, and some are designed so that they can be worn hung from silk cords. The emphasis is on variety of colour and geometric motifs, which are usually inset, or framed by inset lines of tiny brilliants.

This jade and enamel pendant, designed by Georges Fouquet c.1920, is characteristically symmetrical. Like many of his pieces it combines precious and non-precious materials.

RAYMOND TEMPLIER (FRENCH, 1891-1968)

Templier was another Parisian jeweler designing for the luxury market. He worked for the family firm, which was founded by his grandfather in 1849. He made brooches, pins, bangles, pendants and earrings using rigorously geometric forms. Like Fouquet, Templier was fond of elongated forms in which circles are combined with verticals, many of which were inspired by the modern American skyline. Strong contrasts are achieved by use of matt and polished surfaces. White gold and platinum are also contrasted with pavé set brilliants to give a black and white effect.

These pendant earrings from 1928 suggest Manhattan skyscrapers, and like many other decorative arts at this time show the strong influence of the Modernist designers working in the United States, such as Norman bel Geddes (see p.191).

•A number of Templier's brooches and pins are made out of platinum and decorated with superimposed enamelled triangles.

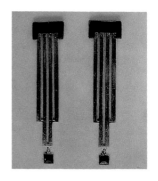

Desprès generally avoided bright colours, preferring greys, blacks and browns. Contrast is achieved through the use of strong relief elements, patination and irregular surfaces, as seen in this 1930 brooch.

JEAN DESPRÈS (FRENCH, 1889-1980)

Desprès' work adopts more of a Modernist, almost futuristic, approach than Fouquet's, and makes very little use of gemstones, employing instead semi-precious stones and expensive metals. He concentrated on brooches and solid, chunky rings in abstract geometric patterns influenced by Cubism and African masks. His work is usually signed "J. Desprès".

Many of Desprès' jewelry designs recall machine components. This brooch from 1930 is typical, possibly inspired by his period in an aircraft factory during the First World War.

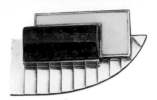

Shapes as well as surfaces and colours were contrasted: lines and curves are juxtaposed in this 1930 brooch, which also shows Desprès' fondness for bloodstone, which he often set against ivory and silver.

GERARD SANDOZ (FRENCH, born 1902)

Marks Pieces are usually marked and may bear the signature of both father and son. The niello and silver cigarette case is signed "GERARD SANDOZ; the lighter and cigarette case are signed "Gerard Sandoz and G. Roger Sandoz".

Sandoz, who trained with his father, Gustave Roger-Sandoz, is among the most inventive craftsmen of the Art Deco period, and one of the most commercial. He hand-made small, individual, luxury items, such as fine quality lighters, boxes and cigarette cases, as well as pendants and brooches, which belong almost exclusively to the 1920s.

Materials Unusually for work made for a luxury market, very little emphasis is placed on precious stones, although precious metals, such as gold, are sometimes used. Sandoz is particularly noted for his use of eggshell, lacquer and niello work, and for his juxtaposition of materials and surfaces to give a textured effect. Niello is the term used for silver and black lacquerwork made by letting in thin lacquer onto a silver surface, which is then polished. Niello work was popularized in Russia in the 19th century and was favoured in Europe during the 1920s and '30s.

This cigarette case, made in around 1925, is typical of Sandoz's work in its use of niello and its highly geometric pattern of industrial gears and other motifs suggestive of modern machine components.

This matching lighter and cigarette case were designed by Gerard Sandoz in around 1925 and display typically geometric and Cubist elements. The form is clean and simple, with contrasting primary colours used for decorative effect.

JEAN GOULDEN (FRENCH, 1878-1947)

This *champlevé* enamelled silver box is dated 1928. The geometric decoration is more sparse than on the cigarette box on the right, and the colours more subdued. The squares are mottled, as is the cream coloured ground, and the lid interior, which is in turquoise.

Primarily an enameller, Jean Goulden produced table lamps, clocks and other decorative items. Some of his designs were executed by Jean Dunand (see p.56), from whom Goulden learned the craft of enamelling.

Most of Goulden's enamel designs were executed on silver or other precious metals, using the *champlevé* technique in which the silver is cut into and the enamels laid in the cloissons, or reservoirs. Although the use of enamel was quite common during this period, Goulden was unusual in introducing texture through the use of degraded or irregular surfaces. Another characteristic of Goulden's enamel work is that he uses areas of the base metal, in this case silver, as part of the decoration. Geometric patterns invariably dominate.

Typically on this cigarette box from 1927 the enamel design has been applied over a silver ground, using the *champlevé* method. The irregular surface gives a grained effect.

Marks Most of Goulden's items are signed. The cigarette box above is engraved with Jean Goulden XXIV, 1927 on the base.

•There are other jewelled items available which, despite their use of less expensive materials and lack of a well-known signature, are nicely made and evocative of the time, and collectable today.

PAUL-EMILE BRANDT (SWISS, dates unknown)

Materials Brandt's designs of the 1920s and '30s are strongly geometric, using materials such as gold and platinum combined with precious stones to create a luxury item. Although similar to Sandoz's work, Brandt's pieces tend to make more use of precious stones and more clearly defined areas of opposing colour. He specialized in eggshell lacquer decoration, which is used on the compact on the right. His work often has a strong symmetrical element and may incorporate a chevron motif. Black enamel and onyx were particularly popular.

Paul Brandt made small luxury items such as boxes, cigarette cases and jewelry, especially bracelets, clips and bracelet-watches. The items that turn up for sale most frequently are those that contain an element of lacquerwork. These often contrast a crackled eggshell with enamel in colours of brilliant red or black. Many reflect African designs.

Marks The compact below is engraved, "Paul Brandt", and comes in a pouch stamped "Paul Brandt Artist Decorateur Joaillier".

This compact from the late 1920s combines eggshell and lacquer work. The symmetrical element of Brandt's designs is clearly evident.

Above This rectangular compact in lacquered tinplate is probably French as it uses a clever photoprinting technique to simulate crushed eggshell, which was very much a French forte. The piece is very lightweight, even flimsy, but it does fit the purpose for which it was intended, and at first glance appears to be made of expensive materials. The handles at the top allow it to be hung on a chain. Although there is no mark, the strong period feel still makes it collectable.

PRINTS AND POSTERS

By the end of the 19th century, increased industrialization and the subsequent need for advertising had led to a vast growth in the importance of the poster as a means of communication. Letter-press was replaced by modern techniques, such as lithography which was particularly strong in France. Jules Chéret, among others, covered *fin de siècle* Paris in striking posters to such an extent that a law was introduced to prevent their being posted. These are a fascinating pictorial record of the time, as are Toulouse-Lautrec's posters of Parisian lowlife. Posters were never as popular elsewhere as they were in France. The artists of the Austrian Secession designed boldly geometric posters, with simple precision-design lettering to advertise exhibitions mounted by the movement. In the United States, Maxfield Parrish applied American Art Nouveau motifs to his commercial art. As well as mass-produced graphic art he also designed covers for magazines such as *Harper's*, *Life* and *Scribners Magazine*. Magazine covers and prints taken from magazines (printed ephemera) are currently very inexpensive. The original artwork is occasionally available, but is rare and usually commands a high price.

1920s and '30s posters primarily promoted travel, art exhibitions and sports meetings, and occasionally political propaganda. Designs are unfussy, with emphasis on a strong central image. Colours were brighter than before, and new typefaces were used. Again, the French designs are most striking; the most innovative designer, Adolphe Cassandre, used strong colours and an unusual sense of perspective. Paul Colin is the most important name in theatre advertising, known for his advertisements for Josephine Baker. Other French artists who worked on posters include Erté and Jean Dupas, many of whose lithographs have been converted into posters. Icart's posters were purely decorative and not promotional. In Britain, London Transport commissioned a series of posters from leading artists which often show contemporary pursuits or people visiting places such as seaside resorts, made more accessible by the railways. The development of Hollywood led to film posters, in colour and often using two-tone artwork, and mainly by unknown artists. Few have survived, although they were originally produced in large numbers (every cinema would have had one).

Poster production methods include engraving, done with a knife straight onto the plate; and etching, where the plate is covered with wax, the design drawn into it, then the whole plate dipped in acid, which eats into the areas not covered by the wax. Etchings look more like a drawing; engravings have a more stilted appearance, and an embossed effect. Lithographs are made by applying wax or an ink-resistant chemical to a stone surface, which is then covered with ink, so that exposed areas are coloured while others are left untouched. The ink lies on the surface, which, unlike an etching, is completely flat. Photogravure is used to reproduce an etching or engraving: the item is photographed and the photographic negative applied to copper plate; the image is then etched or engraved. When examined under a magnifier, the image is revealed as a matrix of tiny dots.

Several points may affect the value of a poster. Among lesser artists, the quality of graphics is important: a stunning image will be valuable even if anonymous. Condition is vital, although the value of a poster by a prominent artist will not be dramatically affected by bad condition. Posters in pristine condition command a premium. Pieces with tears and creases are of little collectable value. Acceptable damage includes minor fading or some loss of the paper around the edges. Some auction houses use letters to denote condition, ranging from "A", for those in very good condition, through to "D" for serious damage. Some were personalized by overprinting – for example, a firm might add a calendar. This does not always devalue a piece, but purists may prefer the clean print. Tears can be prevented from ripping further with the use of acid-free tape. Sellotape or dry mounting (sticking the poster to a backing board) should not be used: they are damaging and irreversible. When buying any backed poster, ensure the glue used is vegetable based which, because it is water soluble, is reversible. When framing, glaze with plexiglass rather than glass, which, lighter to hang, is less dangerous should it crack. Avoid posters that are badly "light stained" (faded by exposure to strong light), or have prominent blemishes. Restoration should always be done by a specialist. The colour blocks on modern reproductions are formed of hundreds of little dots and are fairly easily distinguished from a lithograph, which has solid colours and crayon lines.

Above Manufacture Royale Corsets, by T. Privat Livemont, c.1897
Right Nord Express by Adolphe Cassandre, c.1930

PARISIAN LIFE

The posters of Henri de Toulouse-Lautrec and Jules Chéret are as synonymous with Paris at the turn of the Century as the Moulin Rouge, the Can-Can and the Eiffel Tower. Their bold designs appeared along the boulevards of Paris, turning them into a huge open-air art gallery. Many of their posters informed the public of the capital's theatrical attractions and of culinary and alcoholic delights, and other products, such as kerosene.

Above Chéret often produced more than one poster to advertise a product – this example, recommending Saxoleine, a popular brand of lamp oil, is one of 14 designs.

This poster, one of 10 different Chéret posters advertising Geraudel's throat pastilles, is an early design, from c.1890. It displays characteristics typical of Chéret's later work, such as strong colours and emphasis on the foreground subject.
•Although Chéret produced a few long, thin posters, most are the same proportions as the Saxoleine poster.

Right *Le Figaro*, a lithographic poster by Jules Chéret 1904; 23 x 32in/58.5 x 81.25cm

JULES CHÉRET (FRENCH, 1836-1932)

Although essentially a commercial artist, Chéret is recognized today as the father of the poster. His exuberant designs perfectly reflected the mood of *fin-de-siècle* Paris. Posters had previously been produced using the letterpress method, whereby designs were printed from a raised, inked surface. By drawing his designs directly onto stone, Chéret developed the use of lithography as a creative medium. He began to produce lithographic posters in 1858. A seven-year stay in England introduced him to new methods of mass production using coloured blocks, and in 1866 he began to produce posters on his own press, Imprimerie Chaix. He left the press in 1881, although he continued to design posters.

Chéret's style is distinctive, and many of his designs are strikingly similar. Lettering dominated many early posters, but from around 1885, his focus shifted to figures and products. These later posters are more exciting and more collectable, and usually feature female subjects. Unlike Mucha (see p.216), who emphasized the sensuality of his female figures, Chéret's women are usually vibrant and lively, and are never nude. Like the advertisement at the top of the page for the Paris newspaper, *Le Figaro*, his later designs are full of movement, with minimal detail and simplified outlines.

Value Chéret's work is quite common, and only a few of his posters are really valuable. Each of his 1,000 poster designs was printed in large numbers. Good examples command a higher premium. There are no known fakes, and reproductions are easy to spot.
•All of Chéret's designs were printed on cheap paper, so condition is very important.
•Posters are signed and sometimes dated, but should also bear the name of the printer, Chaix. Other designers used Chaix, but none produced work as accomplished or as valuable as Chéret's.

HENRI DE TOULOUSE-LAUTREC (FRENCH, 1864-1901)

Born an aristocrat, Toulouse-Lautrec suffered an accident as a boy which left him a dwarf. He frequented the seedier places of Paris, including Montmartre and Le Moulin Rouge. He is best known for posters depicting Parisian night-life and low-life, but also promoted exhibitions and retailers, and worked for various periodicals.
•Proofs, or trial impressions made at an early stage, lack any lettering. They are rare and valuable and sought after by print and poster collectors. Contemporary catalogues should record the number of copies made at each stage of proofing. Lautrec often addded amusing little sketches on the stone, not included on the final version.

Left Toulouse-Lautrec's posters have been faked and copied more than those of any other posterist of the age. This poster, first printed in 1893, was reissued in 1904 with subtle differences — for example, in the choice of colour. The Swiss produced a series of reproduction lithographs in the 1950s, clearly marked as such and with a distinctive stamp, although this is sometimes soaked off.

THEOPHILE ALEXANDRE STEINLEN (SWISS, 1859-1923)

Steinlen came to Paris in 1881. He was greatly influenced by Henri de Toulouse-Lautrec and attempted to portray the daily life of the ordinary people of Paris. His work tends not to be as well-documented as that of some of his more commercially-orientated contemporaries. Although he did some commercial work he was foremost an artist and painter.

Original or reproduction? Several checks can be made: genuine posters were done on the stone, colour by colour, and a thin band of overlapping colours can usually be seen along the bottom edge. This colour difference is evened out on lithographs and photographic reproductions, leaving a single band of colour. Good quality paper indicates a "fake". Colours should be checked against a known original as they can seldom be precisely reproduced.
Condition Posters were dispatched folded, so fold marks are common, but may be more distinct on some works than on others. Distinct fold marks are undesirable. Some posters have been trimmed and this seriously reduces their value. Sizes can often be checked in catalogues.

Steinlen's posters were well-executed, with a well-blended variety of good, strong colours. He was particularly fond of drawing cats — here they are advertising milk. Dogs are also common in his poster designs. Many of Steinlen's subjects can be identified: the girl in this poster is his daughter, Collette. This poster shows Steinlen's preference for lettering. His work is always signed.

Above Toulouse-Lautrec's most usual subjects were theatrical women, often ugly in appearance — the woman in this poter advertising *La Revue Blanche* is Missia Natanson, the wife of its co-director, and is relatively attractive when compared to other Lautrec figures. Typically, lettering is simple, almost haphazard.

This poster advertises a Parisian printing service, Charles Verneau, and was, obviously enough, printed by the self-same firm, responsible for many other Steinlen posters. However, Steinlen also used other printers, most notably Ch. Wall & Cie, Paris.

BELLE ÉPOQUE MASTERWORKS

The turn of the century was greeted with both hope and trepidation. It signalled a new freedom – women became more emancipated, communications improved and there was generally a mood of optimism – which was reflected in the decorative arts of the day. Alphonse Mucha designed posters featuring maidens imbued with strong elements of symbolism, often adorned with exotic jewelry, and set against highly ornamental backgrounds. He advertised a variety of products, and even managed to depict the most mundane objects, such as Job cigarette papers, in an exotic manner. Eugène Grasset worked in a similar style, but in a more limited palette and he tended to portray more earthy women. His work displays a stronger Japanese influence than that either of Mucha or T. Privat-Livemont. Many of his posters display a disturbing realism, which is perhaps most notable in his poster featuring a drug addict, another "product" of the new age.

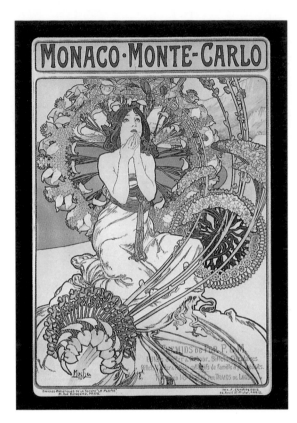

Monaco Monte-Carlo, a lithographic poster by Alphonse Mucha 1897; ht 43in/109cm

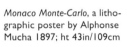

ALPHONSE MUCHA (CZECH, 1860-1939)

Mucha produced several versions of some posters, perhaps varying some of the details. This piece, announcing the performance of de Musset's *Lorenzaccio* with Sarah Bernhardt in 1896, appeared in at least two sizes using different colours. Some versions omit the garter on the right leg or vary other small details. The arch framing the subject is typical, as is the busy design.
•Mucha's posters are nearly always "signed in the block", (as a part of the design). He sometimes countersigned the completed poster by hand.
•Mucha's work is rarely in perfect condition: colours and gilding tend to wear. Tears are not crucial, but damage to the central image can reduce value.
•Mucha produced calendars and albums of decorative motifs, containing life sketches and designs for jewelry, furniture and floral panels. The albums contain 72 plates and are usually found complete.

Mucha worked as a scene painter in Vienna and first came to prominence in the 1890s when he was commissioned by Sarah Bernhardt to design posters for her, and later, costumes, jewelry and stage sets. Most of his collectable work was executed between 1890 and 1910.

The woman in the *Monaco Monte-Carlo* poster at the top of the page is typical of Mucha's better known posters, with her scant clothing and long, flowing hair. He also depicted women in diaphanous robes or more complicated drapery and with their hair *en chignon*. Most are reminiscent of Sarah Bernhardt, although he used other models in some sittings, as the actress had only one leg. The flower garlands symbolize the wheels of the train linked by rail lines. The lettering was done by Mucha himself.

Authenticity The *Monaco Monte-Carlo* poster is relatively large and, as a lithograph stone could not be made to such large dimensions, would have been printed on two sheets of paper. Posters of this size are very difficult to fake successfully: for this reason the majority of fakes tend to be of the smaller designs that can be produced on one stone.

T. PRIVAT-LIVEMONT (BELGIAN, 1861-1936)

Verification and valuation Privat-Livemont used cheap paper. His work is usually signed and often dated. Posters were always made to precise measurements, which can be checked if there is any doubt. His work is not known to have been faked, and reproductions are obvious. His posters are rare and popular. Those he produced to promote Absinthe Robette are especially sought after, particularly in. the United States.

Motifs Typically Art Nouveau motifs, such as sunflowers, recur, and the robes of the *Pépiniéristes* echo the work of the Pre-Raphaelites. The palette reflects the Art Nouveau preoccupation with the organic, with tones of red, green and blue, or early neutrals. Any lettering is also in a distinctive Art Nouveau style.

Privat-Livemont opened a design studio in 1890. Like most poster designers of the period, his work was promotional, for products such as tea, biscuits, chocolate, corsets, cocoa and alcohol, especially Absinthe Robette.

Privat-Livemont's work, although similar to that of Mucha, tends to be less sensual. His subjects are usually women, often with flowing hair, and possibly appearing semi-nude or semi-veiled. Some figures are romanticized. In this poster, entitled *Pépiniéristes*, the women hardly look like the nursery gardeners they are intended to be. Other subjects are anatomically incorrect, perhaps with excessively curved backs, or are drawn out of perspective.

This poster is advertising Bec Auer light, a type of gas lamp mantle which had an extra-bright light. Privat-Livemont also promoted seaside resorts and exhibitions in his posters.

His subjects can appear slightly strange: the clumsy, frowning features of the woman above are very different to the typical advertising beauty of the time.

EUGÈNE SAMUEL GRASSET (SWISS, 1841-1917)

Collecting Grasset is not currently popular and good examples of his work can be acquired at very low prices. Being rare, some damage is acceptable, and strength of colour will always be a more important consideration than condition.

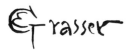

This Swiss-born architect and designer was influenced by Pre-Raphaelite art, medieval architecture and Japanese art. He settled in Paris where he designed posters featuring feminine, old-fashioned women, rather than the more stylized and modern female subjects of other Art Nouveau posterists. He used a palette of mainly subdued tones.

•Some Grasset posters have been later backed with linen, to strengthen the inferior paper.

Marks Grasset's signature usually consists of a capital "EG" followed by "rasset" (see left). The mark may appear in reverse. Most of his work was printed by Chaix, the printer also used by Chéret (p.214).

The woman in this lithograph hides demurely behind a fan. The poster features Grasset's typical, somewhat limited palette of bold, strong tones of yellow, green and blue, outlined in black.

NEW WORLD POSTERISTS

Edward Penfield was the first designer to introduce the artistic poster into America, with the very original designs he created for *Harper's* window bills. Soon promotional posters became very popular, and were often produced in limited editions, acknowledging their potential as artistic items in their own right. Maxfield Parrish, an excellent book illustrator and artist, recognized the strength of the medium and became a prolific posterist. In his commercial art designs he combined accepted Art Nouveau motifs, such as scantily-clad diaphanous women, with strongly American themes and environments, often incorporating an incongruous mixture of both traditional and modern ideas. Among other leading and influential posterists working in America at this time were Will Bradley and the English-born Louis Rhead.

Right A Maxfield Parrish poster for the August 1896 edition of *The Century Magazine*

This 1896 poster designed for the Poster Show held at the Pennsylvania Academy of Fine Arts shows Parrish's potential as one of America's leading turn-of-the-century artists. The flat colours and bold images attract immediate attention, as does the simple and easy-to-read message. The subdued colours and simple images were soon to give way to the brighter colours and more complex later designs.
•Parrish's original artwork is extremely rare and commands prices comparable to that of the minor Impressionists.
•Many of Parrish's later poster designs were made for reproduction as billboards, for magazines and as window cards.

MAXFIELD PARRISH (AMERICAN, 1870-1966)

Parrish learned modern printing methods, such as the chromo-lithographic process, at the Pennsylvania Academy of Fine Arts. He designed theatre sets, book illustrations and typography, as well as magazine covers for *Harper's*, *Life*, and *Scribners Magazine*. However, what is mostly available today is his mass-produced graphic art, including posters, labels and calendars. Not entirely happy with having to produce illustrations to other people's ideas, Parrish stopped producing advertising posters in around 1900, and did not return to them until around 1915. He stopped completely in 1930, to concentrate on painting.

Poster designs Parrish was a strong landscape artist and he frequently combined European symbolism with American imagery, setting androgynous, often naked, beauties or fantastic medieval characters against his American landscapes. The prize-winning design at the top of the page for a poster competition in 1886, features the profile of a nude woman sitting on the grass, typically set against an American landscape.

•The award-winning *Century Magazine* poster design above became one of the most widely reproduced posters in America at the time. It was used, for example, a few years later for an edition of *Scribner's Magazine*.
•Although Parrish recognized that posters which used minimal backgrounds and bold colours were more efficient as an advertising medium, he found it difficult to break away from the busy landscape backgrounds he was famous for, and which his commissioners required.

Other designs Parrish often incorporated self-portraits into his work – for example, in a poster entitled *Fit For a King*, advertising Fisk Tyres. Others were based on nursery rhymes and fairy tales, or reflected Parrish's interest in good living and eating and featured subjects associated with food.

Collecting and marks Maxfield Parrish's best-known and most collectable work is a series of chromo-lithographic prints published between 1915 and 1925 by companies that included New York Graphics, Charles Scribner & Sons, Reinthal and Newman, and the Edward Gross Company, many under arrangement with the advertising lithograph firm of Rusling Wood in New York, which acted as his exclusive agent for many years. The borders of a print may bear a company mark, a facsimile of Parrish's signature, and, very occasionally, an edition number.

In 1918 Parrish began a long-standing commission for the General Electric Mazda Lamp calendar, which made him a household name. He produced a painting every year until

1930. This design for the 1919 calendar shows how Parrish adapted symbolic figures to the advertising medium; the woman, representing the Spirit of the Night, is illuminated by a new-fangled light made by the General Electric Company. Her simple gown, and the garb of her attendants, show a medieval influence.
•The posters for General Electric were finely executed to a very high standard by Forbes Lithograph Manufacturing Co. This particular example was lithographed using 12 different colours.
•Calendars were in two sizes – 38 x 18in (96.5 x 46cm) for professional use and 19 x 8½in (48 x 21.5cm), for public use.

WILLIAM BRADLEY (AMERICAN, 1868-1962)

Born in Boston, Bradley was the son of a cartoonist and a self-taught printer. He was interested in printing from a very early age and at 15 was foreman at *Iron Ore Magazine*, Massachusetts. In 1895 he set up the Wayside Press, and in 1896 published the first issue of his art Journal *Bradley: His Book*. When his business was taken over by the University Press, Boston in 1896, he opened a design and art service in New York. His commissions included cover designs and posters for the *Inland Printer* in Chicago and covers for *Harper's Weekly*, *Harper's Bazaar* and *Harper's Young People*.

In his poster designs, Bradley was influenced by the *Morte d'Arthur* illustrations of English designer Aubrey Beardsley and by the designs of William Morris.

Bradley is best-known for his series of five posters for the *Chicago Chap Book*, produced in the 1890s. The fine elegant writing on this poster is typical. The Japanese influence is apparent in the bold blocks of colour, particularly black. He incorporated Art Nouveau and aesthetic motifs in his work, but always managed to retain a freshness which was often missing in the posters of his English contemporary, Beardsley.

EDWARD PENFIELD (AMERICAN, 1866-1925)

Edward Penfield has been called America's premier poster artist. Like Maxfield Parrish, he is best known as a commercial graphic artist and book illustrator but, unlike Parrish, he used traditional printing methods such as woodblock and lino cuts. Between 1891 and 1901 Penfield was art director for the prestigious *Harper's Magazine*. Much of his printing work displays a Japanese influence – for example, many of his women are depicted with eyes and mouths which have a distinctly Japanese character.

Marks Penfield's signature on the poster on the right appears in the top left hand corner, and is clearly inspired by Toulouse-Lautrec's. Most of his work is signed with his name in full.

Each year between 1893 and 1901, Penfield produced advertising posters for

Harper's. Some show the influence of European poster artists, particularly of Henri de Toulouse-Lautrec (see p.215). This is evident in the style, subject matter and palette of this poster. In many of his posters Penfield manages to create a stylish design out of a commonplace scene: here the woman is reading a book. Like Toulouse-Lautrec, Penfield was sometimes criticised for portraying women who were too plain. However, his posters were often enlivened by the inclusion of animals (one design for the March edition of *Harper's* depicts a mad hare).

THE SECESSIONISTS

In the Art Nouveau period the poster work emanating from the Secessionists in Vienna and Charles Rennie Mackintosh in Glasgow offered a striking contrast to the designs of the Paris posterists of the time. The schools of Glasgow and Vienna always admired and shared each other's relatively insular approach to design, which they considered pure and reasoned and far-removed from the neurotic excesses of the Parisian posterists. They replaced the curvilinear excesses advocated by such designers as Alphonse Mucha (see p.216) with designs that had a stronger perpendicular emphasis and more severe lines.

The Vienna Secession was formed in 1897 by disillusioned members of the Viennese Society of Visual Arts. From 1899 the group, including Josef Olbrich, Josef Hoffmann, Otto Wagner and Koloman Moser, worked from a new building called the *Ver Sacrum*, depicted in the poster on the left, where they also exhibited their work. Both building and poster were designed by Olbrich. Other chief designers include Ferdinand Andri, Gustav Klimt and Alfred Roller. Their posters display strong, geometric motifs, bold colouring and angular graphics. The distinctive lettering on the posters on this page is characteristic. The sharp lines, strikingly different from the flowing organic style of other posters of the period, set a style that influenced artists well into the Art Deco period.

Secession, a lithograph designed by Josef Maria Olbrich 1898; 29 x 18in /75.5 x 46.5 cm

Availability and value As members of an innovative, intellectual movement, the Vienna Secessionists appealed to an exclusive market within the limits of Vienna itself and relatively few copies of their posters were produced. The influence of the Secessionists on subsequent art movements has made their work highly sought-after today. Examples of their work will be costly, whatever their condition, although perfect examples will raise the highest prices. Faded colours will obviously lower a poster's value – the gold in the *Secession* lithograph above has faded quite badly, although the black is strikingly bold.

Marks Olbrich's poster is clearly marked but other artists' marks are not so obvious. The printer's name usually appears in the same lettering, with the words "Druch ..." (printed by) and "Wein" (Vienna). Printers used by the Secessionists included A. Berger and Gesellschaft Für Graphsche Industrie.

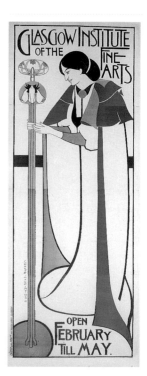

Koloman Moser (1868-1918) designed this poster in 1903 for the *Ver Sacrum* journal of posters by the Secessionists. The lines are typically angular, and the image striking and geometrically inspired, with the writing given as much emphasis as the picture. The three figures, representing writing, painting and music, are integral to the design.

Right Although based in Glasgow, Charles Rennie Mackintosh's posters had affinities with those produced in Vienna at the same time. His work is extremely rare today. This poster from 1895 was produced for the Glasgow School of Arts. Posters by his followers at the Glasgow School were very influential, particularly following The Eighth Secessionist Exhibition at Munich in 1900.

ART AND THE EROTIC

Many of Icart's etchings and drypoint works are single nude or semi-nude studies, although not all of them are explicitly erotic. This one, executed in 1932, and in English entitled *My Model*, shares an air of naughtiness and exuberance with the *Attic Room*, featured below.

The image of the 1930's woman was probably most successfully and prolifically depicted in art by the French artist, Louis Icart, who, following a style already adopted by Joseph Lorenzl (see p.165) and Bruno Zach (see p.168) for their sculptures, portrayed highly erotic women, who were both sexually attractive and defiantly independent. His style, so different from that used by Adolphe Cassandre in his promotional posters (p.227), was imitated by many others, including William Ablett, Maurice Millière and Kaby and Miçao Kono.

LOUIS ICART (FRENCH, 1850-1950)

Louis Icart trained as a printer and worked for a Parisian postcard company before setting up his own atelier in 1908 to print magazines and fashion leaflets. In the 1920s and '30s he produced hundreds of lithographs and etchings, and a number of oils and gouaches, most of which have an air of eroticism about them, either faint or explicit. The etching of *Leda and the Swan* at the top of the page has openly sexual connotations.

Icart depicted hundreds of women in his works; these are invariably the "modern", wealthy, woman of the 1920s and '30s in Paris. Figures are often idealized, with hair curled according to the fashion of the day, and eye shadow usually quite prominent. When not naked, they tend to wear scant lingerie or romantic flowing gowns. Subjects are often engaged in "modern" activities. Sleek and speedy animals feature, sometimes interacting with the female subject in a somewhat erotic way. Horses, lions and butterflies also appear. Two or three colours or tones usually predominate. The soft, shaded focus of the prints featured on this page is characteristic of his work. Primary colours and solid blocks are avoided.

Icart's works were enormously popular in America, although some, like *Leda and the Swan*, were considered too risqué for its more reserved market. After a visit in 1922 Icart began to produce some etchings especially for distribution there, setting up a Louis Icart Society. This etching and drypoint poster, sold under the English name of the *Attic Room* in America, is signed in the lower right hand corner "Copyright 1940 by L. Icart, Paris, New York", indicating that it was marketed in both countries.

Reproductions

It is important to differentiate between the original works, which were mostly drypoint and etching executed in copperplate, and later photogravures (photographic reproductions) of the lithographs which are not collectable: the late reproductions are flat to the touch and have a lack of clarity; under close inspection their dot composition is evident.

•Most of Icart's posters have French titles, which sometimes appear in copperplate script on the front of the work.

THE ART OF FASHION

Many illustrators working in the fashion industry made an important contribution to style in the Art Deco years. The fashion guru Paul Poiret initiated this move when he produced his fashion catalogue illustrated by recognized artists. Contributions were made by Jean Dupas, "Erté", George Barbier, Georges Lepape and Gordon Conway, all of whom also worked for the fashion periodical, *La Gazette du Bon Ton*, which combined the work of leading writers and artists. Erté and Barbier were primarily fashion designers, creating many of the costumes for the *Folies Bergères* and the *Casino de Paris*, whereas the work of Jean Dupas and Gordon Conway was essentially promotional. Several minor artists also made contributions to the many fashion magazines of the time, but remain largely anonymous.

Spring Fashions are here!

Collecting and marks

Dupas worked in a variety of media, including watercolours, pencil and pastel on paper – which all tend to command higher prices than the posters. Oils in particular are usually very expensive. Some posters exist as limited edition lithographs. Dupas' work is always dated and signed "Jean Dupas" at the bottom of the image.

A Jean Dupas fashion poster 1929; 3½ x 47½ in /90 x 120cm

JEAN DUPAS (FRENCH, 1882-1964)

This coloured lithograph from 1930 shows Dupas' distinctive treatment of architecture, with figures set in idyllic situations and simplified classical buildings with columns.
•The advertising element is usually separated from the picture, in simple lettering underneath or above, in the manner of a slogan. Some works had the appropriate slogans added to them later.

Dupas was a painter and poster artist who trained at the major Paris Schools. For the world of fashion he designed posters for a variety of clients, including a series of advertisements for the American department store Saks Fifth Avenue and Arnold Constable. He also produced a series of posters for London Transport and a series advertising various public parks, including Hyde Park in London, as well as designing catalogue covers and large murals.

Dupas' pictures are characterized by their highly individual treatment of subjects, especially women, who are very idealized and rendered in highly decorative detail. Dupas tended to dehumanize his characters, turning them into pretty, sharp-faced but sometimes expressionless mannequins. Women are always slender, willowy, demure and young, with striking features – usually high foreheads with aquiline noses, and tranquil expressions. They are always pale with rouged cheeks. The typically pure, virginal mood is often reinforced by the inclusion of white doves somewhere in the work, as in the English fashion poster at the top of the page. Hair tends to be in a classical 18th century type of style. Foliage is also distinctive, with exaggerated towering trees and feather-like leaves, as in the poster on the left. Colours are usually quite subdued.

"ERTÉ" – ROMAIN DE TIRTOFF (RUSSIAN, 1892-1990)

Erté (the name is derived from the French pronunciation of the R and T in the artist's initials) was one of the leading graphic artists, illustrators and fashion designers of his day. In addition to costumes, he designed stage sets and magazine covers. He was strongly influenced by the French music halls and by the success of the *Ballet Russe*. This influence is clearly evident in his costumes, which tend to be scant, are invariably bizarre and theatrical, and often incorporate exotic headdresses with feathers or motifs. Many garments have long sweeping trains. Women usually wear jewelry and their figures tend to be idealized and their faces stylized. Hair, where it is visible, is usually short and not elaborately coiffured: nothing is allowed to detract from the extravagant costumes and headdress. Figures are frequently raised on stage-like platforms or plinths, emphasizing the theatricality of the design. Much of Erté's work features pale silhouettes set against dark backgrounds, as in all the figures featured here. He also painted some simpler silhouettes, and not just of women – there are a few male figures as well. Silhouettes occasionally appear as several images superimposed on each other.

Four designs by Erté for jewelry, clockwise from top left, *New Moon*, *Lucky Star*, *Four Leaf Clover* and *Wishbone*, all executed in gouache and gold paint on paper.

As well as creating designs for fashion magazines such as *Vogue*, and other leading magazines of the 1920s and '30s, Erté provided the accompanying illustrations for stories that appeared in *Cosmopolitan* magazine. Between 1914/15 and 1936 he designed the covers for *Harper's Bazaar*. This poster in gouache was a design for the October 1927 cover.

Collecting Erté was a prolific designer and his work has survived in quantity. A favourite combination was gouache on paper or board, combined with gold paint, to give a jewel-like quality. The original gouaches of the 1920s and '30s are much sought-after, as are the drawings that went towards the finished design and which were preserved by the artist. Original prints are all highly collectable. Some of his designs have been reproduced in bronze in the United States in recent years. Erté's work is extremely well-documented, and a *catalogue raisonné* is available.

Marks Apart from its individual style, Erté's work is recognizable by its distinct script signature, which usually appears in the corner of the work. Some designs are numbered and stamped. Many carry a wealth of information: the design above is signed and dated, and is stamped on the reverse "Composition Originale". It also carries the title *Robes Nouvelles*.

GEORGE BARBIER (FRENCH, 1882-1932)

Another leading French artist, Barbier designed fashion plates and posters, and illustrations for books, often in the form of pochoir prints. The finest ones were produced as woodcuts by F. L. Schmied.

Barbier's women are generally full figured and sensual, and are often set against a background which is very subtle if not totally plain, as here. As a fashion illustrator, his approach could be daring: in this 1922 gouache, *Elegante en robe du soir bleue*, he shows only part of the dress being advertised.

Barbier's style shows a strong Japanese influence, exemplified here in *Le miroir rouge* of 1923 by the use of flat blocks of colour and an Oriental-looking subject.
•Characteristically, the work is signed and dated in the bottom right-hand corner.

GEORGES LEPAPE (FRENCH, 1887-1971)

From about 1910 Lepape's work appeared in fashion albums such as *Les Choses* and French magazines, notably *La Gazette du Bon Ton*; and his illustrations also adorned many of the covers of *Vogue* magazine in America. Other examples of his work are in the form of book illustrations, posters and advertising brochures.

In their day Lepape's illustrations would have been regarded as strikingly modern and inventive: subjects are placed in the perfect contemporary situation – for example, against skyscrapers. Women were liberated from the tame domestic environments of earlier years and allowed to make a playground of this urban city setting.

Lepape was first and foremost a fashion illustrator and this emerges in all his work. In this *Vogue* illustration of 1928, the costume interacts strikingly with the setting, the woman assuming a skyscraper figure.
•Lepape paid careful attention to detail and this can often help in dating a picture – for example, the short pearls on the lady here belong to the late 1920s.

In a similar style to that of the poster, above, is this cover for *Vogue* magazine, from around 1927, where the woman's hat is lit by one of the skyscrapers in the background. In both cases the colours have been carefully chosen to further highlight the costumes. In both pictures the main figure dominates the composition, and the background is simplified.

Marks Most of Lepape's work is dated and signed with his surname, usually in a bottom corner.

Pochoir prints

From the end of the 19th century in France, gouache originals, such as those by Lepape and other artists of the period, were often reproduced in the form of pochoir prints, using a technique which combines stencils and hand painting. The result far outstripped the technique of machine printing and, in the hands of a skilled printer, could be a very close match to the original. The prints were reproduced in large quantities and, as individual pages, are modestly priced. Complete issues of the magazines in which they featured are, however, rare and expensive. Some of the prints were issued separately in a larger picture size, and some of those that come on the market are still in their original frames.

GORDON CONWAY (AMERICAN, 1894-1956)

Another stylish and versatile fashion illustrator was Gordon Conway, who did her first work for *Vanity Fair* in New York. From 1920 to 1934 she worked in London for *The Tatler* and other magazines, as well as designing for revues, Paris plays and a number of British films. In 1934 she returned to the United States. Like that of Dryden (see p.226) Conway's work has been recently rediscovered and prices are likely to rise. Her illustrations are usually signed with her full name.

Left The sophisticated, modern, self-possessed subject of *Woman With Leopard* (1924) is typical of Conway's women, who, with their geometric hairstyles, stylized faces and cool poses, epitomize the jazz age. Her works often incorporate exotic elements.

Above Conway's work is instantly recognizable for its use of bold, contrasting colours, stylized figures and two-dimensional design elements – all features of this poster from around 1925. Much of her work reveals the influence of Lepape and Barber.

MINOR FASHION POSTERISTS

There are many collectable fashion posters today which are not by the leading designers. Loose fashion plates and contemporary magazines with colour illustrations probably provide the best opportunity for putting together a collection of graphics at a very low cost. Many are well-executed and attractive, but suffer in value because they are by an unknown or little-known artist. When collecting, avoid any pictures that have been pasted on board, as this renders them almost valueless. Ideally, they should be unmounted.

Below This plate from *La Vie Parisienne*, shows a typically idealized woman of the time with dark bobbed hair, orientalized expression and pendant earrings, but it lacks the depth and definition of work by the leading French artists.

Several lesser-known artists contributed to the *Gazette du Bon Ton*. The print on the left from that journal is typical of the period in its use of perspective for dramatic effect: the model's exaggerated height adds to her glamour. In the well-balanced composition on the right, the fabrics being advertised stand out from a simple background.

NEW POSTERS FOR NEW PRODUCTS

Just as the Art Nouveau poster designers were given the challenge of promoting contemporary articles such as the bicycle, so too were posterists during the 1920s asked to promote the new technology and products of their time. The then recent innovation of the automobile was advertised in the posters of the Austrian, Ernst Dryden, for Bugatti, but perhaps the most striking images of the period are by the French artists – Adolphe Cassandre in particular used strong colours and an unusual sense of perspective for his posters, and Paul Colin became the most important name in the area of theatre advertising, particularly known for his posters advertising the actress Josephine Baker.

Dryden poster for the *Paris Matinal* newspaper c.1928; ht 61 x 43in/155 x 108.5cm

Dryden's clever use of restrained colours and his imaginative integration of the picture and lettering are clearly seen in this 1927 advertisement. The combination of the relaxed and the dramatic is typical, as is the way in which the subject stands out strongly against a plain background: in other examples the background may be presented on a smaller-scale. Colours are often restricted to just two tones.

•Dryden often included an element of wit in his work. This is apparent in both this example and the Paris Matinal poster in the main picture.

ERNST DRYDEN (AUSTRIAN, 1883-1938)

Dryden was born Ernst Deutsch, and changed his name in 1919. He was a pupil of Gustav Klimt, and became a prominent illustrator and costume designer. From 1926 he designed covers for the Parisian fashion magazine Die Dame of which he was art director, as well as designing advertisements for a range of international clients, including Persil, Bugatti and Cinzano. In 1933 Dryden moved to Hollywood, where he designed sets and costumes for many major films.

In this unfinished artwork for a poster of 1928, advertising Farben paints the lady is typically chic, with idealized features, conjuring up an air of elegance.

This striking red and white poster design for *Cinzano* is characteristically imaginative and humerous. It is signed in the bottom right corner.

Collecting Dryden

Very little of Dryden's work had appeared on the market before 1976 when 40,000 drawings, sketches and posters were discovered. This has led to a reassessment of his work and prices are rising accordingly. The earlier works with the Deutsch signature, are easier to find than those from 1919 onwards, which are signed "Dryden" or "dryden" with a small circular eye of the "d". The original artwork appears on the market from time to time, but is more expensive than the posters. The Cinzano design is the original and at 14x10in (35x25cm) is three times smaller than the posters.

ADOLPHE J. M. CASSANDRE (FRENCH, 1901-68)

Cassandre was born Jean-Marie Mouron, but adopted the pseudonym at the beginning of his career. He was one of the first to take up the language of formal art movements such as Cubism and apply them to the more popular medium of the advertising poster. He is best known for his striking travel posters, many of which show ships and trains.

Collecting Although Cassandre's work includes posters, lithographs and cover designs for the magazine Harper's Bazaar, his original designs and drawings are rarely offered for sale. Even the posters are quite scarce (in recent years they have most frequently been found in poster sales in New York). Of his three best-known works, that advertising the liner Normandie commands a top price, followed by that for the Etoile du Nord railway service, which uses an abstract interpretation of railway tracks to give a feeling of speed, space and distance. The poster for the Nord Express railway service also commands a good price.

•The technical execution of the prints tends to be masterful: surface brush or collage marks are usually invisible, and it is even difficult to distinguish hand lettering from type.

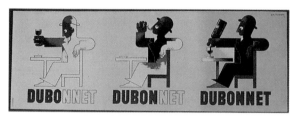

Cassandre's work is often humorous and innovative. In this *Dubonnet* poster (1934) the product is not shown, but its effect is depicted using a cartoon-strip technique.

This advertisement for the liner *Normandie* from 1936 celebrates the modernity of the ship, rather than emphasizing the luxurious aspects of the cruise. Like many Cassandre posters, the image is stark and forceful. Typically, subtle shading gives the subject a metallic impression and a sense of speed – a popular preoccupation at this time. His use of perspective is also distinctive and shows a Japanese influence in its simplification and elimination of superfluous details. Lettering is often bold, clear type, usually sans serif – without cross lines finishing off the strokes of the letters.

PAUL COLIN (FRENCH, 1892-1985)

Like Cassandre, this French artist designed travel posters, but his work also included theatre programme covers and posters advertising performers as well as cigarettes and other products. Nearly all Colin's work features human figures, that are sometimes highly stylized and sometimes caricatured. In 1926 he opened the Ecole Paul Colin. He is best known for his posters to advertise visiting jazz musicians at the *Folies Bergères* and other venues, and for his 1925 series on the actress Josephine Baker, who was appearing in the *Revue Nègre*. His often light-hearted illustrative style is neither as austere nor as sophisticated as that of Cassandre, nor is his work as collectable.

This poster from c.1936, advertising *Weekend* cigarettes, shows three smart smokers in deck chairs, and is typical of Colin's spirited, angular style. It shows how his work epitomized important aspects of the 1920s and '30s poster generally. This is particularly evident in its overhead view and the way the composition is tilted towards the diagonal. Also characteristic of the time is the use of strong colours in unlikely combinations.

RUGS & TEXTILES

The Victorians extended their general tendency to equate elaboration with beauty to their textiles, and developed a bewildering variety of patterns. Their eclectic approach led to the revival of many styles, such as Classical, Gothic, Renaissance, Elizabethan, Moorish and Rococo. However, whilst borrowing heavily from the past, the top designers created something essentially their own. Dark colours gradually replaced the light chintzes and silk damasks of the earlier years. Materials became heavier, giving a richer, more sombre effect, and patterns were more complex and exuberant, with shaded architectural and *trompe l'œil* motifs and ever more naturalistic flowers. Fully pictorial, three-dimensional designs of railway stations, the Crystal Palace, children and dogs – often surrounded by floral wreaths – reached their peak at the time of the 1851 Great Exhibition. Widely criticized, these gave way in the 1860s to simpler, flat patterns based on geometric or historic ornament, with more restrained floral designs.

The Japanese influence was strong in the Aesthetic period of the 1870s and '80s, and pre-empted many of the later Art Nouveau designs. Textiles by William Morris and Liberty in Britain were particularly successful. Attempts to revive fine stitchery came from the Church, whose vestments and alter furnishings were designed by architects. From 1872, the Royal School of Needlework commissioned designs from Morris, Burne-Jones, Walter Crane, Selwyn Image and others, and within a few years "art needlework" had replaced the earlier Berlin woolwork. As with printed and woven textiles, English country flowers predominated, together with a revival of later 17th and early 18th century crewelwork, with designs imitating the "tree of life" (wrongly called Jacobean), Japanese-style flora and fauna, the Italian Renaissance, and Cretan and Turkish embroideries. In the 1890s, appliqué embroidery tended to replace fine stitchery. Samplers were often worked in coloured wools rather than in silk and were consequently coarser. Bobbin lace designs were drawn on vellum and placed on a pillow. Pins were placed upright along the lines of the pattern and the lace was built up by bobbin-weighted threads which were twisted around them. Needlepoint lace was made with needle and thread using buttonhole and other embroidery stitches, drawn thread work and cutwork. Competition from machine-made lace meant that hand-made lace tended to be made by amateurs. Machine embroidery in white thread was used on muslin and fine cotton for handkerchiefs, collars and cuffs and panels of christening robes and as the basis for machine-made lace.

The Modernist movement had much less effect on rugs and textiles than it did on other decorative and applied arts in the 1920s and '30s. However, the designs of William Morris did prompt a revival of textiles and rugs in Britain and Europe. The best British rugs were commissioned; others, often symmetrical, joined by one seam and usually in sombre colours with abstract motifs, were imported from Belgium. French rugs were made to commission by the top designers, who included Jacques-Émile Ruhlmann, Paul Follot, Jules Leleu and the firm of Süe et Mare. Similarly in America, Donald Deskey, Gilbert Rohde and Eugene Schoen turned to textiles. Of other designers, Ruth Reeves designed some rugs for W. & J. Sloane that evoked American city life, as well as a series dominated by Cubist and geometric motifs. Many rugs from the 1920s and '30s were in autumnal and subdued tones or delicate pastels. Edward McKnight-Kauffer's rugs in bold primary colours are exceptions. Designers dispensed with fringes and borders, and with the symmetry of earlier designs. Besides African-inspired geometric designs, the French in particular continued to use stylized floral motifs in *millefiori* (thousand flower) designs, often showing the influence of artists such as Paul Cézanne and Raoul Dufy, whose distinctive palettes complemented the furnishings of "modern" interiors.

Art Deco rugs vary in shape. They were well-made and solid, with canvas backing, intended for use on floors, rather than for wall hangings. The pile is regular, as they tended to be machine-woven, usually in wool. They are often signed by the designer, which is rare in any other period. The wool is subject to fading, so strong colours are often at a premium. Examine the back to determine the density of knots – the more knots per square inch the better.

Above A Hammersmith hand-knotted Morris & Co carpet, c.1890
Right A Bruno da Silva Bruhns wool rug, c.1925

EARLY AND HIGH VICTORIAN TEXTILES

The Victorian period saw a great expansion in the textile industry, with materials being produced using a combination of new machine methods and traditional hand-made techniques. The Victorian love of embellishment, which was evident in everything from furniture to ceramics, was equally prevalent in textiles, with many designers looking to the past for inspiration. Embroidery was popular, particularly Berlin woolwork, as was bobbin and needlepoint lace, and crochet and braid laces.

A chalice veil of cream and gold silk damask by A. W. Pugin c.1848-50; 22½ x 22½in/57 x 57cm

This block-printed chintz with its crisply-drawn flowers on a white ground dates from 1835-40 and is typical of the early Victorian period. Machine-printed patterned grounds were also introduced at this time, the most popular being a simple all-over dot or pin design, known as "Stormont" ground, or an all-over, vermicular pattern.
•A textile design popular in the late 1840s was that of a continuous cascade of mixed flowers printed vertically, in the middle, or on the sides of a fabric.

TEXTILES

Traditional textiles

Among the most popular traditional textiles of the 1830s and '40s were luxury silk damasks with formalized flowers and leaves in pale colours. But these were luxury items and the more characteristic furnishing fabrics were power-loom woven in a mixture of cotton and worsted wool, or silk and wool, in darker colours. The fabric used for these early textiles was often challet, a fine worsted woollen material with a distinct sheen which enhanced the colours' brilliance. The patterns became increasingly more exuberant and naturalistic, using elaborate shading to make the flowers stand out from the ground. This reached a peak in 1851, when the extravagance was then replaced by more delicate patterns.

The classical style prevalent during the Regency period gradually gave way to the revival of a number of historical styles, which included Gothic, Elizabethan, Rococo and the Moorish or Alhambresque.

Gothic This style was based mainly on the formal patterns of 15th and 16th century damasks and velvets, and its chief exponent in the 1840s was the architect, A. W. N. Pugin (see p.26). The patterns usually have an ogival structure with stylized, scrolling leaves and heraldic motifs, such as a *fleur-de-lys*. The chalice at the top of the page is typical. Pugin also designed a number of ecclesiastical textiles for the new Gothic-inspired churches. He was a purist who believed in adhering strictly to authentic prototypes and deplored the use of shaded architectural motifs, and the imitation of one material by another, such as printed chintz blinds designed to imitate a series of stained glass windows.
Exotic Used mainly in cheaper, roller-printed fabrics, this style included pictorial chintzes with a variety of romantic, historical and commemorative designs vignetted in floral wreaths. "Portuguese print" textiles depicting unusual groups of exotic flowers, animals and figures printed in bright colours on striped grounds were made for export to South America and elsewhere.
Elizabethan This style first emerged in around 1834, and became increasingly popular in the 1840s and '50s. Some designs were purely abstract with bands of strapwork, cartouches and brackets. Others incorporated flowers with strapwork that was shaded to give a three-dimensional effect.

Moorish This style was inspired by Owen Jones's influential book, *Plans, Elevations, Sections and Details of the Alhambra* (1842). The intricate, interlaced patterns of delicately carved stonework, which operated on two or three intermingled planes, was copied on woven textiles, usually in primary colours. Geometric designs representing tilework are also found, and vertical stripes of Moorish ornament introduced into floral patterns.

Rococo In the so-called "Louis Quatorze" style, Rococo scrolls and cartouches, shaded to give the appearance of relief, were incorporated into floral designs, notably for carpets.

This woven silk textile called *Maharanee* (c.1872), was created by Owen Jones, one of the finest Victorian designers. He produced woven silk based on classical ornament, often with Moorish designs, and patterns derived from Indian decoration, as here. Jones's celebrated *Grammar of Ornament* (1856) illustrated every known type of European ornament from prehistoric times to the Renaissance, together with examples from ancient Egypt, Assyria, Persia, India and China.

EMBROIDERY

Samplers Berlin woolwork samplers were usually long narrow strips of canvas, bound in ribbon, worked with a variety of canvas stitches. Rectangular samplers, with the alphabet, a pious verse, or various other motifs, were also made throughout the Victorian period, more often worked in wool than silk.

Until the 1870s Berlin woolwork was the most popular type of domestic embroidery, but attempts by the church to revive fine stitchery, together with the establishment of the Royal School of Needlework, led to the prevalence of "art needlework", designed by architects and such designers as William Morris, Walter Crane, and Edward Burne-Jones.

Death was commemorated in needlework and samplers, which were often executed by children. This Berlin woolwork sampler is headed "In Affectionate Remembrance of Ellen Walker Who died December 5th 1853 Aged 69". The three verses are framed by symbols associated with death.

Pictorial designs on Berlin woolwork include biblical subjects, designs after Landseer, or romantic subjects taken from the novels of Sir Walter Scott, such as this panel from 1840, depicting a scene from *The Talisman*. The panels were often mounted in fire-screens or under glass as table tops, and were also used to upholster chair backs and seats. Smaller items include hand-screens and slipper tops. Parts of the pattern were sometimes worked in a looped stitch which was then cut to resemble a velvet pile. Designs were also worked wholly or partly in glass beads. There is usually one stitch to each square, which is evident in the outline of the motifs here.

Berlin woolwork This was the most popular embroidery between the 1830s and the 1870s and was so-called because the patterns and wools emanated from Berlin. The designs were worked in wool, sometimes with silk, in tent or cross-stitch on square meshed canvas, copied from patterns on squared paper. Many designs were floral, depicting roses, lilies-of-the-valley, poppies, water-lilies and other popular flowers, naturalistically treated, and often combined with exotic birds.

This four-leaf screen decorated in hand embroidery was designed by May Morris and produced by Morris and Company (see p.235), who also produced a number of designs by J. H. Dearle.

Designers at Templeton's included Bruce Talbert (see p.234) who created this portière c.1878. Templeton's wares often show a Japanese influence, with a broad border at the bottom, narrower borders at the sides, and a repeating pattern of flowers or ornament in the centre. The flowers may be stylized or conventional and, as here, may be combined with a band of geometric ornament.
•The Royal School of Needlework made embroidered portières, also with a Japanese flavour and featuring cranes, bamboo and *prunus* blossom, or the Jacobean "tree of life" pattern.
•Morris & Co. made hangings decorated with vine leaves, flowering and fruiting trees and large floral sprays, designed by May Morris, J. H. Dearle or William Morris.

The development of the Jacquard loom made it possible to manufacture Paisley shawls with complex all-over patterns in rich, dark colours (usually dominated by red). They often had a central motif surrounded by scrolling patterns filled with Indian-inspired floral and leaf ornament, similar to that of this shawl, and broad borders depicting an elongated *boteh* (pine cone) pattern each end.
•Similar designs were produced in Norwich and France at around the same period, so it is often difficult to make precise attributions.

Screens From the 1870s hand embroidery was often used to decorate three- and four-leaf screens. Many were produced by the Royal School of Needlework, including designs by Selwyn Image (1840-1930) representing the Four Seasons and also figures of Greek and Roman goddesses. Japanese-inspired designs with water-plants, cranes and wildlfowl with sprays of chrysanthemum or *prunus* blossom were popular, and Liberty and other firms imported authentic examples of Japanese screens.

Crossley mosaics A purely Victorian innovation, these velvet-like pictures and rugs, said to be the invention of a German refugee, were produced by John Crossley & Son of Halifax, between 1850 and 1869. The designs, similar to those of Berlin woolwork, were worked out on squared paper. Threads of coloured worsted wool, one for each square of the pattern, were attached longitudinally to vertical frames, and by a complicated process cut into thin vertical slices and stuck to a linen backing, giving a depth of about 4mm.

As with Berlin woolwork, the subjects of Crossley mosaics were often inspired by the paintings of Sir Edwin Landseer and others; Robbie Burns and Highland Mary shown here, were popular. As in other media, royalty were featured: there is a Crossley mosaic portrait of the Prince of Wales in a sailor suit.

Panels and portières
Textile hangings were especially popular in the Aesthetic period when they were often used as curtains in doorways. One firm which specialized in these portières was James Templeton & Sons of Glasgow. Their wares were made of wool and silk and were woven on Jacquard looms.

SHAWLS

The heyday of the shawl was in the 1850s and '60s when the ever-increasing width of crinoline made it difficult to wear a coat. The earliest silk and wool shawls had a cream ground with a narrow, coloured border at the sides and a broad border at each end. Some were square with a plain or patterned centre of tiny stylized flowers or sprigs. Printed shawls made of fine muslin or gauze were preferred for summer wear. Kashmiri-inspired shawls had been woven in Edinburgh and Norwich from the late 1770s, but were first woven in Paisley, Scotland, during the early 19th century and enjoyed a boom there from the 1840s until the late 1860s.

LACE AND WHITEWORK

Honiton lace Made from fine white cotton, this was the most sought-after British lace of the Victorian period, especially when it was chosen by Queen Victoria for her wedding veil and the flouncings and trimmings on her dress. A fine bobbin (or pillow) lace, designs consist mainly of naturalistic sprays, mostly floral, although shells and butterflies often feature.

Bobbin lace The Honiton lace made all over Devon and the East Midlands tended to be in simpler patterns, and was used mainly for trimmings, insertions and borders. Torchon lace, a coarse open-textured bobbin lace in narrow lengths with geometric designs, was also made in the East Midlands.

Irish lace Irish lace includes Carrickmacross, introduced in 1816, made by applying fine cambric to machine-made net and adding embroidery stitches. Scrolling designs of flowers and leaves or delicate floral sprays were popular; borders are often edged in tiny loops. Limerick lace, introduced in 1829, was worked on a machine net ground, usually with delicate floral designs. Crochet laces were an Irish speciality, with floral designs and usually some petals standing free from the ground giving a three-dimensional effect. Pieces are often edged with little scalloped points.

Nottingham lace Nottingham lace-makers produced fine machine-made lace curtains with elaborate designs, as well as dress accessories. In the 1880s, chemical lace was produced by embroidering fabric by machine, then dipping it into a chemical which dissolved the ground. These designs tended to be geometric and rather coarse.

Whitework This fine embroidery in white thread on muslin or fine cotton was used on dresses, christening robes, collars and cuffs. Pioneered by Mrs Jameson of Ayrshire in around 1814, it is also known as "Ayrshire" embroidery. The more specialized "Mountmellick" embroidery was usually worked on a white cotton satin jean in white knitting cotton, using satin stitch, chain and feather stitches and French knots to give a raised effect. Designs are naturalistic; often passion flowers, blackberries, ferns, oak leaves and acorns. It was used on bedspreads, pillow cases and costumes, and although first popular in the 1850s, enjoyed a revival in the '80s.

Patterns on whitework are mostly floral – for example roses, thistle, shamrocks, sprigs and leaves. This border is a good example.

Broiderie Anglaise By 1850 *broiderie anglaise*, also known from 1880 as "Madeira work", began to replace Ayrshire work in popularity. Designs of conventionalized flowers and leaves consisted of cut holes sewn round in buttonhole stitch.

These patterns show the looped and scalloped edges typical of *broiderie anglaise* work. The designs came from one of many contemporary embroidery manuals published in the 19th century.

The best examples of Honiton lace include raised elements, worked by "sewing in" threads into the existing pinholes, as in the veined leaves incorporated into the Honiton cuff and collars here. Typically, motifs are clearly outlined and fairly detailed. Net grounds were initially hand-made, but from c.1825 were increasingly machine-made.

Foreign lace Imported Maltese lace, in fairly coarse, often silk, thread with repeating patterns of stylized flowers and leaves, was much copied in England. Venetian lace, with its three-dimensional raised scrolling designs united by bars, often in ecru (a light brown colour achieved through the use of a dyed thread or by dipping the finished lace in tea) was collected and copied by amateur lace-workers, amongst whom lace-making was a popular pastime.

THE AESTHETIC AND ARTS & CRAFTS STYLES

Dragonfly, part of a woven silk tissue by Bruce Talbert c.1875

The Aesthetic Movement of the 1870s and '80s saw a revival of the decorative arts. One of the main influences was Japanese. In textiles and embroidery work, tertiary, rather than primary colours were preferred, of olive and greyish greens, yellows and pale turquoise. Some textiles designed by Christopher Dresser and Bruce Talbert are in red and gold on a black background, simulating the effect of Japanese lacquer. Further inspiration came from classical, Medieval and Renaissance art. The designs of William Morris and his assistant, J. H. Dearle, were very influential in Europe and America, as were those of Liberty's. Other important Aesthetic textile designers include Walter Crane and Lewis F. Day.

Right Some of Godwin's designs have a rigid geometrical structure, enclosing highly conventionalized flowers reduced to a flat, circular form against a background of Japanese ornament. Here, this treatment has been applied to sunflowers, one of his most typical motifs. The stiff leaves display a medieval influence.

EDWARD WILLIAM GODWIN (ENGLISH, 1833-86)

The sketchbooks of the architect E. W. Godwin are filled with drawings of Japanese badges and ornaments which inspired the textiles he designed for Warner and Sons in the early 1870s. These are some of the finest textiles of the Aesthetic period. Godwin's favoured motifs include sunflowers, peacocks, king-fishers and sparrows, all treated in a Japanese manner. (See also p.30 for Godwin's furniture designs.)

BRUCE TALBERT (ENGLISH 1838-81)

Right Much of the embroidery at this time was floral, the favourite motifs being sunflowers, lilies, daffodils, iris, tulips, daisies, primroses and wild roses, together with *prunus* and apple blossom, fruit, particularly pomegranates, and sprays of chrysanthemum. This detail from a design by E. D. Bradby shows an exquisitely embroidered white lily.

Even more prolific and influential as a textile designer was Bruce Talbert (see p.29), whose designs are similar to those of Godwin. Many of his textiles are all-over patterns of leaves and blossom, the flowers being conventionalized shapes with flat petals. The *Dragonfly* design on a woven silk tissue at the top of the page shows dragonflies hidden amongst an all-over pattern of peach-blossom, leaves and fruit. Like Godwin, Talbert favoured sunflowers, either stylized or drawn with botanical accuracy.

Embroidery Embroidery of the period, known as "art needlework", became as popular as the earlier Berlin woolwork (see p.231). It was used to adorn table covers and cloths, mats and doillies, sideboard cloths, chair backs, mantel borders and fire-screens. Curtains, bedspreads, piano covers and hangings provided great scope for the ambitious art needlewoman and were worked on linen and cotton twill, serge, and velvet, often in crewel wools.

Aesthetic motifs
Renaissance-type patterns with dolphins, grotesque beasts, *putti* and scroll-work were favoured – particularly by Walter Crane – as well as designs based on Turkish, Persian, and Cretan embroideries. Figural panels from the Aesthetic period, notably those by Selwyn Image, were depicted in classical or medieval dress, worked either in outline, in shades of brown, or in appliqué.

MORRIS AND CO. (ENGLISH, 1861-1940)

The pattern of this printed cotton textile, *The Strawberry Thief*, designed by Morris in 1883, was printed by the indigo discharge method, whereby a bleach is used to remove the blue dye, leaving traces on the reverse.
•Many of Morris's patterns have been reproduced, all screen- or machine- printed in modern, chemical dyes which look more uniform than the original vegetable colours.

The poet, writer, socialist and designer, William Morris is chiefly remembered today for his textiles and wallpapers. His firm was founded in 1861 to produce a variety of products including furniture (see p.31). Morris designed his first textile, *The Jasmine Trellis*, in 1868. He created over 50 designs for printed and woven textiles, together with designs for embroideries, carpets and tapestries. Usually printed by hand from wood-blocks using vegetable dyes, such as madder and indigo, they were attractive even when the colours had faded.

Embroidery In the 1860s and '70s Morris produced designs for church embroidery, for the Royal School of Needlework, and for individual houses. However, most extant examples date from after 1885, when Morris's daughter, May, took charge of the firm's embroidery section, producing, together with Morris's chief assistant, J. H. Dearle, finished embroideries and designs traced out for the customers to work themselves.

Carpets In the 1870s Morris made a number of designs for machine-made carpets and in 1880 he set up carpet looms in Hammersmith to produce hand-knotted rugs influenced by Persian and other Eastern carpets. Pieces have approximately 25 knots to the square inch. These carpets were expensive, but of such high quality that many have survived.

Morris designed few complete tapestries and usually concentrated on backgrounds and borders. Figural designs were provided by Edward Burne-Jones. The background of *Flora*, woven in 1881, was supplied by J. H. Dearle, but Morris was designed the original, in a larger format with a background of acanthus leaves. Dearle's backgrounds tend to be stiffer and coarser than Morris's, and lack their complexity.

LIBERTY AND CO (ENGLISH, 1875-Present)

From around 1900, Liberty designs became more formal, with Glasgow-style roses, as in this example. Spade- or heart-shaped leaves, formalized trees or berries and grapes with squared-up leaves were also popular, with plain grounds rather than the earlier, densely patterned ones.
•Originally intended as furnishing fabrics, in the 1960s many Liberty designs were revived for dresses and scarves, and are still in production today. These are usually printed on silk or wool, rather than on the cotton or velveteen of the original designs.

Since its foundation, Liberty has been famous for its textiles. The earliest were silks imported from the East, either plain or printed with Indian- or Japanese-inspired designs. In the 1880s the firm introduced its "Art Fabrics", incorporating English-style Art Nouveau elements into Aesthetic designs. The firm commissioned work from leading artists, including Christopher Dresser, Walter Crane, Lindsay Butterflies and C. F. A. Voysey. (See also p.33 for Liberty furniture and p.184 for their metalwork.)

Although Liberty had its own print-works at Merton Abbey, the textiles were usually produced by outside firms, and most of the designers, not credited by Liberty, also worked for other companies. It is possible to find examples of Victorian Liberty fabrics with the original maker's label.
•Some designs were produced for Liberty by the Silver Studio during the 1890s. Those by Arthur Silver tend to display swirling, sinuous lines, often with a marked discrepancy of scale. Harry Napper, also at the Silver Studio, produced some designs for Liberty in the 1900's.

This cloth of *Birds and Berries* (c.1897) is typical of Voysey's designs for Liberty, which often featured sinuous lines. The stylized effect is partly achieved by the precision with which the pattern is drawn, further emphasized by a heavy outline. Typically, the colours are flat. Birds in flight or on branches were recurring Voysey motifs, often as flat silhouettes. Birds by William Morris are more realistic.

QUILTS

Quilts were very popular both in Britain and the United States during the Victorian period. Quilt-making was a traditional activity carried out in the homes of all but the very rich, using techniques and designs passed down from generation to generation. In many cases the quilts were made into bedcovers for special occasions, particularly for young girls' dowries, when the first would be started on the announcement of the engagement, and the final white quilt finished for the wedding night.

A fine American, mid-19th century pieced and appliquéd *broderie perse* quilt

AMERICAN QUILTS

This quilt is a fine example of a pieced cotton Amish quilt, and dates from the early 20th century. The squares of purple, black, beige, green, blue and white are arranged in a *Wild Goose Chase* pattern.

•Quilts can be categorized according to their pattern, technique and region of origin. Value rests on the skills and inventiveness of the needle-woman who made them, often without a sewing machine.

American quilt-making came into its own at the start of the 19th century and most quilts seen on today's market were made between then and the 1930s. Wool and silks were scarce and expensive in America but cotton was plentiful, so originally many quilts were made up from scraps of left-over fabrics to save money. Quilt-making was especially popular in rural settlements and some of the best pieces were made by women in the mid-Atlantic states such as Maryland and the Carolinas. Superbly-crafted quilts were also made by the German-speaking communities of the northeast, such as the Mennonites, the Amish and the so-called Pennsylvania Dutch, and these examples preserve traditional European designs and techniques. Pennsylvania Dutch quilts are typically boldly coloured and patterned in a style that evokes central European folk art.

Patterns American quilts were often given picturesque pattern names. Perhaps the most well-known design of the mid-19th century is the "log cabin"– a pieced quilt, rustic in flavour and usually composed of identical small, square blocks arranged with a diagonal emphasis. The stitching involved anchoring the squares to a base fabric. Log cabin quilts were often made from inexpensive cotton or wool; examples tend to be small.
•Patterns took on a new lease of life during Centennial year – designs often featured symbols of the American Republic, such as stars and stripes.

The "Album" (or "Albumen") pattern illustrated here in this appliqué quilt was also popular in the mid-19th century. These quilts are the work of several women, who were often from a religious community or an extended family, and each of whom would produce a small, square panel. When these had been stitched together, the piece was finally sewn to a fabric ground. Sometimes the individual makers signed and dated their panels.
•Among the finest of all American quilts were those that imitated delicate Italian *trapunto* patterns. The technique relies solely on the stitching for its decorative effect, and is applied to a monochrome ground.
•As in other areas of American crafts during the 1870s, Japanese art also made an impact on quilt-making, although such examples are very rare.

Crazy quilts Crazy quilts date from the 1870s and '80s, and were particularly fashionable in the late 1880s, when people could buy the components in kit form. The most popular examples are those that combine a high standard of needlework with imaginative compositions.

As seen in this example, crazy quilts were made from odd scraps of fabric (usually silk or elaborately printed), cut and arranged at random. This piece incorporates a souvenir ribbon from the New Orleans exposition of 1884. The result is made more "crazy" by a variety of stitching techniques.

BRITISH QUILTS

In Britain, "Box" patterns which simulated three-dimensional cubes as in this mid-19th century quilt were favoured, along with "log cabin" designs of oblong patches.
•Traditional, stitched quilts were also popular in Britain. These consisted of two layers of fabric with a blanket or padding between them. They were common in northern England and often had patterns of running feathers, cables, fans or bellows. "Strippy" or striped quilts were also popular in the North. These were decorated with full-length border patterns, or small rows of shells and roses.

In Britain, the main centres for quilt-making were in Durham, Wales and the West Country. The traditional hexagonal patchwork quilts continued to be made throughout the Victorian period but often with scraps of silk and velvet instead of cotton. A type of patchwork known as *broderie perse* or Cretonne appliqué was made from about 1850 by sewing groups of flowers, birds and leaves cut from printed cotton onto a black ground. This type was also popular in America – the quilt at the top of the previous page is a good example.

Designs Appliqué and pieced quilts with repeated motifs in squared multiples, and patterns such as the Star of Bethlehem, were an American speciality, but similar examples were made in England.

Another quilt variety which was popular in Britain as well as in America in the 1880s was the "Japanese" or "crazy" patchwork – made up of irregularly shaped, randomly arranged pieces, some with a flower or other motif, joined together by featherstitch (see above right).
•Quilts that were made in Wales usually had borders set in rectangular frames with a round centre, while West Country varieties tended to feature a round centre with fan corners.

This detail from a "mosaic" patchwork hanging exemplifies a type of quilt that consisted of various coloured shapes cut from felt or tailors' cuttings and joined at the edges with almost invisible stitches. The designs were usually pictorial, with a strange mixture of religious and secular subjects derived from various sources such as popular prints and tinsel theatrical pictures.

ART DECO RUGS

In the early 20th century the rug enjoyed a revival. No longer merely a decorative floor cover unrelated to the decor and furnishings of the room, it was elevated to the status of a work of art. Decorative effect took precedence over utility and practicality. The best rugs were commissioned from major designers, including Betty Joel in England and Bruno da Silva Bruhns in France. Rug shapes became varied and motifs more geometrical and simple, with colours tending towards pastels. Fringes, popular before 1920, were no longer a feature. Inspiration came from Africa, while others showed a Mayan or Aztec influence.

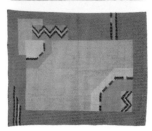

Right A rug designed by Da Silva Bruhns c.1928; 152 × 114in/386 × 289.5cm

BRUNO DA SILVA BRUHNS (FRENCH, dates unknown)

Many of Bruhns' designs exhibit an Aztec or Mayan influence. Motifs usually have a degree of intricacy. Piano key and comb effects often appear in his work. Motifs are occasionally given a thin outline. Bruhns was influenced by many cultures and idioms: he was adapting Colonial motifs as early as the 1920s, and in the mid-20s and '30s he added American-Indian and North African motifs and Cubistic elements. Colours are subtle and muted rather than violent, and though they may contrast, never clash but are well-blended and harmonious. Quality is always high in Bruhns' carpets.

Bruhns worked in Paris, where many of his pieces were manufactured by the Savonnerie works. He contributed to many exhibitions. His rugs, in hand-knotted wool, are characterized by a preference for geometric motifs and layouts with circles or polka dot motifs for his asymmetrical designs, as seen in the rug above.

Signatures and authenticity Bruhns used his full signature and/or monogram. The rug above, fairly typically, has both – the signature along the side and the initials across the top. A carpet signed by Bruhns is almost certainly genuine, as fakes are not known to have been produced. The design sketches he made for his rugs and carpets are also collectable. These are usually framed and may also bear his signature.

BETTY JOEL (CHINESE, 1896-1984)

This rug from c.1930-5, shows Joel's preference for circles and stepped effects. (These also appear in her furniture, see p.57). Designs were often asymmetrical, as here. The palette is subtle and harmonious; colours are not outlined, but laid one over the other. The rugs were made in China and signed with a Chinese-looking monogram.

A contemporary of Bruhns, Betty Joel was born in China and went to live in England in 1919, where she opened a furniture and textile shop. She later moved to Surrey and took showrooms in Knightsbridge, London. During the 1920s her work followed a fine line between the traditional and the avant-garde, becoming more geometric and simpler in the 1930s. She was not a prolific rug maker; most pieces were commissioned, and thus of high quality and very expensive.

EDWARD MCKNIGHT KAUFFER (AMERICAN, 1890-1954)

McKnight Kauffer was American-born, but he spent the major part of his working life in Britain. He collaborated with his wife, Marion Dorn, on commercial rug designs for the British firm Wilton Royal Carpets as well as working to commission for a very select market. Many rugs were designed to act as an integral part of a room setting, and were intended to complement other aspects of the interior design.

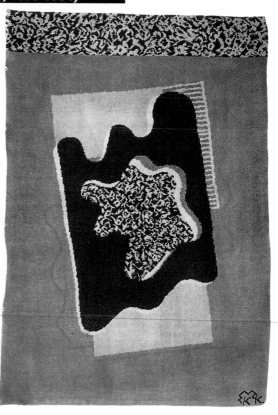

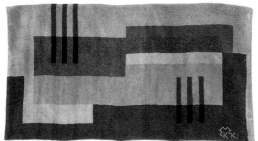

Above Kauffer's work is strongly Modernist. This rug is typical in its use of an asymmetrical design of rectangular motifs with red and black bands. It makes use of the interplay between horizontals and verticals: curved elements are absent. Typically, Kauffer's monogram is clearly visible in the bottom right-hand corner. •Kauffer was also a posterist: his best-known designs are for London Transport and Shell.

Right Kauffer's rugs feature vivid, often unusual shades and combinations; this rug with its Cubist angular and curvilinear elements, is relatively subdued. Stripes and blocks of colour may overlap, and as in Bruhn's rugs, use is made of a comb effect, seen on both examples here. The interplay of shape and form gives Kauffer's rugs a strong three-dimensional quality.

MARION DORN (BRITISH, 1900-64)

Kauffer's wife, Dorn, was a very different type of designer from her husband. Her rugs show greater sensitivity to the textile medium, using more organic colours, rather than imposing the ideas of formal art movements. She was known as the "architect of floors", and her rugs were sold through the London department store Fortnum and Mason. Some rugs were made as commissions for large London hotels. In 1934 she established her own firm, Marion Dorn Ltd., specializing in custom-designed and handmade rugs. She made more rugs than Kauffer. Dorn's designs are less strongly rectilinear than those by Kauffer, and often feature interlaced circles loop patterns, sometimes symmetrical and sometimes free-flowing. Knot and puzzle effects are also common, as are waves.

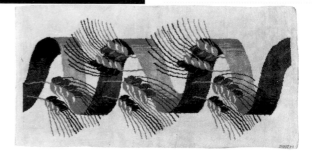

This rug is typical of Dorn's work, incorporating organic imagery with a sweeping curved line. Her colours are subtle and subdued, tending towards autumnal tones, especially shades of brown and grey. On some pieces the pile is cut to give a textural, layered effect. Her rugs are usually signed "DORN" in block letters. Both Kauffer's and Dorn's rugs should also carry the factory label.

The Mrybor Studio Among other influential and now collectable rugs of the Art Deco period are those made in the Myrbor studio in Northern Africa in the ten years or so from 1925. The designs were the work of several artists, such as Jean Lurcat, Fernand Léger, Joan Miró and Jean Arp.

GLOSSARY

Acid-cutting A method of decorating glass by which an object is coated with wax or another acid-resistant substance, then incised with a fine steel point and dipped in acid.

Aesthetic Movement An artistic movement prevalent in Britain c.1860-c.1880, which advocated a return to a harmony of form and function in design and decoration.

Alexandrite A glass type named after a greenish gemstone that seems to change to red or reddish-brown in certain light. Lalique (see p.90) sold glasswares of the same name, cut to reveal the underlying pigment, giving the impression of changing colour.

Amboyna Mottled, highly grained wood of an Indonesian tree.

Appliqué The decorative application of a second fabric to the main fabric ground.

Aquatint Method of etching whereby acidic resin is applied to a copper plate and heated so that areas acquire a pitted surface which then transfers ink to paper.

Arts and Crafts A late-19thC artistic movement, led by William Morris (see pp.29-33), which advocated a return to medieval standards of craftsmanship and simplicity of design.

Automata A term covering a variety of mechanical toys, usually clockwork, popular during the 18th and 19thC.

Bakelite Synthetic resin, or plastic. Usually in dark colours.

Batik A form of stylized animal and floral design inspired by Javanese textiles.

Bauhaus style In the style of the German Bauhaus movement – that is, designed according to the demands of machine production, relating construction to function.

Bentwood Solid or laminated wood, steamed and bent into a curvilinear shape. First used in the 18thC, it was favoured by Wiener Werkstätte craftsmen.

Biscuit The term for unglazed porcelain fired only once.

Britannia metal A 19thC pewter substitute, which was an alloy of tin, antimony and a trace of copper.

Burmese ware A type of American art glass made by combining gold and uranium oxides, patented in 1885 by the Mount Washington Glass Works (p.78).

Cameo glass Decorative glass formed by laminating together two or more layers of glass, often of varying colours, which are wheel-carved or etched to make a design in relief.

Car mascot Ornamental badge or device to be mounted on a car radiator cap.

Case furniture Furniture intended primarily as a receptacle, such as chests of drawers.

Cased glass (overlay) Similar to cameo glass, but with the design on the outer layer cut away rather than in relief.

Chasing A method of embossing or engraving metal, especially silver.

Chryselephantine An expensive combination of ivory and a metal, usually bronze.

Cire perdue ("lost wax") The French term for a process of casting sculpture that results in unique casts.

Cold painting A technique for decorating bronze whereby coloured enamels are annealed or painted on to the metal.

Copper electrotyping A more refined version of the electroplating process.

Crazing The break-up of a glazed surface into a fine network of cracks, either intentionally or as a result of age.

Crackled glaze (craquelure) A deliberate cracked effect achieved by firing ceramics to a precise temperature.

Cubism A formal art movement characterized by distortion, angularity, geometric arrangements and features of African sculpture.

Davenport A small decorative writing desk with a sloped top and drawers below.

Decalcomania Victorian glass wares decorated by amateurs with a variety of scraps and pictures.

Dinanderie Work in non-precious metals.

Earthenware The term for pottery not vitrified (i.e. treated to achieve a glassy surface). Hence, all pottery except stoneware.

Ebonized wood Wood stained to resemble ebony.

Electroplating The process whereby silver is electronically deposited on a copper, nickel silver or Britannia metal base.

Entrelac A type of interlaced decoration used on jewelry. Of Celtic origin, its use was revived by Arts and Crafts designers.

Épergne A type of ornamental glass flower stand, produced mainly in Stourbridge (p.66).

Etching A type of engraving in which the design, drawn with a needle on a copper plate coated with an acid-resistant, is dipped in acid, then used to transfer ink to paper.

Favrile From the Old English word meaning "hand-made", the term for a type of iridescent glass developed by Tiffany (pp.84-5).

Flatback A term for Staffordshire portrait figures with flat, undecorated backs, designed to stand against a wall or on a mantelpiece.

Flatware The technical term for any flat or shallow tableware, such as plates, more specifically applied to cutlery.

Galuchat Sharkskin used in Art Deco furniture by Paul Iribe and others.

Gesso A ground made from plaster mixed with size, used to prepare a panel or canvas for gilding.

Glaze The smooth, shiny coating to soft-paste porcelain or stoneware.

Gouache Opaque watercolour painting. Pigments are bound with glue.

Hallmarks The marks stamped on silver or gold pieces when passed at assay (the test for quality). Books are available that list all the relevant dates, places and maker's marks. However, while hallmarks are a good guide to age and authenticity, they should not be regarded as definitive, as they can be worn, faked, or even let in from another piece.

Hard-paste porcelain Porcelain made using the ancient Chinese combination of kaolin and petuntse.

Impressed Indented, as opposed to incised.

Incised Decoration or maker's mark cut or scratched into the surface, rather than impressed.

Indigo A blue vegetable-based dye used in the colouring of textiles.

Intaglio carving A type of carving whereby forms are sunken into, as opposed to moulded onto, a surface.

Ironstone china Hard white earthenware made to imitate that patented by Masons (p.102).

Ivorene Worthless plastic substance resembling ivory.

Iznik A type of boldy coloured Turkish pottery.

Jardinière A plant container made from a variety of materials including glass or pottery.

Jugendstil The term for German and Austrian design in the Art Nouveau style. Named after the Munich-based publication, *Jugend*.

Latticinio A type of decoration on glasswares which consists of thin white canes of opaque glass moulded on to a piece to create a latticework or lace effect.

Letterpress A printing method whereby ink is transferred from raised surfaces to paper by pressure; replaced by lithography.

Limed oak Oak coated with lime which is then brushed off to leave a white residue in the grain.

Lithograph A print taken from a stone on which a design is drawn in ink and fixed. The remaining porous areas are treated with water so that the printing ink adheres only to the design, which is then transferred to paper.

Lustreware Pottery with a polished surface produced using metallic pigments, usually silver or copper.

Macassar A rare form of ebony.

Madder The red vegetable-based dye used in the colouring of textiles.

Majolica Painted, brightly-coloured earthenware produced in large quantities in Britain and Europe from c.1850 (pp.106-7).

Maquette A rough wax or clay model for a sculpture.

Marquetrie de verre A glass-making process whereby pieces of coloured glass are pressed into the warm, soft body of a piece and rolled in. The insertions are wheel carved.

Marquetry Furniture decoration in which shapes are cut into a sheet of wood veneer and inlaid with other woods or materials.

Martelé The French for "hammered"; the term for silverware with a fine hammered surface produced first in France and revived by the American Gorham Corporation during the Art Nouveau period.

Millefiori A glass-making technique whereby canes of coloured glass are arranged in bundles so that the cross-section creates a pattern. Slices of *millefiori* canes can be used as decoration, or fused together to form hollow wares.

Modernism/Functionalism International movement in 1930s furniture design. Clean lines and the cube shape were emphasized.

Nailsea glass A type of wares produced at the Nailsea works and elsewhere in England, decorated by the fusing or splashing on to the glass body of pieces of coloured or white enamel (p.66).

Novelty or "fancy" glass The elaborately coloured and novel glass produced by several factories from the mid-19thC.

Opalescence A translucent white quality in glass; a reddish core is visible when held up to the light.

Opaline glass The semi-opaque white (opalescent) glass produced in 19thC France.

Parian Porcelain with a matt, white body resembling marble, developed as a substitute for the white biscuit figures popularized by Sèvres and others in the 18th and early 19thC.

Pâte-de-cristal Near-transparent glass made of powdered glass paste which has been fused in a mould.

Pâte-de-verre Translucent glass similar to *pâte-de-cristal* but with a lower proportion of lead.

Pâte-sur-pâte A form of ceramic decoration developed at Sèvres (see pp.122-3)

whereby white slip is applied and fired in layers, building up a cameo effect.

Patina The fine layer or surface sheen on metal or furniture that results with time, use or chemical corrosion.

Patination Alteration to the surface appearance of metal caused by time, use or chemical corrosion.

Pavé Setting Stones set so close together that no backing material is visible.

Peachblow The American term for shaded glass similar to Burmese ware, with an inner layer of opalescent glass giving the appearance of glazed porcelain.

Planished A smooth finish to metalwork achieved by hammering or rolling.

Plique-à-jour An enamelling method whereby a backed, many-celled mould is filled with translucent enamel of different colours. When the backing is removed, the finished piece resembles stained glass.

Plywood Form of laminated wood with the grain of alternate layers set at right angles.

Pochoir Reproduction process using different stencils for each colour of a print, applied over a black and white reproduction of the original.

Pontil mark The mark left by the iron rod upon which some glass is supported for final shaping after blowing.

Pressed glass, or **slagware** Glass items produced in a mechanical press mould.

Quercitron A yellow vegetable-based dye used in the colouring of textiles.

Raku Form of Japanese earthenware covered with a thick lead glaze.

Repoussé The term describing relief metalwork decoration created by hammering on the reverse side.

Reticulated Thinly-walled porcelain pieces with intricate pierced decoration produced by Worester Royal Porcelain in the late 19thC.

Rock crystal A form of engraved lead glass cut and polished to simulate the natural facets of actual rock crystal.

Sand-cast A method of casting bronze in a mould made from pounded quartz and sand.

Scrimshaw The term for carved items made from shell or bone, usually by mariners, popular in the United States in the 19thC.

Secessionist The term for the movement formed in opposition to established artistic taste which surfaced in Munich, Berlin and Vienna toward the end of the 19thC, and which initiated the Art Nouveau movement.

Sgraffito A form of earthenware decoration incised through slip, revealing the ground beneath.

Shades Peculiarly Victorian table decorations of imitation flowers, stuffed birds or miniature figures covered by a glass dome.

Shagreen A type of untanned leather, originally made from the skin of the shagri, a Turkish wild ass, soaked in lime water and dyed. By the 19thC it was made mainly of sharkskin.

Signed in the stone or **in the block** A term describing a poster or print, the signature of which is designed as a part of the stone from which the design was printed.

"Silvered" glass Items produced by injecting silver between two layers of glass.

Slip A smooth dilution of clay and water used in the making and decoration of pottery.

Slip-trailed decoration A form of ceramic decoration involving thin trails of slip trailed across the body of a piece.

Slipware Earthenware decorated with designs trailed in or incised through slip.

Socle The block or slab that forms the lowest part of the pedestal of a sculpture or decorative vase.

Soft-paste porcelain Porcelain made using a combination of kaolin and powdered glass, soapstone or calcined bone.

Stilt mark The mark left on the base of some pottery by supports used during firing.

Stoneware Non-porous pottery, a hybrid of earthenware and porcelain, made of clay and a fusible substance.

Streamlining A style with flowing curved lines and aerodynamic form, prevalent in 1930s American design.

Studio glass One-off pieces made by designers and glass-makers in collaboration.

Transfer-printing Method by which a design is printed in ink on an engraved copper plate and transferred to paper, which is then pressed on the ceramic surface while still wet.

Triple soufflé ("blowout") glass A variation of mould blowing, this method involves the overlaying of glass in the mould and then pumping in air at very high pressure, pressing the glass into the recesses of the mould.

Tube-lining A form of ceramic decoration whereby thin trails of slip are applied as outlines to areas of coloured glaze.

Underglaze The coloured decorative layer applied under the main glaze.

Vase parlante A form of vase produced by Emile Gallé (see pp.72-3) the decoration of which includes an engraved quote from a literary work.

Vaseline glass A cloudy, yellow and oily-looking glass, similar in appearance to vaseline, developed during the 19thC.

Vellum Fine calf or lambskin parchment used to cover some furniture or books.

Vitro porcelain British art glass made from slag, crysolite and glass metal, giving a streaked opaque green effect, with purple veining.

Verdigris The green or bluish patina formed on copper, brass, or bronze.

Weld A yellow vegetable-based dye used in textiles.

Whitework The name for a type of fine embroidery in white thread on muslin or fine cotton pioneered in Ayrshire c.1814. Also known as "Ayrshire embroidery".

Woodcut A print made by drawing the design on the surface of a block of wood and cutting away the parts to remain white in the picture. The surface is then inked and transferred to paper.

Ziggurat Stepped pyramid-shaped pedestal of marble or onyx for small bronze figures.

SELECTED DESIGNERS & MANUFACTURERS

Aalto, Alvar (1898-1976)
Finnish Modernist architect and furniture designer. Director of **Finmar** and founder of Artek (1931), furnishing companies.
Adnet, Jacques and Jean (b.1900)
French cabinet makers working in a distinctly Modernist and avant-garde style. Used wood and metal, and smoked glass. Jacques was director of *La Compagnie des Art Français* and Jean was at *La Maîtresse*, where he became a sales manager for *Galeries Lafayette*.
Alcock, Samuel (dates unknown)
English potter; his factory at Corbridge operated 1830-1859.
Alix, Charlotte (dates unknown)
Member of the *Union des Artistes Modernes*, established in 1930 to promote Modernist movement. Produced luxurious glass furniture with Louis Sognot for the Palace of the Maharajah of Indore.
Amstelhoek (1894-1910)
Dutch ceramics, metalwork and furniture workshop.
Arabia (1874-present)
Helsinki-based porcelain factory, founded as a subsidiary of **Rörstrand**. Became independent in 1916. Mass-produced vases with leaf or geometric motifs in Art Nouveau style. Marks: various, including ARABIA, impressed, AA, or A, and factory name, and sometimes a crown.
Argy-Rousseau, Gabriel (1885-1953)
French designer of *pâte-de-verre* and *pâte-de-cristal* glass objects.

Artificers' Guild (1901-1942)
London-based metalworking firm founded by Nelson Dawson.
Ashbee, Charles R. (1863-1942)
English architect and designer associated with the Arts and Crafts movement. In 1888, founded the **Guild of Handicraft** in order to perpetuate the ideals of medieval craft guilds. Ashbee and Guild marks are stamped.
Baccarat (established 1764)
Alsatian glassworks famous for its paperweights. Marks: stamped or etched.

Bailey, C. J. C. (mid-late 19thC)
London potter, who bought Fulham Pottery, making earthenware and saltware jugs and mugs for domestic use, sometimes with heraldic or Japanese-inspired designs, incised or impressed. Marks usually incorporate the name Bailey.
Bailey, E. H. (1788-1867)
English artist and sculptor in the Neo-classical style.

E. Bakalowits & Sohne (1845)
Viennese glass retailer of avant-garde pieces by leading designers such as Koloman Moser.
Barnsley, Sydney (1865-1926), and Ernest (1863-1926)
Furniture designers and co-founders of the Bath Cabinet Makers Co. Ltd. Pieces unmarked.
Barye, Antoine-Louis (1796-1875)
French animalier. Favoured the *cire perdue* method of casting, resulting in unique casts.
Bath Cabinet Makers Co. Ltd. (dates unknown)
Cabinet designers working in Art Nouveau style, similar to Liberty, with stylized floral decoration and rose motifs. Sold through Heal's in London. Pieces often have a tag bearing design details.
Bauhaus (1919-1933)
German design school. Founded by the architect Walter Gropius, it included architects, engineers, designers, sculptors and painters, who sought to relate form to function and aesthtic qualities to the demands of machine production.
Bayes, Gilbert (1872-1953)
English sculptor working in a style that combined Art Nouveau and medieval influences.
Belleek (est. 1863)
Irish ceramics firm. Specialized in openwork baskets. Wares often impressed on the underside with "Belleek". From 1863 to c.1880, Belleek wares also carried a printed black mark of a seated Irish wolfhound, harp and round tower. After 1880, "County Fermanagh" was added.
Belter, John Henry (1804-63)
German-born cabinet-maker active in the United States. Gave his name to a style of large-scale, elaborate Rococo furniture.
Benson, William Arthur Smith (1854-1924)
English architect, furniture and metalwork designer. Best known for his light fittings and tableware. Close friend of **William Morris**, of whose Merton Abbey workshop he became managing Director in 1896. Marks: stamped.
Bergman, Franz (dates unknown)
Austrian sculptor whose cold-painted bronzes represent Arab figures or exotic figures. Mark: "Namgreb" (name backwards).
Berlin (est. 1751)
German porcelain factory. Marks: in mid-19thC painted red orb or underglaze blue painted sceptre; plaques also carry initials KPM.
Bevan, Charles (active 1860s)
English designer and manufacturer of furniture, specializing in Gothic-revival style.
Bindesbøll, Thorfvald (1846-1908)
Leading Danish ceramist, glass-maker and silver worker, creating designs in Danish-Japanese taste.

Bing & Grondahl Porcellaensfabrik (1853-present)
Danish producer of Art Nouveau stoneware and earthenware.
Bing, Siegfried (1838-1905)
Parisian publisher, art dealer and sponsor.
Böch Frères (est. 1841)
Belgian ceramics firm: a branch of the German company Villeroy & Boch. Produced brightly decorated crackled white wares.

Bonheur, Rosa (1822-99) and Isidore (1817-1901)
French brother and sister animaliers.
Boston and Sandwich Glass Company (est. 1826)
American glass manfacturers. Made pressed glass novelties and a huge variety of glass paperweights. Later incorporated into New England Glass Company.
Maison Boucheron (1858-present)
Parisian jewelry manufacturer, founded by Frederick Boucheron (1830-1902). Mark: French hallmark stamped with Boucheron Paris or simply initial B.
Bouraine, Marcel (dates unknown)
French sculptor, best known for his Amazon figures in bronze. Mark: "M.A. Bouraine".
Bouval, Maurice (d.1920)
French sculptor and metalworker known for bronze lamps and busts of female figures.
Brandt, Edgar-William (1880-1960)
French designer and metalworker, best known for his fine wrought iron work, sometimes burnished or painted a silver colour.

E BRANDT

Brannam, Charles (1855-1937)
English art potter. Pieces are often signed and dated.
Breuer, Marcel (1902-81)
Hungarian-born architect and furniture designer; studied interior design at the Bauhaus. Used wood and tubular steel in his designs. Moved from England to the United States in 1937. Unmarked, but his designs for Thonet and DIM have makers' labels and PEL and Standard-Mobel catalogues note some of his steel chairs.
Brownfield, Wm (active 1850-91)
English potter in Staffordshire. Made high-quality earthenware and porcelain, largely for export. Marks: double globe with BROWNFIELD & SON COBRIDGE STAFFS on ribbon, or WB or BROWNFIELD impressed.
Bugatti, Carlo (1855-1940)
Italian furniture designer and craftsman.

Bugatti, Rembrandt (1885-1916)
Italian animalier known for bronze wildlife sculptures.
Burges, William (1827-81)
English architect and furniture designer in the early Gothic style.
Burgun, Schverer (1711-present)
The only German producer of Art Nouveau cameo glass. Also produced some wares for Emile Gallé.
Buthaud, René (1886-1986)
French painter and artist potter, best known for African-inspired decoration. Marks: "R. Buthaud" painted; "RB" incised or painted.
Butler, Frank A. (late 19th-early 20th century)
English pottery decorator. Worked for **Doulton** in a distinctive style sometimes involving bosses formed by relief modelling.
Cantagalli, Ulisse (d.1901)
Italian potter. Produced copies of early Italian majolica. Mark: rebus of crowing cock.
Carder, Frederick (1864-1963)
British-born glass designer for Stevens & Williams and later Art Director at **Steuben**.
Cardew, Michael (1901-1983)
English artist potter working in earthenware slip, pupil of **Bernard Leach**. Worked from Winchcombe Pottery in Gloucestershire, 1926-39. Experimented with tin glazes.

Carlton Ware (est. 1897)
Brand name used by Wiltshaw & Robinson, a pottery founded in 1897 in Stoke-on-Trent. Marks: "W&R/STOKE ON TRENT" forming a circle which encloses a swallow, topped by a crown; "Carlton ware" hand painted over name and address of firm.
Cartier (est. 1897)
Paris jewelers. Opened in London (1903), New York (1912).

Cartier

Cassandre, Adolphe-Jean-Marie Mouron, (1901-68)
French artist and leading posterist in a geometrical manner.

A.M. CASSANDRE

Century Guild, (est. c.1882)
English Arts and Crafts society of designers, artists, architects and metalworkers, founded by **Arthur Mackmurdo** to restore responsibility for the decorative crafts to the artist from the tradesman. Marks: on metalwork, hammered; on textiles, printed initials.
Chalon, Louis (dates unknown)
French sculptor, whose wares usually feature a female figure.

Cheret, Jules (1836-1932)
French graphic artist credited as the father of the modern poster.

Cheuret, Albert (dates unknown)
French sculptor, working in Art Nouveau and Art Deco styles, producing functional work, featuring naturalist motifs. Mark: ALBERT CHEURET, incise cast.

Chiparus, Dimitri (Dèmetre) (dates unknown)
Rumanian-born sculptor who worked in Paris in the 1920s.

Christian, Desiré (born 1846)
French silverware designer; chief artistic designer at **Burgun, Schverer** until 1896. Opened firm with his brother and son.

Christofle, Orfevrèrie (1829)
Metalworkers, founded in Paris.

Cliff, Clarice (1899-1972)
English potter, designer and decorator. Art director at Wilkinson's Royal Staffordshire Pottery and its subsidiary, Newport Pottery. Cliff also decorated wares designed by other artists. Mark: black printed pottery mark, name of design and facsimile signature.

Coalbrookdale (active 19thC)
English iron foundry near Ironbridge, Shropshire. Largest 19thC manufacturer of iron furniture. Some designs by **Christopher Dresser**.

Coalport (est. 1796)
English ceramics firm. Produced Sèvres-style wares, some bearing paintings of exotic birds. Some are marked Coalport AD 1750.

Cole, Sir Henry (1808-82)
English designer and artistic reformer. Set up Felix Art Manufacturers which put forward designs which were aesthetically pleasing, using mass-production techniques. Instrumental in organization of 1851 Great Exhibition.

Colenbrander, Theodorus A.C. (1841-1930)
Dutch porcelain decorator and designer for **Rozenburg**.

Colin, Paul (born 1892)
French designer and posterist, most renowned designs being for *Les Ballets Suédois* and *Le Ballet Nègre*. Mark: printed signature.

Colinet, Jeanne Robert (dates unknown)
French sculptor. Mark: "J. R. Colinet".

Collcutt, Thomas E. (1840-1924)
Worked primarily for **Collinson and Lock**, specializing in ebonized furniture.

Collinson & Lock (est. 1870, absorbed into Gillow, 1897)
London furniture makers in the Aesthetic style. Designers included **Talbert**, **Godwin** and **Collcutt**.

Colonna, Edward (b.1862)
German architect and designer associated with the Paris School.

Cooper, Susie (born 1902)
English potter. Designed for A. E.

Gray & Co. (c.1925), especially bright geometrical forms. Formed her own company in 1932.

Cotswold School
Association of English furniture designers, led by Ernest Gimson and the Barnsley brothers.

Couper, James & Sons (dates unknown)
Scottish glassmaking firm best known for "Clutha" glass.

J. G. Crace & Sons (1745-1899)
London-based furniture makers known for their Gothic-revival pieces designed by, among others, **Godwin**, **Pugin** and **Voysey**.

Crane, Walter (1845-1915)
English painter, graphic artist and designer associated with the Arts and Crafts movement. Designed pottery and tiles for Wedgwood, Minton, Pilkington and Maw & Co. Painted monogram. Designed textiles for **Morris and Co.**

Crossley (active 19thC)
English textile and carpet maker at Halifax, Yorkshire. Pioneer of mechanization in weaving.

Dammouse, Albert (1848-1926)
Glassmaker and master of *pâte-de-verre*. Mark: impressed.

Daum Frères (1875-present)
Nancy glassworks founded by brothers, Auguste (1853-1909) and Antonin (1864-1930); made fine vases and lamps. Marks: relief cut, etched or painted.

Dawson, Nelson (1859-1942)
English painter, silversmith, jeweler and co-founder of the **Artificers' Guild**.

Dearle, John Henry (1890-1932)
English porcelain decorator. Pieces usually signed.

Decoeur, Émile (1876-1953)
French artist studio potter.

Décorchement, François-Emile (1880-1971)
French glassmaker, exponent of *pâte-de-verre* and *pâte-de-cristal*.

22

de Feure, Georges (1868-1928)
French furniture and ceramics designer associated with the Paris School. Mark: signature, either painted or etched.

de Morgan, William (1839-1917)
English ceramic designer connected with the Arts and Crafts Movement. Founded the William de Morgan Pottery (1872) and other works. Marks: impressed.

Denislow, William Walter (dates unknown)
American metalwork designer associated with the **Roycrofters**.

Derby (c.1749-present)
Renowned English porcelain factory. Variety of marks incorporating the word Derby.

Deskey, Donald (1894-1989)
American architect and designer, using geometric motifs. Mark: "Deskey Vollmer".

De Stijl (1917-31)
Influential Dutch association of artists, favouring primary colours and abstract, rectangular forms, and rejecting ornament.

Deutscher Werkbund (est. 1907)
Association of artists, architects, manufacturers and writers formed in Munich.

Doat, Taxile (b.1851)
French porcelain designer and decorator for **Sèvres**.

Dorn, Marion (1899-1964)
American-born textile designer, living in London. Rug designs made by Wilton Royal Carpet Factory.

DORN

Doulton & Co. (1815-present)
Lambeth-based producer of commercial and industrial stoneware and porcelain figures, including saltglazeware. Marks: printed, impressed or painted. **Doulton Lambeth Potteries**, their art department, were pottery manufacturers founded by Henry Doulton and John Sparkes, head of the Lambeth School of Art.

Dresser, Christopher (1834-1904)
Scottish-born botanist, designer and writer. Most famous for silver and metalwork designs for various firms, including **Elkington**, **Coalbrookdale** and **Benham and Froud**. Marks: on glass – etched ; on metalwork – stamped.

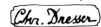

Dryden, Ernst (dates unknown)
Leading Austrian graphic designer. Marks: "Deutsch"; "Dryden".

Dufrêne, Maurice (1876-1955)
French designer of furniture, ceramics, metal, glass and carpets. Later work included Modernist designs using tubular steel. Had a shop in *Galeries Lafayette*.

Dupas, Jean (1882-1964)
French painter, muralist and poster artist. Mark: dated and signed "Jean Dupas" at the bottom.

Durand, Victor (1870-1931)
American glass artist. Produced primarily iridescent wares for the Vineland Glass Manufacturing Co.

Eastlake, Charles L. (1836-1906)
English architect and furniture designer of the Gothic revival.

Elkington & Co. (c.1830-present)
English silversmith founded by George Elkington, who, with his cousin Henry, patented their electroplating process in 1840. Marks: stamped.

Ellis, Harvey (1852-1904)
English-born architect and designer associated with **Gustav Stickley**.

Elton, Sir Edmund (1846-1920)
English baronet and self-taught potter. Produced art pottery on his Somerset estate, first as the Sunflower Pottery, then under the name Elton Ware. Mark: painted.

Etling, Edmund et cie (active 1920s and '30s)
Paris firm which commissioned and distributed glass, bronze and ivory by many designers.

Falguière, Jean-Alexander-Joseph (1831-1900)
French Art Nouveau sculptor.

Farhner, Theodor (1868-1928)
German jeweler; mass-produced fine jewelry in an abstract Art Nouveau style.

Feuillâtre, Eugène (1870-1916)
French designer of jewelry specialized in *plique-à-jour* enamelwork. Mark: engraved.

Feuillatre

Finmar (est. 1934/5)
Finnish furniture manufacturers headed by Alvar Aalto, producing items in laminated wood. Unmarked, although the *Decorative Arts Journal* shows the full range of their wares, and pieces made by Aalto in Finland are maked "Aalto Möbler, Svensk Kvalitet Sprodurt".

Fisher, Alexander (1864-1936)
English enamelling artist known for fine silver plaques.

Foley (later Shelley) (1892-1925)
Staffordshire pottery and producer of decorative earthenwares and bone china.

Follot, Paul (1877-1941)
French interior decorator and designer and early exponent of Art Deco. Pieces unmarked, but some have characteristic "Follot rose".

Fox (active mid 19thC)
London-based family firm of silversmiths. Charles Fox Junior took over from his father c.1822; joined by sons Charles (C.T.) and George c.1841

Fouquet, Georges (1862-1957)
Innovative French jewelry designer. Joined his father's Paris firm in 1891 and took over in 1895, on his father's retirement.

G. FOUQUET

Frankl, Paul (1886-1958)
Austrian architect and furniture designer; settled in the United States in 1914. Used Calfornian redwood, and silver leaf in his predominantly city-style designs. Mark: metal tag with name of manufacturer.

Fratin, Christophe (1800-64)
German-born sculptor and ani-

malier who worked in France. Famous for anthropomorphic pieces.

Fremiet Emanuel (1824-1910) French sculptor and animalier, who made popular, sentimental pieces.

Gaillard, Eugène (active 1895-1911) French furniture designer and associate of the Paris School.

Gaillard, Lucien (born 1861) French jeweler and silversmith, famous for fine hand-made work in unusual materials.

Gallé, Emile (1846-1904) French designer and glassworker; considered the greatest of glass craftsmen. Marks: on glass – large variety of etched marks; on furniture – signature in marquetry.

Gantcheff (active 1920s) French firm making *dinanderie* wares in Paris in the 1920s. Signed on the footrim.

R. & S. Garrard (c.1819-present) London retailer and jeweller, appointed Crown Jewellers in 1843. 19th century wares are marked "RG".

Gesmar, Charles (1900-28) French artist and posterist: designed posters for *Folies-Bergère*.

Gibson, John (1790-1866) English sculptor working strictly in the Neo-Classical style.

Gilbert, Sir Alfred (1854-1934) English sculptor and exponent of the "New Sculpture", who marks the first transition from the Victorian style to Art Nouveau.

Gillow (established 1695, active today as Waring and Gillow). Established in Lancaster, England by Robert Gillow. Specialized in reproducing fine quality antique furniture.

Godwin, Edward W. (1833-86) English designer in the Aesthetic style.

Goldscheider, Marcel (1855-1953) Viennese ceramics manufacturer; mass-produced Art Nouveau vases and later Art Deco figures.

Gorham Corporation (1813-present) Important American silversmiths and jewellers. Produced mainly decorative tablewares in the Rococo style. Marks: stamped.

Goupy, Marcel (1886-1954) French artist and glass and pottery designer. Mark: signature.

Grainger, G. & Co. (est. 1801, absorbed into Worcester Royal Porcelain Co. 1899) Founded in Worcester, Grainger

---

initially followed the Rococo style. Later diversified into domestic and reticulated wares, often with pâte-sur-pâte decoration. Mark (1889-1902 – ROYAL CHINA WORKS WORCESTER surrounding G & Co ESTABLISHED 1801.

Grasset, Eugène S. (1841-1917) Swiss-born architect, designer and posterist.

Greene Brothers: Charles Sumner (1868-1957) and **Henry Mather** (1870-1954) American furniture designers. Worked to commission, mainly in Honduras mahogany.

Gropius, Walter (1883-1969) German architect, founder of the **Bauhaus** and director until 1928. Exponent of Modernim. His multi-combination modular furniture (1927) was highly influential.

Groult, André (1884-1967) French interior decorator and furniture designer who used luxurious embellishments (velvet, ivory, and sharkskin) in his rhythmic furniture designs.

Grueby, William H. (1867-1925) American potter. Founded Grueby Faïence Company at Boston, Massachusetts in 1894. Produced tiles, bases and art pottery.

Guild of Handicraft (1888-1908) British silverworking guild famous for exquisite silverware.

Gurschner, Gustav (b.1873) Bavarian sculptor and metalworker.

Gustavsberg (established 1827) Swedish factory on island of Farsta, producing faïence and creamware transfer-printed, in English style. Also Argentaware. Marks: GUSTAVSBERG and an anchor (1820-60), SSF printed within a rule from 1930.

Hadley, James (1837-1903) English ceramic modeller and designer. Worked at Worcester. Notable for pieces in the Kate Greenaway and Japanese style. Later sold own porcelain as Hadley ware, continued by his sons until sold to Worcester in 1905.)

Hagenauer (established 1898) Austrian foundry based in Vienna, known for its face masks and figures inspired by Negro art.

Handel (1885-1936) American glassworks.

Harris, Kate (active c.1890-1910) English metalwork designer in the Art Nouveau style.

Heal, Sir Ambrose (1872-1959) English cabinet-maker and director of family firm, Heal & Son. He used many woods in his designs and, eventually, steel and aluminium. Mark: stamped or labelled company name.

Heals, Gordon Russell (1892-1980) English furniture designer who specialized in pale veneers.

Henry, J. S. (c.1880-c.1900) London cabinet-makers best-known for "Quaint" furniture, a trade version of Art Nouveau that combined elements of the **Glasgow School**, European Art Nouveau and Arts and Crafts.

Herter Brothers (est. 1865) American furniture makers founded in New York by the half-brothers Gustave and Christian. The latter's pieces, inspired by the English Aesthetic movement, are the most important.

Hobbs, Brockunier and Co. (1845-1887) American glass company founded in West Virginia by James B. Barnes. Famous for Peachblow wares. Also produced spangled, crackled and pressed glass.

Hoffmann, Josef (1870-1956) Architect, designer, founder member of the Vienna Secession.

Holland & Sons (est. early 18thC) London-based furniture makers of high-quality pieces for royal residences. Pieces reflect the 18thC designs of Adam and Chippendale.

Howell & James (active 19thC) London pottery retailers who sold undecorated wares which were then painted by amateurs and offered for sale. Base wares often came from reputable factories and can be misleadingly stamped to infer factory decoration.

Hueck, Eduard (est. 1864) German metalwork firm. Some wares designed by **Josef Olbrich**.

Hunebelle, André (active 1920s) French glass artist inspired by Lalique. Mark: "A. Hunebelle", impressed.

Hunt & Roskill (est. 1843) Formerly Storr & Mortimer. Important silversmith headed by Storr's nephew, the silversmith, John Samuel Hunt.

Hurten, Charles F. (1813-1901) German-born ceramic decorator. Worked in France and England, for Sèvres and Copeland among others. Produced mainly realistic paintings of flora and fauna.

Hutton, William & Sons (1800-1923) English producer of silver, pewter and Britannia metal.

Image, Selwyn (1849-1930) English illustrator and designer. Designed panels and inlay decoration, often for **Mackmurdo** and the **Century Guild**. Marks: printed initials.

Isokon Furniture Co. (est. 1931) English furniture manufacturers, established by Jack Pritchard. Made mass-produced items in the modern style.

Jackson and Graham (est. 1840, absorbed by Collinson & Lock,

1885) English cabinet-makers renowned for their excessively ornate pieces.

Jackson & Sons (active 19thC) English furniture makers who specialized in *papier-mâché* furniture.

Jennens & Bettridge (active 1816-64) British furniture makers, best known for *papier-mâché* furniture.

Jensen, Georg (1866-1935) Danish silversmith specializing in high-quality silverware and jewelry. Mark: stamped.

Joel, Betty (1896-1984) English furniture and rug designer of functional pieces for the smaller home. Company mark: on furniture, signatures of designer and craftsman with date on card under glass; on rugs, woven monogram.

Jones, George (died 1893) English potter. Worked at the **Minton** factory before founding the Trent Pottery.

Jones, Owen (1809-74) English architect, designer and illustrator. Superintendent of Works at 1851 Great Exhibition.

Kauba, Carl (dates unknown) Viennese sculptor working in Art Nouveau style, most notable for his studies of North American Indians.

Kayser Sohn (1894-c.1904) German metalwork foundry. producing fine pewter.

Kerr & Binns (1852-62) The partnership that in 1862 became the **Royal Worcester Porcelain Co.** Made mainly table wares in porcelain.

King, Jessie Marion (1876-1949) Scottish illustrator and designer of ceramics and jewelry, including designs for **Liberty's** Cymric range.

JESSIE·M·KING

Kipp, Karl (dates unknown) American metalworker and designer in the Secessionist style. Director of Roycrofters from 1908.

Knowles, Taylor & Knowles (est. 1854) American pottery at East Liverpool, Ohio. Produced cream coloured earthenware and semi-porcelain. Marks: star-shaped motif or bison and KT & K in a rectangle or circle.

Knox, Archibald (1864-1933) Manx metalwork designer, notably of Liberty's Cymric range.

Korschann, Charles (b.1872) Bohemian sculptor, mainly of female figural bronzes.

La Faguays, Pierre (dates unknown) French sculptor.

Lalique, René (1860-1945) French master jeweler and glassmaker, famous for his scent bottles. The Lalique works also producd glass screens, lamps, innovative car mascots, fountains and lights. Marks: "R Lalique" used during Lalique's lifetime, the "R" being dropped after his death.

R LALIQUE

Laporte-Blairsy, Leo (1865-1923) French sculptor of functional, decorative pieces, especially lighting.

Larche, Raoul-François (1860-1912) French sculptor known for gilt-bronze female figures.

Läuger, Max (1864-1952) German architect, engineer, sculptor and ceramist.

Leach, Bernard (1887-1979) English architect potter. Decoration included stamped, stencilled, inlaid modelled and slip work. Made raku earthenware using a Japanese technique of hand-modelling.

Le Corbusier, Charles Edouard Jeanneret (1887-1965) Swiss Modernist architect and designer; became French citizen in 1930. Designed machine-made goods for mass market, using tubular steel with leather and hides.

Legrain, Pierre (1889-1929) Leading French Art Deco furniture designer, often showing an African influence. Used expensive and unusual materials.

Legras (1864-present) French glassmaking firm; produced cameo wares and commercial glass similar to **Daum** and **Müller Frères**.

Leighton, Frederick Lord (1830-96) English painter, sculptor and pioneer of the "New Sculpture".

Lenoble, Émile (1876-1939) French artist potter influenced by Oriental ceramics.

Léonard, Agathon (born 1841) French ceramist and sculptor. Made Art Nouveau-style biscuit figures and gilt-bronze statuettes.

Leyendecker, Frank and Joseph (1877-1924; 1874-1951) Prolific American commercial and graphic artists in a distinctively American style.

Liberty & Co. (1875-present) English retail firm established by Arthur Lasenby to sell fine British-made goods and Oriental art and fabrics, later expanding to include ceramics, metalwork and furniture.

Limoges (mid 19thC-present) French ceramics centre, mass-produced Art Deco porcelain.

Lindsberg, C.F. (1860-1909) Danish ceramicist and decorator at **Royal Copenhagen**.

Loetz (1836-1939) Bohemian producers of high-quality art glass.

Logan, George (dates unknown) British furniture designer, working for **Wylie and Lockhead**.

Lonhuda (established 1892) American art pottery. From c.1890 produced pieces resembling the successful **Rookwood** wares. Marks: impressed.

Lorenzl, Josef (dates unknown) Austrian sculptor.

Luce, Jean (1895-1964) French designer. Sold porcelain and faience tablewares from his Paris store, 1920s. Mark: painted crossed "LL" in rectangle.

McCallum & Hodson (19thC) English manufacturers of *papier-mâché* furniture.

McKnight-Kauffer, Edward (1890-1954) American artist and posterist working in Britain; designed posters for London Underground.

Macintyre & Co. (1847-present) Staffordshire pottery; employed William Moorcroft as a designer.

Mackennal, Sir Edgar Bertram (1863-1931) Australian sculptor inspired by French Symbolism and Romanticism.

Mackintosh, Charles Rennie (1868-1928) Scottish architect, designer. Formed the "Glasgow Four" with **Margaret Mackintosh**, Frances Macdonald and J.H. McNair.

Mackintosh, Margaret (1865-1933) Designer and metalworker, wife of C.R. Mackintosh and member of the "Glasgow Four".

Mackmurdo, Arthur Heygate (1851-1942) English architect and founder of the **Century Guild**. Marks: hammered initials.

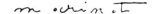

Marcus, Herman (dates unknown) Finest American jeweler of the Art Nouveau period; founded Marcus and Co. in 1900 and perfected the *plique-à-jour* method.

Marinot, Maurice (1882-1960) French painter, sculptor and glass designer; produced mostly vases.

Marshall, Mark V. (died 1912) English designer, **Doulton** potter and sculptor, best known for grotesque animal jugs.

Mason, C. J. (1813-62) English potter and founder of Masons. Patented ironstone in 1813, and was the foremost maker.

Masriera Brothers (1872-1958) Spanish jewelers influenced by

French Art Nouveau, particularly the work of **Lalique**.

Massier, Clement (1845-1917) French ceramicist and producer of earthenware with iridescent or lustre decoration.

Maw & Co. (second half of 19thC) Largest English tile manufacturer of the 19thC, based in Shropshire. Produced tiles using a number of processes and styles, including majolica, mosaic and moulded relief. Later expanded into general ceramic production.

Meeks, Joseph and Son (1797-1868) New York cabinet maker, producing Rococo style parlour furniture and rosewood cabinet furniture in Neo-gothic style.

Meissen (c.1710-present) Prominent German ceramics factory; traditional forms were applied with Art Nouveau decoration.

Mêne, Pierre Jules (1810-79) Prominent and prolific French animalier.

Mies van der Rohe, Ludwig (1886-1969) German Modernist architect and an innovative and influential furniture designer. Vice-president of **Deutscher Werkbund**, 1926; 1930-33 director of the **Bauhaus**; 1937 moved to America. Pieces unmarked.

Miklos, Gustave (1888-1967) Hungarian sculptor, best known for his all-bronze primitive figures made in limited editions.

Minton & Co. (1793-present, from 1873, Mintons Ltd) Staffordshire pottery; produced earthenware, art pottery and porcelain Marks: printed.

Moigniez, Jules (1835-94) French animalier best known for his bird sculptures.

Moorcroft, William (1872-1945) Head of Art Pottery Department of Macintyre & Co. Best known for "Florian" ware vases. Mark: signature or monogram.

Morris, William (1834-96) English poet, writer, socialist and designer. Founded Marshall, Faulkner and Co. in 1861 (became Morris and Co.) to execute his designs for furniture, textiles and wallpapers.

Mount Washington Glass Company (est. 1837) American glassworks established near Boston by William L. Libbey. Produced art glass and was closely associated with the American Aesthetic Movement.

Moser, Koloman (1868-1918) Austrian artist and designer of furniture, ceramics and glass; founder member of the Vienna Secession and co-founder of the Wiener Werkstätte

Mucha, Alphonse (1860-1939) Czech artist commissioned by the actress Sarah Bernhardt to design posters, stage sets and costumes.

Müller, Albin (1871-1941) German architect and designer known for useful stonewares with moulded decoration.

Müller Frères (active c.1900-36) French glassmaking firm run by **Henri** and **Désiré** Müller. Marks: etched or relief cut.

Murray, Keith (1893-1981) New Zealand-born architect and designer, settled in England 1935. Designed silver and pottery and, from 1932, glass. Marks: "Keith Murray" over *fleur-de-lys*.

Murrle Bennet & Co. (1884-present) Anglo-German mass-producer of jewelry. Marks: stamped.

Nancy School A group of artists and designers inspired by the work of **Gallé** and **Majorelle** in Nancy towards the end of the 19thC.

Nash, Paul (1889-1946) English painter and illustrator. A war artist in both World Wars, he was a central figure in the British avant-garde movement and formed Unit One in 1933 to popularize Modernist thinking.

Navarre, Henri (1885-1970) French glass artist. His sculptural, textured vases and bowls were influence by **Marinot**. Mark: "Henri Navarre.

H.NAVARRE

Neffe (est. 1815) Bohemian glassworks; produced useful geometric wares.

Nekola, Karel (active from c.1880) Bohemian artist and potter. From 1883 worked at the Fife Pottery decorating **Wemyss** ware, with which his name, and that of his son, Joseph (died 1952) are now synonymous.

Newcomb College Pottery (c.1895-1945) American producer of art pottery-with incised floral patterns.

New England Glass Co. (1818-88)

American glass company. Produced coloured art glass.

Ohr, George E. (1857-1918) American studio art potter and founder of the Biloxi Art Pottery in Mississippi. Unconventional forms and lustrous glazes. Marks: impressed.

Olbrich, Josef Maria (1867-1908) Architect, designer and founder member of the Vienna Secession.

Orrefors (est. 1898) Swedish glassworks. From 1915 produced decorative glasswares designed by Edvard Hald and Simon Gate, amongst others.

Owens, J. B. (died 1934) American potter and founder of J. B. Owens Pottery at Roseville, Ohio. Made majolica wares and copies of **Rookwood**. Marks: Roseville, impressed; J. B. Owens, printed.

Palme-König (est. 1786) Bohemian glassmakers; produced fine-quality Art Nouveau iridescent glass wares and table glass in forms popularized by **Loetz**.

Paris School Artists and designers associated with the Parisian publisher and dealer, **Samuel Bing**.

Parrish, Maxfield (1870-1966) American posterist, illustrator and stage designer in the Art Nouveau style.

Pèche, Dagobert (1887-1923) Austrian designer of ceramics and metalwork, and co-director of the **Wiener Werkstätte**.

Penfield, Edward (1866-1925) American graphic artist, posterist and illustrator.

Phoenixville Pottery (c.1867-1902) American pottery, the largest and most influential manufacturer of American majolica.

Pindar, Bourne & Co. (est. 1862, taken over by **Doulton & Co.** 1882) Pottery manufacturers in Burslem, Staffordshire, producing mainly tablewares. Japanese-inspired design is typical. Mark: PINDER BOURNE & Co/NILE St/BURSLEM.

Poertzel, Otto (born 1876) German sculptor. Mark: "Prof. Poertzel".

Poole Pottery (est. 1873) Originally Carter, Stabler & Adams. Partnership formed 1921 at Poole, Dorset. Traded as Poole Pottery Ltd from 1963.

Powell, Harry J. (active c.1880-c.1910) English glass artist and designer; director of James Powell & Sons 1880-1914.

Powell, James & Sons (c.1830-1980) Innovative London glasshouse, influential in the late 19thC. Acquired Whitefriars Glassworks in 1883. Designers included Philip Webb and Joseph Leicester. Marks: stamped.

Powolny, Michael (1871-1954) Austrian ceramics decorator and founder of Wiener Keramik factory. Marks: painted or impressed.

Practical Equipment Limited (1920s/30s) English manufacturer of tubular steel frame chairs and steel and glass furnishings.

Pratt, F. & R. (active 19thC) Staffordshire pottery which perfected the technique of mulit-coloured printing on a white earthenware base, now often referred to as Prattware. Some pieces are marked "F & R PRATT FENTON", impressed.

Preiss, Ferdinand (1882-1943) German sculptor. Opened foundry in 1906. Mark: "F Preiss"; foundry mark "PK".

Primavera (1920s/30s) Pottery department of the *Au Printemps* store in Paris.

Pritchard, Jack (born 1899) English manufacturer of laminated wood furniture, distributed through his **Isokon** retail outlet.

Privat-Livemont, T. (1861-1936) Belgian commercial artist and posterist.

Prouvé, Victor (1858-1943) French painter, sculptor and designer in the Art Nouveau style.

Prutscher, Otto (1880-1949) Designer for the **Wiener Werkstätte** of distinctive glass, jewelry and silver. Wares unsigned.

Pugin, Augustus Welby Northmore (1812-52) English furniture designer whose work epitomizes the Gothic revival in Britain. Produced solid and utilitarian furniture, usually of oak.

Quezal (1901-25) American glassmaking firm inspired by **Tiffany**.

Rateau, Armand-Albert (1882-1938) French interior decorator and furniture designer. Work epitomized by fine decoration in patinated bronze, lacquer, marble and ivory.

Riessner, Stellmacher and Kessel (R.S.K.) (est. 1892)

Bohemian ceramics firm; main contribution to Art Nouveau was the "Amphora" range.

Rietveld, Gerrit T. (1888-1964) Dutch architect and furniture designer. Joined De Stijl, the Dutch artists' association, in 1919; the geometric forms, primary colours and revealed construction of his furniture epitomize the work of the group.

Ricketts, Charles de Sousy (1866-1931) English sculptor whose Art Nouveau style was inspired by the work of the Frenchman, Rodin.

Ridgway, Edward John (active early 19thC-c.1872) Staffordshire potter best known for tea and dessert services in bone china, earthenware and stoneware. Mark: Staffordshire knot.

Rivière, Guiraud (dates unknown) French sculptor and metalworker. Mark: "GUIRAUD-RIVIÈRE".

Robinson & Leadbetter (1856-1924) Staffordshire pottery renowned for its Parian ware. Victorian pieces are marked with an "RL" surrounded by an oval border.

Rockingham (c.1826-420) English porcelain factory at Swinton, Yorkshire. Mark: a griffen; red on wares made before 1830, puce thereafter.

Rode, Godfried (1862-1937) Danish ceramic decorator at **Royal Copenhagen**. Famous for underglaze seascapes.

Rohlfs, Charles (1853-1936) American actor, stove maker and designer of furniture, particularly in oak. Mark: burned initials.

Rookwood (1880-1960) American pottery founded in Cincinnatti by Maria Longworth Nichols. Best known of the American producers. Foremost maker of fine Art Nouveau pottery.

Rörstrand (est. 1726) Prominent Swedish pottery: producer of bold designs under the influence of French Art Nouveau.

Rosenthal, Philip (d.1937) German potter and founder of the Rosenthal factory, producer of high-quality tablewares in the Art Nouveau style. Marks: printed.

Roseville Company (1890-mid-1940s) American pottery established on the site of **J. B. Owens'** Pottery; produced wares similar to **Rookwood's** Standard glaze wares.

Royal Copenhagen (1773-present) Danish factory, making Chinese-style porcelain with crystalline glazes and stoneware. Arnold Krog (director from 1885) introduced innovative glazing and decorative techniques. Marks: crown and three waves motif with "Danmark" or "Royal Copenhagen."

Royal Dux (1860-mid-20thC) Bohemian ceramicists known for their classically-inspired figures.

Roycrofters, The (1895-1938) American craft community founded by Elbert Hubbard (1856-1917) to produce simple furniture in the Mission style, textiles and metalwork.

Rozenburg (1883-1916) Pottery whose "eggshell" porcelain is considered foremost Dutch contribution to Art Nouveau.

Ruhlmann, Jacques-Émile (1879-1933) French painter, master-cabinetmaker from 1925. Mark: branded signature.

Rundell, Bridge & Rundell (1805-39) London gold and silversmiths. Crown Jewellers before **Garrard**. Designers included John Flaxman and Philip Storr.

Sabino, Marius Ernest (active 1920s and '30s) French glass architect inspired by **Lalique**. Mark: "Sabino, France".

Saunders, Gaulbert (active mid-19thC) Furniture designer in the Gothic style.

Scheurich, Paul (born 1883) Porcelain modeller, born in New York: worked in Germany.

Sèvres (1750-present) Renowned French ceramics factory, whose Art Nouveau pieces are acknowledged as the finest of the period.

Shelley Potteries (1872-1966) The name from 1925 of Foley, pottery firm estalished 1860 in Staffordshire, England.

Silver Studio (1880-1965) London design studio opened by Arthur Silver (1853-96). Known for wallpapers and textiles.

Sognot, Louis (dates unknown) French Art Deco cabinet maker, working in simple styles, with plain, unadorned surfaces.

Solon, Leon V. (1872-1957) English ceramic designer and director of **Mintons**, 1900-09.

Sowerby (1847-1972) English glassworks in Gateshead on Tyne famous for pressed glass and vitro-porcelain in the Aesthetic style. Mark: a peacock's head.

Spencer, Edward Napier Hitchcock (1872-1938) English metalworker and co-founder of the **Artificers' Guild**.

Stabler, Phoebe (died 1955) English sculptor and designer.

Made ceramic figures, enamels and jewelry with her husband Harold. Mark: STABLER, HAMMER-SMITH, LONDON" with date and mould number.

Staite-Murray, William (1881-1962)
English engineer, painter and potter. Influenced by Japanese artist-potter, Shoji Hamada, he made stoneware with scratched or brushed decoration and partial glazing.

Steinlen, Théophile-Alexandre (1859-1923)
Swiss-born, naturalized French, artist whose postes reflected his socialist principles and love of animals, particularly dogs and cats.

Steuben GlassWorks (1903-present)
New York-based glassworks founded by Howkes family and Frederick Carder.

Steuben

Stevens & Williams (c.1830-present)
Glassmakers at Stourbridge in England, best known for fine cameo wares. Later Brierley Royal Crystal. Mark: either impressed "Stevens & Williams" or "S&W".

Stickley Brothers, L. and J. G. (1891-1910)
George and Albert, brothers of Gustav, made oak furniture in a style popularized by **Gustav**, but of inferior quality.

Stickley, Gustav (1847-1942)
American furniture designer; produced pieces with an Arts and Crafts feel, notably his range of "Craftsman furniture".

Storr, Paul (active early 19thC)
Most famous 19thC English silversmith. Best known for Neo-classical pieces in silver-gilt.

Stourbridge
English glass-making centre in the Midlands known for cameo glass by Thomas Webb & Sons and novelty, or "fancy", glass produced by several factories.

Süe, Louis (1875-1968) and **André Mare** (1887-1932)
French furniture, carpet and textile designers who collaborated on ornate furniture in the French high Deco style. Unmarked.

Summers, Gerald (dates unknown)
British Art Deco furniture designer.

Talbert, Bruce (1838-81)
Scottish-born architect and furniture designer. Designs tend to be massive and profusely inalid, showing elements of both the Neo-gothic and the Aesthetic styles.

Taylor, Ernest Archibald (1874-1951)
Scottish painter and furniture designer.

Taylor, Smith & Taylor (est. 1896)
American pottery at East Liverpool, Ohio. Produced earthenware and ironstone china. Marks: impressed.

Teague, Walter Dorwin (1883-1960)
American industrial designer. Work includes Modernist art glass for **Steuben**.

Teco (c.1902-c.1923)
Part of Gates Potteries, and Illinois terracotta, tile and brick firm founded by William Day Gates.

Templeton, James (born 1802)
Scottish textile and carpet manufacturer. Founded factory in Glasgow in 1839, which still produces carpets on the biggest looms in Britain.

Thompson, Robert "Mouseman" (died 1955)
British cabinet maker who followed the principles of the Cotswold School. Work mainly in oak and largely undecorated. The figure of a mouse, usually in relief, but sometimes carved into a niche, became his trademark.

Thonet Brothers (Gebrüder Thonet, Thonet Fréres) (est. 1853)
Furniture manufacturers. Designed and manufactured bentwood furniture. Largely for export. Designers included **Le Corbusier** and **Mies van der Rohe**. Marks: variations on name, stamped or on label.

Thuret, André (1898-1965)
French glass artist. His sculptural designs were inventive.

Thornycroft, Sir William Hamo (1850-1925)
English exponent of the New Sculpture, who drew his subjects mainly from Greek mythology.

Tiffany & Co. (1837-present)
American jeweler and retailer founded by Charles Louis Tiffany (812-1902) and John B. Mill Young. Now established in Geneva, Paris, New York and London. Marks: stamped.

Tiffany, Louis Comfort (1848-1933)
Founder of Louis C. Tiffany in the United States. Initially designed interiors but is now better known for glasswares, particularly lamps.

Toft, Albert (1862-1949)
English sculptor of bronze figural pieces, mainly of ethereal, cloaked female subjects.

Toulouse-Lautrec, Henri de 1864-1901)
Renowned French commercial artist and posterist; depicted the seedier nightlife of Paris.

Ungar Brothers (1872-c.1910)
American firm of 5 brothers who produced an impressive range of Art Nouveau silver. Most wares designed by Emma L. Dickinson.

Van Briggle, Artus (1869-1904)
American potter. Worked initially for **Rookwood**; founded the Van Briggle Pottery Co. in 1902.

Van de Hoef, Christian Johannes (1875-1933)
Dutch sculptor, medallist and ceramist, the main designer at **Amstelhoek**. Mark: painted.

Van de Velde, Henri (1863-1957)
Belgian architect and designer; worked with **Samuel Bing** and at **Meissen**.

Van Erp, Dirk (1860-1933/53)
Dutch-born metalworker.

Vever (1821-1982)
Leading French Art Nouveau retailer and jewelers.

Villanis, Emmanuele (dates unknown)
French sculptor of female figural forms in an Art Nouveau style.

Villeroy and Boch (1836-present)
German producer of stoneware art pottery.

Vineland Glass Manufacturing Company (dates unknown)
American glassmaking firm with strong ties with **Quezal**.

Voysey, Charles A. (1847-1941)
English architect. Designed interiors, wallpapers, textiles and furniture.

Wahliss, Ernst (1863-1930)
Bohemian potter influenced by **Michael Powolny**.

Walton, George (1867-1933)
Scottish designer of interiors and furniture.

Walter, Alméric (1859-1942)
French Art Nouveau and Art Deco glass artist; worked primarily in *pâte-de-verre*.

Waugh, Sidney B. (1904-63)
American sculptor and glass designer. Designer for **Steuben Glass Works**, 1933. Marks: engraved series numbers on limited edition pieces.

Webb, Thomas & Sons (1856-present)
Stourbridge-based glassworks whose glass includes Burmese ware, cameo glass, rock crystal and overlay. Marks: printed or etched.

Wedgwood, Josiah, & Sons (1759-present)
Renowned English pottery founded in Staffordshire by Josiah Wedgwood. Produced an extensive range of decorative and useful wares.

Weduwe N.S.A. Brantjes & Co. (1895-1904)
Dutch ceramics factory.

Whitefriars Glass Works (c.1680-present)
Influential London glasshouse bought by **James Powell & Sons** in 1833.

Wiener Werkstätte (Vienna Workshops) (1903-32)
Series of Austrian craft workshops founded by **Kolomon Moser** and **Josef Hoffmann**, which sought to combine utility and aesthetic qualities in furniture, metalwork and building designs.

William Watt & Co. (active 1865-85)
London-based furniture makers known for pieces in the Anglo-Japanse style.

Wilkinson, A. J. Ltd (est. 1896)
English pottery company. Factories included Royal Staffordshire Pottery. **Clarice Cliff** was art director, although the company also produced the designs of other artists – for example, Vanessa Bell and Duncan Grant.

Worcester Royal Porcelain Co. (active 1783-1902)
English porcelain factory. Became the Worcester Royal Porcelain Co. in 1862, producing a wide variety of excellent porcelain wares. Important designers included James Hadley and Thomas Bott.

Wright, Frank Lloyd (1867-1959)
American architect and designer, father of the Prairie Shool of architecture. Used pure forms, modern materials and modern techniques. Pieces are unsigned but usually well-documented.

Zach, Bruno (dates unknown)
Austrian sculptor, best known for his erotic figures. Mark: "Zach"

Wüttembergischer Metallwarenfabrik (W.M.F.) (1880-present)
Austrian metalwork foundry; produced decorative and domestic metalwork. Marks: stamped.

[WMF mark] WMFB

Zanesville Pottery (1882-1949)
American pottery established by Samuel A. Weller (1851-1925) to · produce art pottery in the style of **Lonhuda**, closely resembling **Rookwood** standard ware. By 1925 Weller owned three factories. Mark: WELLER, impressed, usually with the name of the style; also Weller Faïence, incised.

Zijl, Lambertus (dates unknown)
Dutch sculptor and ceramicist employed by **Amstelhoek**.

Zsolnay (est. 1862)
Hungarian ceramics firm; helped the development of Art Nouveau in eastern Europe.

BIBLIOGRAPHY

GENERAL

Adburgham, Alison, et al, *Liberty's 1875-1975*, catalogue of an exhibition at the Victoria and Albert Museum, London, 1975

Liberty's: A Biography of a Shop, London, 1975

Amaya, Mario, *Art Nouveau*, London and New York, 1966

Anscombe, Isabelle and Charlotte Gere, *Arts and Crafts in Britain and America*, London, 1978

Arwas, Victor, *Art Deco*, 1980

Aslin, Elizabeth, *The Aesthetic Movement, Prelude to Art Nouveau*, London, 1969

Battersby, Martin, *The World of Art Nouveau*, London, 1968

The Decorative Twenties, 1971

Bauhaus, Exhibition Catalogue, Royal Academy, 1973

Becker, Vivienne, *Art Nouveau Jewelry*, London, 1985

Brohan, Karl H., *Kunsthandwerk I. Jugendstil, Werkbund - Art Deco*, Berlin 1976

British Art and Design 1900-1960

Brunhammer, Yvonne, *The Nineteen Twenties Style*, 1966

Clarke, Robert Judson, *The Arts and Crafts Movement in America 1876- 1916*, Exhibition Catalogue, Princeton, 1972

Aspects of the Arts and Crafts Movement in America, Record of the Art Museum, Princeton University, Vol. 34, No. 2, 1975

Cooper Hewitt Museum, *Vienna Moderne 1898-1918*, New York, 1978

Duncan, Alistair, *Louis Majorelle – Master of Art Nouveau Design*, London, 1991

Deutsche Keramik Des 20 Jahrhunderts, Catalogue of the Hetjens Museums; Dusseldorf, vols I and II, 1985

Dufrêne, Maurice, *Art Deco Interiors*, London

Duncan, Alistair, *American Art Deco*, 1986

Exhibition Catalogue, *Art and Design in Europe and America 1800-1900*, Victoria and Albert Museum, London, 1987

Exhibition Catalogue, *Art Nouveau Belgium/France*, Institute for the Arts, Rice University, Houston, 1976

Exhibition Catalogue, *Christopher Dresser 1834-1904*, London, 1972

Exhibition Catalogue, *The Amsterdam School*, Gemeente Museum, the Hague, 1975

Exhibition Catalogue, *Vienna - Turn of the Century*, Fischer Fine Art, London, 1979

Fanelli, Giovanni, and Ezio Godoli, *Art Nouveau Postcards*, New York, 1987

Field, Rachel, *Victoriana*, London, 1988

Fine Art Society, *The Architect-Designers Pugin to Mackintosh*, London, 1981

French,Y., *The Great Exhibition*, London, 1950

Garner, Philippe, *Phaidon Encyclopedia of Decorative Arts*, Oxford, 1978

Gibbs-Smith C.H., *The Great Exhibtion of 1851: A Commemorative Album*, London, 1950

Gilbert, Alfred, *Royal Academy of Arts 1986*, Exhibition Catalogue

Halen, Widar, Christopher Dresser, Oxford, 1990

Hanks, David A., *The Decorative Designs by Frank Lloyd Wright*, 1979

Haslam, Malcolm, *Arts and Crafts*, London, 1988

Marks and Monograms of the Modern Movement 1815-1930, London, 1977

Henderson, Philip, *William Morris*, London, 1967

Hillier, Bevis, *The World of Art Deco*, 1971

Home, Bea, *Antiques from the Victorian Home*, London, 1973

International Exhibition Foundation, *Art Nouveau Jewelry by Rene Lalique*, Washington D.C., 1985-1986

Kaplan, Wendy, (Ed.) *Encyclopaedia of Arts and Crafts The International Arts Movement 1850-1920*, London, 1989

Klein, Dan and Margaret Bishop, *Decorative Art 1880-1980*, Oxford, 1986

Kunst Diesich Nutzlihuh Macht, Industrial Design at the Neue Sammlung Museum, Munich, 1985

Laver, J., *Victoriana*, London, 1972

Leidelmeijer, Frans and Daan van der Cingel, *Art Nouveau and Art Deco in the Netherlands*, Amsterdam, 1983

Marks and Monograms of the Modern Movement 1815-1930, London, 1977

Lesieutre, Alain, *Art Deco*, 1974

May, John, *Victoria Remembered*, London, 1983

Metropolitan Museum of Art, *In Pursuit of Beauty*, New York, 1986

Morris, Barbara, *Liberty Design*, London, 1989

Naylor, Gillian, *The Arts and Crafts Movement*, London, 1971

Neurwirth, Walter, *Wiener Werkstätte*, Vienna 1984

Pevsner, Nikolaus, *High Victorian Design: A study of the exhibits of 1851*, 1951

Priestly, J.B., *Victoria's Heyday*, London, 1972

Royal Academy, *Vienna Seccession, Art Nouveau to 1970*, London, 1971

Rutherford, Jessica and Bedoc, Stella, *Art Nouuveau, Art Deco and the Thirties; the Ceramic, Glass and Metalwork Collections at Brighton Musueum*, 1986

Strong, Roy, *The Collector's Encyclopedia Victoriana to Art Deco*, London, 1974

The Thirties, Exhibition Catalogue, The Hayward Gallery, 1979

Tilbrook, A.J., *The Designs of Archibald Knox for Liberty & Co.*, London, 1976

Ward Lock, *Dictionary of Turn of the Century Antiques*, London, 1974

Warren, Geoffrey, *All Colour Book of Art Nouveau*, London 1972

Watkinson, Ray, *William Morris as a Designer*, London, 1967

Pre-Raphaelite Art and Design, London, 1970

Weisberg, Gabriel P., *Art Nouveau Bing - Paris Style 1900*, New York, 1986

FURNITURE

Alison, Filippo, *Charles Rennie Mackintosh - Chairs*, London, 1978

The Architectural Association, *PEL and Tubular Steel Furniture of the Thirties*, 1977, London

Aslin, Elizabeth, *19th Century English Furniture*, London, 1962

Beard, Geoffrey W., *Nineteenth Century Cameo Glass*, Monmouthshire, 1956

Billcliffe, Roger, *Charles Rennie Mackintosh, Furniture and Interiors*, Guildford 1979

Cooper, Jeremy, *Victorian and Edwardian Furniture and Interiors*, London, 1987

Duncan, Alastair, *Art Deco Furniture*, 1984

Exhibition Catalogue, *Architect-Designers Pugin to Mackintosh*, The Fine Art Society, London 1981

Hanks, David A., *The Decorative Designs of Frank Lloyd Wright*, London, 1979

Hayward, Helena, *World Furniture*, 1977

Heller, Carl Benno, *Art Nouveau Furniture*, Kirchdorf, 1990

Johnson, Stewart, *Eileen Gray: Designer 1879-1976*, 1979, London

Page, Marion *Furniture Designed by Architects*, 1980

Sembach, Leuthauser, Gossel, *Twentieth Century Furniture Design*, Cologne (not dated)

Stimpson, Miriam, *Modern Furniture Classics*, 1987

Wilk, Christopher, *Marcel Breuer – Furniture and Interiors*, 1981

GLASS

Amaya, Mario, *Tiffany Glass*, London, 1967

Arwas, Victor, *Glass – Art Nouveau to Art Deco*, 1977

Bayer, Patricia and Waller, Mark, *The Art of René Lalique*, 1988

British Glass Between the Wars Exhibition Catalogue, Broadfield House Glass Museum, 1987

Davis, Derek C. and Keith Middlemas, *Coloured Glass*, London, 1968

Dawes, Nicholas M., *Lalique Glass*, 1986

Decelle, Phillipe, *Sabino – Catalogue Raisonné*, 1987

Dodsworth, Roger, *Glass and Glassmakers*, Risborough, 1982

Duncan, Alistair, Martin Eidelburg and Neil Harris, *The Masterworks of Louis Comfort Tiffany*, New York, 1990

Davis, Derek, *English Bottles and Decanters 1650-1900*, London, 1972

Garner, Philippe, *Emile Gallé*, London, 1976

Gardner, Paul V., *The Glass of Frederick Carder*, New York, 1971

George, S. and Helen McKearin, *American Glass*, New York, 1968

Glass in Sweden 1915-1916, various authors, 1986

Grover, Ray and Lee, *Art Glass Nouveau*, Rutland, Vermont, 1968

Carved and Decorated European Art Glass, Vermont, 1970

George, S. and Helen McKearin, *American Glass*, New York, 1968

Grover, Ray and Lee, *Art Glass Nouveau*. Vermont, 1967

Haynes, E. Barrington, *Glass Through the Ages*, London, 1948

Hilschenz-Mlynek, Helga, and Ricke, Helmut, *Glass*, 1985

Janneau, Guillaume, *Modern Glass*, 1931

Klein, Dan, and Lloyd, Ward, *History of Glass*, 1988

Koch, Robert, *Louis C. Tiffany's Glass - Bronzes - Lamps*, New York, 1971

Louis C. Tiffany, Rebel in Glass, New York, 1974

Lalique – A Century of Glass for a Modern World, Exhibiion Catalogue

Lee, Ruth Webb, *Nineteenth Century Art Glass*, New York, 1952

Marchilhac, Felix, *R. Lalique – Catalogue Raisonné*, 1989

Mortimer, Tony L., *Lalique Jewellery and Glassware*, 1989

Neustadt, Egon, *The Lamps of Tiffany*, New York, 1970

Newark, Tim, *The Art of Emile Gallé*, London, 1989

O'Looney, Betty, *Victorian Glass*,

London, 1972
Opie, Jennifer, *Scandinavian Ceramics and Glass in the Twentieth Century*, 1989
Paul, Tessa, *The Art of Louis Comfort Tiffany*, London, 1987
Percy, C.V., *The Glass of Lalique*, 1977
Potter, Norman and Douglas Jackson, *Tiffany*, London, 1988
Revi, Albert Christian, *Nineteenth Century Glass, its Genesis and Development*, New York, 1967
American Art Nouveau Glass, Nashville, Tennessee 1968
American Pressed Glass and Figure Bottles, New York, 1964
Slack. R., *English Pressed Glass 1830-1900*, London, 1987
Wakefield, Hugh, *19th Century British Glass*, London, 1961
Wotley, Raymond, *Pressed Flint-Glass*, Risborough, 1986
Carnival Glass, Risborough, 1983

CERAMICS

Atterbury, Paul, *Moorcroft Pottery*, London 1987
Dictionary of Minton, Woodbridge, 1989
Austwick, J. and B., *The Decorated Tile*, London, 1980
Barnard, Julian, *Victorian Ceramic Tiles*, London, 1972
Batkin, Maureen, *Wedgwood Ceramics, 1846-1959*, London, 1982
Bergesen, V., *Majolica British Continental and American Wares*, London, 1989
Berthoud, M., *Daniel – Porcelain*, Bridgenorth, 1980
Catley, Brian, *Art Deco and Other Figures*, 1978
Cecil, V., *Minton Majolica*, London, 1982
Charleston, R.J., *World Ceramics*, Feltham, 1968
Susie Cooper Productions, Exhibition Catalogue
Cox and Cox, *Rockingham Pottery and Porcelain*, London, 1983
Cross, A.J., *Pilkingtons Royal Lancastrian Pottery and Tiler*, 1980
Dawes, Nicholas M., *Majolica*, New York, 1990
Dennis, Richard, *Doulton Stoneware and Terracotta 1870-1925*, London, 1971
Doulton Pottery Stoneware Terracotta 1870-1928, London, 1971
Doulton Pottery Lambeth to Burslem 1873-1939, London, 1975
Royal Doulton 1815-1965, London, 1965
The Parian Phenomenan, London, 1989
Eyles, Desmond, *The Doulton Lambeth Wares*, 1975
The Doulton Burslem Wares, 1980
Eyles and Dennis, *Royal Doulton*

Figures, 1978
Evans, Paul F., *Art Pottery of the United States*, New York, 1974
Exhibition Catalogue, *William Moorcroft and Walter Moorcroft*, London, 1973
Frelinghuysen, Alice Cooney, *American Porcelain 1770-1920*, Metropolitan Museum of Art, New York Exhibition, 1989
Gaunt, W. and M.D.E. Clayton-Stamm, *William de Morgan*, London, 1971
Haslam, M. *English Art Pottery 1865-1915*, Woodbridge, 1975
Godden, G.A., *An Illustrated Encyclopaedia of British Pottery and Porcelain*, London, 1968
Goddens Encyclopaedia of British Pottery and Porcelain Marks, 1978
Coalport and Coalbrookdale Porcelain, London, 1970
Encyclopaedia of British Pottery and Porcelain Marks, London, 1964
The Illustrated Guide to Mason's Ironstone China, London, 1971
Ridgway Porcelains, London, 1972
Staffordshire Porcelain, St Albans, 1983
Victorian Porcelain, London, 1961
Griffin, L. & Meisel, L.K. and S.P., *Clarice Cliff – The Bizarre Affair*, 1988
Haggar, R.G., *Staffordshire Chimney Ornaments*, London, 1955
Hall, John, *Staffordshire Portrait Figures*, London, 1972
Haslam, Malcolm, *English Art Pottery 1865-1915*, Woodbridge, 1975
The Martin Brothers Potters, London, 1978
Hawes, Lloyd E., *The Dedham Pottery*, Massachusetts, 1969
Henzke, Lucile, *American Art Pottery*, New Jersey, 1970
Hughes, G.B., *Victorian Pottery and Porcelain*, London, 1959
Kunst & Antiquilaten, *Rozenburg 1883-1917*, Munich, 1984
Le Vine, J.R.A, *Linthorpe Pottery*, Yorkshire, 1970
Locket, T.A., *Victorian Tiles*, Woodridge
Lukins, Jocelyn, *Doulton for the Collector*, 1989
Mankowitz, Wolf, *Wedgwood*, London, 1953
Neuwirth, Waltraud, *Osterreichisches Keramik des Jugendstils*, Munich, 1974
Wiener Keramik, Braunschwig, 1974
Oliver, Anthony, *Staffordshire Pottery – The Tribal Art of England*, London, 1981
The Victorian Staffordshire Figure, London, 1971
Peck, Herbert, *The Book of*

Rookwood Pottery, New York, 1968
Pugh, P.D.Gordon, *Staffordshire Portrait Figures*, London, 1970
Rogers de Rin Collection, The, *Wemyss Ware 1880-1915*, Exhibition at Sotheby's, London, 1976
Royal Copenhagen Porcelain, 200 years of, Catalogue of an exhibition circulated by the Smithsonian Institute, 1974-1976
Sandon, H. and J., *Graingers Worcester Porcelain*, London, 1989
Sandon, Henry, *Royal Worcester Porcelain*, London, 1973
Shinn, Charles and Dorrie, *The Illustrated Guide to Victorian Parian China*, London, 1971
Thomas, E. Lloyd, *Victorian Art Pottery*, London, 1974
Twitchett, J. and B. Bailey, *Royal Crown Derby Porcelain*, Woodbridge, 1978
Victoria and Albert Museum, *Catalogue of works by William de Morgan*, London, 1921
Wakefield, Hugh, *Victorian Pottery*, London, 1962
Watson, *Collecting Clarice Cliff*, 1988
Williams Wood, Cyril, *Staffordshire Pot Lids and their Potters*, London, 1972
Winstone, Victor, *Royal Copenhagen*, London, 1984

SCULPTURE

Arwas, Victor, *Art Deco Sculpture*, 1975
Beattie, Susan, *The New Sculpture*, London, 1983
Catley, Brian, *Art Deco and Other Figures*, 1978
Cooper, Jeremy, *Nineteenth Century Romantic Bronzes*, Devon, 1974
Handley-Read, Charles, *British Sculpture, 1850-1914*, London, 1968
Horsewell, Jane, *Bronze Sculptures of 'Les animaliers'*, Suffolk, 1971
Mackay, J. *The Animaliers*, London, 1973
Saulnier, C. *Antoine-Louis Barye*, London, 1926
Shepherd Gallery, The, *Western European Bronzes of the 19th Century*, USA, 1972

SILVER & METALWORK

Blair, Claude, *The History of Silver*, New York, 1987
Bury, Shirley, *Victorian Electroplate*, London, 1971
Hughes, G. Bernard, *Small Antique Silverware (including flatware)*, London, 1957
Jones, Mark, *The Art of the Medal*, 1979
Wardle, Patricia, *Victorian Silver and Silver-Plate*, London, 1963

Krekel-Aalberse, Annelies, *Art Nouveau and Art Deco Silver*, 1989

JEWELRY

Bayer, Patricia, and Mark Waller, *The Art of René Lalique*, London, 1988
Becker, Vivienne, *The Jewellery of René Lalique*, Exhibition Catalogue, London, 1987
Bury, Shirley, *Jewellery 1789-1910* (Volume II 1862-1910), Woodbridge, 1990
Cooper, Jeremy, *Nineteenth Century Romantic Bronzes*, Devon, 1974
The Delorenzo Gallery, *Jean Dunand*, New York, 1985
Flower, Margaret, *Victorian Jewellery*, London, 1967
Gabardi, Melissa, *Art Deco Jewellery*, 1989
Gere, Charlotte, *Victorian Jewellery Design*, London, 1970
Peter, Mary, *Collecting Victorian Jewellery*, London, 1970
Mortimer, Tony, *Lalique Jewellery and Glassware*, London, 1989

TEXTILES

Godden, G.A., *Stevengraphs and Other Victorian Silk Pictures*, London 1971
Morris, Barbara, *Victorian Embroidery*, London, 1962

POSTERS

Lipmann, Anthony, *Divinely Elegant – The World of Ernst Dryden*, 1989
Ludwig, Coy, *Maxfield Parrish*, 1973
Schnessel, Michael S., *Icart*, 1976

MISCELLANEOUS

Melvin, Andrew, *William Morris: Wallpapers and Designs*, London, 1971
Pinto, Edward, *Treen and other Wooden Bygones*, London, 1969
Pinto, Edward and Eva, *Tunbridge and Scottish Souvenir Woodware*, London, 1970

INDEX

Page numbers in **bold** refer to main entries. *Italic* numbers refer to the illustrations

Cubism 18, 22, 51, 171, 186, 209, 210, 225, 228, 238, 239
Cundall, Charles 121
cut glass 71
Cuzner, Bernard 183
Cymric silver 182, *182*, 183, 196, 206, *206*, 207
Czech bottles 93, *93*

Daimler, Gottlieb 21
Daly, Matthew 117, *117*
Damousse, Albert 88
Daniel, H. & R. 102
Danish metalwork 188, *188*
Darby, Abraham and Alfred 181
Daum Factory 88, *94*, 96, *96*, 172, *192*
Daum Frères 34, 64, 72, 74-5, *74-5*, 77
Daurat, Maurice 187
Davidson, George 9, 64, 71, *71*
Dawson, Edith 177
Dawson, Nelson 176, 177
Day, Lewis F. 234
De Gregory, Waylan 139
De Morgan, William 100, 110, *110*, 118, 134
Deakin, James and Son 172
Dearle, J.H. 232, 234, 235, *235*
Decoeur, Emile 123
Décorchement, François-Émile 88, **89**, *89*, 96
Delft ware 124
Della Robbia Pottery 109, *109*
Denislow, William Walter 179
"Depression glass" 64
Derby 103
Derbyshire, John 71
Deskey, Donald 58, **61**, *61*, 62, 190, 228
Després, Jean 20, *20*, 209, 210, *210*, 211
Diaghilev, Sergei 18
diamond jewelry 199-200, *199-200*
Dickens, Charles 102
DIM 59
Dimoline of Bristol 25
dinanderie 56, 172, 192, *193*, 194
Distel 125, *125*
Doat, Taxile 122-3, *122-3*
Doccia 107
Dodd, William J. 119
Dorn, Marion 239, *239*
Doucet, Jacques 52, *53*
Doulton & Co. 12, 17, 108, 110, **113**, *113*, 116, *116*, 128, **132-3**, *132-3*, 148
Dressler, Christopher 8, **68**, *68*, 108, *109*, 111, *111*, 172, 180, *180*, 181, *181*, 234, 235
Dressler, Conrad 109
Dreyfuss, Henry 191
Dryden, Ernst 19, **224**, *224*, 227
Duesbury, William 116
Duffner and Kimberly 87
Dunand, Jean 9, 13, 21, 22, 54, **55-6**, *55-6*, 172, 192, **193**, *193*, 194, 211
Dunlop, John 21
Dupas, Jean 21, 123, 136, 212, **222**, *222*
Durand, Victor 64, 87
Dutch ceramics **124-5**, *124-5*

earthenware 100, **106-7**, *106-7*, 124, *125*, 130, *136*, 137, 142
Eastlake, Charles Locke 28, *28*, 30
École de Paris 100
Edison, Thomas 20, 84
Edwards & Roberts 22
eggshell 55
electrical items 195, *195*
electroplate 172, **174-5**, *187*
Elizabethan-style textiles **230**, *230*
Elkington and Co. 157, **174-5**, *174-5*

Ellis, Harvey *33*
Ellison Glassworks 71
Elton Ware 100, **112**, *112*
embroidery **231-2**, *231-2*, **234**, *234*, **235**
enamel 177, *177*, 202, 203, *203*, 211, *211*
enamelled glass 64, 74, *76*, 96, *96*
engraved glass 64, 67, **97-9**, *97-9*
épergnes, glass **66**, *66*
Erickson, Ruth 118, *118*
Erté 16-17, 19, 212, 222, **223**, *223*
Eskey and Amodec 61
Etchells, Frederick 50
Etling, Edmund et Cie **92**, 163, 167
Etruscan wares 107, *107*
exhibitions 12
Exposition Internationale de l'Est de la France (1909) 53

Fabergé, Carl 203
Fachschüle Haida *83*
Fahrner, Theodor **207**, *207*
faïence **113**
Falguière 160
Farquharson, Clyne 97, **99**, *99*
fashion **16-17**
fashion illustration **222-3**, *222-3*
Favrile glass 79, 84, 85, 87
Ferrobrandt Inc. 192
Feuillâtre, Eugène 202, **203**, *203*
Feure, Georges de 12, 13, 22, 36, **37**, *37*, 100
figures, ceramic 105, *105*, **128-33**, *128-33*, *135*, *137*
see also sculpture
Finch, Arthur 138
Finmar Ltd 58, **63**, *63*
Fisher, Alexander 176, **177**, *177*, 196
Fitzgerald, J.A. 27
Fjerdingsstad, Christian 187
flashed glasswares 69
Flaxman, John 150, 175
"flint" glass 71
Florian ware 100, *113*
Folch 102
Foley, John Henry **152**, *152*
Follot, Paul **51-2**, *51-2*, 187, 228
Fontaine, Anne Marie 123, *123*
Forbes Lithograph Manufacturing Co. 219
Ford, Henry 21
Forsyth, Gordon 121, *121*
Forter, Ursin 32
Fouquet, Georges 9, 196, 202, **204-5**, *205*, **209**, *209*, 210, 211
Fox, Charles and George **175**, *175*
Fox, George Ernest 66
France: glass 67, *67*, **72-7**, *72-7*
jewelry **202-5**, *202-5*
metalwork **186-7**, *186-7*
posters **214-15**, *214-15*
Frank, Jean Michel **55**, *55*
Frankl, Paul 18, 19, 58, **61-2**, *61-2*
Fratin, Christopher **154**, *154*
Fremiet, Emanuel **154**, *154*
Frishmuth, Whitney 150
Fry, Roger 50, 51
Fuller, Loïe 18, **158**, 159, *159*
furniture **22-63**

Gaillard, Eugène 12, 13, **36**, *36*
Gaillard, Lucien 202, **203**, *203*
Galuchat, M. 53
Gallé, Emile 9, 12, 22, 34, *34*, 35, 64, **72-3**, *72-3*, 74, *76*, 77, 94
Gallé Studios **53**, *53*
Gates, William Day 119
Gaudí, Antoni y Cornet 42, **43**, *43*
Gautrait, Lucien 204
La Gazette du Bon Ton 17
German ceramics 124, **126-7**, *126-7*

Geyer, Karl 185
Gibson, John 150, **152**, *152*
Gilbert, Sir Alfred 150, **156**, *156*, 157
Gillows & Co. 12, 28
Gimson, Ernest 13, 22, 32, **48**, *48*
Glasgow Four 44-5
Glasgow School 22, 40, 44-5, *220*
glass **64-99**
Godwin, Edward William 8, 28, **29**, *29*, **234**, *234*
Goebel, Anna 100
gold 196
Goldscheider 18, 19, 128, **129-30**, *129*
Goldscheider, Arthur 166
Goldscheider, Friedrich 165
Goode, Thomas & Co. **120**, *120*
Gorham Corporation 172, **178**, *178*, 179
Gothic Revival 8, **13**, **26-8**, *26-8*, **230**, *230*
Goulden, Jean 17, 209, **211**, *211*
Goupy, Marcel 18, 94, **95**, *95*
Graal glass 64, *97*, 98
Grace, J.G. 29
Grant, Duncan 50, 51
Grasset, Eugène Samuel 204, 216, **217**, *217*
Gray, A.E. & Co. 142
Gray, Eileen 53, 58, **60**, *60*
Gray-Stan 94, **95**, *95*
Graydon Stannus, Mrs 95, *95*
Great Exhibition (1851) 12, 22, 25, *67*, 100, 150, 152, 172, 174, 228
Greenaway, Kate 115
Greene, Charles & Henry **32**, *32*
Greener, Henry 9, **71**, *71*
Gregory (Mary) glass 67
gres de Flanders 127
Griffen, Smith and Hill 107, *107*
Gropius, Walter 22, 59, 63
Groult, André 54, **55**, *55*
Grueby Faïence Co. 100, **117-18**, *117-18*
Guild of Handicraft 13, 70, **176-7**, *176-7*, 206
Guimard, Hector 12, 22, **36**, *36*
Guiraud-Rivière, Maurice 54
Gurschner, Gustav 80, 150, 158, **161**, *161*
Gustavsberg 107

Hadley, James 100, 115
Haga, N.V. 125
Hagenauer 17, *17*, 18, *151*, 169, *169*
Hague School 124, 125
hair jewelry 200
Hald, Edvard *97*, 98
Hall China Company 100
Hallin, F. August 135
Hamada, Shoji 146, 147, *147*, 148
Hamilton, Cuthbert 50, 148
Handel Company 84, **86**, *86*
Harradine, Lesley *133*
Harris, Kate 172, 182, **184**, *184*
Hartgring, W.P. 124
Haseler, W.H. & Co. 182, 183
Hawkes family 79, 98
Heal, Ambrose 57
Heal & Son 54, **57**, *57*
Hébrard foundry 155
Hegermann-Lindencrone, Effie 135
Heiligenstein, Auguste 95
Heron, Robert 120
Herter Brothers 22, 29, **30**, *30*
Hertschel, Julius Konrad 126
Hicks and Meigh 102
High Victorian style 25, *25*
Hiroshige 8
Hobbs, Brockunier 79, *79*
Hodgetts, Joshua 69
Hoeker, W. 125
Hoffmann, Josef 9, 22, 33, **40-1**, *40*, 50, 51, 82, **83**, *83*, 130, **189**, *189*, 220

Hokusai 8
Holbein, Albrecht *207*
Holland & Sons 28
Holliday, Henry 27
Holzer-Defanti, C. *131*
Honiton lace **233**, *233*
Horner, Charles 9, 196, 206
Horta, Victor 38, **39**, *39*
Howard, F. *114*
Hubbard, Elbert 179
Huber, Patrik *207*
Hucenreuther 100
Hueck, Eduard 127
Hunt, John Samuel 175
Hunt & Roskill 175, *175*
Hutton, William 17, 182, **184**, *184*

Icart, Louis 212, **221**, *221*
Iles, Frank 110
Image, Selwyn *31*, 228, 232, 234
Imperial Glass Factory 64
Ingres, J.A.D. *116*
intercalaires 74, *74*, 94
International Silver Co. **190-1**, *190-1*
Iribe, Paul 18, 19, **52-3**, *52-3*
iridescent ceramics 134, *134*
iridescent glass 64, **80-1**, *80-1*, 84, 85, 87, *87*
Irish lace 233
iron work 172, *179*, 181, **192-3**, *192*
ironstone 100, 102, 103, *103*
Isokon 22, 58, 59, **63**, *63*
Iznik wares *72*, 74, 110, *112*, 115, *124*

Jack, George 31
Jackson and Graham 25, *25*, 28
Japanese influences 8, 13
ceramics 100, 102, 106, *111*, 115, 116, 117, 124
furniture 29, 30
glass 71
jewelry 202, 208
metalwork 172, 178, 192
posters and prints 216, 219, *219*, *226*
textiles 228, 232, 234, 237
japanning, *papier-mâché* 24, *24*
Jennens, Aaron 24, *24*, 25
Jennens & Bettridge 12
Jensen, Georg 21, 172, *173*, 187, **188**, *188*
jewelry 16, **196-211**
Jobling and Co. 92, **93**, *93*
Joel, Betty 19, 20, 22, 54, **57**, *57*, **238**, *238*
Johnson Administration building *60*
Jones, George **106**, *106*, 107
Jones, Owen 25, 231, *231*
Jouve, Paul 21, 170
Joyce, Richard 121
Jugendstil 127, *127*, 185
jugs, relief-moulded **104**, *104*
Just 188

Kassler, Walter 162
Kayser & Sohn 172, 182, **185**, *185*
Kayserzinn wares 183, 185, *185*
Kazhütte 100
Kélety, Alex 170
Keller, Joseph 69
Kendrick, George P. 118
Keramis 138
Kerr and Binns 115
Khyn, Knud 100
King, Jessie M. **206**, *206*
Kipp, Karl 179
Kirschner, Maria *83*
Kiss, Paul 172, **193**, *193*
Klimt, Gustav 40, 220, 224
Knight, Laura *141*
Knox, Archibald **182-3**, *182-3*, 196, 206, 207
Kodak 20, 45, 191

251

ACKNOWLEDGMENTS

The publishers would like to thank the following
auction houses, museums, dealers, collectors
and other sources for supplying pictures for use
in this book or for allowing their pieces
to be photographed.

2 B; 4 B; 5t CNY; 5b SNY; 6t CG; 6c SG; 6b SL;
7t SM; 7c CSK; 7b SL; 12 SNY; 13 B; 16t B; 16b
SL; 17t CL; 17b CL; 18t CNY; 18b CNY; 19t
CNY; 19b B; 20t B; 20b CNY; 21t B; 21b B; 22
CL; 23 SNY; 24tl CL; 24bl&r CL; 25l CE; 25tr B;
25br SL; 26t FAS; 26c SL; 26b SL; 27t SL; 27c CL;
27b SL; 28tl B; 28bl CL; 28r SL; 29tl CL; 29bl CL;
29r SL; 30tl CNY; 30bl CL; 30tr B&B; 30br CL;
31l SL; 31tr SL; 31br SL; 32tl RPB; 32cl CNY;
32bl CNY; 32r CL; 33tl CNY;33bl CNY; 33r
CNY; 34l CNY; 34tr CG; 34r SM; 35t CNY; 35c
CNY; 35b SM; 36tl SM; 36bl CG; 36tr SL; 36bl
CNY; 37tl CM; 37bl SM; 37tr P; 37br PL; 38l SM;
38tr CG; 38br SM; 39tl SM; 39c SM; 39tr CNY;
39br SM; 40t CNY; 40bl SM; 40br SL; 41l CL;
41tr P; 41br CNY; 42t CL; 42l CL; 43l CNY ; 43tr
SL; 43cr CM; 43br SNY; 44t SM; 44bl SL; 44r SL;
45t CL;45c SL; 45br SL; 46t CNY; 46c CNY; 46b
CNY; 47tl CL; 47bl SL; 47tr SL; 47br CL; 48tl P;
48bl P; 48tr FAS; 49t SL; 49c CL; 49b CL; 50l SL;
50c SL; 50b SL; 51l CA; 51c CA; 51r CNY; 52t M;
52c SM; 52b CNY; 53tl SNY; 53tr SL; 53c SL; 53b
SL; 54t CNY; 54r SM; 55tl CNY; 55bl SM; 55tr
SNY; 55br SNY; 56t SNY; 56b SM; 57t SM; 57c
CL; 57bl CL; 57br CL; 58 CL; 59t SM; 59c SM;
59bl SM; 59br SNY; 60tl CNY; 60cl SL; 60bl CNY;
60tr CNY; 60brCNY; 61tSL; 61b WF; 62 tl CNY;
62tr CNY; 62c CNY; 62b CNY; 63t SL; 63c SL;
63b SL; 64 B; 65 B; 66t MB; 66bl MB; 66t&br MB;
67t SL; 67cl EK/MB; 67br MB; 67cr MB; 68tr SL;
68cl CL; 68bl SL; 68cr CL; 69t MB; 69c MP; 69b
MP; 70tl CL; 70bl CL; 70tr CL; 70br P; 71t PC;
71tr PC, 71br PC;72t P; 72b CL; 72r SL; 73tl CL:
73bl CNY; 73tr CL; 73cr HF; 73br CL; 74tl P;
74cl SM; 74tr CNY; 74br SL; 75t HF; 75bl CG;
75br HB; 76tl HF; 76bl CNY; 76r CG; 77l CNY;
77c SM; 77r SM; 78t Cor; 78bl SNY; 78r Cor;
79tr Cor; 79cl SNY; 79b SNY; 79cr SNY; 80t CG;
80l CL; 80r SL; 81tl MB; 81bl MB; 81tr MB; 81br
SL; 82t CA; 82cl CL; 82bl CA; 82br CNY; 83tl SL;
83bl SL; 83tc SL; 83bc CA; 83tr SL; 83br SL; 84t
CNY; 84bl CNY; 84r CNY; 85 SNY; 85bl SNY;
85cl CNY; 85tr SNY; 85cr SNY; 85br SNY; 86tl
Hib; 86bl SNY; 86c Hib; 86c Hib; 86r Hib; 87t
CNY; 87c CNY; 87r CNY; 88t CNY; 88c SM; 88b
SM; 89tl SNY; 89bl SM; 89tr CNY; 89br SM; 90tl
B; 90bl B; 90cr SL; 90br CNY; 91t SL; 91cl B; 91br
SL; 92tl 92 Bx4; 93t B; 93c B; 93bl B; 93br B; 94t
CG; 94c CM; 94b SNY; 95t CSK; 95c RD; 95bl
CNY; 95br SNY; 96tB; 96c CM; 96r CNY; 97t
CG; 97cl CG; 97cr SNY; 97b CNY; 98t CG; 98bl
Cor; 98br SNY; 99tSL; 99cr Cor; 99bl CL; 99brB;
100B; 101MB; 102t MB; 102c MB; 102b MB; 103t
SL; 103c SL; 103b EK/MB; 104t SL; 104b MB;
105tl&r MB; 105bl MB; 105cr RD;
105br MB; 106t CE; 106cl SL; 106bl DB; 106cr
MB; 107t SL; 107cl, cb,br Sil; 108t MB; 108b SL;
109tl&r Tor; 109bl CL; 109br CL; 110t SL; 110bl
SL; 110br SL; 111t CL; 111c CL; 111b MB; 113tr
MB; 113cl MB; 113br CL; 114t SL; 114b SL; 115tr
LG; 115cl SL; 115cr B; 115br SL; 116t SL; 116ct
RD; 116cb SL; 116b MB; 117t Met; 117c SNY;
117b CNY; 118tl CNY; 118bl CNY; 118tr DR;
118br CNY; 119t DR; 119c CNY; 119b CNY;
120t DL; 120cl RDr; 120b B; 121tl B; 121tr B;
121bl CL; 121br B; 122t Sev; 122bl Sev; 122tr SL;
122br HF; 123tc SM; 123tl GM; 123bl SL; 123tr B;
123br MB; 124t SL; 124cl SL; 124r CA; 125tr
V&A; 125tl CA; 125c NK; 125b NK; 126t P; 126c
SM; 126b HF; 127t BG; 127c SL; 127b CL; 128t
SL; 128b SNY;129tl SNY; 129cl SL; 129b B; 129tr
SL; 129cr SL; 130tl CL; 130b MB; 130tr CL; 131tl

SL; 131tr SL; 131b SL; 132tl CL; 132tr SL; 132c B;
132b B; 133t B; 133bl B; 133bc B; 133br B; 134t
CG; 134ct HF; 134cbB; 134bB;135tCNY; 135cHF;
135bRC; 136tCNY; 136blSL; 136rSL; 137tlB;
137trB; 138tSNY; 138cCNY; 138bB139tx3B;
139b CNY; 140t CL; 140cl CL; 140cr B; 140bl CL;
140br B; 141t P; 141tr&bx3 B; 142 B; 143tx2 CL;
143bl B; 143cb SL; 143br B; 143cr CSK; 144tr
CSK; 144c B; 144b B; 145t B; 145b CNY; 146t B;
146c CL; 146b B; 147tl B; 147tr CL; 147bl B;
147br B; 148t SL; 148bl SL; 149t B; 149c B; 149b B;
150 B; 151 B; 152t SL; 152lc SL; 152bl FAS; 152r
SL; 153t SL; 153b SL; 154tl SL; 154lc SL; 154bl SL;
154tr SL; 154br SL; 155tl SL; 155lc SG; 155tr SL;
155b SG; 156t SL; 156bl SL; 156r SL; 156tr B;
157tr B; 157cr SL; 157br P; 158t SL; 158c SL;
158b SL; 159tr SL; 159tl CNY; 159bl SL; 159br
CNY; 160t SL; 160c SL; 160r CL; 161tl CL;
161tCL; 161tr CNY; 161br SNY; 162t CNY; 162l
SL; 162cr SL; 162b SM; 163t SM; 163l CNY; 163b
SL; 164tt CL; 164r SL; 164b CNY; 165l SL; 165r
CNY; 166tl B; 166bl SL; 166r SM; 167t SL; 167c
SL; 167b SL; 168tl B; 168tr CNY; 168b SL; 169t
CL; 169bx3 SL; 170t CNY; 171c SNY; 171b CM;
170t HA; 170bx2 NM; 172 B; 173 B; 174t RP/MB;
174bx2 MB; 175b CL; 175tr SL; 175cr MMB;
175br SL; 176t CL; 176b SL; 177t SL; 177l SL;
177c SL; 177cr CL; 177b SL; 178t CNY; 178lc
CNY; 178lb CNY; 178bc CNY; 179t CNY; 179l
CNY; 179b CNY; 180t H&W; 180c MB; 180b CL;
181t CL; 181c SL; 181b CL; 182t SL; 182lc SL;
182b SL; 183tl SL; 183lc CNY; 183b SL; 183tr SL;
183rc SL; 184tl SL; 184b NH; 184r NH; 185t SL;
185c SL; 185b RPB; 186t CNY; 186c CNY; 186b
SNY; 187t CNY; 187r CL; 187cl CNY; 187b SM;
188t CL; 188bl SL; 188r CNY; 189tl SM; 189bl
CN Y; 189tr SL; 189br SNY; 190t WF; 190b B;
191t CL; 191l MG; 191b CNY; 191r CNY; 192t
CNY; 192l CNY; 192r CNY; 193CNY; 193CNY;
193b B; 194 CG; 194 CG; 194lc NT; 194b CNY;
196 B; 197 B;198x5 CSKJ;199x5 CSK; 200x4 CSK;
201t RJS; 201l CG; 201br TC; 202t CG; 202b SL;
202r CG; 203tl SL; 203bl SNY; 203br CNY; 204tl
SL; 204cr CG; 204b SL; 205l SM; 205tc SG; 205tr
SL; 205b SG; 206x3 SL; 207x4 SL; 208t SG; 208lc
SG; 208b SM; 209tx2 SL; 209b Col; 210tl SM;
210lb SM; 210cb SM; 210cb SNY; 210r SNY; 211tl
SNY; 211tr CG; 211bc SL; 211b NT; 212 JR; 213
SL; 214t CL; 214lx2 CL; 215t CSK; 215lt CNY;
215lb P; 215br CSK; 216t CNY; 216l SL; 217t
CSK; 217c RB; 217 CSK; 218l CNY; 218r MPT;
219t P; 219c B; 219 CSK; 220t P; 220lb P; 220r
CSK; 221tl CNY; 221tr CL; 221b CL; 222t CNY;
222b CNY;223t SNY; 223b SNY; 224tl SM; 224c
B; 224r SM; 224b B; 225tl CS; 139tr CS; 225bx3
B; 226t B; 226l B; 226bc B; 226br B; 227t CNY;
227l P; 227b P; 228 CL; 229 CL; 230t V&A; 230b
PC;231t PC; 231l PC; 231cb PC; 232l SL; 232tr
PC; 232c PC; 232b P; 233x3 PC; 234t WF; 234c
WF; 234b PC; 235tl V&A; 235tr SL; 235bl WAG;
235br WAG; 236t SL; 236b SNY; 158t SNY;
237l PC; 237br PC; 237rc CNY; 238t CNY;
238lx3 SM; 238bl SL; 239tl SL; 239tr SL; 239b
V&A

KEY

b bottom, c centre l left r right t top

B   Bonham's London
BAL   Bridgeman Art Library
B&B   Butterfield & Butterfield, Los Angeles
BG   Bethnal Green Museum
BEB   Judith Bebber
CA   Christie's Amsterdam
CE   Christie's East
CL   Christie's, London
CG   Christie's, Geneva
CNY   Christie's, New York

Col   Antique Collectors Club
Cor   Corning Museum of Glass, New York
CS   Charles Spencer
CSK   Christie's, South Kensington
DB   David Battie
DDC   Donald and Diane Cameron
DL   Dr Laird
DR   David Rago Arts and Crafts, New Jersey
EHA   Goria Gibson
EK   Eric Knowles
FAS   Fine Art Society
FF   Fan-Fayre
FG   Frances Gertler
GM   Galerie Moderne
HA   Hirschl & Adler Galleries, Inc, New York
H&W   Haslam & Whiteway Ltd, London
HF   Habsburg Fedman
Hib   John and Carole Hibel – H & D Press, Inc
JL   Jocelyn Lukins
JR   Jack Rennart
LG   L Greenwold, Stow-on-the-Wold
MB   Mitchell Beazley
MG   Maison Gerard, New York
MM   Metropolitan Museum of Art, New York
MP   Michael Parkington Collection, on loan to
        the Broadfield House Glass Museum,
        Kingswinford, Stourbridge
NH   The Nicholas Harris Gallery, London
ND   Nicholas Dawes, New York
NK   Nederlands Keramickmusuem,
        Leeuwarden
NM   National Museum of Amerian Art,
        Smithsonian Institution
NT   Noel Tovey, L'Odeon
P   Phillips, London
PC   Private Collection
P(C)   Phillips Cardiff
PB   Patricia Bayer
RB   Richard Barclay
RC   Royal Copenhagen
RD   Royal Doulton
RPB   Royal Pavilion Art Gallery and Museums,
        Brighton
RdR   Rogers de Rin Antiques, London
RJS   Ruth and Joseph Sataloff
RP   Richard Price
Sev   Le Pavillon de Sèvres Ltd, London
SF/MB   Stephen Furniss, Asters Antiques, Shere,
        Surrey
Sil   Dr and Mrs Howard Silby
SL   Sotheby's, London
SM   Sotheby's, Monaco
SNY   Sotheby's, New York
TC   Tiffany Collection/Stephen B.Leek
Tor   Torquay Pottery Collectors Society
V&A   Victoria and Albert Museum
WAG   Whitworth Art Gallery, Manchester
WF   Warner Fabrics, plc
WEF   The Wolfsonian Foundation, Miami,
        Florida
Wil   Williamson Art Gallery, Birkenhead

The illustration on p.218tr was provided courtesy
of The American Illustrators Gallery and the
Maxfield Parrish family trust, New York

Thanks are due to the following for their
generous help in the preparation of this book:
Bob Lawrence, Gallery 25
Clive Stewart Lockhart
Noel Tovey
Barbara Morris
Jim Collingridge (Jewelry)

Special thanks are due to Nicholas Dawes
for his invaluable contribution to the
American sections of the book.